# Readings in English Literature

# Readings in English Literature

L. Joseph

CYBER TECH PUBLICATIONS
4264/3, Ansari Road, Daryaganj, New Delhi-110002 (India)
Ph.: 011-23244078. Fax: 011-23280028
E-Mail: cyberpublicationsdelhi@yahoo.com

**Readings in English Literature**

**L. Joseph**



First Edition 2009



*Published by :*

**G.S. Rawat** for **Cyber Tech Publications**

4264/3, Ansari Road, Daryaganj, New Delhi-110002 (India)

Ph.: 011-23244078. Fax: 011-23280028

E-Mail: cyberpublicationsdelhi@yahoo.com

*Printed at :*

# Preface

In an enquiry embracing the history of motives, causes, and ends, it is often far less important to dwell on "leading" personalities and on the main tendencies of literary production, than to consider subsidiary movements and writers below the highest rank, and to trace, in apparently arid periods, processes which were often carried on, as it were, underground, or seemed to be such as could safely be ignored. It cannot be too often urged that there are few, if any, isolated phenomena; the voices may be voices crying in the wilderness, but they belong to those who prepare the way. While, therefore, anxious that not less than justice shall be dealt out to the works of betterknown writers, the editors have tried so to plan these volumes that something more than the mere justice with which works designed on a smaller scale have had to content themselves may be given to less known writers and to so-called fugitive literature.

In the interest both of the general reader and of the student, it has been decided to insert footnotes below the text, where references seem required. These have been kept as brief as possible, in order that they may not distract attention. Further notes are, in special cases, added in the appendix and bibliographies at the end of the volume. The names of a few writers not dealt with in the text will be found in the bibliographies; but these names have not, it is hoped, been forgotten in the index. And the birth and death dates of most of the English writers mentioned in the text will be found in the index, rather than in the body of the work.

An occasional attempt has been made to give the student some assistance by means of critical hints in the bibliographies, and to point out where he may best obtain fuller information of a more special nature than can possibly be given within the limits of a general history. To attempt an exhaustive treatment of any one writer, however eminent or however insignificant, to supply analyses of well-known books which are, or should be, on the same shelves as those which may hold these volumes, or to devote much space to the repetition of biographical facts-all this has seemed to lie outside the scope of the present work.

However there is no dearth of books on the subject, but still I am confident that this work has its unique style and language the readers will derive pleasure going through it. Your valuable suggestions are always heartily welcome.

—***Author***

# Contents

1

# How to Study and Judge Literature

## ASPECTS OF LITERARY STUDY

Such a study of Literature as that for which the present book is designed includes two purposes, contributing to a common end. In the first place (I), the student must gain some general knowledge of the conditions out of which English literature has come into being, as a whole and during its successive periods, that is of the external facts of one sort or another without which it cannot be understood. This means chiefly:

(1) tracing in a general way, from period to period, the social life of the nation, and

(2) getting some acquaintance with the lives of the more important authors.

The principal thing, however (II), is the direct study of the literature itself. This study in turn should aim first at an understanding of the literature as an expression of the authors' views of life and of their personalities and especially as a portrayal and interpretation of the life of their periods and of all life as they have seen it; it should aim further at an appreciation of each literary work as a product of Fine Art, appealing with peculiar power both to our minds and to our emotions, not least to the sense of Beauty and the whole higher nature. In the present book, it should perhaps be added, the word Literature is generally interpreted in the strict sense, as including only writing of permanent significance and beauty.

The outline discussion of literary qualities which follows is intended to help in the formation of intelligent and appreciative judgments.

## SUBSTANCE AND FORM

The most thoroughgoing of all distinctions in literature, as in the other Fine Arts, is that between (1) Substance, the essential content and meaning of the work, and (2) Form, the manner in which it is expressed (including narrative structure, external style, in poetry verse-form, and many related matters). This distinction should be kept in mind, but in what follows it will not be to our purpose to emphasize it.

### General Matters

1. First and always in considering any piece of literature a student should ask himself the question already implied: Does it present a true portrayal of life--of the permanent elements in all life and in human nature, of the life or thought of its own particular period, and (in most sorts of books) of the persons, real or imaginary, with whom it deals? If it properly accomplishes this main purpose, when the reader finishes it he should feel that his understanding of life and of people has been increased and broadened. But it should always be remembered that truth is quite as much a matter of general spirit and impression as of literal accuracy in details of fact. The essential question is not, Is the presentation of life and character perfect in a photographic fashion? but Does it convey the underlying realities?
2. Other things being equal, the value of a book, and especially of an author's whole work, is proportional to its range, that is to the breadth and variety of the life and characters which it presents.
3. A student should not form his judgments merely from what is technically called the dogmatic point of view, but should try rather to adopt that of historical criticism. This means that he should take into account the limitations imposed on every author by the age in which he lived. If you find that the poets of the Anglo-Saxon 'Beowulf' have given a clear and interesting picture of the life of our barbarous ancestors of the sixth or seventh century A. D., you should not blame them for a lack of the finer elements of feeling and expression which after

a thousand years of civilization distinguish such delicate spirits as Keats and Tennyson.

4. It is often important to consider also whether the author's personal method is objective, which means that he presents life and character without bias; or subjective, coloring his work with his personal tastes, feelings and impressions. Subjectivity may be a falsifying influence, but it may also be an important virtue, adding intimacy, charm, or force. 5. Further, one may ask whether the author has a deliberately formed theory of life; and if so how it shows itself, and, of course, how sound it is.

**Intellect, Emotion, Imagination, and Related Qualities**

Another main question in judging any book concerns the union which it shows:

(1) of the Intellectual faculty, that which enables the author to understand and control his material and present it with directness and clearness; and

(2) of the Emotion, which gives warmth, enthusiasm, and appealing human power.

The relative proportions of these two faculties vary greatly in books of different sorts. Exposition (as in most essays) cannot as a rule be permeated with so much emotion as narration or, certainly, as lyric poetry. In a great book the relation of the two faculties will of course properly correspond to form and spirit. Largely a matter of Emotion is the Personal Sympathy of the author for his characters, while Intellect has a large share in Dramatic Sympathy, whereby the author enters truly into the situations and feelings of any character, whether he personally likes him or not.

Largely made up of Emotion are: (1) true Sentiment, which is fine feeling of any sort, and which should not degenerate into Sentimentalism (exaggerated tender feeling); (2) Humor, the instinctive sense for that which is amusing; and (3) the sense for Pathos. Pathos differs from Tragedy in that Tragedy (whether in a drama or elsewhere) is the suffering of persons who are able to struggle against it, Pathos the suffering of those persons (children, for instance) who are merely helpless victims. Wit, the brilliant perception of incongruities, is a matter of Intellect and the complement of Humor.

**Imagination and Fancy**

Related to Emotion also and one of the most necessary elements in the higher forms of literature is Imagination, the faculty of making what is absent or unreal seem present and real, and revealing the hidden or more subtile forces of life. Its main operations may be classified under three heads:

1. Pictorial and Presentative. It presents to the author's mind, and through him to the minds of his readers, all the elements of human experience and life (drawing from his actual experience or his reading).
2. Selective, Associative, and Constructive. From the unorganized material thus brought clearly to the author's consciousness Imagination next selects the details which can be turned to present use, and proceeds to combine them, uniting scattered traits and incidents, perhaps from widely different sources, into new characters, stories, scenes, and ideas. The characters of 'Silas Marner,' for example, never had an actual existence, and the precise incidents of the story never took place in just that order and fashion, but they were all constructed by the author's imagination out of what she had observed of many real persons and events, and so make, in the most significant sense, a true picture of life.
3. Penetrative and Interpretative. In its subtlest operations, further, Imagination penetrates below the surface and comprehends and brings to light the deeper forces and facts--the real controlling instincts of characters, the real motives for actions, and the relations of material things to those of the spiritual world and of Man to Nature and God.

Fancy may for convenience be considered as a distinct faculty, though it is really the lighter, partly superficial, aspect of Imagination. It deals with things not essentially or significantly true, amusing us with striking or pleasing suggestions, such as seeing faces in the clouds, which vanish almost as soon as they are discerned. Both Imagination and Fancy naturally express themselves, often and effectively, through the use of metaphors, similes, and suggestive condensed language. In painful contrast to them stands commonplaceness, always a fatal fault.

## IDEALISM, ROMANCE, AND REALISM

Among the most important literary qualities also are Idealism, Romance, and Realism. Realism, in the broad sense, means simply the presentation of the actual, depicting life as one sees it, objectively, without such selection as aims deliberately to emphasize some particular aspects, such as the pleasant or attractive ones. (Of course all literature is necessarily based on the ordinary facts of life, which we may call by the more general name of Reality.) Carried to the extreme, Realism may become ignoble, dealing too frankly or in unworthy spirit with the baser side of reality, and in almost all ages this sort of Realism has actually attempted to assert itself in literature.

Idealism, the tendency opposite to Realism, seeks to emphasize the spiritual and other higher elements, often to bring out the spiritual values which lie beneath the surface. It is an optimistic interpretation of life, looking for what is good and permanent beneath all the surface confusion. Romance may be called Idealism in the realm of sentiment. It aims largely to interest and delight, to throw over life a pleasing glamor; it generally deals with love or heroic adventure; and it generally locates its scenes and characters in distant times and places, where it can work unhampered by our consciousness of the humdrum actualities of our daily experience. It may always be asked whether a writer of Romance makes his world seem convincingly real as we read or whether he frankly abandons all plausibility. The presence or absence of a supernatural element generally makes an important difference. Entitled to special mention, also, is spiritual Romance, where attention is centered not on external events, which may here be treated in somewhat shadowy fashion, but on the deeper questions of life. Spiritual Romance, therefore, is essentially idealistic.

### Dramatic Power

Dramatic power, in general, means the presentation of life with the vivid active reality of life and character which especially distinguishes the acted drama. It is, of course, one of the main things to be desired in most narrative; though sometimes the effect sought may be something different, as, for instance, in romance and poetry, an atmosphere of dreamy beauty. In a drama, and to some extent in other forms of narrative, dramatic power culminates in the ability to bring out the great crises with supreme effectiveness.

### Characters

There is, generally speaking, no greater test of an author's skill than his knowledge and presentation of characters. We should consider whether he makes them (1) merely caricatures, or (2) type characters, standing for certain general traits of human nature but not convincingly real or especially significant persons, or (3) genuine individuals with all the inconsistencies and half-revealed tendencies that in actual life belong to real personality. Of course in the case of important characters, the greater the genuine individuality the greater the success.

But with secondary characters the principles of emphasis and proportion generally forbid very distinct individualization; and sometimes, especially in comedy (drama), truth of character is properly sacrificed to other objects, such as the main effect. It may also be asked whether the characters are simple, as some people are in actual life, or complex, like most interesting persons; whether they develop, as all real people must under the action of significant experience, or whether the author merely presents them in brief situations or lacks the power to make them anything but stationary. If there are several of them it is a further question whether the author properly contrasts them in such a way as to secure interest. And a main requisite is that he shall properly motivate their actions, that is make their actions result naturally from their characters, either their controlling traits or their temporary impulses.

### Structure

In any work of literature there should be definite structure. This requires, (1) Unity, (2) Variety, (3) Order, (4) Proportion, and (5) due Emphasis of parts. Unity means that everything included in the work ought to contribute directly or indirectly to the main effect. Very often a definite theme may be found about which the whole work centers, as for instance in 'Macbeth,' The Ruin of a Man through Yielding to Evil. Sometimes, however, as in a lyric poem, the effect intended may be the rendering or creation of a mood, such as that of happy content, and in that case the poem may not have an easily expressible concrete theme.

Order implies a proper beginning, arrangement, progress, and a definite ending. In narrative, including all stories whether in prose or verse and also the drama, there should be traceable a Line of Action, comprising generally: (1) an Introduction, stating the necessary preliminaries; (2) the Initial Impulse, the event which really sets in motion this particular story; (3) a Rising Action; (4) a Main Climax. Sometimes (generally, in Comedy) the Main Climax is identical with the Outcome; sometimes (regularly in Tragedy) the Main Climax is a turning point and comes near the middle of the story. In that case it really marks the beginning of the success of the side which is to be victorious at the end (in Tragedy the side opposed to the hero) and it initiates (5) a Falling Action, corresponding to the Rising Action, and sometimes of much the same length, wherein the losing side struggles to maintain itself. After (6) the Outcome, may come (7) a brief tranquilizing Conclusion. The Antecedent Action is that part of the characters' experiences which precedes the events of the story. If it has a bearing, information about it must be given either in the Introduction or incidentally later on. Sometimes, however, the structure just indicated may not be followed; a story may begin in the middle, and the earlier part may be told later on in retrospect, or incidentally indicated, like the Antecedent Action.

If in any narrative there is one or more Secondary Action, a story which might be separated from the Main Action and viewed as complete in itself, criticism should always ask whether the Main and Secondary Actions are properly unified. In the strictest theory there should be an essential connection between them; for instance, they may illustrate different and perhaps contrasting aspects of the general theme. Often, however, an author introduces a Secondary Action merely for the sake of variety or to increase the breadth of his picture--in order to present a whole section of society instead of one narrow stratum or group. In such cases, he must generally be judged to have succeeded if he has established an apparent unity, say by mingling the same characters in the two actions, so that readers are not readily conscious of the lack of real structural unity.

Other things to be considered in narrative are: Movement, which, unless for special reasons, should be rapid, at least not slow and broken; Suspense; general Interest; and the questions whether or not there are good situations and good minor climaxes, contributing to the interest; and whether or not motivation is good, apart from that which results from character, that is whether events are properly represented as happening in accordance with the law of cause and effect which inexorably governs actual life. But it must always be remembered that in such writing as Comedy and Romance the strict rules of motivation must be relaxed, and indeed in all literature, even in Tragedy, the idealization, condensation, and heightening which are the proper methods of Art require them to be slightly modified.

## Descriptive Power

Usually secondary in appearance but of vital artistic importance, is the author's power of description, of picturing both the appearance of his characters and the scenes which make his background and help to give the tone of his work. Perhaps four subjects of description may be distinguished: 1. External Nature. Here such questions as the following are of varying importance, according to the character and purpose of the work: Does the author know and care for Nature and frequently introduce descriptions? Are the descriptions concrete and accurate, or on the other hand purposely general (impressionistic) or carelessly superficial? Do they give fine variations of appearance and impression, such as delicate shiftings of light and shade and delicate tones of color? Are they powerfully sensuous, that is do they appeal strongly to the physical senses, of sight (color, light, and movement), sound (including music), smell, taste, touch, and general physical sensation? How great is their variety? Do they deal with many parts of Nature, for example the sea, mountains, plains, forests, and clouds? Is the love of external beauty a passion with the author?

What is the author's attitude toward Nature--(1) does he view Nature in a purely objective way, as a mass of material things, a series of material phenomena or a mere embodiment of sensuous beauty; or (2) is there symbolism or mysticism in his attitude, that is--does he view Nature with awe as a spiritual power; or (3) is he thoroughly subjective, reading his own moods into Nature or using Nature chiefly for the expression of his moods? Or again, does the author describe with merely expository purpose, to make the background of his work clear? 2. Individual Persons and Human Life: Is the author skilful in descriptions of personal appearance and dress? Does he produce his impressions by full enumeration of details, or by emphasis on prominent or characteristic details? How often and how fully does he describe scenes of human activity (such as a street scene, a social gathering, a procession on the march)? 3. How frequent and how vivid are his descriptions of the inanimate background of human life--buildings, interiors of rooms, and the rest? 4. Does the author skilfully use description to create the general atmosphere in which he wishes to invest his work--an atmosphere of cheerfulness, of mystery, of activity, or any of a hundred other moods?

### Style

Style in general means 'manner of writing.' In the broad sense it includes everything pertaining to the author's spirit and point of view--almost everything which is here being discussed. More narrowly considered, as 'external style,' it designates the author's use of language. Questions to be asked in regard to external style are such as these: Is it good or bad, careful or careless, clear and easy or confused and difficult; simple or complex; terse and forceful (perhaps colloquial) or involved and stately; eloquent, balanced, rhythmical; vigorous, or musical, languid, delicate and decorative; varied or monotonous; plain or figurative; poor or rich in connotation and poetic suggestiveness; beautiful, or only clear and strong? Are the sentences mostly long or short; periodic or loose; mostly of one type, such as the declarative, or with frequent introduction of such other forms as the question and the exclamation?

### Poetry

Most of what has thus far been said applies to both Prose and Poetry. But in Poetry, as the literature especially characterized in general by high Emotion, Imagination, and Beauty, finer and more delicate effects are to be sought than in Prose. Poetry, generally speaking, is the expression of the deeper nature; it belongs peculiarly to the realm of the spirit. On the side of poetical expression such imaginative figures of speech as metaphors and similes, and such devices as alliteration, prove especially helpful. It may be asked further of poetry, whether the meter and stanza structure are appropriate to the mood and thought and so handled as to bring out the emotion effectively; and whether the sound is adapted to the sense (for example, musical where the idea is of peace or quiet beauty). If the sound of the words actually imitates the sound of the thing indicated, the effect is called Onomatopoeia. Among kinds of poetry, according to form, the most important are: (1) Narrative, which includes many subordinate forms, such as the Epic. (2) Lyric. Lyric poems are expressions of spontaneous emotion and are necessarily short. (3) Dramatic, including not merely the drama but all poetry of vigorous action. (4) Descriptive, like Goldsmith's 'Deserted Village' and Tennyson's 'Dream of Fair Women.' Minor kinds are: (5) Satiric; and (6) Didactic.

Highly important in poetry is Rhythm, but the word means merely 'flow,' so that rhythm belongs to prose as well as to poetry. Good rhythm is merely a pleasing succession of sounds. Meter, the distinguishing formal mark of poetry and all verse, is merely rhythm which is regular in certain fundamental respects, roughly speaking is rhythm in which the recurrence of stressed syllables or of feet with definite time-values is regular. There is no proper connection either in spelling or in meaning between rhythm and rime (which is generally misspelled 'rhyme'). The adjective derived from 'rhythm' is 'rhythmical'; there is no adjective from 'rime' except 'rimed.' The word 'verse' in its general sense includes all writing in meter. Poetry is that verse which has real literary merit. In a very different and narrower sense 'verse' means 'line' (never properly 'stanza').

**Classicism and Romanticism**

Two of the most important contrasting tendencies of style in the general sense are Classicism and Romanticism. Classicism means those qualities which are most characteristic of the best literature of Greece and Rome. It is in fact partly identical with Idealism. It aims to express the inner truth or central principles of things, without anxiety for minor details, and it is by nature largely intellectual in quality, though not by any means to the exclusion of emotion. In outward form, therefore, it insists on correct structure, restraint, careful finish and avoidance of all excess. 'Paradise Lost,' Arnold's 'Sohrab and Rustum,' and Addison's essays are modern examples. Romanticism, which in general prevails in modern literature, lays most emphasis on independence and fulness of expression and on strong emotion, and it may be comparatively careless of form. The Classical style has well been called sculpturesque, the Romantic picturesque. The virtues of the Classical are exquisiteness and incisive significance; of the Romantic, richness and splendor. The dangers of the Classical are coldness and formality; of the Romantic, over-luxuriance, formlessness and excess of emotion.

# 2

# The Britons and the Anglo-saxons

The two earliest of the nine main divisions of English Literature are by far the longest--taken together are longer than all the others combined--but we shall pass rather rapidly over them. This is partly because the amount of thoroughly great literature which they produced is small, and partly because for present-day readers it is in effect a foreign literature, written in early forms of English or in foreign languages, so that to-day it is intelligible only through special study or in translation.

## THE BRITONS

The present English race has gradually shaped itself out of several distinct peoples which successively occupied or conquered the island of Great Britain. The earliest one of these peoples which need here be mentioned belonged to the Celtic family and was itself divided into two branches. The Goidels or Gaels were settled in the northern part of the island, which is now Scotland, and were the ancestors of the present Highland Scots. On English literature they exerted little or no influence until a late period. The Britons, from whom the present Welsh are descended, inhabited what is now England and Wales; and they were still further subdivided, like most barbarous peoples, into many tribes which were often at war with one another. Though the Britons were conquered and chiefly supplanted later on by the Anglo-Saxons, enough of them, as we shall see, were spared and intermarried with the victors to transmit something of their racial qualities to the English nation and literature.

The characteristics of the Britons, which are those of the Celtic family as a whole, appear in their history and in the scanty late remains of their literature. Two main traits include or suggest all the others: first, a vigorous but fitful emotionalism which rendered them vivacious, lovers of novelty, and brave, but ineffective in practical affairs; second, a somewhat fantastic but sincere and delicate sensitiveness to beauty. Into impetuous action they were easily hurried; but their momentary ardor easily cooled into fatalistic despondency. To the mysterious charm of Nature--of hills and forests and pleasant breezes; to the loveliness and grace of meadow-flowers or of a young man or a girl; to the varied sheen of rich colors--to all attractive objects of sight and sound and motion their fancy responded keenly and joyfully; but they preferred chiefly to weave these things into stories and verse of supernatural romance or vague suggestiveness; for substantial work of solider structure either in life or in literature they possessed comparatively little faculty. Here is a description (exceptionally beautiful, to be sure) from the story 'Kilhwch and Olwen':

'The maid was clothed in a robe of flame-colored silk, and about her neck was a collar of ruddy gold, on which were precious emeralds and rubies. More yellow was her head than the flowers of the broom, and her skin was whiter than the foam of the wave, and fairer were her hands and her fingers than the blossoms of the wood anemone amidst the spray of the meadow fountain. The eye of the trained hawk, the glance of the three-mewed falcon, was not brighter than hers. Her bosom was more snowy than the breast of the white swan, her cheeks were redder than the reddest roses. Who beheld her was filled with her love. Pour white trefoils sprang up wherever she trod. And therefore was she called Olwen.'

This charming fancifulness and delicacy of feeling is apparently the great contribution of the Britons to English literature; from it may perhaps be descended the fairy scenes of Shakspere and possibly to some extent the lyrical music of Tennyson.

## THE ROMAN OCCUPATION

Of the Roman conquest and occupation of Britain (England and Wales) we need only make brief mention, since it produced virtually no effect on English literature. The fact should not be forgotten that for over three hundred years, from the first century A. D. to the beginning of the fifth, the island was a Roman province, with Latin as the language of the ruling class of Roman immigrants, who introduced Roman civilization and later on Christianity, to the Britons of the towns and plains. But the interest of the Romans in the island was centered on other things than writing, and the great bulk of the Britons themselves seem to have been only superficially affected by the Roman supremacy. At the end of the Roman rule, as at its beginning, they appear divided into mutually jealous tribes, still largely barbarous and primitive.

The Anglo-Saxons. Meanwhile across the North Sea the three Germanic tribes which were destined to form the main element in the English race were multiplying and unconsciously preparing to swarm to their new home. The Angles, Saxons, and Jutes occupied territories in the region which includes parts of the present Holland, of Germany about the mouth of the Elbe, and of Denmark. They were barbarians, living partly from piratical expeditions against the northern and eastern coasts of Europe, partly from their flocks and herds, and partly from a rude sort of agriculture. At home they seem to have sheltered themselves chiefly in unsubstantial wooden villages, easily destroyed and easily abandoned; For the able-bodied freemen among them the chief occupation, as a matter of course, was war.

Strength, courage, and loyalty to king and comrades were the chief virtues that they admired; ferocity and cruelty, especially to other peoples, were necessarily among their prominent traits when their blood was up; though among themselves there was no doubt plenty of rough and ready companionable good-humor. Their bleak country, where the foggy and unhealthy marshes of the coast gave way further inland to vast and somber forests, developed in them during their long inactive winters a sluggish and gloomy mood, in which, however, the alternating spirit of aggressive enterprise was never quenched. In religion they had reached a moderately advanced state of heathenism, worshipping especially, it seems, Woden, a 'furious' god as well as a wise and crafty one; the warrior Tiu; and the strong-armed Thunor (the Scandinavian Thor); but together with these some milder deities like the goddess of spring, Eostre, from whom our Easter is named. For the people on whom they fell these barbarians were a pitiless and terrible scourge; yet they possessed in undeveloped form the intelligence, the energy, the strength--most of the qualities of head and heart and body--which were to make of them one of the great world-races.

## THE ANGLO-SAXON CONQUEST AND SETTLEMENT

The process by which Britain became England was a part of the long agony which transformed the Roman Empire into modern Europe. In the fourth century A. D. the Angles, Saxons, and Jutes began to harry the southern and eastern shores of Britain, where the Romans were obliged to maintain a special military establishment against them. But early in the fifth century the Romans, hard-pressed even in Italy by other barbarian invaders, withdrew all their troops and completely abandoned Britain. Not long thereafter, and probably before the traditional date of 449, the Jutes, Angles, and Saxons began to come in large bands with the deliberate purpose of permanent settlement. Their conquest, very different in its methods and results from that of the Romans, may roughly be said to have occupied a hundred and fifty or two hundred years.

The earlier invading hordes fixed themselves at various points on the eastern and southern shore and gradually fought their way inland, and they were constantly augmented by new arrivals. In general the Angles settled in the east and north and the Saxons in the south, while the less numerous Jutes, the first to come, in Kent, soon ceased to count in the movement. In this way there naturally came into existence a group of separate and rival kingdoms, which when they were not busy with the Britons were often at war with each other. Their number varied somewhat from time to time as they were united or divided; but on the whole, seven figured most prominently, whence comes the traditional name 'The Saxon Heptarchy' (Seven Kingdoms). The resistance of the Britons to the Anglo-Saxon advance was often brave and sometimes temporarily successful. Early in the sixth century, for example, they won at Mount Badon in the south a great victory, later connected in tradition with the legendary name of King Arthur, which for many years gave them security from further aggressions. But in the long run their racial defects proved fatal; they were unable to combine in permanent and steady union, and tribe by tribe the newcomers drove them slowly back; until early in the seventh century the Anglo-Saxons were in possession of nearly all of what is now England, the exceptions being the regions all along the west coast, including what has ever since been, known as Wales.

Of the Roman and British civilization the Anglo-Saxons were ruthless destroyers, exulting, like other barbarians, in the wanton annihilation of things which they did not understand. Every city, or nearly every one, which they took, they burned, slaughtering the inhabitants. They themselves occupied the land chiefly as masters of scattered farms, each warrior established in a large rude house surrounded by its various outbuildings and the huts of the British slaves and the Saxon and British bondmen. Just how largely the Britons were exterminated and how largely they were kept alive as slaves and wives, is uncertain; but it is evident that at least a considerable number were spared; to this the British names of many of our objects of humble use, for example mattoc and basket, testify.

In the natural course of events, however, no sooner had the Anglo-Saxons destroyed the (imperfect and partial) civilization of their predecessors than they began to rebuild one for themselves; possessors of a fertile land, they settled down to develop it, and from tribes of lawless fighters were before long transformed into a race of farmer-citizens. Gradually trade with the Continent, also, was reestablished and grew; but perhaps the most important humanizing influence was the reintroduction of Christianity.

The story is famous of how Pope Gregory the Great, struck by the beauty of certain Angle slave-boys at Rome, declared that they ought to be called not Angli but Angeli (angels) and forthwith, in 597, sent to Britain St. Augustine (not the famous African saint of that name), who landed in Kent and converted that kingdom. Within the next two generations, and after much fierce fighting between the adherents of the two religions, all the other kingdoms as well had been christianized. It was only the southern half of the island, however, that was won by the Roman missionaries; in the north the work was done independently by preachers from Ireland, where, in spite of much anarchy, a certain degree of civilization had been preserved.

These two types of Christianity, those of Ireland and of Rome, were largely different in spirit. The Irish missionaries were simple and loving men and won converts by the beauty of their lives; the Romans brought with them the architecture, music, and learning of their imperial city and the aggressive energy which in the following centuries was to make their Church supreme throughout the Western world. When the inevitable clash for supremacy came, the king of the then-dominant Anglian kingdom, Northumbria, made choice of the Roman as against the Irish Church, a choice which proved decisive for the entire island. And though our personal sympathies may well go to the finer-spirited Irish, this outcome was on the whole fortunate; for only through religious union with Rome during the slow centuries of medieval rebirth could England be bound to the rest of Europe as one of the family of cooperating Christian states; and outside that family she would have been isolated and spiritually starved.

One of the greatest gifts of Christianity, it should be observed, and one of the most important influences in medieval civilization, was the network of monasteries which were now gradually established and became centers of active hospitality and the chief homes of such learning as was possible to the time.

## ANGLO-SAXON POETRY

The Anglo-Saxons doubtless brought with them from the Continent the rude beginnings of poetry, such as come first in the literature of every people and consist largely of brief magical charms and of rough 'popular ballads' (ballads of the people). The charms explain themselves as an inevitable product of primitive superstition; the ballads probably first sprang up and developed, among all races, in much the following way. At the very beginning of human society, long before the commencement of history, the primitive groups of savages who then constituted mankind were instinctively led to express their emotions together, communally, in rhythmical fashion. Perhaps after an achievement in hunting or war the village-group would mechanically fall into a dance, sometimes, it might be, about their village fire. Suddenly from among the inarticulate cries of the crowd some one excited individual would shout out a fairly distinct rhythmical expression. This expression, which may be called a line, was taken up and repeated by the crowd; others might be added to it, and thus gradually, in the course of generations, arose the regular habit of communal composition, composition of something like complete ballads by the throng as a whole. This procedure ceased to be important everywhere long before the literary period, but it led to the frequent composition by humble versifiers of more deliberate poems which were still 'popular' because they circulated by word of mouth, only, from generation to generation, among the common people, and formed one of the best expressions of their feeling.

At an early period also professional minstrels, called by the Anglo-Saxons scops or gleemen, disengaged themselves from the crowd and began to gain their living by wandering from village to village or tribe to tribe chanting to the harp either the popular ballads or more formal poetry of their own composition. Among all races when a certain stage of social development is reached at least one such minstrel is to be found as a regular retainer at the court of every barbarous chief or king, ready to entertain the warriors at their feasts, with chants of heroes and battles and of the exploits of their present lord. All the earliest products of these processes of 'popular' and minstrel composition are everywhere lost long before recorded literature begins, but the processes themselves in their less formal stages continue among uneducated people (whose mental life always remains more or less primitive) even down to the present time.

Out of the popular ballads, or, chiefly, of the minstrel poetry which is partly based on them, regularly develops epic poetry. Perhaps a minstrel finds a number of ballads which deal with the exploits of a single hero or with a single event. He combines them as best he can into a unified story and recites this on important and stately occasions. As his work passes into general circulation other minstrels add other ballads, until at last, very likely after many generations, a complete epic is formed, outwardly continuous and whole, but generally more or less clearly separable on analysis into its original parts. Or, on the other hand, the combination may be mostly performed all at once at a comparatively late period by a single great poet, who with conscious art weaves together a great mass of separate materials into the nearly finished epic.

Not much Anglo-Saxon poetry of the pagan period has come down to us. By far the most important remaining example is the epic 'Beowulf,' of about three thousand lines. This poem seems to have originated on the Continent, but when and where are not now to be known. It may have been carried to England in the form of ballads by the Anglo-Saxons; or it may be Scandinavian material, later brought in by Danish or Norwegian pirates. At any rate it seems to have taken on its present form in England during the seventh and eighth centuries. It relates, with the usual terse and unadorned power of really primitive poetry, how the hero Beowulf, coming over the sea to the relief of King Hrothgar, delivers him from a monster, Grendel, and then from the vengeance of Grendel's only less formidable mother.

Returned home in triumph, Beowulf much later receives the due reward of his valor by being made king of his own tribe, and meets his death while killing a fire-breathing dragon which has become a scourge to his people. As he appears in the poem, Beowulf is an idealized Anglo-Saxon hero, but in origin he may have been any one of several other different things. Perhaps he was the old Germanic god Beowa, and his exploits originally allegories, like some of those in the Greek mythology, of his services to man; he may, for instance, first have been the sun, driving away the mists and cold of winter and of the swamps, hostile forces personified in Grendel and his mother. Or, Beowulf may really have been a great human fighter who actually killed some especially formidable wild beasts, and whose superhuman strength in the poem results, through the similarity of names, from his being confused with Beowa.

This is the more likely because there is in the poem a slight trace of authentic history.

'Beowulf' presents an interesting though very incomplete picture of the life of the upper, warrior, caste among the northern Germanic tribes during their later period of barbarism on the Continent and in England, a life more highly developed than that of the Anglo-Saxons before their conquest of the island.

About King Hrothgar are grouped his immediate retainers, the warriors, with whom he shares his wealth; it is a part of the character, of a good king to be generous in the distribution of gifts of gold and weapons. Somewhere in the background there must be a village, where the bondmen and slaves provide the daily necessaries of life and where some of the warriors may have houses and families; but all this is beneath the notice of the courtly poet.

The center of the warriors' life is the great hall of the king, built chiefly of timber. Inside, there are benches and tables for feasting, and the walls are perhaps adorned with tapestries. Near the center is the hearth, whence the smoke must escape, if it escapes at all, through a hole in the roof. In the hall the warriors banquet, sometimes in the company of their wives, but the women retire before the later revelry which often leaves the men drunk on the floor. Sometimes, it seems, there are sleeping-rooms or niches about the sides of the hall, but in 'Beowulf' Hrothgar and his followers retire to other quarters. War, feasting, and hunting are the only occupations in which the warriors care to be thought to take an interest.

The spirit of the poem is somber and grim. There is no unqualified happiness of mood, and only brief hints of delight in the beauty and joy of the world. Rather, there is stern satisfaction in the performance of the warrior's and the sea-king's task, the determination of a strong-willed race to assert itself, and do, with much barbarian boasting, what its hand finds to do in the midst of a difficult life and a hostile nature. For the ultimate force in the universe of these fighters and their poets (in spite of certain Christian touches inserted by later poetic editors before the poem crystallized into its present form) is Wyrd, the Fate of the Germanic peoples, cold as their own winters and the bleak northern sea, irresistible, despotic, and unmoved by sympathy for man. Great as the differences are, very much of this Anglo-Saxon pagan spirit persists centuries later in the English Puritans.

For the finer artistic graces, also, and the structural subtilties of a more developed literary period, we must not, of course, look in 'Beowulf.' The narrative is often more dramatic than clear, and there is no thought of any minuteness of characterization. A few typical characters stand out clearly, and they were all that the poet's turbulent and not very attentive audience could understand. But the barbaric vividness and power of the poem give it much more than a merely historical interest; and the careful reader cannot fail to realize that it is after all the product of a long period of poetic development.

## THE ANGLO-SAXON VERSE-FORM

The poetic form of 'Beowulf' is that of virtually all Anglo-Saxon poetry down to the tenth century, or indeed to the end, a form which is roughly represented in the present book in a passage of imitative translation two pages below. The verse is unrimed, not arranged in stanzas, and with lines more commonly end-stopped (with distinct pauses at the ends) than is true in good modern poetry. Each line is divided into halves and each half contains two stressed syllables, generally long in quantity. The number of unstressed syllables appears to a modern eye or ear irregular and actually is very unequal, but they are really combined with the stressed ones into 'feet' in accordance with certain definite principles.

At least one of the stressed syllables in each half-line must be in alliteration with one in the other half-line; and most often the alliteration includes both stressed syllables in the first halfline and the first stressed syllable in the second, occasionally all four stressed syllables. (All vowels are held to alliterate with each other.) It will be seen therefore that (1) emphatic stress and (2) alliteration are the basal principles of the system. To a present-day reader the verse sounds crude, the more so because of the harshly consonantal character of the Anglo-Saxon language; and in comparison with modern poetry it is undoubtedly unmelodious. But it was worked out on conscious artistic principles, carefully followed; and when chanted, as it was meant to be, to the harp it possessed much power and even beauty of a vigorous sort, to which the pictorial and metaphorical wealth of the Anglo-Saxon poetic vocabulary largely contributed.

This last-named quality, the use of metaphors, is perhaps the most conspicuous one in the style, of the Anglo-Saxon poetry. The language, compared to that of our own vastly more complex time, was undeveloped; but for use in poetry, especially, there were a great number of periphrastic but vividly picturesque metaphorical synonyms (technically called kennings). Thus the spear becomes 'the slaughter-shaft'; fighting 'hand-play'; the sword 'the leavings of the hammer' (or 'of the anvil'); and a ship 'the foamy-necked floater.' These kennings add much imaginative suggestiveness to the otherwise over-terse style, and often contribute to the grim irony which is another outstanding trait.

## The Northumbrian Period

The Anglo-Saxons were for a long time fully occupied with the work of conquest and settlement, and their first literature of any importance, aside from 'Beowulf,' appears at about the time when 'Beowulf' was being put into its present form, namely in the seventh century. This was in the Northern, Anglian, kingdom of Northumbria (Yorkshire and Southern Scotland), which, as we have already said, had then won the political supremacy, and whose monasteries and capital city, York, thanks to the Irish missionaries, had become the chief centers of learning and culture in Western Christian Europe. Still pagan in spirit are certain obscure but, ingenious and skillfully developed riddles in verse, representatives of one form of popular literature only less early than the ballads and charms. There remain also a few pagan lyric poems, which are all not only somber like 'Beowulf' but distinctly elegiac, that is pensively melancholy.

They deal with the hard and tragic things in life, the terrible power of ocean and storm, or the inexorableness and dreariness of death, banishment, and the separation of friends. In their frequent tender notes of pathos there may be some influence from the Celtic spirit. The greater part of the literature of the period, however, was Christian, produced in the monasteries or under their influence. The first Christian writer was Caedmon (pronounced Kadmon), who toward the end of the seventh century paraphrased in Anglo-Saxon verse some portions of the Bible. The legend of his divine call is famous.

The following is a modern rendering of the hymn which is said to have been his first work:

*Now must we worship the heaven-realm's Warder, The Maker's might and his mind's thought, The glory-father's work as he every wonder, Lord everlasting, of old established. He first fashioned the firmament for mortals, Heaven as a roof, the holy Creator. Then the midearth mankind's Warder, Lord everlasting, afterwards wrought, For men a garden, God almighty.*

After Caedmon comes Bede, not a poet but a monk of strong and beautiful character, a profound scholar who in nearly forty Latin prose works summarized most of the knowledge of his time. The other name to be remembered is that of Cynewulf (pronounced Kinnywulf), the author of some noble religious poetry (in Anglo-Saxon), especially narratives dealing with Christ and Christian Apostles and heroes. There is still other Anglo-Saxon Christian poetry, generally akin in subjects to Cynewulf's, but in most of the poetry of the whole period the excellence results chiefly from the survival of the old pagan spirit which distinguishes 'Beowulf Where the poet writes for edification he is likely to be dull, but when his story provides him with sea-voyages, with battles, chances for dramatic dialogue, or any incidents of vigorous action or of passion, the zest for adventure and war rekindles, and we have descriptions and narratives of picturesque color and stern force.

Sometimes there is real religious yearning, and indeed the heroes of these poems are partly medieval hermits and ascetics as well as quick-striking fighters; but for the most part the Christian Providence is really only the heathen Wyrd under another name, and God and Christ are viewed in much the same way as the Anglo-Saxon kings, the objects of feudal allegiance which is sincere but rather self-assertive and worldly than humble or consecrated.

On the whole, then, Anglo-Saxon poetry exhibits the limitations of a culturally early age, but it manifests also a degree of power which gives to Anglo-Saxon literature unquestionable superiority over that of any other European country of the same period.

## THE WEST-SAXON, PROSE, PERIOD

The horrors which the Anglo-Saxons had inflicted on the Britons they themselves were now to suffer from their still heathen and piratical kinsmen the 'Danes' or Northmen, inhabitants or the Scandinavian peninsula and the neighboring coasts. For a hundred years, throughout the ninth century, the Danes, appearing with unwearied persistence, repeatedly ravaged and plundered England, and they finally made complete conquest of Northumbria, destroyed all the churches and monasteries, and almost completely extinguished learning. It is a familiar story how Alfred, king from 871 to 901 of the southern kingdom of Wessex (the land of the West Saxons), which had now taken first place among the Anglo-Saxon states, stemmed the tide of invasion and by ceding to the 'Danes' the whole northeastern half of the island obtained for the remainder the peace which was the first essential for the reestablishment of civilization.

Peace secured, Alfred, who was one of the greatest of all English kings, labored unremittingly for learning, as for everything else that was useful, and he himself translated from Latin into Anglo-Saxon half a dozen of the best informational manuals of his time, manuals of history, philosophy, and religion. His most enduring literary work, however, was the inspiration and possibly partial authorship of the 'Anglo-Saxon Chronicle,' a series of annals beginning with the Christian era, kept at various monasteries, and recording year by year (down to two centuries and a half after Alfred's own death), the most important events of history, chiefly that of England. Most of the entries in the 'Chronicle' are bare and brief, but sometimes, especially in the accounts of Alfred's own splendid exploits, a writer is roused to spirited narrative, occasionally in verse; and in the tenth century two great battles against invading Northmen, at Brunanburh and Maldon, produced the only important extant pieces of Anglo-Saxon poetry which certainly belong to the West Saxon period.

For literature, indeed, the West-Saxon period has very little permanent significance. Plenty of its other writing remains in the shape of religious prose--sermons, lives and legends of saints, biblical paraphrases, and similar work in which the monastic and priestly spirit took delight, but which is generally dull with the dulness of medieval commonplace didacticism and fantastic symbolism. The country, too, was still distracted with wars. Within fifty years after Alfred's death, to be sure, his descendants had won back the whole of England from 'Danish' rule (though the 'Danes,' then constituting half the population of the north and east, have remained to the present day a large element in the English race). But near the end of the tenth century new swarms of 'Danes' reappeared from the

Baltic lands, once more slaughtering and devastating, until at last in the eleventh century the 'Danish' though Christian Canute ruled for twenty years over all England. In such a time there could be little intellectual or literary life.

But the decline of the Anglo-Saxon literature speaks also partly of stagnation in the race itself. The people, though still sturdy, seem to have become somewhat dull from inbreeding and to have required an infusion of altogether different blood from without. This necessary renovation was to be violently forced upon them, for in 1066 Duke William of Normandy landed at Pevensey with his army of adventurers and his ill-founded claim to the crown, and before him at Hastings fell the gallant Harold and his nobles. By the fortune of this single fight, followed only by stern suppression of spasmodic outbreaks, William established himself and his vassals as masters of the land. England ceased to be Anglo-Saxon and became, altogether politically, and partly in race, Norman-French, a change more radical and far-reaching than any which it has since undergone.

# 3

# The Norman-french Period

## THE NORMANS

The Normans who conquered England were originally members of the same stock as the 'Danes' who had harried and conquered it in the preceding centuries--the ancestors of both were bands of Baltic and North Sea pirates who merely happened to emigrate in different directions; and a little farther back the Normans were close cousins, in the general Germanic family, of the Anglo-Saxons themselves. The exploits of this whole race of Norse sea-kings make one of the most remarkable chapters in the history of medieval Europe. In the ninth and tenth centuries they mercilessly ravaged all the coasts not only of the West but of all Europe from the Rhine to the Adriatic. 'From the fury of the Norsemen, good Lord, deliver us!' was a regular part of the litany of the unhappy French.

They settled Iceland and Greenland and prematurely discovered America; they established themselves as the ruling aristocracy in Russia, and as the imperial body-guard and chief bulwark of the Byzantine empire at Constantinople; and in the eleventh century they conquered southern Italy and Sicily, whence in the first crusade they pressed on with unabated vigor to Asia Minor. Those bands of them with whom we are here concerned, and who became known distinctively as Normans, fastened themselves as settlers, early in the eleventh century, on the northern shore of France, and in return for their acceptance of Christianity and acknowledgment of the nominal feudal sovereignty of the French king were recognized as rightful possessors of the large province which thus came to bear the name of Normandy. Here by intermarriage with the native women they rapidly developed into a race which while retaining all their original courage and enterprise took on also, together with the French language, the French intellectual brilliancy and flexibility and in manners became the chief exponent of medieval chivalry.

The different elements contributed to the modern English character by the latest stocks which have been united in it have been indicated by Matthew Arnold in a famous passage ('On the Study of Celtic Literature'): 'The Germanic [Anglo-Saxon and 'Danish'] genius has steadiness as its main basis, with commonness and humdrum for its defect, fidelity to nature for its excellence. The Norman genius, talent for affairs as its main basis, with strenuousness and clear rapidity for its excellence, hardness and insolence for its defect.' The Germanic (Anglo-Saxon and 'Danish') element explains, then, why uneducated Englishmen of all times have been thick-headed, unpleasantly self-assertive, and unimaginative, but sturdy fighters; and the Norman strain why upper-class Englishmen have been self-contained, inclined to snobbishness, but vigorously aggressive and persevering, among the best conquerors, organizers, and administrators in the history of the world.

## SOCIAL RESULTS OF THE CONQUEST

In most respects, or all, the Norman conquest accomplished precisely that racial rejuvenation of which, as we have seen, Anglo-Saxon England stood in need. For the Normans brought with them from France the zest for joy and beauty and dignified and stately ceremony in which the Anglo-Saxon temperament was poor--they brought the love of light-hearted song and chivalrous sports, of rich clothing, of finely-painted manuscripts, of noble architecture in cathedrals and palaces, of formal religious ritual, and of the pomp and display of all elaborate pageantry. In the outcome they largely reshaped the heavy mass of Anglo-Saxon life into forms of grace and beauty and brightened its duller surface with varied and brilliant colors.

For the Anglo-Saxons themselves, however, the Conquest meant at first little else than that bitterest and most complete of all national disasters, hopeless subjection to a tyrannical and contemptuous foe. The Normans were not heathen, as the 'Danes' had been, and they were too few in number to wish to supplant the conquered people; but they imposed themselves, both politically and socially, as stern and absolute masters. King William confirmed in their possessions the few Saxon nobles and lesser land-owners who accepted his rule and did not later revolt; but both pledges and interest compelled him to bestow most of the estates of the kingdom, together with the widows of their former holders, on his own nobles and the great motley throng of turbulent fighters who had made up his invading army.

In the lordships and manors, therefore, and likewise in the great places of the Church, were established knights and nobles, the secular ones holding in feudal tenure from the king or his immediate great vassals, and each supported in turn by Norman men-at-arms; and to them were subjected as serfs, workers bound to the land, the greater part of the Saxon population. As visible signs of the changed order appeared here and there throughout the country massive and gloomy castles of stone, and in the larger cities, in place of the simple Anglo-Saxon churches, cathedrals lofty and magnificent beyond all Anglo-Saxon dreams. What sufferings, at the worst, the Normans inflicted on the Saxons is indicated in a famous passage of the 'Anglo-Saxon Chronicle,' an entry seventy years subsequent to the Conquest, of which the least distressing part may be thus paraphrased:

'They filled the land full of castles. They compelled the wretched men of the land to build their castles and wore them out with hard labor. When the castles were made they filled them with devils and evil men. Then they took all those whom they thought to have any property, both by night and by day, both men and women, and put them in prison for gold and silver, and tormented them with tortures that cannot be told; for never were any martyrs so tormented as these were.'

## THE UNION OF THE RACES AND LANGUAGES

That their own race and identity were destined to be absorbed in those of the Anglo-Saxons could never have occurred to any of the Normans who stood with William at Hastings, and scarcely to any of their children. Yet this result was predetermined by the stubborn tenacity and numerical superiority of the conquered people and by the easy adaptability of the Norman temperament. Racially, and to a less extent socially, intermarriage did its work, and that within a very few generations. Little by little, also, Norman contempt and Saxon hatred were softened into tolerance, and at last even into a sentiment of national unity. This sentiment was finally to be confirmed by the loss of Normandy and other French possessions of the Norman-English kings in the thirteenth century, a loss which transformed England from a province of the Norman Continental empire and of a foreign nobility into an independent country, and further by the wars ('The Hundred Years' War') which England-Norman nobility and Saxon yeomen fighting together--carried on in France in the fourteenth century.

In language and literature the most general immediate result of the Conquest was to make of England a trilingual country, where Latin, French, and Anglo-Saxon were spoken separately side by side. With Latin, the tongue of the Church and of scholars, the Norman clergy were much more thoroughly familiar than the Saxon priests had been; and the introduction of the richer Latin culture resulted, in the latter half of the twelfth century, at the court of Henry II, in a brilliant outburst of Latin literature. In England, as well as in the rest of Western Europe, Latin long continued to be the language of religious and learned writing--down to the sixteenth century or even later.

French, that dialect of it which was spoken by the Normans--Anglo-French (English-French) it has naturally come to be called--was of course introduced by the Conquest as the language of the governing and upper social class, and in it also during the next three or four centuries a considerable body of literature was produced.

Anglo-Saxon, which we may now term English, remained inevitably as the language of the subject race, but their literature was at first crushed down into insignificance. Ballads celebrating the resistance of scattered Saxons to their oppressors no doubt circulated widely on the lips of the people, but English writing of the more formal sorts, almost absolutely ceased for more than a century, to make a new beginning about the year 1200. In the interval the 'Anglo-Saxon Chronicle' is the only important document, and even this, continued at the monastery of Peterboro, comes to an end in 1154, in the midst of the terrible anarchy of Stephen's reign.

It must not be supposed, notwithstanding, that the Normans, however much they despised the English language and literature, made any effort to destroy it. On the other hand, gradual union of the two languages was no less inevitable than that of the races themselves. From, the very first the need of communication, with their subjects must have rendered it necessary for the Normans to acquire some knowledge of the English language; and the children of mixed parentage of course learned it from their mothers.

The use of French continued in the upper strata of society, in the few children's schools that existed, and in the law courts, for something like three centuries, maintaining itself so long partly because French was then the polite language of Western Europe. But the dead pressure of English was increasingly strong, and by the end of the fourteenth century and of Chaucer's life French had chiefly given way to it even at Court.

As we have already implied, however, the English which triumphed was in fact English-French--English was enabled to triumph partly because it had now largely absorbed the French. For the first one hundred or one hundred and fifty years, it seems, the two languages remained for the most part pretty clearly distinct, but in the thirteenth and fourteenth centuries English, abandoning its first aloofness, rapidly took into itself a large part of the French (originally Latin) vocabulary; and under the influence of the French it carried much farther the process of dropping its own comparatively complicated grammatical inflections--a process which had already gained much momentum even before the Conquest. This absorption of the French was most fortunate for English. To the Anglo-Saxon vocabulary--vigorous, but harsh, limited in extent, and lacking in fine discriminations and power of abstract expression, was now added nearly the whole wealth of French, with its fullness, flexibility, and grace. As a direct consequence the resulting language, modern English, is the richest and most varied instrument of expression ever developed at any time by any race.

## THE RESULT FOR POETRY

For poetry the fusion meant even more than for prose. The metrical system, which begins to appear in the thirteenth century and comes to perfection a century and a half later in Chaucer's poems combined what may fairly be called the better features of both the systems from which it was compounded. We have seen that Anglo-Saxon verse depended on regular stress of a definite number of quantitatively long syllables in each line and on alliteration; that it allowed much variation in the number of unstressed syllables; and that it was without rime.

French verse, on the other hand, had rime (or assonance) and carefully preserved identity in the total number of syllables in corresponding lines, but it was uncertain as regarded the number of clearly stressed ones. The derived English system adopted from the French (1) rime and (2) identical line-length, and retained from the Anglo-Saxon (3) regularity of stress. (4) It largely abandoned the Anglo-Saxon regard for quantity and (5) it retained alliteration not as a basic principle but as an (extremely useful) subordinate device. This metrical system, thus shaped, has provided the indispensable formal basis for making English poetry admittedly the greatest in the modern world.

## THE ENGLISH DIALECTS

The study of the literature of the period is further complicated by the division of English into dialects. The Norman Conquest put a stop to the progress of the West-Saxon dialect toward complete supremacy, restoring the dialects of the other parts of the island to their former positions of equal authority. The actual result was the development of three groups of dialects, the Southern, Midland (divided into East and West) and Northern, all differing among themselves in forms and even in vocabulary. Literary activity when it recommenced was about equally distributed among the three, and for three centuries it was doubtful which of them would finally win the first place.

In the outcome success fell to the East Midland dialect, partly through the influence of London, which under the Norman kings replaced Winchester as the capital city and seat of the Court and Parliament, and partly through the influence of the two Universities, Oxford and Cambridge, which gradually grew up during the twelfth and thirteenth centuries and attracted students from all parts of the country. This victory of the East

Midland form was marked by, though it was not in any large degree due to, the appearance in the fourteenth century of the first great modern English poet, Chaucer. To the present day, however, the three dialects, and subdivisions of them, are easily distinguishable in colloquial use; the common idiom of such regions as Yorkshire and Cornwall is decidedly different from that of London or indeed any other part of the country.

## THE ENGLISH LITERATURE AS A PART OF GENERAL MEDIEVAL EUROPEAN LITERATURE

One of the most striking general facts in the later Middle Ages is the uniformity of life in many of its aspects throughout all Western Europe. It was only during this period that the modern nations, acquiring national consciousness, began definitely to shape themselves out of the chaos which had followed the fall of the Roman Empire. The Roman Church, firmly established in every corner of every land, was the actual inheritor of much of the unifying power of the Roman government, and the feudal system everywhere gave to society the same political organization and ideals. In a truer sense, perhaps, than at any later time, Western Europe was one great brotherhood, thinking much the same thoughts, speaking in part the same speech, and actuated by the same beliefs. At least, the literature of the period, largely composed and copied by the great army of monks, exhibits everywhere a thorough uniformity in types and ideas.

We of the twentieth century should not allow ourselves to think vaguely of the Middle Ages as a benighted or shadowy period when life and the people who constituted it had scarcely anything in common with ourselves. In reality the men of the Middle Ages were moved by the same emotions and impulses as our own, and their lives presented the same incongruous mixture of nobility and baseness. Yet it is true that the externals of their existence were strikingly different from those of more recent times. In society the feudal system--lords with their serfs, towns struggling for municipal independence, kings and nobles doing, peaceably or with violence, very much what they pleased; a constant condition of public or private war; cities walled as a matter of course for protection against bands of robbers or hostile armies; the country still largely covered with forests, wildernesses, and fens; roads infested with brigands and so bad that travel was scarcely possible except on horseback; in private life, most of the modern comforts unknown, and the houses, even of the wealthy, so filthy and uncomfortable that all classes regularly, almost necessarily, spent most of the daylight hours in the open air; in industry no coal, factories, or large machinery, but in the towns guilds of workmen each turning out by hand his slow product of single articles; almost no education except for priests and monks, almost no conceptions of genuine science or history, but instead the abstract system of scholastic logic and philosophy, highly ingenious but highly fantastic; in religion no outward freedom of thought except for a few courageous spirits, but the arbitrary dictates of a despotic hierarchy, insisting on an ironbound creed which the remorseless process of time was steadily rendering more and more inadequate--this offers some slight suggestion of the conditions of life for several centuries, ending with the period with which we are now concerned.

In medieval literature likewise the modern student encounters much which seems at first sight grotesque. One of the most conspicuous examples is the pervasive use of allegory. The men of the Middle Ages often wrote, as we do, in direct terms and of simple things, but when they wished to rise above the commonplace they turned with a frequency which to-day appears astonishing to the devices of abstract personification and veiled meanings. No doubt this tendency was due in part to an idealizing dissatisfaction with the crudeness of their actual life (as well as to frequent inability to enter into the realm of deeper and finer thought without the aid of somewhat mechanical imagery); and no doubt it was greatly furthered also by the medieval passion for translating into elaborate and fantastic symbolism all the details of the Bible narratives. But from whatever cause, the tendency hardened into a ruling convention; thousands upon thousands of medieval manuscripts seem to declare that the world is a mirage of shadowy forms, or that it exists merely to body forth remote and highly surprising ideas.

Of all these countless allegories none was reiterated with more unwearied persistence than that of the Seven Deadly Sins (those sins which in the doctrine of the Church lead to spiritual death because they are wilfully committed). These sins are: Covetousness, Unchastity, Anger, Gluttony, Envy, Sloth, and, chief of all, Pride, the earliest of all, through which Lucifer was moved to his fatal rebellion against God, whence spring all human ills. Each of the seven, however, was interpreted as including so many related offences that among them they embraced nearly the whole range of possible wickedness. Personified, the Seven Sins in themselves almost dominate medieval literature, a sort of shadowy evil pantheon.

Moral and religious questions could scarcely be discussed without regard to them; and they maintain their commanding place even as late as in Spenser's 'Faerie Queene,' at the very end of the sixteenth century. To the Seven Sins were commonly opposed, but with much less emphasis, the Seven Cardinal Virtues, Faith, Hope, Charity (Love), Prudence, Temperance, Chastity, and Fortitude. Again, almost as prominent as the Seven Sins was the figure of Fortune with her revolving wheel, a goddess whom the violent vicissitudes and tragedies of life led the men of the Middle Ages, in spite of their Christianity, to bring over from classical literature and virtually to accept as a real divinity, with almost absolute control in human affairs. In the seventeenth century Shakspere's plays are full of allusions to her, but so for that matter is the everyday talk of all of us in the twentieth century.

## LITERATURE IN THE THREE LANGUAGES

It is not to the purpose in a study like the present to give special attention to the literature written in England in Latin and French; we can speak only briefly of that composed in English. But in fact when the English had made its new beginning, about the year 1200, the same general forms flourished in all three languages, so that what is said in general of the English applies almost as much to the other two as well.

## RELIGIOUS LITERATURE

We may virtually divide all the literature of the period, roughly, into (1) Religious and (2) Secular. But it must be observed that religious writings were far more important as literature during the Middle Ages than in more recent times, and the separation between religious and secular less distinct than at present. The forms of the religious literature were largely the same as in the previous period. There were songs, many of them addressed to the Virgin, some not only beautiful in their sincere and tender devotion, speaking for the finer spirits in an age of crudeness and violence, but occasionally beautiful as poetry. There were paraphrases of many parts of the Bible, lives of saints, in both verse and prose, and various other miscellaneous work. Perhaps worthy of special mention among single productions is the 'Cursor Mundi' (Surveyor of the World), an early fourteenth century poem of twenty-four thousand lines ('Paradise Lost' has less than eleven thousand), relating universal history from the beginning, on the basis of the Biblical narrative. Most important of all for their promise of the future, there were the germs of the modern drama in the form of the Church plays; but to these we shall give special attention in a later chapter.

## SECULAR LITERATURE

In secular literature the variety was greater than in religious. We may begin by transcribing one or two of the songs, which, though not as numerous then as in some later periods, show that the great tradition of English secular lyric poetry reaches back from our own time to that of the Anglo-Saxons without a break. The best known of all is the 'Cuckoo Song,' of the thirteenth century, intended to be sung in harmony by four voices:

*Sumer is icumen in; Lhude sing, cuccu! Groweth sed and bloweth med And springth the wde nu. Sing, cuccu! Awe bleteth after lomb, Lhouth after calve cu. Bulluc sterteth, bucke verteth; Murie sing, cuccu! Cuccu, cuccu, Wel singes thu, cuccu; Ne swik thu never nu.*

Summer is come in; loud sing, cuckoo! Grows the seed and blooms the mead [meadow] and buds the wood anew. Sing, cuckoo! The ewe bleats for the lamb, lows for the calf the cow. The bullock gambols, the buck leaps; merrily sing, cuckoo! Cuckoo, cuckoo, well singest thou, cuckoo; cease thou never now.

The next is the first stanza of 'Alysoun' ('Fair Alice'):

*Bytuene Mersh ant Averil, When spray beginnth to springe, The lutel foul hath hire wyl On hyre lud to synge. Ieh libbe in love-longinge For semlokest of alle thinge; He may me blisse bringe; Icham in hire baundoun. An hendy hap ichabbe ybent; Iehot from hevene it is me sent; From alle wymmen mi love is lent Ant lyht on Alysoun.*

Between March and April, When the sprout begins to spring, The little bird has her desire In her tongue to sing. I live in love-longing For the fairest of all things; She may bring me bliss; I am at her mercy. A lucky lot I have secured; I think from heaven it is sent me; From all women my love is turned And is lighted on Alysoun.

There were also political and satirical songs and miscellaneous poems of various sorts, among them certain 'Bestiaries,' accounts of the supposed habits of animals, generally drawn originally from classical tradition, and most of them highly fantastic and allegorized in the interests of morality and religion. There was an abundance of extremely realistic coarse tales, hardly belonging to literature, in both prose and verse. The popular ballads of the fourteenth century we must reserve for later consideration. Most numerous of all the prose works, perhaps, were the Chronicles, which were produced generally in the monasteries and chiefly in the twelfth and thirteenth centuries, the greater part in Latin, some in French, and a few in rude English verse. Many of them were mere annals like the Anglo-Saxon Chronicle, but some were the lifelong works of men with genuine historical vision. Some dealt merely with the history of England, or a part of it, others with that of the entire world as it was known to medieval Europe. The majority will never be withdrawn from the obscurity of the manuscripts on which the patient care of their authors inscribed them; others have been printed in full and serve as the main basis for our knowledge of the events of the period.

## THE ROMANCES

But the chief form of secular literature during the period, beginning in the middle of the twelfth century, was the romance, especially the metrical (verse) romance. The typical romances were the literary expression of chivalry. They were composed by the professional minstrels, some of whom, as in Anglo-Saxon times, were richly supported and rewarded by kings and nobles, while others still wandered about the country, always welcome in the manor-houses. There, like Scott's Last Minstrel, they recited their sometimes almost endless works from memory, in the great halls or in the ladies' bowers, to the accompaniment of occasional strains on their harps. For two or three centuries the romances were to the lords and ladies, and to the wealthier citizens of the towns, much what novels are to the reading public of our own day.

By far the greater part of the romances current in England were written in French, whether by Normans or by French natives of the English provinces in France, and the English ones which have been preserved are mostly translations or imitations of French originals. The romances are extreme representatives of the whole class of literature of all times to which they have given the name. Frankly abandoning in the main the world of reality, they carry into that of idealized and glamorous fancy the chief interests of the medieval lords and ladies, namely, knightly exploits in war, and lovemaking. Love in the romances, also, retains all its courtly affectations, together with that worship of woman by man which in the twelfth century was exalted into a sentimental art by the poets of wealthy and luxurious Provence in Southern France. Side by side, again, with war and love, appears in the romances medieval religion, likewise conventionalized and childishly superstitious, but in some inadequate degree a mitigator of cruelty and a restrainer of lawless passion. Artistically, in some respects or all, the greater part of the romances are crude and immature.

Their usual main or only purpose is to hold attention by successions of marvellous adventures, natural or supernatural; of structure, therefore, they are often destitute; the characters are ordinarily mere types; and motivation is little considered. There were, however, exceptional authors, genuine artists, masters of meter and narrative, possessed by a true feeling for beauty; and in some of the romances the psychological analysis of love, in particular, is subtile and powerful, the direct precursor of one of the main developments in modern fiction.

The romances may very roughly be grouped into four great classes. First in time, perhaps, come those which are derived from the earlier French epics and in which love, if it appears at all, is subordinated to the military exploits of Charlemagne and his twelve peers in their wars against the Saracens. Second are the romances which, battered salvage from a greater past, retell in strangely altered romantic fashion the great stories of classical antiquity, mainly the achievements of Alexander the Great and the tragic fortunes of Troy. Third come the Arthurian romances, and fourth those scattering miscellaneous ones which do not belong to the other classes, dealing, most of them, with native English heroes. Of these, two, 'King Horn' and 'Havelok,' spring direct from the common people and in both substance and expression reflect the hard reality of their lives, while 'Guy of Warwick' and 'Bevis of Hampton,' which are among the best known but most tedious of all the list, belong, in their original form, to the upper classes.

Of all the romances the Arthurian are by far the most important. They belong peculiarly to English literature, because they are based on traditions of British history, but they have assumed a very prominent place in the literature of the whole western world. Rich in varied characters and incidents to which a universal significance could be attached, in their own time they were the most popular works of their class; and living on vigorously after the others were forgotten, they have continued to form one of the chief quarries of literary material and one of the chief sources of inspiration for modern poets and romancers. It seems well worth while, therefore, to outline briefly their literary history.

The period in which their scene is nominally laid is that of the Anglo-Saxon conquest of Great Britain. Of the actual historical events of this period extremely little is known, and even the capital question whether such a person as Arthur ever really existed can never receive a definite answer. The only contemporary writer of the least importance is the Briton (priest or monk), Gildas, who in a violent Latin pamphlet of about the year 550 ('The Destruction and Conquest of Britain') denounces his countrymen for their sins and urges them to unite against the Saxons; and Gildas gives only the slightest sketch of what had actually happened. He tells how a British king (to whom later tradition assigns the name Vortigern) invited in the Anglo-Saxons as allies against the troublesome northern Scots and Picts, and how the Anglo-Saxons, victorious against these tribes, soon turned in furious conquest against the Britons themselves, until, under a certain Ambrosius Aurelianus, a man 'of Roman race,' the Britons successfully defended themselves and at last in the battle of Mount Badon checked the Saxon advance.

Next in order after Gildas, but not until about the year 800, appears a strangely jumbled document, last edited by a certain Nennius, and entitled 'Historia Britonum' (The History of the Britons), which adds to Gildas' outline traditions, natural and supernatural, which had meanwhile been growing up among the Britons (Welsh). It supplies the names of the earliest Saxon leaders, Hengist and Horsa (who also figure in the 'Anglo-Saxon Chronicle'), and narrates at length their treacherous dealings with Vortigern. Among other stories we find that of Vortigern's tower, where Gildas' Ambrosius appears as a boy of supernatural nature, destined to develop in the romances into the great magician Merlin. In Nennius' book occurs also the earliest mention of Arthur, who, in a comparatively sober passage, is said, some time after the days of Vortigern, to have 'fought against the Saxons, together with the kings of the Britons, but he himself was leader in the battles.' A list, also, is given of his twelve victories, ending with Mount Badon.

It is impossible to decide whether there is really any truth in this account of Nennius, or whether it springs wholly from the imagination of the Britons, attempting to solace themselves for their national overthrow; but it allows us to believe if we choose that sometime in the early sixth century there was a British leader of the name of Arthur, who by military genius rose to high command and for a while beat back the Saxon hordes. At most, however, it should be clearly realized, Arthur was probably only a local leader in some limited region, and, far from filling the splendid place which he occupies in the later romances, was but the hard-pressed captain of a few thousand barbarous and half-armed warriors.

For three hundred years longer the traditions about Arthur continued to develop among the Welsh people. The most important change which took place was Arthur's elevation to the position of chief hero of the British (Welsh) race and the subordination to him, as his followers, of all the other native heroes, most of whom had originally been gods. To Arthur himself certain divine attributes were added, such as his possession of magic weapons, among them the sword Excalibur. It also came to be passionately believed among the Welsh that he was not really dead but would some day return from the mysterious Other World to which he had withdrawn and reconquer the island for his people.

It was not until the twelfth century that these Arthurian traditions, the cherished heritage of the Welsh and their cousins, the Bretons across the English Channel in France, were suddenly adopted as the property of all Western Europe, so that Arthur became a universal Christian hero. This remarkable transformation, no doubt in some degree inevitable, was actually brought about chiefly through the instrumentality of a single man, a certain English archdeacon of Welsh descent, Geoffrey of Monmouth. Geoffrey, a literary and ecclesiastical adventurer looking about for a means of making himself famous, put forth about the year 1136, in Latin, a 'History of the Britons' from the earliest times to the seventh century, in which, imitating the form of the serious chronicles, he combined in cleverly impudent fashion all the adaptable miscellaneous material, fictitious, legendary, or traditional, which he found at hand. In dealing with Arthur, Geoffrey greatly enlarges on Gildas and Nennius; in part, no doubt, from his own invention, in part, perhaps, from Welsh tradition. He provides Arthur with a father, King Uther, makes of Arthur's wars against the Saxons only his youthful exploits, relates at length how Arthur conquered almost all of Western Europe, and adds to the earlier story the figures of Merlin, Guenevere, Modred, Gawain, Kay, and Bedivere. What is not least important, he gives to Arthur's reign much of the atmosphere of feudal chivalry which was that of the ruling class of his own age.

Geoffrey may or may not have intended his astonishing story to be seriously accepted, but in fact it was received with almost universal credence. For centuries it was incorporated in outline or in excerpts into almost all the sober chronicles, and what is of much more importance for literature, it was taken up and rehandled in various fashions by very numerous romancers. About twenty years after Geoffrey wrote, the French poet Wace, an English subject, paraphrased his entire 'History' in vivid, fluent, and diffuse verse. Wace imparts to the whole, in a thorough-going way, the manners of chivalry, and adds, among other things, a mention of the Round Table, which Geoffrey, somewhat chary of the supernatural, had chosen to omit, though it was one of the early elements of the Welsh tradition.

Other poets followed, chief among them the delightful Chretien of Troyes, all writing mostly of the exploits of single knights at Arthur's court, which they made over, probably, from scattering tales of Welsh and Breton mythology. To declare that most romantic heroes had been knights of Arthur's circle now became almost a matter of course. Prose romances also appeared, vast formless compilations, which gathered up into themselves story after story, according to the fancy of each successive editor. Greatest of the additions to the substance of the cycle was the story of the Holy Grail, originally an altogether independent legend. Important changes necessarily developed. Arthur himself, in many of the romances, was degraded from his position of the bravest knight to be the inactive figurehead of a brilliant court; and the only really historical element in the story, his struggle against the Saxons, was thrust far into the background, while all the emphasis was laid on the romantic achievements of the single knights.

### LAGHAMON'S 'BRUT'

Thus it had come about that Arthur, originally the national hero of the Welsh, and the deadly foe of the English, was adopted, as a Christian champion, not only for one of the medieval Nine Worthies of all history, but for the special glory of the English race itself. In that light he figures in the first important work in which native English reemerges after the Norman Conquest, the 'Brut' (Chronicle) wherein, about the year 1200, Laghamon paraphrased Wace's paraphrase of Geoffrey.

Laghamon was a humble parish priest in Worcestershire, and his thirty-two thousand half-lines, in which he imperfectly follows the Anglo-Saxon alliterative meter, are rather crude; though they are by no means dull, rather are often strong with the old-time Anglo-Saxon fighting spirit. In language also the poem is almost purely Saxon; occasionally it admits the French device of rime, but it is said to exhibit, all told, fewer than a hundred words of French origin. Expanding throughout on Wace's version, Laghamon adds some minor features; but English was not yet ready to take a place beside French and

Latin with the reading class, and the poem exercised no influence on the development of the Arthurian story or on English literature.

## SIR GAWAIN AND THE GREEN KNIGHT

We can make special mention of only one other romance, which all students should read in modern translation, namely, 'Sir Gawain (pronounced Gaw'-wain) and the Green Knight.' This is the brief and carefully constructed work of an unknown but very real poetic artist, who lived a century and more later than Laghamon and probably a little earlier than Chaucer. The story consists of two old folk-tales, here finely united in the form of an Arthurian romance and so treated as to bring out all the better side of knightly feeling, with which the author is in charming sympathy. Like many other medieval writings, this one is preserved by mere chance in a single manuscript, which contains also three slightly shorter religious poems (of a thousand or two lines apiece), all possibly by the same author as the romance. One of them in particular, 'The Pearl,' is a narrative of much fine feeling, which may well have come from so true a gentleman as he. The dialect is that of the Northwest Midland, scarcely more intelligible to modern readers than Anglo-Saxon, but it indicates that the author belonged to the same border region between England and Wales from which came also Geoffrey of Monmouth and Laghamon, a region where Saxon and Norman elements were mingled with Celtic fancy and delicacy of temperament. The meter, also, is interesting--the Anglo-Saxon unrimed alliterative verse, but divided into long stanzas of irregular length, each ending in a 'bob' of five short riming lines.

'Sir Gawain and the Green Knight' may very fittingly bring to a close our hasty survey of the entire Norman-French period, a period mainly of formation, which has left no literary work of great and permanent fame, but in which, after all, there were some sincere and talented writers, who have fallen into forgetfulness rather through the untoward accidents of time than from lack of genuine merit in themselves.

# 4

# The End of the Middle Ages

## POLITICAL AND SOCIAL CONDITIONS

Of the century and a half, from 1350 to 1500, which forms our third period, the most important part for literature was the first fifty years, which constitutes the age of Chaucer.

The middle of the fourteenth century was also the middle of the externally brilliant fifty years' reign of Edward III. In 1337 Edward had begun the terrible though often-interrupted series of campaigns in France which historians group together as the Hundred Tears' War, and having won the battle of Crecy against amazing odds, he had inaugurated at his court a period of splendor and luxury. The country as a whole was really increasing in prosperity; Edward was fostering trade, and the towns and some of the town-merchants were becoming wealthy; but the oppressiveness of the feudal system, now becoming outgrown, was apparent, abuses in society and state and church were almost intolerable, and the spirit which was to create our modern age, beginning already in Italy to move toward the Renaissance, was felt in faint stirrings even so far to the North as England.

The towns, indeed, were achieving their freedom. Thanks to compact organization, they were loosening the bonds of their dependence on the lords or bishops to whom most of them paid taxes; and the alliance of their representatives with the knights of the shire (country gentlemen) in the House of Commons, now a separate division of Parliament, was laying the foundation of the political power of the whole middle class. But the feudal system continued to rest cruelly on the peasants. Still bound, most of them, to the soil, as serfs of the land or tenants with definite and heavy obligations of service, living in dark and filthy hovels under indescribably unhealthy conditions, earning a wretched subsistence by ceaseless labor, and almost altogether at the mercy of masters who regarded them as scarcely better than beasts, their lot was indeed pitiable.

Nevertheless their spirit was not broken nor their state so hopeless as it seemed. It was by the archers of the class of yeomen (small free-holders), men akin in origin and interests to the peasants, that the victories in the French wars were won, and the knowledge that this was so created in the peasants an increased self-respect and an increased dissatisfaction. Their groping efforts to better their condition received strong stimulus also from the ravages of the terrible Black Death, a pestilence which, sweeping off at its first visitation, in 1348, at least half the population, and on two later recurrences only smaller proportions, led to a scarcity of laborers and added strength to their demand for commutation of personal services by money-payments and for higher wages. This demand was met by the ruling classes with sternly repressive measures, and the socialistic Peasants' Revolt of John Ball and Wat Tyler in 1381 was violently crushed out in blood, but it expressed a great human cry for justice which could not permanently be denied.

Hand in hand with the State and its institutions, in this period as before, stood the Church. Holding in the theoretical belief of almost every one the absolute power of all men's salvation or spiritual death, monopolizing almost all learning and education, the Church exercised in the spiritual sphere, and to no small extent in the temporal, a despotic tyranny, a tyranny employed sometimes for good, sometimes for evil. As the only even partially democratic institution of the age it attracted to itself the most ambitious and able men of all classes. Though social and personal influence were powerful within its doors, as always in all human organizations, nevertheless the son of a serf for whom there was no other means of escape from his servitude might steal to the nearest monastery and there, gaining his freedom by a few months of concealment, might hope, if he proved his ability, to rise to the highest position, to become abbot, bishop or perhaps even Pope.

Within the Church were many sincere and able men unselfishly devoting their lives to the service of their fellows;

but the moral tone of the organization as a whole had suffered from its worldly prosperity and power. In its numerous secular lordships and monastic orders it had become possessor of more than half the land in England, a proportion constantly increased through the legacies left by religious-minded persons for their souls' salvation; but from its vast income, several times greater than that of the Crown, it paid no taxes, and owing allegiance only to the Pope it was in effect a foreign power, sometimes openly hostile to the national government. The monasteries, though still performing important public functions as centers of education, charity, and hospitality, had relaxed their discipline, and the lives of the monks were often scandalous. The Dominican and Franciscan friars, also, who had come to England in the thirteenth century, soon after the foundation of their orders in Italy, and who had been full at first of passionate zeal for the spiritual and physical welfare of the poor, had now departed widely from their early character and become selfish, luxurious, ignorant, and unprincipled.

Much the same was true of the 'secular' clergy (those not members of monastic orders, corresponding to the entire clergy of Protestant churches). Then there were such unworthy charlatans as the pardoners and professional pilgrims, traveling everywhere under special privileges and fleecing the credulous of their money with fraudulent relics and preposterous stories of edifying adventure. All this corruption was clear enough to every intelligent person, and we shall find it an object of constant satire by the authors of the age, but it was too firmly established to be easily or quickly rooted out.

## 'MANDEVILLE'S VOYAGE'

One of the earliest literary works of the period, however, was uninfluenced by these social and moral problems, being rather a very complete expression of the naive medieval delight in romantic marvels. This is the highly entertaining 'Voyage and Travels of Sir John Mandeville.' This clever book was actually written at Liege, in what is now Belgium, sometime before the year 1370, and in the French language; from which, attaining enormous popularity, it was several times translated into Latin and English, and later into various other languages. Five centuries had to pass before scholars succeeded in demonstrating that the asserted author, 'Sir John Mandeville,' never existed, that the real author is undiscoverable, and that this pretended account of his journeyings over all the known and imagined world is a compilation from a large number of previous works. Yet the book (the English version along with the others) really deserved its long-continued reputation.

Its tales of the Ethiopian Prester John, of diamonds that by proper care can be made to grow, of trees whose fruit is an odd sort of lambs, and a hundred other equally remarkable phenomena, are narrated with skilful verisimilitude and still strongly hold the reader's interest, even if they no longer command belief. With all his credulity, too, the author has some odd ends of genuine science, among others the conviction that the earth is not flat but round. In style the English versions reflect the almost universal medieval uncertainty of sentence structure; nevertheless they are straightforward and clear; and the book is notable as the first example in English after the Norman Conquest of prose used not for religious edification but for amusement (though with the purpose also of giving instruction). 'Mandeville,' however, is a very minor figure when compared with his great contemporaries, especially with the chief of them, Geoffrey Chaucer.

## GEOFFREY CHAUCER, 1338-1400

Chaucer (the name is French and seems to have meant originally 'shoemaker') came into the world probably in 1338, the first important author who was born and lived in London, which with him becomes the center of English literature. About his life, as about those of many of our earlier writers, there remains only very fragmentary information, which in his case is largely pieced together from scattering entries of various kinds in such documents as court account books and public records of state matters and of lawsuits. His father, a wine merchant, may have helped supply the cellars of the king (Edward III) and so have been able to bring his son to royal notice; at any rate, while still in his teens Geoffrey became a page in the service of one of the king's daughters-in-law.

In this position his duty would be partly to perform various humble work in the household, partly also to help amuse the leisure of the inmates, and it is easy to suppose that he soon won favor as a fluent story-teller. He early became acquainted with the seamy as well as the brilliant side of courtly life; for in 1359 he was in the campaign in France and was taken prisoner. That he was already valued appears from the king's subscription of the equivalent of a thousand dollars of present-day money toward his ransom; and after his release he was transferred to the king's own service, where about 1368 he was promoted to the rank of esquire. He was probably already married to one of the queen's ladies-in-waiting. Chaucer was now thirty years of age, and his practical sagacity and knowledge of men had been recognized; for from this time on he held important public positions.

He was often sent to the Continent--to France, Flanders, and Italy--on diplomatic missions; and for eleven years he was in charge of the London customs, where the uncongenial drudgery occupied almost all his time until through the intercession of the queen he was allowed to perform it by deputy. In 1386 he was a member of Parliament, knight of the shire for Kent; but in that year his fortune turned--he lost all his offices at the overthrow of the faction of his patron, Duke John of Gaunt (uncle of the young king, Richard II, who had succeeded his grandfather, Edward III, some years before). Chaucer's party and himself were soon restored to power, but although during the remaining dozen years of his life he received from the Court various temporary appointments and rewards, he appears often to have been poor and in need. When Duke Henry of Bolingbroke, son of John of Gaunt, deposed the king and himself assumed the throne as Henry IV, Chaucer's prosperity seemed assured, but he lived after this for less than a year, dying suddenly in 1400. He was buried in Westminster Abbey, the first of the men of letters to be laid in the nook which has since become the Poets' Corner.

Chaucer's poetry falls into three rather clearly marked periods. First is that of French influence, when, though writing in English. he drew inspiration from the rich French poetry of the period, which was produced partly in France, partly in England. Chaucer experimented with the numerous lyric forms which the French poets had brought to perfection; he also translated, in whole or in part, the most important of medieval French narrative poems, the thirteenth century 'Romance of the Rose' of Guillaume de Lorris and Jean de Meung, a very clever satirical allegory, in many thousand lines, of medieval love and medieval religion.

This poem, with its Gallic brilliancy and audacity, long exercised over Chaucer's mind the same dominant influence which it possessed over most secular poets of the age. Chaucer's second period, that of Italian influence, dates from his first visit to Italy in 1372-3, where at Padua he may perhaps have met the fluent Italian poet Petrarch, and where at any rate the revelation of Italian life and literature must have aroused his intense enthusiasm. From this time, and especially after his other visit to Italy, five years later, he made much direct use of the works of Petrarch and Boccaccio and to a less degree of those of their greater predecessor, Dante, whose severe spirit was too unlike Chaucer's for his thorough appreciation.

The longest and finest of Chaucer's poems of this period, 'Troilus and Criseyde' is based on a work of Boccaccio; here Chaucer details with compelling power the sentiment and tragedy of love, and the psychology of the heroine who had become for the Middle Ages a central figure in the tale of Troy. Chaucer's third period, covering his last fifteen years, is called his English period, because now at last his genius, mature and self-sufficient, worked in essential independence. First in time among his poems of these years stands 'The Legend of Good Women,' a series of romantic biographies of famous ladies of classical legend and history, whom it pleases Chaucer to designate as martyrs of love; but more important than the stories themselves is the Prolog, where he chats with delightful frankness about his own ideas and tastes.

The great work of the period, however, and the crowning achievement of Chaucer's life, is 'The Canterbury Tales.' Every one is familiar with the plan of the story (which may well have had some basis in fact): how Chaucer finds himself one April evening with thirty other men and women, all gathered at the Tabard Inn in Southwark (a suburb of London and just across the Thames from the city proper), ready to start next morning, as thousands of Englishmen did every year, on a pilgrimage to the shrine of St. Thomas a Becket at Canterbury. The travelers readily accept the proposal of Harry Bailey, their jovial and domineering host, that he go with them as leader and that they enliven the journey with a story-telling contest (two stories from each pilgrim during each half of the journey) for the prize of a dinner at his inn on their return.

Next morning, therefore, the Knight begins the series of tales and the others follow in order. This literary form--a collection of disconnected stories bound together in a fictitious framework--goes back almost to the beginning of literature itself; but Chaucer may well have been directly influenced by Boccaccio's famous book of prose tales, 'The Decameron' (Ten Days of Story-Telling). Between the two works, however, there is a striking contrast, which has often been pointed out. While the Italian author represents his gentlemen and ladies as selfishly fleeing from the misery of a frightful plague in Florence to a charming villa and a holiday of unreflecting pleasure, the gaiety of Chaucer's pilgrims rests on a basis of serious purpose, however conventional it may be.

Perhaps the easiest way to make clear the sources of Chaucer's power will be by means of a rather formal summary.

1. *His Personality.* Chaucer's personality stands out in his writings plainly and most delightfully. It must be borne in mind that, like some others of the greatest poets, he was not a poet merely, but also a man of practical affairs, in the eyes of his associates first and mainly a courtier, diplomat, and government official. His wide experience of men and things is manifest in the life-likeness and mature power of his poetry, and it accounts in part for the broad truth of all but his earliest work, which makes it essentially poetry not of an age but for all time. Something of conventional medievalism still clings to Chaucer in externals, as we shall see, but in alertness, independence of thought, and a certain directness of utterance, he speaks for universal humanity. His practical experience helps to explain as well why, unlike most great poets, he does not belong primarily with the idealists.

Fine feeling he did not lack; he loved external beauty--some of his most pleasing passages voice his enthusiasm for Nature; and down to the end of his life he never lost the zest for fanciful romance. His mind and eye were keen, besides, for moral qualities; he penetrated directly through all the pretenses of falsehood and hypocrisy; while how thoroughly he understood and respected honest worth appears in the picture of the Poor Parson in the Prolog to 'The Canterbury Tales.' Himself quiet and self-contained, moreover, Chaucer was genial and sympathetic toward all mankind. But all this does not declare him a positive idealist, and in fact, rather, he was willing to accept the world as he found it--he had no reformer's dream of 'shattering it to bits and remoulding it nearer to the heart's desire.'

His moral nature, indeed, was easy-going; he was the appropriate poet of the Court circle, with very much of the better courtier's point of view. At the day's tasks he worked long and faithfully, but he also loved comfort, and he had nothing of the martyr's instinct. To him human life was a vast procession, of boundless interest, to be observed keenly and reproduced for the reader's enjoyment in works of objective literary art. The countless tragedies of life he noted with kindly pity, but he felt no impulse to dash himself against the existing barriers of the world in the effort to assure a better future for the coming generations. In a word, Chaucer is an artist of broad artistic vision to whom art is its own excuse for being. And when everything is said few readers would have it otherwise with him; for in his art he has accomplished what no one else in his place could have done, and he has left besides the picture of himself, very real and human across the gulf of half a thousand years. Religion, we should add, was for him, as for so many men of the world, a somewhat secondary and formal thing. In his early works there is much conventional piety, no doubt sincere so far as it goes; and he always took a strong intellectual interest in the problems of medieval theology; but he became steadily and quietly independent in his philosophic outlook and indeed rather skeptical of all definite dogmas.

Even in his art Chaucer's lack of the highest will-power produced one rather conspicuous formal weakness; of his numerous long poems he really finished scarcely one. For this, however, it is perhaps sufficient excuse that he could write only in intervals hardly snatched from business and sleep. In 'The Canterbury Tales' indeed, the plan is almost impossibly ambitious; the more than twenty stories actually finished, with their eighteen thousand lines, are only a fifth part of the intended number. Even so, several of them do not really belong to the series; composed in stanza forms, they are selected from his earlier poems and here pressed into service, and on the average they are less excellent than those which he wrote for their present places (in the rimed pentameter couplet that he adopted from the French).

2. *His Humor*. In nothing are Chaucer's personality and his poetry more pleasing than in the rich humor which pervades them through and through. Sometimes, as in his treatment of the popular medieval beast-epic material in the Nun's Priest's Tale of the Fox and the Cock, the humor takes the form of boisterous farce; but much more often it is of the finer intellectual sort, the sort which a careless reader may not catch, but which touches with perfect sureness and charming lightness on all the incongruities of life, always, too, in kindly spirit. No foible is too trifling for Chaucer's quiet observation; while if he does not choose to denounce the hypocrisy of the Pardoner and the worldliness of the Monk, he has made their weaknesses sources of amusement (and indeed object-lessons as well) for all the coming generations.

3. He is one of the greatest of all narrative poets. Chaucer is an exquisite lyric poet, but only a few of his lyrics have come down to us, and his fame must always rest largely on his narratives. Here, first, he possesses unfailing fluency. It was with rapidity, evidently with ease, and with masterful certainty, that he poured out his long series of vivid and delightful tales. It is true that in his early, imitative, work he shares the medieval faults of wordiness, digression, and abstract symbolism; and, like most medieval writers, he chose rather to reshape material from the great contemporary store than to invent stories of his own. But these are really very minor matters. He has great variety, also, of narrative forms: elaborate allegories; love stories of many kinds; romances, both religious and secular; tales of chivalrous exploit, like that related by the Knight; humorous extravaganzas; and jocose renderings of coarse popular material--something, at least, in virtually every medieval type.

4. The thorough knowledge and sure portrayal of men and women which, belong to his mature work extend through, many various types of character. It is a commonplace to say that the Prolog to 'The Canterbury Tales' presents in its twenty

portraits virtually every contemporary English class except the very lowest, made to live forever in the finest series of character sketches preserved anywhere in literature; and in his other work the same power appears in only less conspicuous degree.

5. His poetry is also essentially and thoroughly dramatic, dealing very vividly with life in genuine and varied action. To be sure, Chaucer possesses all the medieval love for logical reasoning, and he takes a keen delight in psychological analysis; but when he introduces these things (except for the tendency to medieval diffuseness) they are true to the situation and really serve to enhance the suspense. There is much interest in the question often raised whether, if he had lived in an age like the Elizabethan, when the drama was the dominant literary form, he too would have been a dramatist.

6. As a descriptive poet (of things as well as persons) he displays equal skill. Whatever his scenes or objects, he sees them with perfect clearness and brings them in full life-likeness before the reader's eyes, sometimes even with the minuteness of a nineteenth century novelist. And no one understands more thoroughly the art of conveying the general impression with perfect sureness, with a foreground where a few characteristic details stand out in picturesque and telling clearness.

7. Chaucer is an unerring master of poetic form. His stanza combinations reproduce all the well-proportioned grace of his French models, and to the pentameter riming couplet of his later work he gives the perfect ease and metrical variety which match the fluent thought. In all his poetry there is probably not a single faulty line. And yet within a hundred years after his death, such was the irony of circumstances, English pronunciation had so greatly altered that his meter was held to be rude and barbarous, and not until the nineteenth century were its principles again fully understood. His language, we should add, is modern, according to the technical classification, and is really as much like the form of our own day as like that of a century before his time; but it is still only early modern English, and a little definitely directed study is necessary for any present-day reader before its beauty can be adequately recognized.

The main principles for the pronunciation of Chaucer's language, so far as it differs from ours, are these: Every letter should be sounded, especially the final e (except when it is to be suppressed before another vowel). A large proportion of the rimes are therefore feminine. The following vowel sounds should be observed: Stressed a like modern a_ in father. Stressed _e_ and _ee_ like _e_ in _fete_ or _ea_ in breath. Stressed _i_ as in _machine_, _oo_ like _o_ in _open_. _u_ commonly as in _push_ or like _oo_ in _spoon_, _y_ like _i_ in _machine_ or _pin_ according as it is stressed or not. _ai_, _ay_, _ei_, and _ey_ like _ay_ in _day_. _au_ commonly like _ou_ in _pound_, _ou_ like _oo_ in _spoon_. _-ye_ (final) is a diphthong. _g_ (not in _ng_ and not initial) before _e_ or _i_is like _j_.

Lowell has named in a suggestive summary the chief quality of each of the great English poets, with Chaucer standing first in order: 'Actual life is represented by Chaucer; imaginative life by Spenser; ideal life by Shakspere; interior life by Milton; conventional life by Pope.' We might add: the life of spiritual mysticism and simplicity by Wordsworth; the completely balanced life by Tennyson; and the life of moral issues and dramatic moments by Robert Browning.

## JOHN GOWER

The three other chief writers contemporary with Chaucer contrast strikingly both with him and with each other. Least important is John Gower (pronounced either Go-er or Gow-er), a wealthy landowner whose tomb, with his effigy, may still be seen in St. Savior's, Southwark, the church of a priory to whose rebuilding he contributed and where he spent his latter days. Gower was a confirmed conservative, and time has left him stranded far in the rear of the forces that move and live. Unlike Chaucer's, the bulk of his voluminous poems reflect the past and scarcely hint of the future. The earlier and larger part of them are written in French and Latin, and in 'Vox Clamantis' (The Voice of One Crying in the Wilderness) he exhausts the vocabulary of exaggerated bitterness in denouncing the common people for the insurrection in which they threatened the privileges and authority of his own class. Later on, perhaps through Chaucer's example, he turned to English, and in 'Confessio Amantis' (A Lover's Confession) produced a series of renderings of traditional stories parallel in general nature to 'The Canterbury Tales.' He is generally a smooth and fluent versifier, but his fluency is his undoing; he wraps up his material in too great a mass of verbiage.

## THE VISION CONCERNING PIERS THE PLOWMAN

The active moral impulse which Chaucer and Gower lacked, and a consequent direct confronting of the evils of the age, appear vigorously in the group of poems written during the last forty years of the century and known from the title in some of the manuscripts as 'The Vision of William Concerning Piers the Plowman.' From the sixteenth century, at least, until very lately this work, the various versions of which differ greatly, has been supposed to be the single poem of a single author, repeatedly enlarged and revised by him; and ingenious inference has constructed for this supposed author a brief but picturesque biography under the name of William Langland. Recent investigation, however, has made it seem at least probable that the work grew, to its final form through additions by several successive writers who have not left their names and whose points of view were not altogether identical.

Like the slightly earlier poet of 'Sir Gawain and the Green Knight,' the authors belonged to the region of the Northwest Midland, near the Malvern Hills, and like him, they wrote in the Anglo-Saxon verse form, alliterative, unrimed, and in this case without stanza divisions. Their language, too, the regular dialect of this region, differs very greatly, as we have already implied, from that of Chaucer, with much less infusion from the French; to the modern reader, except in translation, it seems uncouth and unintelligible. But the poem, though in its final state prolix and structurally formless, exhibits great power not only of moral conviction and emotion, but also of expression--vivid, often homely, but not seldom eloquent.

The 'first passus' begins with the sleeping author's vision of 'a field full of folk' (the world), bounded on one side by a cliff with the tower of Truth, and on the other by a deep vale wherein frowns the dungeon of Wrong. Society in all its various classes and occupations is very dramatically presented in the brief description of the 'field of folk,' with incisive passing satire of the sins and vices of each class. 'Gluttonous wasters' are there, lazy beggars, lying pilgrims, corrupt friars and pardoners, venal lawyers, and, with a lively touch of realistic humour, cooks and their 'knaves' crying, 'Hot pies!' But a sane balance is preserved--there are also worthy people, faithful laborers, honest merchants, and sincere priests and monks. Soon the allegory deepens. Holy Church, appearing, instructs the author about Truth and the religion which consists in loving God and giving help to the poor.

A long portrayal of the evil done by Lady Meed (love of money and worldly rewards) prepares for the appearance of the hero, the sturdy plowman Piers, who later on is even identified in a hazy way with Christ himself. Through Piers and his search for Truth is developed the great central teaching of the poem, the Gospel of Work--the doctrine, namely, that society is to be saved by honest labor, or in general by the faithful service of every class in its own sphere. The Seven Deadly Sins and their fatal fruits are emphasized, and in the later forms of the poem the corruptions of wealth and the Church are indignantly denounced, with earnest pleading for the religion of practical social love to all mankind.

In its own age the influence of 'Piers the Plowman' was very great. Despite its intended impartiality, it was inevitably adopted as a partisan document by the poor and oppressed, and together with the revolutionary songs of John Ball it became a powerful incentive to the Peasant's Insurrection. Piers himself became and continued an ideal for men who longed for a less selfish and brutal world, and a century and a half later the poem was still cherished by the Protestants for its exposure of the vices of the Church. Its medieval form and setting remove it hopelessly beyond the horizon of general readers of the present time, yet it furnishes the most detailed remaining picture of the actual social and economic conditions of its age, and as a great landmark in the progress of moral and social thought it can never lose its significance.

## THE WICLIFITE BIBLE

A product of the same general forces which inspired 'Piers the Plowman' is the earliest in the great succession of the modern English versions of the Bible, the one connected with the name of John Wiclif, himself the first important English precursor of the Reformation. Wiclif was born about 1320, a Yorkshireman of very vigorous intellect as well as will, but in all his nature and instincts a direct representative of the common people. During the greater part of his life he was connected with Oxford University, as student, teacher (and therefore priest), and college head. Early known as one of the ablest English thinkers and philosophers, he was already opposing certain doctrines and practices of the Church when he was led to become a chief spokesman for King Edward and the nation in their refusal to pay the tribute which King John, a century and a half before, had promised to the Papacy and which was now actually demanded.

As the controversies proceeded, Wiclif was brought at last to formulate the principle, later to be basal in the whole Protestant movement, that the final source of religious authority is not the Church, but the Bible. One by one he was led to attack also other fundamental doctrines and institutions of the Church--transubstantiation, the temporal possessions of the Church, the Papacy, and at last, for their corruption, the four orders of friars. In the outcome the Church proved too strong for even Wiclif, and Oxford, against its will, was compelled to abandon him; yet he could be driven no farther than to his parish of Lutterworth, where he died undisturbed in 1384.

His connection with literature was an unforeseen but natural outgrowth of his activities. Some years before his death, with characteristic energy and zeal, he had begun to spread his doctrines by sending out 'poor priests' and laymen who, practicing the self-denying life of the friars of earlier days, founded the Lollard sect. [Footnote: The name, given by their enemies, perhaps means 'tares.'] It was inevitable not only that he and his associates should compose many tracts and sermons for the furtherance of their views, but, considering their attitude toward the Bible, that they should wish to put it into the hands of all the people in a form which they would be able to understand, that is in their own vernacular English. Hence sprang the Wiclifite translation. The usual supposition that from the outset, before the time of Wiclif, the Church had prohibited translations of the Bible from the Latin into the common tongues is a mistake; that policy was a direct result of Wiclif's work.

In England from Anglo-Saxon times, as must be clear from what has here already been said, partial English translations, literal or free, in prose or verse, had been in circulation among the few persons who could read and wished to have them. But Wiclif proposed to popularize the entire book, in order to make the conscience of every man the final authority in every question of belief and religious practice, and this the Church would not allow. It is altogether probable that Wiclif personally directed the translation which has ever since borne his name; but no record of the facts has come down to us, and there is no proof that he himself was the actual author of any part of it--that work may all have been done by others. The basis of the translation was necessarily the Latin 'Vulgate' (Common) version, made nine hundred years before from the original Hebrew and Greek by St. Jerome, which still remains to-day, as in Wiclif's time, the official version of the Roman church. The first Wiclifite translation was hasty and rather rough, and it was soon revised and bettered by a certain John Purvey, one of the 'Lollard' priests.

Wiclif and the men associated with him, however, were always reformers first and writers only to that end. Their religious tracts are formless and crude in style, and even their final version of the Bible aims chiefly at fidelity of rendering. In general it is not elegant, the more so because the authors usually follow the Latin idioms and sentence divisions instead of reshaping them into the native English style. Their text, again, is often interrupted by the insertion of brief phrases explanatory of unusual words. The vocabulary, adapted to the unlearned readers, is more largely Saxon than in our later versions, and the older inflected forms appear oftener than in Chaucer; so that it is only through our knowledge of the later versions that we to-day can read the work without frequent stumbling. Nevertheless this version has served as the starting point for almost all those that have come after it in English, as even a hasty reader of this one must be conscious; and no reader can fail to admire in it the sturdy Saxon vigor which has helped to make our own version one of the great masterpieces of English literature.

## THE FIFTEENTH CENTURY

With Chaucer's death in 1400 the half century of original creative literature in which he is the main figure comes to an end, and for a hundred and fifty years thereafter there is only a single author of the highest rank. For this decline political confusion is the chief cause; first, in the renewal of the Hundred Years' War, with its sordid effort to deprive another nation of its liberty, and then in the brutal and meaningless War of the Roses, a mere cut-throat civil butchery of rival factions with no real principle at stake. Throughout the fifteenth century the leading poets (of prose we will speak later) were avowed imitators of Chaucer, and therefore at best only second-rate writers.

Most of them were Scots, and best known is the Scottish king, James I. For tradition seems correct in naming this monarch as the author of a pretty poem, 'The King's Quair' ('The King's Quire,' that is Book), which relates in a medieval dream allegory of fourteen hundred lines how the captive author sees and falls in love with a lady whom in the end Fortune promises to bestow upon him. This may well be the poetic record of King James' eighteen-year captivity in England and his actual marriage to a noble English wife. In compliment to him Chaucer's stanza of seven lines (riming _ababbcc_), which King James employs, has received the name of 'rime royal.'

## THE 'POPULAR' BALLADS

Largely to the fifteenth century, however, belong those of the English and Scottish 'popular' ballads which the accidents of time have not succeeded in destroying. We have already considered the theory of the communal origin of this kind of poetry in the remote pre-historic past, and have seen that the ballads continue to flourish vigorously down to the later periods of civilization. The still existing English and Scottish ballads are mostly, no doubt, the work of individual authors of the fifteenth and sixteenth centuries, but none the less they express the little-changing mind and emotions of the great body of the common people who had been singing and repeating ballads for so many thousand years. Really essentially 'popular,' too, in spirit are the more pretentious poems of the wandering professional minstrels, which have been handed down along with the others, just as the minstrels were accustomed to recite both sorts indiscriminately.

Such minstrel ballads are the famous ones on the battle of Chevy Chase, or Otterburn. The production of genuine popular ballads began to wane in the fifteenth century when the printing press gave circulation to the output of cheap London writers and substituted reading for the verbal memory by which the ballads had been transmitted, portions, as it were, of a half mysterious and almost sacred tradition. Yet the existing ballads yielded slowly, lingering on in the remote regions, and those which have been preserved were recovered during the eighteenth and nineteenth centuries by collectors from simple men and women living apart from the main currents of life, to whose hearts and lips they were still dear. Indeed even now the ballads and ballad-making are not altogether dead, but may still be found nourishing in such outskirts of civilization as the cowboy plains of Texas, Rocky Mountain mining camps, or the nooks and corners of the Southern Alleghenies.

The true 'popular' ballads have a quality peculiarly their own, which renders them far superior to the sixteenth century imitations and which no conscious literary artist has ever successfully reproduced. Longfellow's 'Skeleton in Armor' and Tennyson's 'Revenge' are stirring artistic ballads, but they are altogether different in tone and effect from the authentic 'popular' ones. Some of the elements which go to make this peculiar 'popular' quality can be definitely stated.

1. The 'popular' ballads are the simple and spontaneous expression of the elemental emotion of the people, emotion often crude but absolutely genuine and unaffected. Phrases are often repeated in the ballads, just as in the talk of the common man, for the sake of emphasis, but there is neither complexity of plot or characterization nor attempt at decorative literary adornment--the story and the emotion which it calls forth are all in all. It is this simple, direct fervor of feeling, the straightforward outpouring of the authors' hearts, that gives the ballads their power and entitles them to consideration among the far more finished works of conscious literature. Both the emotion and the morals of the ballads, also, are pagan, or at least pre-Christian; vengeance on one's enemies is as much a virtue as loyalty to one's friends; the most shameful sins are cowardice and treachery in war or love; and the love is often lawless.

2. From first to last the treatment of the themes is objective, dramatic, and picturesque. Everything is action, simple feeling,

or vivid scenes, with no merely abstract moralizing (except in a few unusual cases); and often much of the story or sentiment is implied rather than directly stated. This too, of course, is the natural manner of the common man, a manner perfectly effective either in animated conversation or in the chant of a minstrel, where expression and gesture can do so much of the work which the restraints of civilized society have transferred to words.

3. To this spirit and treatment correspond the subjects of the ballads. They are such as make appeal to the underlying human instincts--brave exploits in individual fighting or in organized war, and the romance and pathos and tragedy of love and of the other moving situations of simple life. From the 'popular' nature of the ballads it has resulted that many of them are confined within no boundaries of race or nation, but, originating one here, one there, are spread in very varying versions throughout the whole, almost, of the world. Purely English, however, are those which deal with Robin Hood and his 'merry men,' idealized imaginary heroes of the Saxon common people in the dogged struggle which they maintained for centuries against their oppressive feudal lords.

4. The characters and 'properties' of the ballads of all classes are generally typical or traditional. There are the brave champion, whether noble or common man, who conquers or falls against overwhelming odds; the faithful lover of either sex; the woman whose constancy, proving stronger than man's fickleness, wins back her lover to her side at last; the traitorous old woman (victim of the blind and cruel prejudice which after a century or two was often to send her to the stake as a witch); the loyal little child; and some few others.

5. The verbal style of the ballads, like their spirit, is vigorous and simple, generally unpolished and sometimes rough, but often powerful with its terse dramatic suggestiveness. The usual, though not the only, poetic form is the four-lined stanza in lines alternately of four and three stresses and riming only in the second and fourth lines. Besides the refrains which are perhaps a relic of communal composition and the conventional epithets which the ballads share with epic poetry there are numerous traditional ballad expressions--rather meaningless formulas and line-tags used only to complete the rime or meter,

the common useful scrap-bag reserve of these unpretentious poets. The license of Anglo-Saxon poetry in the number of the unstressed syllables still remains. But it is evident that the existing versions of the ballads are generally more imperfect than the original forms; they have suffered from the corruptions of generations of oral repetition, which the scholars who have recovered them have preserved with necessary accuracy, but which for appreciative reading editors should so far as possible revise away.

Among the best or most representative single ballads are: The Hunting of the Cheviot (otherwise called The Ancient Ballad of Chevy Chase--clearly of minstrel authorship); Sir Patrick Spens; Robin Hood and Guy of Gisborne; Adam Bell, Clym of the Clough, and William of Cloudeslee; Captain Car, or Edom o' Gordon; King Estmere (though this has been somewhat altered by Bishop Percy, who had and destroyed the only surviving copy of it); Edward, Edward; Young Waters; Sweet William's Ghost; Lord Thomas and Fair Annet. Kinmont Willie is very fine, but seems to be largely the work of Sir Walter Scott and therefore not truly 'popular.'

## SIR THOMAS MALORY AND HIS 'MORTE DARTHUR'

The one fifteenth century author of the first rank, above referred to, is Sir Thomas Malory (the _a_ is pronounced as in _tally_). He is probably to be identified with the Sir Thomas Malory who during the wars in France and the civil strife of the Roses that followed was an adherent of the Earls of Warwick and who died in 1471 under sentence of outlawry by the victorious Edward IV. And some passing observations, at least, in his book seem to indicate that if he knew and had shared all the splendor and inspiration of the last years of medieval chivalry, he had experienced also the disappointment and bitterness of defeat and prolonged captivity. Further than this we know of him only that he wrote 'Le Morte Darthur' and had finished it by 1467.

Malory's purpose was to collect in a single work the great body of important Arthurian romance and to arrange it in the form of a continuous history of King Arthur and his knights. He called his book 'Le Morte Darthur,' The Death of Arthur, from the title of several popular Arthurian romances to which, since they dealt only with Arthur's later years and death, it was properly enough applied, and from which it seems to have passed into general currency as a name for the entire story of Arthur's life.

Actually to get together all the Arthurian romances was not possible for any man in Malory's day, or in any other, but he gathered up a goodly number, most of them, at least, written in French, and combined them, on the whole with unusual skill, into a work of about one-tenth their original bulk, which still ranks, with all qualifications, as one of the masterpieces of English literature. Dealing with such miscellaneous material, he could not wholly avoid inconsistencies, so that, for example, he sometimes introduces in full health in a later book a knight whom a hundred pages earlier he had killed and regularly buried; but this need not cause the reader anything worse than mild amusement. Not Malory but his age, also, is to blame for his sometimes hazy and puzzled treatment of the supernatural element in his material. In the remote earliest form of the stories, as Celtic myths, this supernatural element was no doubt frank and very large, but Malory's authorities, the more skeptical French romancers, adapting it to their own age, had often more or less fully rationalized it; transforming, for instance, the black river of Death which the original heroes often had to cross on journeys to the Celtic Other World into a rude and forbidding moat about the hostile castle into which the romancers degraded the Other World itself. Countless magic details, however, still remained recalcitrant to such treatment; and they evidently troubled Malory, whose devotion to his story was earnest and sincere.

Some of them he omits, doubtless as incredible, but others he retains, often in a form where the impossible is merely garbled into the unintelligible. For a single instance, in his seventh book he does not satisfactorily explain why the valiant Gareth on his arrival at Arthur's court asks at first only for a year's food and drink. In the original story, we can see to-day, Gareth must have been under a witch's spell which compelled him to a season of distasteful servitude; but this motivating bit of superstition Malory discards, or rather, in this case, it had been lost from the story at a much earlier stage. It results, therefore, that Malory's supernatural incidents are often far from clear and satisfactory; yet the reader is little troubled by this difficulty either in so thoroughly romantic a work.

Other technical faults may easily be pointed out in Malory's book. Thorough unity, either in the whole or in the separate stories so loosely woven together, could not be expected; in continual reading the long succession of similar combat after combat and the constant repetition of stereotyped phrases become monotonous for a present-day reader; and it must be confessed that Malory has little of the modern literary craftsman's power of close-knit style or proportion and emphasis in details. But these faults also may be overlooked, and the work is truly great, partly because it is an idealist's dream of chivalry, as chivalry might have been, a chivalry of faithful knights who went about redressing human wrongs and were loyal lovers and zealous servants of Holy Church; great also because Malory's heart is in his stories, so that he tells them in the main well, and invests them with a delightful atmosphere of romance which can never lose its fascination.

The style, also, in the narrower sense, is strong and good, and does its part to make the book, except for the Wiclif Bible, unquestionably the greatest monument of English prose of the entire period before the sixteenth century. There is no affectation of elegance, but rather knightly straightforwardness which has power without lack of ease. The sentences are often long, but always 'loose' and clear; and short ones are often used with the instinctive skill of sincerity. Everything is picturesque and dramatic and everywhere there is chivalrous feeling and genuine human sympathy.

## WILLIAM CAXTON AND THE INTRODUCTION OF PRINTING TO ENGLAND, 1476

Malory's book is the first great English classic which was given to the world in print instead of written manuscript; for it was shortly after Malory's death that the printing press was brought to England by William Caxton. The invention of printing, perhaps the most important event of modern times, took place in Germany not long after the middle of the fifteenth century, and the development of the art was rapid. Caxton, a shrewd and enterprising Kentishman, was by first profession a cloth merchant, and having taken up his residence across the Channel, was appointed by the king to the important post of Governor of the English Merchants in Flanders. Employed later in the service of the Duchess of Burgundy (sister of Edward IV), his ardent delight in romances led him to translate into English a French 'Recueil des Histoires de Troye' (Collection of the Troy Stories).

To supply the large demand for copies he investigated and mastered the new art by which they might be so wonderfully multiplied and about 1475, at fifty years of age, set up a press at Bruges in the modern Belgium, where he issued his 'Recueil,' which was thus the first English book ever put into print. During the next year, 1476, just a century before the first theater was to be built in London, Caxton returned to England and established his shop in Westminster, then a London suburb. During the fifteen remaining years of his life he labored diligently, printing an aggregate of more than a hundred books, which together comprised over fourteen thousand pages.

Aside from Malory's romance, which he put out in 1485, the most important of his publications was an edition of Chaucer's 'Canterbury Tales.' While laboring as a publisher Caxton himself continued to make translations, and in spite of many difficulties he, together with his assistants, turned into English from French no fewer than twenty-one distinct works. From every point of view Caxton's services were great. As translator and editor his style is careless and uncertain, but like Malory's it is sincere and manly, and vital with energy and enthusiasm. As printer, in a time of rapid changes in the language, when through the wars in France and her growing influence the second great infusion of Latin-French words was coming into the English language, he did what could be done for consistency in forms and spelling. Partly medieval and partly modern in spirit, he may fittingly stand at the close, or nearly at the close, of our study of the medieval period.

# 5

# The Medieval Drama

For the sake of clearness we have reserved for a separate chapter the discussion of the drama of the whole medieval period, which, though it did not reach a very high literary level, was one of the most characteristic expressions of the age. It should be emphasized that to no other form does what we have said of the similarity of medieval literature throughout Western Europe apply more closely, so that what we find true of the drama in England would for the most part hold good for the other countries as well.

## JUGGLERS, FOLK-PLAYS, PAGEANTS

At the fall of the Roman Empire, which marks the beginning of the Middle Ages, the corrupt Roman drama, proscribed by the Church, had come to an unhonored end, and the actors had been merged into the great body of disreputable jugglers and inferior minstrels who wandered over all Christendom. The performances of these social outcasts, crude and immoral as they were, continued for centuries unsuppressed, because they responded to the demand for dramatic spectacle which is one of the deepest though not least troublesome instincts in human nature.

The same demand was partly satisfied also by the rude country folk-plays, survivals of primitive heathen ceremonials, performed at such festival occasions as the harvest season, which in all lands continue to flourish among the country people long after their original meaning has been forgotten. In England the folk-plays, throughout the Middle Ages and in remote spots down almost to the present time, sometimes took the form of energetic dances (Morris dances, they came to be called, through confusion with Moorish performances of the same general nature). Others of them, however, exhibited in the midst of much rough-and-tumble fighting and buffoonery, a slight thread of dramatic action.

Their characters gradually came to be a conventional set, partly famous figures of popular tradition, such as St. George, Robin Hood, Maid Marian, and the Green Dragon. Other offshoots of the folk-play were the 'mummings' and 'disguisings,' collective names for many forms of processions, shows, and other entertainments, such as, among the upper classes, that precursor of the Elizabethan Mask in which a group of persons in disguise, invited or uninvited, attended a formal dancing party. In the later part of the Middle Ages, also, there were the secular pageants, spectacular displays (rather different from those of the twentieth century) given on such occasions as when a king or other person of high rank made formal entry into a town. They consisted of an elaborate scenic background set up near the city gate or on the street, with figures from allegorical or traditional history who engaged in some pantomime or declamation, but with very little dramatic dialog, or none.

## TROPES, LITURGICAL PLAYS, AND MYSTERY PLAYS

But all these forms, though they were not altogether without later influence, were very minor affairs, and the real drama of the Middle Ages grew up, without design and by the mere nature of things, from the regular services of the Church.

We must try in the first place to realize clearly the conditions under which the church service, the mass, was conducted during all the medieval centuries. We should picture to ourselves congregations of persons for the most part grossly ignorant, of unquestioning though very superficial faith, and of emotions easily aroused to fever heat. Of the Latin words of the service they understood nothing; and of the Bible story they had only a very general impression. It was necessary, therefore, that the service should be given a strongly spectacular and emotional character, and to this end no effort was spared. The great cathedrals and churches were much the finest buildings of the time, spacious with lofty pillars and shadowy recesses, rich in sculptured stone and in painted windows that cast on the walls and pavements soft and glowing patterns of many colors and shifting forms. The service itself was in great part musical, the confident notes of the full choir joining with the resonant organ-tones; and after all the rest the richly robed priests and ministrants passed along the aisles in stately processions enveloped in fragrant clouds of incense. That the eye if not the ear of the spectator, also, might catch some definite knowledge, the priests as they read the Bible stories sometimes displayed painted rolls which vividly pictured the principal events of the day's lesson.

Still, however, a lack was strongly felt, and at last, accidentally and slowly, began the process of dramatizing the services. First, inevitably, to be so treated was the central incident of Christian faith, the story of Christ's resurrection. The earliest steps were very simple. First, during the ceremonies on Good Friday, the day when Christ was crucified, the cross which stood all the year above the altar, bearing the Savior's figure, was taken down and laid beneath the altar, a dramatic symbol of the Death and Burial; and two days later, on 'the third day' of the Bible phraseology, that is on Easter Sunday, as the story of the Resurrection was chanted by the choir, the cross was uncovered and replaced, amid the rejoicings of the congregation.

Next, and before the Norman Conquest, the Gospel dialog between the angel and the three Marys at the tomb of Christ came sometimes to be chanted by the choir in those responses which are called 'tropes': 'Whom seek ye in the sepulcher, O Christians ?' 'Jesus of Nazareth the crucified, O angel.' 'He is not here; he has arisen as he said. Go, announce that he has risen from the sepulcher.' After this a little dramatic action was introduced almost as a matter of course.

One priest dressed in white robes sat, to represent the angel, by one of the square-built tombs near the junction of nave and transept, and three others, personating the Marys, advanced slowly toward him while they chanted their portion of the same dialog. As the last momentous words of the angel died away a jubilant 'Te Deum' burst from, organ and choir, and every member of the congregation exulted, often with sobs, in the great triumph which brought salvation to every Christian soul.

Little by little, probably, as time passed, this Easter scene was further enlarged, in part by additions from the closing incidents of the Savior's life. A similar treatment, too, was being given to the Christmas scene, still more humanly beautiful, of his birth in the manger, and occasionally the two scenes might be taken from their regular places in the service, combined, and presented at any season of the year. Other Biblical scenes, as well, came to be enacted, and, further, there were added stories from Christian tradition, such as that of Antichrist, and, on their particular days, the lives of Christian saints. Thus far these compositions are called Liturgical Plays, because they formed, in general, a part of the church service (liturgy).

But as some of them were united into extended groups and as the interest of the congregation deepened, the churches began to seem too small and inconvenient, the excited audiences forgot the proper reverence, and the performances were transferred to the churchyard, and then, when the gravestones proved troublesome, to the market place, the village-green, or any convenient field. By this time the people had ceased to be patient with the unintelligible Latin, and it was replaced at first, perhaps, and in part, by French, but finally by English; though probably verse was always retained as more appropriate than prose to the sacred subjects. Then, the religious spirit yielding inevitably in part to that of merrymaking, minstrels and mountebanks began to flock to the celebrations; and regular fairs, even, grew up about them. Gradually, too, the priests lost their hold even on the plays themselves; skilful actors from among the laymen began to take many of the parts; and at last in some towns the trade-guilds, or unions of the various handicrafts, which had secured control of the town governments, assumed entire charge.

These changes, very slowly creeping in, one by one, had come about in most places by the beginning of the fourteenth century. In 1311 a new impetus was given to the whole ceremony by the establishment of the late spring festival of Corpus Christi, a celebration of the doctrine of transubstantiation. On this occasion, or sometimes on some other festival, it became customary for the guilds to present an extended series of the plays, a series which together contained the essential substance of the Christian story, and therefore of the Christian faith. The Church generally still encouraged attendance, and not only did all the townspeople join wholeheartedly, but from all the country round the peasants flocked in. On one occasion the Pope promised the remission of a thousand days of purgatory to all persons who should be present at the Chester plays, and to this exemption the bishop of Chester added sixty days more.

The list of plays thus presented commonly included: The Fall of Lucifer; the Creation of the World and the Fall of Adam; Noah and the Flood; Abraham and Isaac and the promise of Christ's coming; a Procession of the Prophets, also foretelling Christ; the main events of the Gospel story, with some additions from Christian tradition; and the Day of Judgment. The longest cycle now known, that at York, contained, when fully developed, fifty plays, or perhaps even more. Generally each play was presented by a single guild (though sometimes two or three guilds or two or three plays might be combined), and sometimes, though not always, there was a special fitness in the assignment, as when the watermen gave the play of Noah's Ark or the bakers that of the Last Supper. In this connected form the plays are called the Mystery or Miracle Cycles. In many places, however, detached plays, or groups of plays smaller than the full cycles, continued to be presented at one season or another.

Each cycle as a whole, it will be seen, has a natural epic unity, centering about the majestic theme of the spiritual history and the final judgment of all Mankind. But unity both of material and of atmosphere suffers not only from the diversity among the separate plays but also from the violent intrusion of the comedy and the farce which the coarse taste of the audience demanded.

Sometimes, in the later period, altogether original and very realistic scenes from actual English life were added, like the very clever but very coarse parody on the Nativity play in the 'Towneley' cycle. More often comic treatment was given to the Bible scenes and characters themselves. Noah's wife, for example, came regularly to be presented as a shrew, who would not enter the ark until she had been beaten into submission; and Herod always appears as a blustering tyrant, whose fame still survives in a proverb of Shakspere's coinage--'to out-Herod Herod.'

The manner of presentation of the cycles varied much in different towns. Sometimes the entire cycle was still given, like the detached plays, at a single spot, the market-place or some other central square; but often, to accommodate the great crowds, there were several 'stations' at convenient intervals. In the latter case each play might remain all day at a particular station and be continuously repeated as the crowd moved slowly by; but more often it was the, spectators who remained, and the plays, mounted on movable stages, the 'pageant'-wagons, were drawn in turn by the guild-apprentices from one station to another.

When the audience was stationary, the common people stood in the square on all sides of the stage, while persons of higher rank or greater means were seated on temporary wooden scaffolds or looked down from the windows of the adjacent houses. In the construction of the 'pageant' all the little that was possible was done to meet the needs of the presentation. Below the main floor, or stage, was the curtained dressing-room of the actors; and when the play required, on one side was attached 'Hell-Mouth,' a great and horrible human head, whence issued flames and fiendish cries, often the fiends themselves, and into which lost sinners were violently hurled.

On the stage the scenery was necessarily very simple. A small raised platform or pyramid might represent Heaven, where God the Father was seated, and from which as the action required the angels came down; a single tree might indicate the Garden of Eden; and a doorway an entire house. In partial compensation the costumes were often elaborate, with all the finery of the church wardrobe and much of those of the wealthy citizens.

The expense accounts of the guilds, sometimes luckily preserved, furnish many picturesque and amusing items, such as these: 'Four pair of angels' wings, 2 shillings and 8 pence.' 'For mending of hell head, 6 pence.' 'Item, link for setting the world on fire.' Apparently women never acted; men and boys took the women's parts. All the plays of the cycle were commonly performed in a single day, beginning, at the first station, perhaps as early as five o'clock in the morning; but sometimes three days or even more were employed. To the guilds the giving of the plays was a very serious matter. Often each guild had a 'pageant-house' where it stored its 'properties,' and a pageant-master who trained the actors and imposed substantial fines on members remiss in cooperation.

We have said that the plays were always composed in verse. The stanza forms employed differ widely even within the same cycle, since the single plays were very diverse in both authorship and dates. The quality of the verse, generally mediocre at the outset, has often suffered much in transmission from generation to generation. In other respects also there are great contrasts; sometimes the feeling and power of a scene are admirable, revealing an author of real ability, sometimes there is only crude and wooden amateurishness. The medieval lack of historic sense gives to all the plays the setting of the authors' own times; Roman officers appear as feudal knights; and all the heathens (including the Jews) are Saracens, worshippers of 'Mahound' and 'Termagaunt'; while the good characters, however long they may really have lived before the Christian era, swear stoutly by St. John and St. Paul and the other medieval Christian divinities.

The frank coarseness of the plays is often merely disgusting, and suggests how superficial, in most cases, was the medieval religious sense. With no thought of incongruity, too, these writers brought God the Father onto the stage in bodily form, and then, attempting in all sincerity to show him reverence, gilded his face and put into his mouth long speeches of exceedingly tedious declamation.

The whole emphasis, as generally in the religion of the times, was on the fear of hell rather than on the love of righteousness. Yet in spite of everything grotesque and inconsistent, the plays no doubt largely fulfilled their religious purpose and exercised on the whole an elevating influence. The humble submission of the boy Isaac to the will of God and of his earthly father, the yearning devotion of Mary the mother of Jesus, and the infinite love and pity of the tortured Christ himself, must have struck into even callous hearts for at least a little time some genuine consciousness of the beauty and power of the finer and higher life. A literary form which supplied much of the religious and artistic nourishment of half a continent for half a thousand years cannot be lightly regarded or dismissed.

## THE MORALITY PLAYS

The Mystery Plays seem to have reached their greatest popularity in the fourteenth and fifteenth centuries. In the dawning light of the Renaissance and the modern spirit they gradually waned, though in exceptional places and in special revivals they did not altogether cease to be given until the seventeenth century. On the Continent of Europe, indeed, they still survive, after a fashion, in a single somewhat modernized form, the celebrated Passion Play of Oberammergau. In England by the end of the fifteenth century they had been for the most part replaced by a kindred species which had long been growing up beside them, namely the Morality Plays.

The Morality Play probably arose in part from the desire of religious writers to teach the principles of Christian living in a more direct and compact fashion than was possible through the Bible stories of the Mysteries. In its strict form the Morality Play was a dramatized moral allegory. It was in part an offshoot from the Mysteries, in some of which there had appeared among the actors abstract allegorical figures, either good or bad, such as The Seven Deadly Sins, Contemplation, and Raise-Slander.

In the Moralities the majority of the characters are of this sort--though not to the exclusion of supernatural persons such as God and the Devil--and the hero is generally a type-figure standing for all Mankind. For the control of the hero the two definitely opposing groups of Virtues and Vices contend; the commonest type of Morality presents in brief glimpses the entire story of the hero's life, that is of the life of every man.

It shows how he yields to temptation and lives for the most part in reckless sin, but at last in spite of all his flippancy and folly is saved by Perseverance and Repentance, pardoned through God's mercy, and assured of salvation. As compared with the usual type of Mystery plays the Moralities had for the writers this advantage, that they allowed some independence in the invention of the story; and how powerful they might be made in the hands of a really gifted author has been finely demonstrated in our own time by the stage-revival of the best of them, 'Everyman' (which is probably a translation from a Dutch original).

In most cases, however, the spirit of medieval allegory proved fatal, the genuinely abstract characters are mostly shadowy and unreal, and the speeches of the Virtues are extreme examples of intolerable sanctimonious declamation. Against this tendency, on the other hand, the persistent instinct for realism provided a partial antidote; the Vices are often very lifelike rascals, abstract only in name. In these cases the whole plays become vivid studies in contemporary low life, largely human and interesting except for their prolixity and the coarseness which they inherited from the Mysteries and multiplied on their own account. During the Reformation period, in the early sixteenth century, the character of the Moralities, more strictly so called, underwent something of a change, and they were--sometimes made the vehicle for religious argument, especially by Protestants.

**THE INTERLUDES**

Early in the sixteenth century, the Morality in its turn was largely superseded by another sort of play called the Interlude. But just as in the case of the Mystery and the Morality, the Interlude developed out of the Morality, and the two cannot always be distinguished, some single plays being distinctly described by the authors as 'Moral Interludes.' In the Interludes the realism of the Moralities became still more pronounced, so that the typical Interlude is nothing more than a coarse farce, with no pretense at religious or ethical meaning. The name Interlude denotes literally 'a play between,' but the meaning intended (between whom or what) is uncertain. The plays were given sometimes in the halls of nobles and gentlemen, either when banquets were in progress or on other festival occasions; sometimes before less select audiences in the town halls or on village greens.

The actors were sometimes strolling companies of players, who might be minstrels 'or rustics, and were sometimes also retainers of the great nobles, allowed to practice their dramatic ability on tours about the country when they were not needed for their masters' entertainment. In the Interlude-Moralities and Interludes first appears The Vice, a rogue who sums up in himself all the Vices of the older Moralities and serves as the buffoon. One of his most popular exploits was to belabor the Devil about the stage with a wooden dagger, a habit which took a great hold on the popular imagination, as numerous references in later literature testify. Transformed by time, the Vice appears in the Elizabethan drama, and thereafter, as the clown.

## THE LATER INFLUENCE OF THE MEDIEVAL DRAMA

The various dramatic forms from the tenth century to the middle of the sixteenth at which we have thus hastily glanced--folk-plays, mummings and disguisings, secular pageants, Mystery plays, Moralities, and Interludes--have little but a historical importance. But besides demonstrating the persistence of the popular demand for drama, they exerted a permanent influence in that they formed certain stage traditions which were to modify or largely control the great drama of the Elizabethan period and to some extent of later times. Among these traditions were the disregard for unity, partly of action, but especially of time and place; the mingling of comedy with even the intensest scenes of tragedy; the nearly complete lack of stage scenery, with a resultant willingness in the audience to make the largest possible imaginative assumptions; the presence of certain stock figures, such as the clown; and the presentation of women's parts by men and boys. The plays, therefore, must be reckoned with in dramatic history.

# 6

# Period IV the Sixteenth Century the Renaissance and the Reign of Elizabeth

## THE RENAISSANCE

The fifteenth and sixteenth centuries are the period of the European Renaissance or New Birth, one of the three or four great transforming movements of European history. This impulse by which the medieval society of scholasticism, feudalism, and chivalry was to be made over into what we call the modern world came first from Italy. Italy, like the rest of the Roman Empire, had been overrun and conquered in the fifth century by the barbarian Teutonic tribes, but the devastation had been less complete there than in the more northern lands, and there, even more, perhaps, than in France, the bulk of the people remained Latin in blood and in character.

Hence it resulted that though the Middle Ages were in Italy a period of terrible political anarchy, yet Italian culture recovered far more rapidly than that of the northern nations, whom the Italians continued down to the modern period to regard contemptuously as still mere barbarians. By the fourteenth and fifteenth centuries, further, the Italians had become intellectually one of the keenest races whom the world has ever known, though in morals they were sinking to almost incredible corruption. Already in fourteenth century Italy, therefore, the movement for a much fuller and freer intellectual life had begun, and we have seen that by Petrarch and Boccaccio something of this spirit was transmitted to Chaucer. In England Chaucer was followed by the medievalizing fifteenth century, but in Italy there was no such interruption.

The Renaissance movement first received definite direction from the rediscovery and study of Greek literature, which clearly revealed the unbounded possibilities of life to men who had been groping dissatisfied within the now narrow limits of medieval thought. Before Chaucer was dead the study of Greek, almost forgotten in Western Europe during the Middle Ages, had been renewed in Italy, and it received a still further impulse when at the taking of Constantinople by the Turks in 1453 Greek scholars and manuscripts were scattered to the West. It is hard for us to-day to realize the meaning for the men of the fifteenth century of this revived knowledge of the life and thought of the Greek race. The medieval Church, at first merely from the brutal necessities of a period of anarchy, had for the most part frowned on the joy and beauty of life, permitting pleasure, indeed, to the laity, but as a thing half dangerous, and declaring that there was perfect safety only within the walls of the nominally ascetic Church itself.

The intellectual life, also, nearly restricted to priests and monks, had been formalized and conventionalized, until in spite of the keenness of its methods and the brilliancy of many of its scholars, it had become largely barren and unprofitable. The whole sphere of knowledge had been subjected to the mere authority of the Bible and of a few great minds of the past, such as Aristotle. All questions were argued and decided on the basis of their assertions, which had often become wholly inadequate and were often warped into grotesquely impossible interpretations and applications. Scientific investigation was almost entirely stifled, and progress was impossible. The whole field of religion and knowledge had become largely stagnant under an arbitrary despotism.

To the minds which were being paralyzed under this system, Greek literature brought the inspiration for which they longed. For it was the literature of a great and brilliant people who, far from attempting to make a divorce within man's nature, had aimed to 'see life steadily and see it whole,' who, giving free play to all their powers, had found in pleasure and beauty some of the most essential constructive forces, and had embodied beauty in works of literature and art where the significance of the whole spiritual life was more splendidly suggested than in the achievements of any, or almost any, other period. The enthusiasm, therefore, with which the Italians turned to the study of Greek literature and Greek life was boundless, and it constantly found fresh nourishment. Every year restored from forgotten recesses of libraries or from the ruins of Roman villas another Greek author or volume or work of art, and those which had never been lost were reinterpreted with much deeper insight. Aristotle was again vitalized, and Plato's noble idealistic philosophy was once more appreciatively studied and understood. In the light of this new revelation Latin literature, also, which had never ceased to be almost superstitiously studied, took on a far greater human significance.

Vergil and Cicero were regarded no longer as mysterious prophets from a dimly imagined past, but as real men of flesh and blood, speaking out of experiences remote in time from the present but no less humanly real. The word 'human,' indeed, became the chosen motto of the Renaissance scholars; 'humanists' was the title which they applied to themselves as to men for whom 'nothing human was without appeal.' New creative enthusiasm, also, and magnificent actual new creation, followed the discovery of the old treasures, creation in literature and all the arts; culminating particularly in the early sixteenth century in the greatest group of painters whom any country has ever seen, Lionardo da Vinci, Raphael, and Michelangelo.

In Italy, to be sure, the light of the Renaissance had its palpable shadow; in breaking away from the medieval bondage into the unhesitating enjoyment of all pleasure, the humanists too often overleaped all restraints and plunged into wild excess, often into mere sensuality. Hence the Italian Renaissance is commonly called Pagan, and hence when young English nobles began to travel to Italy to drink at the fountain head of the new inspiration moralists at home protested with much reason against the ideas and habits which many of them brought back with their new clothes and flaunted as evidences of intellectual emancipation. History, however, shows no great progressive movement unaccompanied by exaggerations and extravagances.

The Renaissance, penetrating northward, past first from Italy to France, but as early as the middle of the fifteenth century English students were frequenting the Italian universities. Soon the study of Greek was introduced into England, also, first at Oxford; and it was cultivated with such good results that when, early in the sixteenth century, the great Dutch student and reformer, Erasmus, unable through poverty to reach Italy, came to Oxford instead, he found there a group of accomplished scholars and gentlemen whose instruction and hospitable companionship aroused his unbounded delight. One member of this group was the fine-spirited John Colet, later Dean of St. Paul's Cathedral in London, who was to bring new life into the secondary education of English boys by the establishment of St. Paul's Grammar School, based on the principle of kindness in place of the merciless severity of the traditional English system.

Great as was the stimulus of literary culture, it was only one of several influences that made up the Renaissance. While Greek was speaking so powerfully to the cultivated class, other forces were contributing to revolutionize life as a whole and all men's outlook upon it. The invention of printing, multiplying books in unlimited quantities where before there had been only a few manuscripts laboriously copied page by page, absolutely transformed all the processes of knowledge and almost of thought. Not much later began the vast expansion of the physical world through geographical exploration. Toward the end of the fifteenth century the Portuguese sailor, Vasco da Gama, finishing the work of Diaz, discovered the sea route to India around the Cape of Good Hope. A few years earlier Columbus had revealed the New World and virtually proved that the earth is round, a proof scientifically completed a generation after him when Magellan's ship actually circled the globe.

Following close after Columbus, the Cabots, Italian-born, but naturalized Englishmen, discovered North America, and for a hundred years the rival ships of Spain, England, and Portugal filled the waters of the new West and the new East. In America handfuls of Spanish adventurers conquered great empires and despatched home annual treasure fleets of gold and silver, which the audacious English sea-captains, half explorers and half pirates, soon learned to intercept and plunder. The marvels which were constantly being revealed as actual facts seemed no less wonderful than the extravagances of medieval romance; and it was scarcely more than a matter of course that men should search in the new strange lands for the fountain of perpetual youth and the philosopher's stone.

The supernatural beings and events of Spenser's 'Faerie Queene' could scarcely seem incredible to an age where incredulity was almost unknown because it was impossible to set a bound how far any one might reasonably believe. But the horizon of man's expanded knowledge was not to be limited even to his own earth. About the year 1540, the Polish Copernicus opened a still grander realm of speculation (not to be adequately possessed for several centuries) by the announcement that our world is not the center of the universe, but merely one of the satellites of its far-superior sun.

The whole of England was profoundly stirred by the Renaissance to a new and most energetic life, but not least was this true of the Court, where for a time literature was very largely to center. Since the old nobility had mostly perished in the wars, both Henry VII, the founder of the Tudor line, and his son, Henry VIII, adopted the policy of replacing it with able and wealthy men of the middle class, who would be strongly devoted to themselves. The court therefore became a brilliant and crowded circle of unscrupulous but unusually adroit statesmen, and a center of lavish entertainments and display. Under this new aristocracy the rigidity of the feudal system was relaxed, and life became somewhat easier for all the dependent classes. Modern comforts, too, were largely introduced, and with them the Italian arts; Tudor architecture, in particular, exhibited the originality and splendor of an energetic and self-confident age. Further, both Henries, though perhaps as essentially selfish and tyrannical as almost any of their predecessors, were politic and far-sighted, and they took a genuine pride in the prosperity of their kingdom. They encouraged trade; and in the peace which was their best gift the well-being of the nation as a whole increased by leaps and bounds.

## THE REFORMATION

Lastly, the literature of the sixteenth century and later was profoundly influenced by that religious result of the Renaissance which we know as the Reformation. While in Italy the new impulses were chiefly turned into secular and often corrupt channels, in the Teutonic lands they deeply stirred the Teutonic conscience. In 1517 Martin Luther, protesting against the unprincipled and flippant practices that were disgracing religion, began the breach between Catholicism, with its insistence on the supremacy of the Church, and Protestantism, asserting the independence of the individual judgment. In England Luther's action revived the spirit of Lollardism, which had nearly been crushed out, and in spite of a minority devoted to the older system, the nation as a whole began to move rapidly toward change. Advocates of radical revolution thrust themselves forward in large numbers, while cultured and thoughtful men, including the Oxford group, indulged the too ideal hope of a gradual and peaceful reform.

The actual course of the religious movement was determined largely by the personal and political projects of Henry VIII. Conservative at the outset, Henry even attacked Luther in a pamphlet, which won from the Pope for himself and his successors the title 'Defender of the Faith.' But when the Pope finally refused Henry's demand for the divorce from Katharine of Spain, which would make possible a marriage with Anne Boleyn, Henry angrily threw off the papal authority and declared himself the Supreme Head of the Church in England, thus establishing the separate English (Anglican, Episcopal) church. In the brief reign of Henry's son, Edward VI, the separation was made more decisive; under Edward's sister, Mary, Catholicism was restored; but the last of Henry's children, Elizabeth, coming to the throne in 1558, gave the final victory to the English communion.

Under all these sovereigns (to complete our summary of the movement) the more radical Protestants, Puritans as they came to be called, were active in agitation, undeterred by frequent cruel persecution and largely influenced by the corresponding sects in Germany and by the Presbyterianism established by Calvin in Geneva and later by John Knox in Scotland. Elizabeth's skilful management long kept the majority of the Puritans within the English Church, where they formed an important element, working for simpler practices and introducing them in congregations which they controlled. But toward the end of the century and of Elizabeth's reign, feeling grew tenser, and groups of the Puritans, sometimes under persecution, definitely separated themselves from the State Church and established various sectarian bodies. Shortly after 1600, in particular, the

Independents, or Congregationalists, founded in Holland the church which was soon to colonize New England. At home, under James I, the breach widened, until the nation was divided into two hostile camps, with results most radically decisive for literature. But for the present we must return to the early part of the sixteenth century.

## SIR THOMAS MORE AND HIS 'UTOPIA'

Out of the confused and bitter strife of churches and parties, while the outcome was still uncertain, issued a great mass of controversial writing which does not belong to literature. A few works, however, more or less directly connected with the religious agitation, cannot be passed by.

One of the most attractive and finest spirits of the reign of Henry VIII was Sir Thomas More. A member of the Oxford group in its second generation, a close friend of Erasmus, his house a center of humanism, he became even more conspicuous in public life. A highly successful lawyer, he was rapidly advanced by Henry VIII in court and in national affairs, until on the fall of Cardinal Wolsey in 1529 he was appointed, much against his will, to the highest office open to a subject, that of Lord Chancellor (head of the judicial system).

A devoted Catholic, he took a part which must have been revolting to himself in the torturing and burning of Protestants; but his absolute loyalty to conscience showed itself to better purpose when in the almost inevitable reverse of fortune he chose harsh imprisonment and death rather than to take the formal oath of allegiance to the king in opposition to the Pope. His quiet jests on the scaffold suggest the never-failing sense of humor which was one sign of the completeness and perfect poise of his character; while the hair-shirt which he wore throughout his life and the severe penances to which he subjected himself reveal strikingly how the expression of the deepest convictions of the best natures may be determined by inherited and outworn modes of thought.

More's most important work was his 'Utopia,' published in 1516. The name, which is Greek, means No-Place, and the book is one of the most famous of that series of attempts to outline an imaginary ideal condition of society which begins with Plato's 'Republic' and has continued to our own time. 'Utopia,' broadly considered, deals primarily with the question which is common to most of these books and in which both ancient Greece and Europe of the Renaissance took a special interest, namely the question of the relation of the State and the individual. It consists of two parts.

In the first there is a vivid picture of the terrible evils which England was suffering through war, lawlessness, the wholesale and foolish application of the death penalty, the misery of the peasants, the absorption of the land by the rich, and the other distressing corruptions in Church and State. In the second part, in contrast to all this, a certain imaginary Raphael Hythlodaye describes the customs of Utopia, a remote island in the New World, to which chance has carried him. To some of the ideals thus set forth More can scarcely have expected the world ever to attain; and some of them will hardly appeal to the majority of readers of any period; but in the main he lays down an admirable program for human progress, no small part of which has been actually realized in the four centuries which have since elapsed.

The controlling purpose in the life of the Utopians is to secure both the welfare of the State and the full development of the individual under the ascendancy of his higher faculties. The State is democratic, socialistic, and communistic, and the will of the individual is subordinated to the advantage of all, but the real interests of each and all are recognized as identical. Every one is obliged to work, but not to overwork; six hours a day make the allotted period; and the rest of the time is free, but with plentiful provision of lectures and other aids for the education of mind and spirit. All the citizens are taught the fundamental art, that of agriculture, and in addition each has a particular trade or profession of his own.

There is no surfeit, excess, or ostentation. Clothing is made for durability, and every one's garments are precisely like those of every one else, except that there is a difference between those of men and women and those of married and unmarried persons. The sick are carefully tended, but the victims of hopeless or painful disease are mercifully put to death if they so desire. Crime is naturally at a minimum, but those who persist in it are made slaves (not executed, for why should the State be deprived of their services?). Detesting war, the Utopians make a practice of hiring certain barbarians who, conveniently, are their neighbors, to do whatever fighting is necessary for their defense, and they win if possible, not by the revolting slaughter of pitched battles, but by the assassination of their enemies' generals. In especial, there is complete religious toleration, except for atheism, and except for those who urge their opinions with offensive violence.

'Utopia' was written and published in Latin; among the multitude of translations into many languages the earliest in English, in which it is often reprinted, is that of Ralph Robinson, made in 1551.

### THE ENGLISH BIBLE AND BOOKS OF DEVOTION

To this century of religious change belongs the greater part of the literary history of the English Bible and of the ritual books of the English Church. Since the suppression of the Wiclifite movement the circulation of the Bible in English had been forbidden, but growing Protestantism insistently revived the demand for it. The attitude of Henry VIII and his ministers was inconsistent and uncertain, reflecting their own changing points of view. In 1526 William Tyndale, a zealous Protestant controversialist then in exile in Germany, published an excellent English translation of the New Testament. Based on the proper authority, the Greek original, though with influence from Wiclif and from the Latin and German (Luther's) version, this has been directly or indirectly the starting-point for all subsequent English translations except those of the Catholics.

Ten years later Tyndale suffered martyrdom, but in 1535 Miles Coverdale, later bishop of Exeter, issued in Germany a translation of the whole Bible in a more gracious style than Tyndale's, and to this the king and the established clergy were now ready to give license and favor. Still two years later appeared a version compounded of those of Tyndale and Coverdale and called, from the fictitious name of its editor, the 'Matthew' Bible. In 1539, under the direction of Archbishop Cranmer, Coverdale issued a revised edition, officially authorized for use in churches; its version of the Psalms still stands as the Psalter of the English Church. In 1560 English Puritan refugees at Geneva put forth the 'Geneva Bible,' especially accurate as a translation, which long continued the accepted version for private use among all parties and for all purposes among the Puritans, in both Old and New England. Eight years later, under Archbishop Parker, there was issued in large volume form and for use in churches the 'Bishops' Bible,' so named because the majority of its thirteen editors were bishops. This completes the list of important translations down to those of 1611 and 1881, of which we shall speak in the proper place. The Book of Common Prayer, now used in the English Church coordinately with Bible and Psalter, took shape out of previous primers of private devotion, litanies, and hymns, mainly as the work of Archbishop Cranmer during the reign of Edward VI.

Of the influence of these translations of the Bible on English literature it is impossible to speak too strongly. They rendered the whole nation familiar for centuries with one of the grandest and most varied of all collections of books, which was adopted with ardent patriotic enthusiasm as one of the chief national possessions, and which has served as an unfailing storehouse of poetic and dramatic allusions for all later writers. Modern English literature as a whole is permeated and enriched to an incalculable degree with the substance and spirit of the English Bible.

## WYATT AND SURREY AND THE NEW POETRY

In the literature of fine art also the new beginning was made during the reign of Henry VIII. This was through the introduction by Sir Thomas Wyatt of the Italian fashion of lyric poetry. Wyatt, a man of gentle birth, entered Cambridge at the age of twelve and received his degree of M. A. seven years later. His mature life was that of a courtier to whom the king's favor brought high appointments, with such vicissitudes of fortune, including occasional imprisonments, as formed at that time a common part of the courtier's lot. Wyatt, however, was not a merely worldly person, but a Protestant seemingly of high and somewhat severe moral character. He died in 1542 at the age of thirty-nine of a fever caught as he was hastening, at the king's command, to meet and welcome the Spanish ambassador.

On one of his missions to the Continent, Wyatt, like Chaucer, had visited Italy. Impressed with the beauty of Italian verse and the contrasting rudeness of that of contemporary England, he determined to remodel the latter in the style of the former.

Here a brief historical retrospect is necessary. The Italian poetry of the sixteenth century had itself been originally an imitation, namely of the poetry of Provence in Southern France. There, in the twelfth century, under a delightful climate and in a region of enchanting beauty, had arisen a luxurious civilization whose poets, the troubadours, many of them men of noble birth, had carried to the furthest extreme the woman-worship of medieval chivalry and had enshrined it in lyric poetry of superb and varied sweetness and beauty.

In this highly conventionalized poetry the lover is forever sighing for his lady, a correspondingly obdurate being whose favor is to be won only by years of the most unqualified and unreasoning devotion. From Provence, Italy had taken up the style, and among the other forms for its expression, in the twelfth and thirteenth centuries, had devised the poem of a single fourteen-line stanza which we call the sonnet. The whole movement had found its great master in Petrarch, who, in hundreds of poems, mostly sonnets, of perfect beauty, had sung the praises and cruelty of his nearly imaginary Laura.

It was this highly artificial but very beautiful poetic fashion which Wyatt deliberately set about to introduce into England. The nature and success of his innovation can be summarized in a few definite statements.

1. Imitating Petrarch, Wyatt nearly limits himself as regards substance to the treatment of the artificial love-theme, lamenting the unkindness of ladies who very probably never existed and whose favor in any case he probably regarded very lightly; yet even so, he often strikes a manly English note of independence, declaring that if the lady continues obstinate he will not die for her love.

2. Historically much the most important feature of Wyatt's experiment was the introduction of the sonnet, a very substantial service indeed; for not only did this form, like the love-theme, become by far the most popular one among English lyric poets of the next two generations, setting a fashion which was carried to an astonishing excess; but it is the only artificial form of foreign origin which has ever been really adopted and naturalized in English, and it still remains the best instrument for the terse expression of a single poetic thought. Wyatt, it should be observed, generally departs from the Petrarchan

rime-scheme, on the whole unfortunately, by substituting a third quatrain for the first four lines of the sestet. That is, while Petrarch's rime-arrangement is either a b b a a b b a c d c d c d, or a b b a a b b a c d e c d e, Wyatt's is usually a b b a a b b a c d d c e e.

3. In his attempted reformation of English metrical irregularity Wyatt, in his sonnets, shows only the uncertain hand of a beginner. He generally secures an equal number of syllables in each line, but he often merely counts them off on his fingers, wrenching the accents all awry, and often violently forcing the rimes as well. In his songs, however, which are much more numerous than the sonnets, he attains delightful fluency and melody. His 'My Lute, Awake,' and 'Forget Not Yet' are still counted among the notable English lyrics.

4. A particular and characteristic part of the conventional Italian lyric apparatus which Wyatt transplanted was the 'conceit.' A conceit may be defined as an exaggerated figure of speech or play on words in which intellectual cleverness figures at least as largely as real emotion and which is often dragged out to extremely complicated lengths of literal application. An example is Wyatt's declaration (after Petrarch) that his love, living in his heart, advances to his face and there encamps, displaying his banner (which merely means that the lover blushes with his emotion). In introducing the conceit Wyatt fathered the most conspicuous of the superficial general features which were to dominate English poetry for a century to come.

5. Still another, minor, innovation of Wyatt was the introduction into English verse of the Horatian 'satire' (moral poem, reflecting on current follies) in the form of three metrical letters to friends. In these the meter is the terza rima of Dante.

Wyatt's work was continued by his poetical disciple and successor, Henry Howard, who, as son of the Duke of Norfolk, held the courtesy title of Earl of Surrey. A brilliant though wilful representative of Tudor chivalry, and distinguished in war, Surrey seems to have occupied at Court almost the same commanding position as Sir Philip Sidney in the following generation. His career was cut short in tragically ironical fashion at the age of thirty by the plots of his enemies and the dying bloodthirstiness of King Henry, which together led to his execution on a trumped-up charge of treason. It was only one of countless brutal court crimes, but it seems the more hateful because if the king had died a single day earlier Surrey could have been saved.

Surrey's services to poetry were two: 1. He improved on the versification of Wyatt's sonnets, securing fluency and smoothness. 2. In a translation of two books of Vergil's 'Aneid' he introduced, from the Italian, pentameter blank verse, which was destined thenceforth to be the meter of English poetic drama and of much of the greatest English non-dramatic poetry. Further, though his poems are less numerous than those of Wyatt, his range of subjects is somewhat broader, including some appreciative treatment of external Nature. He seems, however, somewhat less sincere than his teacher. In his sonnets he abandoned the form followed by Wyatt and adopted (still from the Italian) the one which was subsequently used by Shakspere, consisting of three independent quatrains followed, as with Wyatt, by a couplet which sums up the thought with epigrammatic force, thus: a b a b c d c d e f e f g g.

Wyatt and Surrey set a fashion at Court; for some years it seems to have been an almost necessary accomplishment for every young noble to turn off love poems after Italian and French models; for France too had now taken up the fashion. These poems were generally and naturally regarded as the property of the Court and of the gentry, and circulated at first only in manuscript among the author's friends; but the general public became curious about them, and in 1557 one of the publishers of the day, Richard Tottel, securing a number of those of Wyatt, Surrey, and a few other noble or gentle authors, published them in a little volume, which is known as 'Tottel's Miscellany.' Coming as it does in the year before the accession of Queen Elizabeth, at the end of the comparatively barren reigns of Edward and Mary, this book is taken by common consent as marking the beginning of the literature of the Elizabethan period. It was the premature predecessor, also, of a number of such anthologies which were published during the latter half of Elizabeth's reign.

## THE ELIZABETHAN PERIOD

The earlier half of Elizabeth's reign, also, though not lacking in literary effort, produced no work of permanent importance.

After the religious convulsions of half a century time was required for the development of the internal quiet and confidence from which a great literature could spring.

At length, however, the hour grew ripe and there came the greatest outburst of creative energy in the whole history of English literature. Under Elizabeth's wise guidance the prosperity and enthusiasm of the nation had risen to the highest pitch, and London in particular was overflowing with vigorous life. A special stimulus of the most intense kind came from the struggle with Spain.

After a generation of half-piratical depredations by the English seadogs against the Spanish treasure fleets and the Spanish settlements in America, King Philip, exasperated beyond all patience and urged on by a bigot's zeal for the Catholic Church, began deliberately to prepare the Great Armada, which was to crush at one blow the insolence, the independence, and the religion of England.

There followed several long years of breathless suspense; then in 1588 the Armada sailed and was utterly overwhelmed in one of the most complete disasters of the world's history. Thereupon the released energy of England broke out exultantly into still more impetuous achievement in almost every line of activity. The great literary period is taken by common consent to begin with the publication of Spenser's 'Shepherd's Calendar' in 1579, and to end in some sense at the death of Elizabeth in 1603, though in the drama, at least, it really continues many years longer.

Several general characteristics of Elizabethan literature and writers should be indicated at the outset.

1. The period has the great variety of almost unlimited creative force; it includes works of many kinds in both verse and prose, and ranges in spirit from the loftiest Platonic idealism or the most delightful romance to the level of very repulsive realism.
2. It was mainly dominated, however, by the spirit of romance.
3. It was full also of the spirit of dramatic action, as befitted an age whose restless enterprise was eagerly extending itself to every quarter of the globe.

4. In style it often exhibits romantic luxuriance, which sometimes takes the form of elaborate affectations of which the favorite 'conceit' is only the most apparent.
5. It was in part a period of experimentation, when the proper material and limits of literary forms were being determined, oftentimes by means of false starts and grandiose failures. In particular, many efforts were made to give prolonged poetical treatment to many subjects essentially prosaic, for example to systems of theological or scientific thought, or to the geography of all England.
6. It continued to be largely influenced by the literature of Italy, and to a less degree by those of France and Spain.
7. The literary spirit was all-pervasive, and the authors were men (not yet women) of almost every class, from distinguished courtiers, like Ralegh and Sidney, to the company of hack writers, who starved in garrets and hung about the outskirts of the bustling taverns.

**PROSE FICTION**

The period saw the beginning, among other things, of English prose fiction of something like the later modern type. First appeared a series of collections of short tales chiefly translated from Italian authors, to which tales the Italian name 'novella' (novel) was applied. Most of the separate tales are crude or amateurish and have only historical interest, though as a class they furnished the plots for many Elizabethan dramas, including several of Shakspere's. The most important collection was Painter's 'Palace of Pleasure,' in 1566. The earliest original, or partly original, English prose fictions to appear were handbooks of morals and manners in story form, and here the beginning was made by John Lyly, who is also of some importance in the history of the Elizabethan drama. In 1578 Lyly, at the age of twenty-five, came from Oxford to London, full of the enthusiasm of Renaissance learning, and evidently determined to fix himself as a new and dazzling star in the literary sky. In this ambition he achieved a remarkable and immediate success, by the publication of a little book entitled 'Euphues and His Anatomie of Wit.' 'Euphues' means 'the well-bred man,' and though there is a slight action, the work is mainly a series of moralizing disquisitions (mostly rearranged from Sir Thomas North's translation of 'The Dial of Princes' of the Spaniard Guevara) on love, religion, and conduct. Most influential, however, for the time-being, was Lyly's style, which is the most conspicuous English example of the later Renaissance craze, then rampant throughout Western Europe, for refining and beautifying the art of prose expression in a mincingly affected fashion.

Witty, clever, and sparkling at all costs, Lyly takes especial pains to balance his sentences and clauses antithetically, phrase against phrase and often word against word, sometimes emphasizing the balance also by an exaggerated use of alliteration and assonance. A representative sentence is this: 'Although there be none so ignorant that doth not know, neither any so impudent that will not confesse, friendship to be the jewell of humaine joye; yet whosoever shall see this amitie grounded upon a little affection, will soone conjecture that it shall be dissolved upon a light occasion.'

Others of Lyly's affectations are rhetorical questions, hosts of allusions to classical history, and literature, and an unfailing succession of similes from all the recondite knowledge that he can command, especially from the fantastic collection of fables which, coming down through the Middle Ages from the Roman writer Pliny, went at that time by the name of natural history and which we have already encountered in the medieval Bestiaries. Preposterous by any reasonable standard, Lyly's style, 'Euphuism,' precisely hit the Court taste of his age and became for a decade its most approved conversational dialect.

In literature the imitations of 'Euphues' which flourished for a while gave way to a series of romances inaugurated by the 'Arcadia' of Sir Philip Sidney. Sidney's brilliant position for a few years as the noblest representative of chivalrous ideals in the intriguing Court of Elizabeth is a matter of common fame, as is his death in 1586 at the age of thirty-two during the siege of Zutphen in Holland. He wrote 'Arcadia' for the amusement of his sister, the Countess of Pembroke, during a period of enforced retirement beginning in 1580, but the book was not published until ten years later.

It is a pastoral romance, in the general style of Italian and Spanish romances of the earlier part of the century. The pastoral is the most artificial literary form in modern fiction. It may be said to have begun in the third century B. C. with the perfectly sincere poems of the Greek Theocritus, who gives genuine expression to the life of actual Sicilian shepherds. But with successive Latin, Medieval, and Renaissance writers in verse and prose the country characters and setting had become mere disguises, sometimes allegorical, for the expression of the very far from simple sentiments of the upper classes, and sometimes for their partly genuine longing, the outgrowth of sophisticated weariness and ennui, for rural naturalness.

Sidney's very complicated tale of adventures in love and war, much longer than any of its successors, is by no means free from artificiality, but it finely mirrors his own knightly spirit and remains a permanent English classic. Among his followers were some of the better hack-writers of the time, who were also among the minor dramatists and poets, especially Robert Greene and Thomas Lodge. Lodge's 'Rosalynde,' also much influenced by Lyly, is in itself a pretty story and is noteworthy as the original of Shakspere's 'As You Like It.'

Lastly, in the concluding decade of the sixteenth century, came a series of realistic stories depicting chiefly, in more or less farcical spirit, the life of the poorer classes. They belonged mostly to that class of realistic fiction which is called picaresque, from the Spanish word 'picaro,' a rogue, because it began in Spain with the 'Lazarillo de Tormes' of Diego de Mendoza, in 1553, and because its heroes are knavish serving-boys or similar characters whose unprincipled tricks and exploits formed the substance of the stories. In Elizabethan England it produced nothing of individual note.

## EDMUND SPENSER, 1552-1599

The first really commanding figure in the Elizabethan period, and one of the chief of all English poets, is Edmund Spenser. [Footnote: His name should never be spelled with a c.] Born in London in 1552, the son of a clothmaker, Spenser past from the newly established Merchant Taylors' school to Pembroke Hall, Cambridge, as a sizar, or poor student, and during the customary seven years of residence took the degrees of B. A. and, in 1576, of M. A. At Cambridge he assimilated two of the controlling forces of his life, the moderate Puritanism of his college and Platonic idealism. Next, after a year or two with his kinspeople in Lancashire, in the North of England, he came to London, hoping through literature to win high political place, and attached himself to the household of Robert Dudley, Earl of Leicester, Queen Elizabeth's worthless favorite. Together with Sidney, who was Leicester's nephew, he was for a while a member of a little group of students who called themselves 'The Areopagus' and who, like occasional other experimenters of the later Renaissance period, attempted to make over English versification by substituting for rime and accentual meter the Greek and Latin system based on exact quantity of syllables. Spenser, however, soon outgrew this folly and in 1579 published the collection of poems which, as we have already said, is commonly taken as marking the beginning of the great Elizabethan literary period, namely 'The Shepherd's Calendar.'

This is a series of pastoral pieces (eclogues, Spenser calls them, by the classical name) twelve in number, artificially assigned one to each month in the year. The subjects are various--the conventionalized love of the poet for a certain Rosalind; current religious controversies in allegory; moral questions; the state of poetry in England; and the praises of Queen Elizabeth, whose almost incredible vanity exacted the most fulsome flattery from every writer who hoped to win a name at her court. The significance of 'The Shepherd's Calendar' lies partly in its genuine feeling for external Nature, which contrasts strongly with the hollow conventional phrases of the poetry of the previous decade, and especially in the vigor, the originality, and, in some of the eclogues, the beauty, of the language and of the varied verse. It was at once evident that here a real poet had appeared. An interesting innovation, diversely judged at the time and since, was Spenser's deliberate employment of rustic and archaic words, especially of the Northern dialect, which he introduced partly because of their appropriateness to the imaginary characters, partly for the sake of freshness of expression. They, like other features of the work, point forward to 'The Faerie Queene.'

In the uncertainties of court intrigue literary success did not gain for Spenser the political rewards which he was seeking, and he was obliged to content himself, the next year, with an appointment, which he viewed as substantially a sentence of exile, as secretary to Lord Grey, the governor of Ireland. In Ireland, therefore, the remaining twenty years of Spenser's short life were for the most part spent, amid distressing scenes of English oppression and chronic insurrection among the native Irish. After various activities during several years Spenser secured a permanent home in Kilcolman, a fortified tower and estate in the southern part of the island, where the romantic scenery furnished fit environment for a poet's imagination. And Spenser, able all his life to take refuge in his art from the crass realities of life, now produced many poems, some of them short, but among the others the immortal 'Faerie Queene.'

The first three books of this, his crowning achievement, Spenser, under enthusiastic encouragement from Ralegh, brought to London and published in 1590. The dedication is to Queen Elizabeth, to whom, indeed, as its heroine, the poem pays perhaps the most splendid compliment ever offered to any human being in verse. She responded with an uncertain pension of L50 (equivalent to perhaps $1500 at the present time), but not with the gift of political preferment which was still Spenser's hope; and in some bitterness of spirit he retired to Ireland, where in satirical poems he proceeded to attack the vanity of the world and the fickleness of men. His courtship and, in 1594, his marriage produced his sonnet sequence, called 'Amoretti' (Italian for 'Love-poems'), and his 'Epithalamium,' the most magnificent of marriage hymns in English and probably in world-literature; though his 'Prothalamium,' in honor of the marriage of two noble sisters, is a near rival to it.

Spenser, a zealous Protestant as well as a fine-spirited idealist, was in entire sympathy with Lord Grey's policy of stern repression of the Catholic Irish, to whom, therefore, he must have appeared merely as one of the hated crew of their pitiless tyrants. In 1598 he was appointed sheriff of the county of Cork; but a rebellion which broke out proved too strong for him, and he and his family barely escaped from the sack and destruction of his tower. He was sent with despatches to the English Court and died in London in January, 1599, no doubt in part as a result of the hardships that he had suffered. He was buried in Westminster Abbey.

Spenser's 'Faerie Queene' is not only one of the longest but one of the greatest of English poems; it is also very characteristically Elizabethan. To deal with so delicate a thing by the method of mechanical analysis seems scarcely less than profanation, but accurate criticism can proceed in no other way.

***Sources and Plan.*** Few poems more clearly illustrate the variety of influences from which most great literary works result. In many respects the most direct source was the body of Italian romances of chivalry, especially the 'Orlando Furioso' of Ariosto, which was written in the early part of the sixteenth century. These romances, in turn, combine the personages of the medieval French epics of Charlemagne with something of the spirit of Arthurian romance and with a Renaissance atmosphere of magic and of rich fantastic beauty. Spenser borrows and absorbs all these things and moreover he imitates Ariosto closely, often merely translating whole passages from his work. But this use of the Italian romances, further, carries with it a large employment of characters, incidents, and imagery from classical mythology and literature, among other things the elaborated similes of the classical epics. Spenser himself is directly influenced, also, by the medieval romances. Most important of all, all these elements are shaped to the purpose of the poem by Spenser's high moral aim, which in turn springs largely from his Platonic idealism.

What the plan of the poem is Spenser explains in a prefatory letter to Sir Walter Ralegh. The whole is a vast epic allegory, aiming, in the first place, to portray the virtues which make up the character of a perfect knight; an ideal embodiment, seen through Renaissance conceptions, of the best in the chivalrous system which in Spenser's time had passed away, but to which some choice spirits still looked back with regretful admiration.

As Spenser intended, twelve moral virtues of the individual character, such as Holiness and Temperance, were to be presented, each personified in the hero of one of twelve Books; and the crowning virtue, which Spenser, in Renaissance terms, called Magnificence, and which may be interpreted as Magnanimity, was to figure as Prince (King) Arthur, nominally the central hero of the whole poem, appearing and disappearing at frequent intervals. Spenser states in his prefatory letter that if he shall carry this first projected labor to a successful end he may continue it in still twelve other Books, similarly allegorizing twelve political virtues. The allegorical form, we should hardly need to be reminded, is another heritage from medieval literature, but the effort to shape a perfect character, completely equipped to serve the State, was characteristically of the Platonizing Renaissance. That the reader may never be in danger of forgetting his moral aim, Spenser fills the poem with moral observations, frequently setting them as guides at the beginning of the cantos.

***The Allegory.*** Lack of Unity. So complex and vast a plan could scarcely have been worked out by any human genius in a perfect and clear unity, and besides this, Spenser, with all his high endowments, was decidedly weak in constructive skill. The allegory, at the outset, even in Spenser's own statement, is confused and hazy. For beyond the primary moral interpretation, Spenser applies it in various secondary or parallel ways. In the widest sense, the entire struggle between the good and evil characters is to be taken as figuring forth the warfare both in the individual soul and in the world at large between Righteousness and Sin; and in somewhat narrower senses, between Protestantism and Catholicism, and between England and Spain.

In some places, also, it represents other events and aspects of European politics. Many of the single persons of the story, entering into each of these overlapping interpretations, bear double or triple roles. Gloriana, the Fairy Queen, is abstractly Glory, but humanly she is Queen Elizabeth; and from other points of view Elizabeth is identified with several of the lesser heroines. So likewise the witch Duessa is both Papal Falsehood and Mary Queen of Scots; Prince Arthur both Magnificence and (with sorry inappropriateness) the Earl of Leicester; and others of the characters stand with more or less consistency for such actual persons as Philip II of Spain, Henry IV of France, and Spenser's chief, Lord Grey. In fact, in Renaissance spirit, and following Sidney's 'Defense of Poesie,' Spenser attempts to harmonize history, philosophy, ethics, and politics, subordinating them all to the art of poetry. The plan is grand but impracticable, and except for the original moral interpretation, to which in the earlier books the incidents are skilfully adapted, it is fruitless as one reads to undertake to follow the allegories. Many readers are able, no doubt, merely to disregard them, but there are others, like Lowell, to whom the moral, 'when they come suddenly upon it, gives a shock of unpleasant surprise, as when in eating strawberries one's teeth encounter grit.'

The same lack of unity pervades the external story. The first Book begins abruptly, in the middle; and for clearness' sake Spenser had been obliged to explain in his prefatory letter that the real commencement must be supposed to be a scene like those of Arthurian romance, at the court and annual feast of the Fairy Queen, where twelve adventures had been assigned to as many knights. Spenser strangely planned to narrate this beginning of the whole in his final Book, but even if it had been properly placed at the outset it would have served only as a loose enveloping action for a series of stories essentially as distinct as those in Malory. More serious, perhaps, is the lack of unity within the single books. Spenser's genius was never for strongly condensed narrative, and following his Italian originals, though with less firmness, he wove his story as a tangled web of intermingled adventures, with almost endless elaboration and digression. Incident after incident is broken off and later resumed and episode after episode is introduced, until the reader almost abandons any effort to trace the main design. A part of the confusion is due to the mechanical plan. Each Book consists of twelve cantos (of from forty to ninety stanzas each) and oftentimes Spenser has difficulty in filling out the scheme. No one, certainly, can regret that he actually completed only a quarter of his projected work. In the six existing Books he has given almost exhaustive expression to a richly creative imagination, and additional prolongation would have done little but to repeat.

Still further, the characteristic Renaissance lack of certainty as to the proper materials for poetry is sometimes responsible for a rudely inharmonious element in the otherwise delightful romantic atmosphere. For a single illustration, the description of the House of Alma in Book II, Canto Nine, is a tediously literal medieval allegory of the Soul and Body; and occasional realistic details here and there in the poem at large are merely repellent to more modern taste.

***The Lack of Dramatic Reality.*** A romantic allegory like 'The Faerie Queene' does not aim at intense lifelikeness--a certain remoteness from the actual is one of its chief attractions.

But sometimes in Spenser's poem the reader feels too wide a divorce from reality. Part of this fault is ascribable to the use of magic, to which there is repeated but inconsistent resort, especially, as in the medieval romances, for the protection of the good characters. Oftentimes, indeed, by the persistent loading of the dice against the villains and scapegoats, the reader's sympathy is half aroused in their behalf. Thus in the fight of the Red Cross Knight with his special enemy, the dragon, where, of course, the Knight must be victorious, it is evident that without the author's help the dragon is incomparably the stronger. Once, swooping down on the Knight, he seizes him in his talons (whose least touch was elsewhere said to be fatal) and bears him aloft into the air. The valor of the Knight compels him to relax his hold, but instead of merely dropping the Knight to certain death, he carefully flies back to earth and sets him down in safety. More definite regard to the actual laws of life would have given the poem greater firmness without the sacrifice of any of its charm.

***The Romantic Beauty.*** General Atmosphere and Description. Critical sincerity has required us to dwell thus long on the defects of the poem; but once recognized we should dismiss them altogether from mind and turn attention to the far more important beauties. The great qualities of 'The Faerie Queene' are suggested by the title, 'The Poets' Poet,' which Charles Lamb, with happy inspiration, applied to Spenser. Most of all are we indebted to Spenser's high idealism. No poem in the world is nobler than 'The Faerie Queene' in atmosphere and entire effect. Spenser himself is always the perfect gentleman of his own imagination, and in his company we are secure from the intrusion of anything morally base or mean. But in him, also, moral beauty is in full harmony with the beauty of art and the senses. Spenser was a Puritan, but a Puritan of the earlier English Renaissance, to whom the foes of righteousness were also the foes of external loveliness. Of the three fierce Saracen brother-knights who repeatedly appear in the service of Evil, two are Sansloy, the enemy of law, and Sansfoy, the enemy of religion, but the third is Sansjoy, enemy of pleasure. And of external beauty there has never been a more gifted lover than Spenser. We often feel, with Lowell, that 'he is the pure sense of the beautiful incarnated.' The poem is a romantically luxuriant wilderness of dreamily or languorously delightful visions, often rich with all the harmonies of form and motion and color and sound.

As Lowell says, 'The true use of Spenser is as a gallery of pictures which we visit as the mood takes us, and where we spend an hour or two, long enough to sweeten our perceptions, not so lcng as to cloy them.' His landscapes, to speak of one particular feature, are usually of a rather vague, often of a vast nature, as suits the unreality of his poetic world, and usually, since Spenser was not a minute observer, follow the conventions of Renaissance literature. They are commonly great plains, wide and gloomy forests (where the trees of many climates often grow together in impossible harmony), cool caves--in general, lonely, quiet, or soothing scenes, but all unquestionable portions of a delightful fairyland. To him, it should be added, as to most men before modern Science had subdued the world to human uses, the sublime aspects of Nature were mainly dreadful; the ocean, for example, seemed to him a raging 'waste of waters, wide and deep,' a mysterious and insatiate devourer of the lives of men.

To the beauty of Spenser's imagination, ideal and sensuous, corresponds his magnificent command of rhythm and of sound. As a verbal melodist, especially a melodist of sweetness and of stately grace, and as a harmonist of prolonged and complex cadences, he is unsurpassable. But he has full command of his rhythm according to the subject, and can range from the most delicate suggestion of airy beauty to the roar of the tempest or the strident energy of battle. In vocabulary and phraseology his fluency appears inexhaustible. Here, as in 'The Shepherd's Calendar,' he deliberately introduces, especially from Chaucer, obsolete words and forms, such as the inflectional ending in -en, which distinctly contribute to his romantic effect. His constant use of alliteration is very skilful; the frequency of the alliteration on w is conspicuous but apparently accidental.

***The Spenserian Stanza.*** For the external medium of all this beauty Spenser, modifying the ottava rima of Ariosto (a stanza which rimes abababcc), invented the stanza which bears his own name and which is the only artificial stanza of English origin that has ever passed into currency. The rime-scheme is ababbcbcc, and in the last line the iambic pentameter gives place to an Alexandrine (an iambic hexameter). Whether or not any stanza form is as well adapted as blank verse or the rimed couplet for prolonged narrative is an interesting question, but there can be no doubt that Spenser's stanza, firmly unified, in spite of its length, by its central couplet and by the finality of the last line, is a discovery of genius, and that the Alexandrine, 'forever feeling for the next stanza,' does much to bind the stanzas together. It has been adopted in no small number of the greatest subsequent English poems, including such various ones as Burns' 'Cotter's Saturday Night,' Byron's 'Childe Harold,' Keats' 'Eve of St. Agnes,' and Shelley's 'Adonais.'

In general style and spirit, it should be added, Spenser has been one of the most powerful influences on all succeeding English romantic poetry. Two further sentences of Lowell well summarize his whole general achievement: 'His great merit is in the ideal treatment with which he glorified common things and gilded them with a ray of enthusiasm. He is a standing protest against the tyranny of the Commonplace, and sows the seeds of a noble discontent with prosaic views of life and the dull uses to which it may be put.'

**ELIZABETHAN LYRIC POETRY**

'The Faerie Queene' is the only long Elizabethan poem of the very highest rank, but Spenser, as we have seen, is almost equally conspicuous as a lyric poet. In that respect he was one among a throng of melodists who made the Elizabethan age in many respects the greatest lyric period in the history of English or perhaps of any literature. Still grander, to be sure, by the nature of the two forms, was the Elizabethan achievement in the drama, which we shall consider in the next chapter; but the lyrics have the advantage in sheer delightfulness and, of course, in rapid and direct appeal.

The zest for lyric poetry somewhat artificially inaugurated at Court by Wyatt and Surrey seems to have largely subsided, like any other fad, after some years, but it vigorously revived, in much more genuine fashion, with the taste for other imaginative forms of literature, in the last two decades of Elizabeth's reign. It revived, too, not only among the courtiers but among all classes; in no other form of literature was the diversity of authors so marked; almost every writer of the period who was not purely a man of prose seems to have been gifted with the lyric power.

The qualities which especially distinguish the Elizabethan lyrics are fluency, sweetness, melody, and an enthusiastic joy in life, all spontaneous, direct, and exquisite. Uniting the genuineness of the popular ballad with the finer sense of conscious artistic poetry, these poems possess a charm different, though in an only half definable way, from that of any other lyrics.

In subjects they display the usual lyric variety. There are songs of delight in Nature; a multitude of love poems of all moods; many pastorals, in which, generally, the pastoral conventions sit lightly on the genuine poetical feeling; occasional patriotic outbursts; and some reflective and religious poems. In stanza structure the number of forms is unusually great, but in most cases stanzas are internally varied and have a large admixture of short, ringing or musing, lines.

The lyrics were published sometimes in collections by single authors, sometimes in the series of anthologies which succeeded to Tottel's 'Miscellany.' Some of these anthologies were books of songs with the accompanying music; for music, brought with all the other cultural influences from Italy and France, was now enthusiastically cultivated, and the soft melody of many of the best Elizabethan lyrics is that of accomplished composers. Many of the lyrics, again, are included as songs in the dramas of the time; and Shakspere's comedies show him nearly as preeminent among the lyric poets as among the playwrights.

Some of the finest of the lyrics are anonymous. Among the best of the known poets are these: George Gascoigne (about 1530-1577), a courtier and soldier, who bridges the gap between Surrey and Sidney; Sir Edward Dyer (about 1545-1607), a scholar and statesman, author of one perfect lyric, 'My mind to me a kingdom is'; John Lyly (1553-1606), the Euphuist and dramatist; Nicholas Breton (about 1545 to about 1626), a prolific writer in verse and prose and one of the most successful poets of the pastoral style; Robert Southwell (about 1562-1595), a Jesuit intriguer of ardent piety, finally imprisoned, tortured, and executed as a traitor; George Peele (1558 to about 1598), the dramatist; Thomas Lodge (about 1558-1625), poet, novelist, and physician; Christopher Marlowe (1564-1593), the dramatist;

Thomas Nash (1567-1601), one of the most prolific Elizabethan hack writers; Samuel Daniel (1562-1619), scholar and critic, member in his later years of the royal household of James I; Barnabe Barnes (about 1569-1609); Richard Barnfield (1574-1627); Sir Walter Ralegh (1552-1618), courtier, statesman, explorer, and scholar; Joshua Sylvester (1563-1618), linguist and merchant, known for his translation of the long religious poems of the Frenchman Du Bartas, through which he exercised an influence on Milton; Francis Davison (about 1575 to about 1619), son of a counsellor of Queen Elizabeth, a lawyer; and Thomas Dekker (about 1570 to about 1640), a ne'er-do-weel dramatist and hack-writer of irrepressible and delightful good spirits.

## THE SONNETS

In the last decade, especially, of the century, no other lyric form compared in popularity with the sonnet. Here England was still following in the footsteps of Italy and France; it has been estimated that in the course of the century over three hundred thousand sonnets were written in Western Europe. In England as elsewhere most of these poems were inevitably of mediocre quality and imitative in substance, ringing the changes with wearisome iteration on a minimum of ideas, often with the most extravagant use of conceits. Petrarch's example was still commonly followed; the sonnets were generally composed in sequences (cycles) of a hundred or more, addressed to the poet's more or less imaginary cruel lady, though the note of manly independence introduced by Wyatt is frequent.

First of the important English sequences is the 'Astrophel and Stella' of Sir Philip Sidney, written about 1580, published in 1591. 'Astrophel' is a fanciful half-Greek anagram for the poet's own name, and Stella (Star) designates Lady Penelope Devereux, who at about this time married Lord Rich. The sequence may very reasonably be interpreted as an expression of Platonic idealism, though it is sometimes taken in a sense less consistent with Sidney's high reputation. Of Spenser's 'Amoretti' we have already spoken. By far the finest of all the sonnets are the best ones (a considerable part) of Shakspere's one hundred and fifty-four, which were not published until 1609 but may have been mostly written before 1600.

Their interpretation has long been hotly debated. It is certain, however, that they do not form a connected sequence. Some of them are occupied with urging a youth of high rank, Shakspere's patron, who may have been either the Earl of Southampton or William Herbert, Earl of Pembroke, to marry and perpetuate his race; others hint the story, real or imaginary, of Shakspere's infatuation for a 'dark lady,' leading to bitter disillusion; and still others seem to be occasional expressionsof devotion to other friends of one or the other sex. Here as elsewhere Shakspere's genius, at its best, is supreme over all rivals; the first recorded criticism speaks of the 'sugared sweetness' of his sonnets; but his genius is not always at its best.

## JOHN DONNE AND THE BEGINNING OF THE 'METAPHYSICAL' POETRY

The last decade of the sixteenth century presents also, in the poems of John Donne, [Footnote: Pronounced Dun] a new and very strange style of verse. Donne, born in 1573, possessed one of the keenest and most powerful intellects of the time, but his early manhood was largely wasted in dissipation, though he studied theology and law and seems to have seen military service. It was during this period that he wrote his love poems. Then, while living with his wife and children in uncertain dependence on noble patrons, he turned to religious poetry. At last he entered the Church, became famous as one of the most eloquent preachers of the time, and through the favor of King James was rapidly promoted until he was made Dean of St. Paul's Cathedral. He died in 1631 after having furnished a striking instance of the fantastic morbidness of the period (post-Elizabethan) by having his picture painted as he stood wrapped in his shroud on a funeral urn.

The distinguishing general characteristic of Donne's poetry is the remarkable combination of an aggressive intellectuality with the lyric form and spirit. Whether true poetry or mere intellectual cleverness is the predominant element may reasonably be questioned; but on many readers Donne's verse exercises a unique attraction. Its definite peculiarities are outstanding:

1. By a process of extreme exaggeration and minute elaboration Donne carries the Elizabethan conceits

almost to the farthest possible limit, achieving what Samuel Johnson two centuries later described as 'enormous and disgusting hyperboles.'

2. In so doing he makes relentless use of the intellect and of verbally precise but actually preposterous logic, striking out astonishingly brilliant but utterly fantastic flashes of wit.
3. He draws the material of his figures of speech from highly unpoetical sources--partly from the activities of every-day life, but especially from all the sciences and school-knowledge of the time. The material is abstract, but Donne gives it full poetic concrete picturesqueness. Thus he speaks of one spirit overtaking another at death as one bullet shot out of a gun may overtake another which has lesser velocity but was earlier discharged. It was because of these last two characteristics that Dr. Johnson applied to Donne and his followers the rather clumsy name of 'Metaphysical' (Philosophical) poets. 'Fantastic' would have been a better word.
4. In vigorous reaction against the sometimes nerveless melody of most contemporary poets Donne often makes his verse as ruggedly condensed (often as obscure) and as harsh as possible. Its wrenched accents and slurred syllables sometimes appear absolutely unmetrical, but it seems that Donne generally followed subtle rhythmical ideas of his own. He adds to the appearance of irregularity by experimenting with a large number of lyric stanza forms--a different form, in fact, for nearly every poem.
5. In his love poems, while his sentiment is often Petrarchan, he often emphasizes also the English note of independence, taking as a favorite theme the incredible fickleness of woman.

In spirit Donne belongs much less to Elizabethan poetry than to the following period, in which nearly half his life fell. Of his great influence on the poetry of that period we shall speak in the proper place.

# 7

# The Drama From about 1550 to 1642

## THE INFLUENCE OF CLASSICAL COMEDY AND TRAGEDY

In previous chapter we left the drama at that point, toward the middle of the sixteenth century, when the Mystery Plays had largely declined and Moralities and Interlude-Farces, themselves decadent, were sharing in rather confused rivalry that degree of popular interest which remained unabsorbed by the religious, political, and social ferment. There was still to be a period of thirty or forty years before the flowering of the great Elizabethan drama, but they were to be years of new, if uncertain, beginnings.

The first new formative force was the influence of the classical drama, for which, with other things classical, the Renaissance had aroused enthusiasm. This force operated mainly not through writers for popular audiences, like the authors of most Moralities and Interludes, but through men of the schools and the universities, writing for performances in their own circles or in that of the Court. It had now become a not uncommon thing for boys at the large schools to act in regular dramatic fashion, at first in Latin, afterward in English translation, some of the plays of the Latin comedians which had long formed a part of the school curriculum. Shortly after the middle of the century, probably, the head-master of Westminister School, Nicholas Udall, took the further step of writing for his boys on the classical model an original farce-comedy, the amusing 'Ralph Roister Doister.' This play is so close a copy of Plautus' 'Miles Gloriosus' and Terence's 'Eunuchus' that there is little that is really English about it; a much larger element of local realism of the traditional English sort, in a classical framework, was presented in the coarse but really skillful 'Gammer Gurton's Needle,' which was probably written at about the same time, apparently by the Cambridge student William Stevenson.

Meanwhile students at the universities, also, had been acting Plautus and Terence, and further, had been writing and acting Latin tragedies, as well as comedies, of their own composition. Their chief models for tragedy were the plays of the first-century Roman Seneca, who may or may not have been identical with the philosopher who was the tutor of the Emperor Nero. Both through these university imitations and directly, Seneca's very faulty plays continued for many years to exercise a great influence on English tragedy. Falling far short of the noble spirit of Greek tragedy, which they in turn attempt to copy, Seneca's plays do observe its mechanical conventions, especially the unities of Action and Time, the use of the chorus to comment on the action, the avoidance of violent action and deaths on the stage, and the use of messengers to report such events. For proper dramatic action they largely substitute ranting moralizing declamation, with crudely exaggerated passion, and they exhibit a great vein of melodramatic horror, for instance in the frequent use of the motive of implacable revenge for murder and of a ghost who incites to it. In the early Elizabethan period, however, an age when life itself was dramatically intense and tragic, when everything classic was looked on with reverence, and when standards of taste were unformed, it was natural enough that such plays should pass for masterpieces.

A direct imitation of Seneca, famous as the first tragedy in English on classical lines, was the 'Gorboduc, or Ferrex and Porrex,' of Thomas Norton and Thomas Sackville, acted in 1562. Its story, like those of some of Shakspere's plays later, goes back ultimately to the account of one of the early reigns in Geoffrey of Monmouth's 'History.' 'Gorboduc' outdoes its Senecan models in tedious moralizing, and is painfully wooden in all respects; but it has real importance not only because it is the first regular English tragedy, but because it was the first play to use the iambic pentameter blank verse which Surrey had introduced to English poetry and which was destined to be the verse-form of really great English tragedy. When they wrote the play Norton and Sackville were law students at the Inner Temple, and from other law students during the following years came other plays, which were generally acted at festival seasons, such, as Christmas, at the lawyers' colleges, or before the Queen, though the common people were also admitted among the audience. Unlike 'Gorboduc,' these other university plays were not only for the most part crude and coarse in the same manner as earlier English plays, but in accordance also with the native English tradition and in violent defiance of the classical principle of Unity, they generally combined tragical classical stories with realistic scenes of English comedy (somewhat later with Italian stories). Nevertheless, and this is the main thing, the more thoughtful members of the Court and University circles, were now learning from the study of classical plays a sense for form and the fundamental distinction between tragedy and comedy.

## THE CHRONICLE-HISTORY PLAY

About twenty years before the end of the century there began to appear, at first at the Court and the Universities, later on the popular stage, a form of play which was to hold, along with tragedy and comedy, an important place in the great decades that were to follow, namely the Chronicle-History Play. This form of play generally presented the chief events in the whole or a part of the reign of some English king. It was largely a product of the pride which was being awakened among the people in the greatness of England under Elizabeth, and of the consequent desire to know something of the past history of the country, and it received a great impulse from the enthusiasm aroused by the struggle with Spain and the defeat of the Armada. It was not, however, altogether a new creation, for its method was similar to that of the university plays which dealt with monarchs of classical history.

It partly inherited from them the formless mixture of farcical humor with historical or supposedly historical fact which it shared with other plays of the time, and sometimes also an unusually reckless disregard of unity of action, time, and place. Since its main serious purpose, when it had one, was to convey information, the other chief dramatic principles, such as careful presentation of a few main characters and of a universally significant human struggle, were also generally disregarded. It was only in the hands of Shakspere that the species was to be moulded into true dramatic form and to attain real greatness; and after a quarter century of popularity it was to be reabsorbed into tragedy, of which in fact it was always only a special variety.

### JOHN LYLY

The first Elizabethan dramatist of permanent individual importance is the comedian John Lyly, of whose early success at Court with the artificial romance 'Euphues' we have already spoken. From 'Euphues' Lyly turned to the still more promising work of writing comedies for the Court entertainments with which Queen Elizabeth was extremely lavish. The character of Lyly's plays was largely determined by the light and spectacular nature of these entertainments, and further by the fact that on most occasions the players at Court were boys. These were primarily the 'children [choir-boys] of the Queen's Chapel,' who for some generations had been sought out from all parts of England for their good voices and were very carefully trained for singing and for dramatic performances.

The choir-boys of St. Paul's Cathedral, similarly trained, also often acted before the Queen. Many of the plays given by these boys were of the ordinary sorts, but it is evident that they would be most successful in dainty comedies especially adapted to their boyish capacity. Such comedies Lyly proceeded to write, in prose. The subjects are from classical mythology or history or English folk-lore, into which Lyly sometimes weaves an allegorical presentation of court intrigue. The plots are very slight, and though the structure is decidedly better than in most previous plays, the humorous sub-actions sometimes have little connection with the main action. Characterization is still rudimentary, and altogether the plays present not so much a picture of reality as 'a faint moonlight reflection of life.'

None the less the best of them, such as 'Alexander and Campaspe,' are delightful in their sparkling delicacy, which is produced partly by the carefully-wrought style, similar to that of 'Euphues,' but less artificial, and is enhanced by the charming lyrics which are scattered through them. For all this the elaborate scenery and costuming of the Court entertainments provided a very harmonious background.

These plays were to exert a strong influence on Shakspere's early comedies, probably suggesting to him: the use of prose for comedy; the value of snappy and witty dialog; refinement, as well as affectation, of style; lyric atmosphere; the characters and tone of high comedy, contrasting so favorably with the usual coarse farce of the period; and further such details as the employment of impudent boy-pages as a source of amusement.

## PEELE, GREENE, AND KYD

Of the most important early contemporaries of Shakspere we have already mentioned two as noteworthy in other fields of literature. George Peele's masque-like 'Arraignment of Paris' helps to show him as more a lyric poet than a dramatist. Robert Greene's plays, especially 'Friar Bacon and Friar Bungay,' reveal, like his novels, some real, though not very elaborate, power of characterization. They are especially important in developing the theme of romantic love with real fineness of feeling and thus helping to prepare the way for Shakspere in a very important particular. In marked contrast to these men is Thomas Kyd, who about the year 1590 attained a meteoric reputation with crude 'tragedies of blood,' specialized descendants of Senecan tragedy, one of which may have been the early play on Hamlet which Shakspere used as the groundwork for his masterpiece.

## CHRISTOPHER MARLOWE, 1564-1593

Peele and Greene were University men who wrote partly for Court or academic audiences, partly for the popular stage. The distinction between the two sorts of drama was still further broken down in the work of Christopher Marlowe, a poet of real genius, decidedly the chief dramatist among Shakspere's early contemporaries, and the one from whom Shakspere learned the most.

Marlowe was born in 1564 (the same year as Shakspere), the son of a shoemaker at Canterbury. Taking his master's degree after seven years at Cambridge, in 1587, he followed the other 'university wits' to London. There, probably the same year and the next, he astonished the public with the two parts of 'Tamburlaine the Great,' a dramatization of the stupendous career of the bloodthirsty Mongol fourteenth-century conqueror. These plays, in spite of faults now conspicuous enough, are splendidly imaginative and poetic, and were by far the most powerful that had yet been written in England. Marlowe followed them with 'The Tragical History of Dr. Faustus,' a treatment of the medieval story which two hundred years later was to serve Goethe for his masterpiece; with 'The Jew of Malta,' which was to give Shakspere suggestions for 'The Merchant of Venice'; and with 'Edward the Second,' the first really artistic Chronicle History play. Among the literary adventurers of the age who led wild lives in the London taverns Marlowe is said to have attained a conspicuous reputation for violence and irreligion. He was killed in 1593 in a reckless and foolish brawl, before he had reached the age of thirty.

If Marlowe's life was unworthy, the fault must be laid rather at the door of circumstances than of his own genuine nature. His plays show him to have been an ardent idealist and a representative of many of the qualities that made the greatness of the Renaissance. The Renaissance learning, the apparently boundless vistas which it had opened to the human spirit, and the consciousness of his own power, evidently intoxicated Marlowe with a vast ambition to achieve results which in his youthful inexperience he could scarcely even picture to himself. His spirit, cramped and outraged by the impassable limitations of human life and by the conventions of society, beat recklessly against them with an impatience fruitless but partly grand. This is the underlying spirit of almost all his plays, struggling in them for expression. The Prolog to 'Tamburlaine' makes pretentious announcement that the author will discard the usual buffoonery of the popular stage and will set a new standard of tragic majesty:

> *From jigging veins of rhyming mother wits, And such conceits as clownage keeps in pay, We'll lead you to the stately tent of war, Where you shall hear the Scythian Tamburlaine Threatening the world with high astounding terms, And scourging kingdoms with his conquering sword.*

Tamburlaine himself as Marlowe presents him is a titanic, almost superhuman, figure who by sheer courage and pitiless unbending will raises himself from shepherd to general and then emperor of countless peoples, and sweeps like a whirlwind over the stage of the world, carrying everywhere overwhelming slaughter and desolation. His speeches are outbursts of incredible arrogance, equally powerful and bombastic. Indeed his blasphemous boasts of superiority to the gods seem almost justified by his apparently irresistible success. But at the end he learns that the laws of life are inexorable even for him; all his indignant rage cannot redeem his son from cowardice, or save his wife from death, or delay his own end. As has been said, 'Tamburlaine' expresses with 'a profound, lasting, noble sense and in grandly symbolic terms, the eternal tragedy inherent in the conflict between human aspiration and human power.'

For several other reasons 'Tamburlaine' is of high importance. It gives repeated and splendid expression to the passionate haunting Renaissance zest for the beautiful. It is rich with extravagant sensuous descriptions, notable among those which abound gorgeously in all Elizabethan poetry. But finest of all is the description of beauty by its effects which Marlowe puts into the mouth of Faustus at the sight of Helen of Troy:

*Was this the face that launched a thousand ships*
*And burnt the topless towers of Ilium?*

Much of Marlowe's strength, again, lies in his powerful and beautiful use of blank verse. First among the dramatists of the popular stage he discarded rime, and taking and vitalizing the stiff pentameter line of 'Gorboduc,' gave it an immediate and lasting vogue for tragedy and high comedy. Marlowe, virtually a beginner, could not be expected to carry blank verse to that perfection which his success made possible for Shakspere; he did not altogether escape monotony and commonplaceness; but he gained a high degree of flexibility and beauty by avoiding a regularly end-stopped arrangement, by taking pains to secure variety of pause and accent, and by giving his language poetic condensation and suggestiveness. His workmanship thoroughly justifies the characterization 'Marlowe's mighty line,' which Ben Jonson in his tribute to Shakspere bestowed on it long after Marlowe's death.

The greatest significance of 'Tamburlaine,' lastly, lies in the fact that it definitely established tragedy as a distinct form on the English popular stage, and invested it with proper dignity.

These are Marlowe's great achievements both in 'Tamburlaine' and in his later more restrained plays. His limitations must also be suggested. Like other Elizabethans he did not fully understand the distinction between drama and other literary forms; 'Tamburlaine' is not so much a regularly constructed tragedy, with a struggle between nearly equal persons and forces, artistically complicated and resolved, as an epic poem, a succession of adventures in war (and love). Again, in spite of the prolog in 'Tamburlaine,' Marlowe, in almost all his plays, and following the Elizabethan custom, does attempt scenes of humor, but he attains only to the coarse and brutal horse-play at which the English audiences had laughed for centuries in the Mystery plays and the Interludes.

Elizabethan also (and before that medieval) is the lack of historical perspective which gives to Mongol shepherds the manners and speech of Greek classical antiquity as Marlowe had learned to know it at the university. More serious is the lack of mature skill in characterization. Tamburlaine the man is an exaggerated type; most of the men about him are his faint shadows, and those who are intended to be comic are preposterous. The women, though they have some differentiating touches, are certainly not more dramatically and vitally imagined. In his later plays Marlowe makes gains in this respect, but he never arrives at full easy mastery and trenchantly convincing lifelikeness either in characterization, in presentation of action, or in fine poetic finish. It has often been remarked that at the age when Marlowe died Shakspere had produced not one of the great plays on which his reputation rests; but Shakspere's genius came to maturity more surely, as well as more slowly, and there is no basis for the inference sometimes drawn that if Marlowe had lived he would ever have equalled or even approached Shakespere's supreme achievement.

## THEATRICAL CONDITIONS AND THE THEATER BUILDINGS

Before we pass to Shakspere we must briefly consider those external facts which conditioned the form of the Elizabethan plays and explain many of those things in them which at the present time appear perplexing.

*[Illustration: TIMON OF ATHENS, v, 4. OUTER SCENE. Trumpets sound. Enter Alcibiades with his Powers before Athens. "Alc. Sound to this Coward, and lascivious Towne, Our terrible approach." Sounds a parly. The Senators appears upon the Wals. Reproduced from The Shakespearean Stage, by V. E. Albright, through the courtesy of the publishers, the Columbia University Press. AN ELIZABETHAN STAGE]*

The medieval religious drama had been written and acted in many towns throughout the country, and was a far less important feature in the life of London than of many other places. But as the capital became more and more the center of national life, the drama, with other forms of literature, was more largely appropriated by it; the Elizabethan drama of the great period was altogether written in London and belonged distinctly to it.

Until well into the seventeenth century, to be sure, the London companies made frequent tours through the country, but that was chiefly when the prevalence of the plague had necessitated the closing of the London theaters or when for other reasons acting there had become temporarily unprofitable. The companies themselves had now assumed a regular organization. They retained a trace of their origin (above, page 90) in that each was under the protection of some influential noble and was called, for example, 'Lord Leicester's Servants,' or 'The Lord Admiral's Servants.'

But this connection was for the most part nominal--the companies were virtually very much like the stock-companies of the nineteenth century. By the beginning of the great period the membership of each troupe was made up of at least three classes of persons. At the bottom of the scale were the boy-apprentices who were employed, as Shakspere is said to have been at first, in miscellaneous menial capacities. Next came the paid actors; and lastly the shareholders, generally also actors, some or all of whom were the general managers. The writers of plays were sometimes members of the companies, as in Shakspere's case; sometimes, however, they were independent.

Until near the middle of Elizabeth's reign there were no special theater buildings, but the players, in London or elsewhere, acted wherever they could find an available place--in open squares, large halls, or, especially, in the quadrangular open inner yards of inns. As the profession became better organized and as the plays gained in quality, such makeshift accommodations became more and more unsatisfactory; but there were special difficulties in the way of securing better ones in London.

For the population and magistrates of London were prevailingly Puritan, and the great body of the Puritans, then as always, were strongly opposed to the theater as a frivolous and irreligious thing--an attitude for which the lives of the players and the character of many plays afforded, then as almost always, only too much reason. The city was very jealous of its prerogatives; so that in spite of Queen Elizabeth's strong patronage of the drama, throughout her whole reign no public theater buildings were allowed within the limits of the city corporation. But these limits were narrow, and in 1576 James Burbage inaugurated a new era by erecting 'The Theater' just to the north of the 'city,' only a few minutes' walk from the center of population. His example was soon followed by other managers, though the favorite place for the theaters soon came to be the 'Bankside,' the region in Southwark just across the Thames from the 'city' where Chaucer's Tabard Inn had stood and where pits for bear-baiting and cock-fighting had long flourished.

The structure of the Elizabethan theater was naturally imitated from its chief predecessor, the inn-yard. There, under the open sky, opposite the street entrance, the players had been accustomed to set up their stage. About it, on three sides, the ordinary part of the audience had stood during the performance, while the inn-guests and persons able to pay a fixed price had sat in the open galleries which lined the building and ran all around the yard.

In the theaters, therefore, at first generally square-built or octagonal, the stage projected from the rear wall well toward the center of an unroofed pit (the present-day 'orchestra'), where, still on three sides of the stage, the common people, admitted for sixpence or less, stood and jostled each other, either going home when it rained or staying and getting wet as the degree of their interest in the play might determine.

The enveloping building proper was occupied with tiers of galleries, generally two or three in number, provided with seats; and here, of course, sat the people of means, the women avoiding embarrassment and annoyance only by being always masked. Behind the unprotected front part of the stage the middle part was covered by a lean-to roof sloping down from the rear wall of the building and supported by two pillars standing on the stage. This roof concealed a loft, from which gods and goddesses or any appropriate properties could be let down by mechanical devices. Still farther back, under the galleries, was the 'rear-stage,' which could be used to represent inner rooms; and that part of the lower gallery immediately above it was generally appropriated as a part of the stage, representing such places as city walls or the second stories of houses. The musicians' place was also just beside in the gallery.

The stage, therefore, was a 'platform stage,' seen by the audience from almost all sides, not, as in our own time, a 'picture-stage,' with its scenes viewed through a single large frame. This arrangement made impossible any front curtain, though a curtain was generally hung before the rear stage, from the floor of the gallery. Hence the changes between scenes must generally be made in full view of the audience, and instead of ending the scenes with striking situations the dramatists must arrange for a withdrawal of the actors, only avoiding if possible the effect of a mere anti-climax. Dead bodies must either get up and walk away in plain sight or be carried off, either by stage hands, or, as part of the action, by other characters in the play. This latter device was sometimes adopted at considerable violence to probability, as when Shakspere makes Falstaff bear away Hotspur, and Hamlet, Polonius. Likewise, while the medieval habit of elaborate costuming was continued, there was every reason for adhering to the medieval simplicity of scenery.

A single potted tree might symbolize a forest, and houses and caverns, with a great deal else, might be left to the imagination of the audience. In no respect, indeed, was realism of setting an important concern of either dramatist or audience; in many cases, evidently, neither of them cared to think of a scene as located in any precise spot; hence the anxious effort of Shakspere's editors on this point is beside the mark. This nonchalance made for easy transition from one place to another, and the whole simplicity of staging had the important advantage of allowing the audience to center their attention on the play rather than on the accompaniments. On the rear-stage, however, behind the curtain, more elaborate scenery might be placed, and Elizabethan plays, like those of our own day, seem sometimes to have 'alternation scenes,' intended to be acted in front, while the next background was being prepared behind the balcony curtain.

The lack of elaborate settings also facilitated rapidity of action, and the plays, beginning at three in the afternoon, were ordinarily over by the dinner-hour of five. Less satisfactory was the entire absence of women-actors, who did not appear on the public stage until after the Restoration of 1660. The inadequacy of the boys who took the part of the women-characters is alluded to by Shakspere and must have been a source of frequent irritation to any dramatist who was attempting to present a subtle or complex heroine.

Lastly may be mentioned the picturesque but very objectionable custom of the young dandies who insisted on carrying their chairs onto the sides of the stage itself, where they not only made themselves conspicuous objects of attention but seriously crowded the actors and rudely abused them if the play was not to their liking. It should be added that from the latter part of Elizabeth's reign there existed within the city itself certain 'private' theaters, used by the boys' companies and others, whose structure was more like that of the theaters of our own time and where plays were given by artificial light.

### SHAKESPEARE, 1564-1616

William Shakspere, by universal consent the greatest author of England, if not of the world, occupies chronologically a central position in the Elizabethan drama. He was born in 1564 in the good-sized village of Stratford-on-Avon in Warwickshire, near the middle of England, where the level but beautiful country furnished full external stimulus for a poet's eye and heart. His father, John Shakspere, who was a general dealer in agricultural products and other commodities, was one of the chief citizens of the village, and during his son's childhood was chosen an alderman and shortly after mayor, as we should call it. But by 1577 his prosperity declined, apparently through his own shiftlessness, and for many years he was harassed with legal difficulties.

In the village 'grammar' school William Shakspere had acquired the rudiments of book-knowledge, consisting largely of Latin, but his chief education was from Nature and experience. As his father's troubles thickened he was very likely removed from school, but at the age of eighteen, under circumstances not altogether creditable to himself, he married Anne Hathaway, a woman eight years his senior, who lived in the neighboring village of Shottery. The suggestion that the marriage proved positively unhappy is supported by no real evidence, but what little is known of Shakspere's later life implies that it was not exceptionally congenial. Two girls and a boy were born from it.

In his early manhood, apparently between 1586 and 1588, Shakspere left Stratford to seek his fortune in London. As to the circumstances, there is reasonable plausibility in the later tradition that he had joined in poaching raids on the deer-park of Sir Thomas Lucy, a neighboring country gentleman, and found it desirable to get beyond the bounds of that gentleman's authority. It is also likely enough that Shakspere had been fascinated by the performances of traveling dramatic companies at Stratford and by the Earl of Leicester's costly entertainment of Queen Elizabeth in 1575 at the castle of Kenilworth, not many miles away. At any rate, in London he evidently soon secured mechanical employment in a theatrical company, presumably the one then known as Lord Leicester's company, with which, in that case, he was always thereafter connected. His energy and interest must soon have won him the opportunity to show his skill as actor and also reviser and collaborator in play-writing, then as independent author; and after the first few years of slow progress his rise was rapid. He became one of the leading members, later one of the chief shareholders, of the company, and evidently enjoyed a substantial reputation as a playwright and a good, though not a great, actor.

This was both at Court (where, however, actors had no social standing) and in the London dramatic circle. Of his personal life only the most fragmentary record has been preserved, through occasional mentions in miscellaneous documents, but it is evident that his rich nature was partly appreciated and thoroughly loved by his associates. His business talent was marked and before the end of his dramatic career he seems to have been receiving as manager, shareholder, playwright and actor, a yearly income equivalent to $25,000 in money of the present time. He early began to devote attention to paying the debts of his father, who lived until 1601, and restoring the fortunes of his family in Stratford.

The death of his only son, Hamnet, in 1596, must have been a severe blow to him, but he obtained from the Heralds' College the grant of a family coat of arms, which secured the position of the family as gentlefolks; in 1597 he purchased New Place, the largest house in Stratford; and later on he acquired other large property rights there. How often he may have visited Stratford in the twenty-five years of his career in London we have no information; but however enjoyable London life and the society of the writers at the 'Mermaid' Tavern may have been to him, he probably always looked forward to ending his life as the chief country gentleman of his native village. Thither he retired about 1610 or 1612, and there he died prematurely in 1616, just as he was completing his fifty-second year.

Shakspere's dramatic career falls naturally into four successive divisions of increasing maturity. To be sure, no definite record of the order of his plays has come down to us, and it can scarcely be said that we certainly know the exact date of a single one of them; but the evidence of the title-page dates of such of them as were hastily published during his lifetime, of allusions to them in other writings of the time, and other scattering facts of one sort or another, joined with the more important internal evidence of comparative maturity of mind and art which shows 'Macbeth' and 'The Winter's Tale,' for example, vastly superior to 'Love's Labour's Lost'--all this evidence together enables us to arrange the plays in a chronological order which is certainly approximately correct.

The first of the four periods thus disclosed is that of experiment and preparation, from about 1588 to about 1593, when Shakspere tried his hand at virtually every current kind of dramatic work. Its most important product is 'Richard III,' a melodramatic chronicle-history play, largely imitative of Marlowe and yet showing striking power. At the end of this period Shakspere issued two rather long narrative poems on classical subjects, 'Venus and Adonis,' and 'The Rape of Lucrece,' dedicating them both to the young Earl of Southampton, who thus appears as his patron.

Both display great fluency in the most luxuriant and sensuous Renaissance manner, and though they appeal little to the taste of the present day 'Venus and Adonis,' in particular, seems to have become at once the most popular poem of its own time. Shakspere himself regarded them very seriously, publishing them with care, though he, like most Elizabethan dramatists, never thought it worth while to put his plays into print except to safeguard the property rights of his company in them. Probably at about the end of his first period, also, he began the composition of his sonnets, of which we have already spoken.

The second period of Shakspere's work, extending from about 1594 to about 1601, is occupied chiefly with chronicle-history plays and happy comedies. The chronicle-history plays begin (probably) with the subtile and fascinating, though not yet absolutely masterful study of contrasting characters in 'Richard II'; continue through the two parts of 'Henry IV,' where the realistic comedy action of Falstaff and his group makes history familiarly vivid; and end with the epic glorification of a typical English hero-king in 'Henry V.'

The comedies include the charmingly fantastic 'Midsummer Night's Dream'; 'The Merchant of Venice,' where a story of tragic sternness is strikingly contrasted with the most poetical idealizing romance and yet is harmoniously blended into it; 'Much Ado About Nothing,' a magnificent example of high comedy of character and wit; 'As You Like It,' the supreme delightful achievement of Elizabethan and all English pastoral romance; and 'Twelfth Night,' where again charming romantic sentiment is made believable by combination with a story of comic realism. Even in the one, unique, tragedy of the period, 'Romeo and Juliet,' the main impression is not that of the predestined tragedy, but that of ideal youthful love, too gloriously radiant to be viewed with sorrow even in its fatal outcome.

The third period, extending from about 1601 to about 1609, includes Shakspere's great tragedies and certain cynical plays, which formal classification mis-names comedies. In these plays as a group Shakspere sets himself to grapple with the deepest and darkest problems of human character and life; but it is only very uncertain inference that he was himself passing at this time through a period of bitterness and disillusion. 'Julius Casar' presents the material failure of an unpractical idealist (Brutus); 'Hamlet' the struggle of a perplexed and divided soul; 'Othello' the ruin of a noble life by an evil one through the terrible power of jealousy; 'King Lear' unnatural ingratitude working its hateful will and yet thwarted at the end by its own excess and by faithful love; and 'Macbeth' the destruction of a large nature by material ambition. Without doubt this is the greatest continuous group of plays ever wrought out by a human mind, and they are followed by 'Antony and Cleopatra,' which magnificently portrays the emptiness of a sensual passion against the background of a decaying civilization.

Shakspere did not solve the insoluble problems of life, but having presented them as powerfully, perhaps, as is possible for human intelligence, he turned in his last period, of only two or three years, to the expression of the serene philosophy of life in which he himself must have now taken refuge. The noble and beautiful romance-comedies, 'Cymbeline,' 'The Winter's Tale,' and 'The Tempest,' suggest that men do best to forget what is painful and center their attention on the pleasing and encouraging things in a world where there is at least an inexhaustible store of beauty and goodness and delight.

Shakspere may now well have felt, as his retirement to Stratford suggests, that in his nearly forty plays he had fully expressed himself and had earned the right to a long and peaceful old age. The latter, as we have seen, was denied him; but seven years after his death two of his fellow-managers assured the preservation of the plays whose unique importance he himself did not suspect by collecting them in the first folio edition of his complete dramatic works.

Shakspere's greatness rests on supreme achievement--the result of the highest genius matured by experience and by careful experiment and labor--in all phases of the work of a poetic dramatist. The surpassing charm of his rendering of the romantic beauty and joy of life and the profundity of his presentation of its tragic side we have already suggested. Equally sure and comprehensive is his portrayal of characters. With the certainty of absolute mastery he causes men and women to live for us, a vast representative group, in all the actual variety of age and station, perfectly realized in all the subtile diversities and inconsistencies of protean human nature.

Not less notable than his strong men are his delightful young heroines, romantic Elizabethan heroines, to be sure, with an unconventionality, many of them, which does not belong to such women in the more restricted world of reality, but pure embodiments of the finest womanly delicacy, keenness, and vivacity. Shakspere, it is true, was a practical dramatist. His background characters are often present in the plays not in order to be entirely real but in order to furnish amusement; and even in the case of the chief ones, just as in the treatment of incidents, he is always perfectly ready to sacrifice literal truth to dramatic effect. But these things are only the corollaries of all successful playwriting and of all art.

To Shakspere's mastery of poetic expression similarly strong superlatives must be applied. For his form he perfected Marlowe's blank verse, developing it to the farthest possible limits of fluency, variety, and melody; though he retained the riming couplet for occasional use (partly for the sake of variety) and frequently made use also of prose, both for the same reason and in realistic or commonplace scenes. As regards the spirit of poetry, it scarcely need be said that nowhere else in literature is there a like storehouse of the most delightful and the greatest ideas phrased with the utmost power of condensed expression and figurative beauty.

In dramatic structure his greatness is on the whole less conspicuous. Writing for success on the Elizabethan stage, he seldom attempted to reduce its romantic licenses to the perfection of an absolute standard. 'Romeo and Juliet, 'Hamlet,' and indeed most of his plays, contain unnecessary scenes, interesting to the Elizabethans, which Sophocles as well as Racine would have pruned away. Yet when Shakspere chooses, as in 'Othello,' to develop a play with the sternest and most rapid directness, he proves essentially the equal even of the most rigid technician.

Shakspere, indeed, although as Ben Jonson said, 'he was not for an age but for all time,' was in every respect a thorough Elizabethan also, and does not escape the superficial Elizabethan faults. Chief of these, perhaps, is his fondness for 'conceits,' with which he makes his plays, especially some of the earlier ones, sparkle, brilliantly, but often inappropriately. In his prose style, again, except in the talk of commonplace persons, he never outgrew, or wished to outgrow, a large measure of Elizabethan self-conscious elegance. Scarcely a fault is his other Elizabethan habit of seldom, perhaps never, inventing the whole of his stories, but drawing the outlines of them from previous works--English chronicles, poems, or plays, Italian 'novels,' or the biographies of Plutarch.

But in the majority of cases these sources provided him only with bare or even crude sketches, and perhaps nothing furnishes clearer proof of his genius than the way in which he has seen the human significance in stories baldly and wretchedly told, where the figures are merely wooden types, and by the power of imagination has transformed them into the greatest literary masterpieces, profound revelations of the underlying forces of life.

Shakspere, like every other great man, has been the object of much unintelligent, and misdirected adulation, but his greatness, so far from suffering diminution, grows more apparent with the passage of time and the increase of study.

The theory persistently advocated during the last half century that Shakspere's works were really written not by himself but by Francis Bacon or some other person can never gain credence with any competent judge. Our knowledge of Shakspere's life, slight as it is, is really at least as great as that which has been preserved of almost any dramatist of the period; for dramatists were not then looked on as persons of permanent importance. There is really much direct contemporary documentary evidence, as we have already indicated, of Shakspere's authorship of the plays and poems. No theory, further, could be more preposterous, to any one really acquainted with literature, than the idea that the imaginative poetry of Shakspere was produced by the essentially scientific and prosaic mind of Francis Bacon.

As to the cipher systems supposed to reveal hidden messages in the plays: First, no poet bending his energies to the composition of such masterpieces as Shakspere's could possibly concern himself at the same time with weaving into them a complicated and trifling cryptogram. Second, the cipher systems are absolutely arbitrary and unscientific, applied to any writings whatever can be made to 'prove' anything that one likes, and indeed have been discredited in the hands of their own inventors by being made to 'prove' far too much. Third, it has been demonstrated more than once that the verbal coincidences on which the cipher systems rest are no more numerous than the law of mathematical probabilities requires. Aside from actually vicious pursuits, there can be no more melancholy waste of time than the effort to demonstrate that Shakspere is not the real author of his reputed works.

**NATIONAL LIFE FROM 1603 TO 1660**

We have already observed that, as Shakspere's career suggests, there was no abrupt change in either life or literature at the death of Queen Elizabeth in 1603; and in fact the Elizabethan period of literature is often made to include the reign of James I, 1603-1625 (the Jacobean period [Footnote: 'Jaco'bus' is the Latin form of 'James.']), or even, especially in the case of the drama, that of Charles I, 1625-1649 (the Carolean period). Certainly the drama of all three reigns forms a continuously developing whole, and should be discussed as such. None the less the spirit of the first half of the seventeenth century came gradually to be widely different from that of the preceding fifty years, and before going on to Shakspere's successors we must stop to indicate briefly wherein the difference consists and for this purpose to speak of the determining events of the period.

Before the end of Elizabeth's reign, indeed, there had been a perceptible change; as the queen grew old and morose the national life seemed also to lose its youth and freshness. Her successor and distant cousin, James of Scotland (James I of England), was a bigoted pedant, and under his rule the perennial Court corruption, striking in, became foul and noisome. The national Church, instead of protesting, steadily identified itself more closely with the Court party, and its ruling officials, on the whole, grew more and more worldly and intolerant. Little by little the nation found itself divided into two great factions; on the one hand the Cavaliers, the party of the Court, the nobles, and the Church, who continued to be largely dominated by the Renaissance zest for beauty and, especially, pleasure; and on the other hand the Puritans, comprising the bulk of the middle classes, controlled by the religious principles of the Reformation, often, in their opposition to Cavalier frivolity, stern and narrow, and more and more inclined to separate themselves from the English Church in denominations of their own.

The breach steadily widened until in 1642, under the arbitrary rule of Charles I, the Civil War broke out. In three years the Puritan Parliament was victorious, and in 1649 the extreme minority of the Puritans, supported by the army, took the unprecedented step of putting King Charles to death, and declared England a Commonwealth. But in four years more the Parliamentary government, bigoted and inefficient, made itself impossible, and then for five years, until his death, Oliver Cromwell strongly ruled England as Protector. Another year and a half of chaos confirmed the nation in a natural reaction, and in 1660 the unworthy Stuart race was restored in the person of the base and frivolous Charles II. The general influence of the forces which produced these events shows clearly in the changing tone of the drama, the work of those dramatists who were Shakspere's later contemporaries and successors.

## BEN JONSON

The second place among the Elizabethan and Jacobean dramatists is universally assigned, on the whole justly, to Ben Jonson, who both in temperament and in artistic theories and practice presents a complete contrast to Shakspere. Jonson, the posthumous son of an impoverished gentleman-clergyman, was born in London in 1573. At Westminster School he received a permanent bent toward classical studies from the headmaster, William Camden, who was one of the greatest scholars of the time. Forced into the uncongenial trade of his stepfather, a master-bricklayer, he soon deserted it to enlist among the English soldiers who were helping the Dutch to fight their Spanish oppressors.

Here he exhibited some of his dominating traits by challenging a champion from the other army and killing him in classical fashion in single combat between the lines. By about the age of twenty he was back in London and married to a wife whom he later described as being 'virtuous but a shrew,' and who at one time found it more agreeable to live apart from him. He became an actor (at which profession he failed) and a writer of plays. About 1598 he displayed his distinguishing realistic style in the comedy 'Every Man in His Humour,' which was acted by Shakspere's company, it is said through Shakspere's friendly influence. At about the same time the burly Jonson killed another actor in a duel and escaped capital punishment only through 'benefit of clergy' (the exemption still allowed to educated men).

The plays which Jonson produced during the following years were chiefly satirical attacks on other dramatists, especially Marston and Dekker, who retorted in kind. Thus there developed a fierce actors' quarrel, referred to in Shakspere's 'Hamlet,' in which the 'children's' companies had some active but now uncertain part. Before it was over most of the dramatists had taken sides against Jonson, whose arrogant and violent self-assertiveness put him at odds, sooner or later, with nearly every one with whom he had much to do. In 1603 he made peace, only to become involved in other, still more, serious difficulties.

Shortly after the accession of King James, Jonson, Chapman, and Marston brought out a comedy, 'Eastward Hoe,' in which they offended the king by satirical flings at the needy Scotsmen to whom James was freely awarding Court positions. They were imprisoned and for a while, according to the barbarous procedure of the time, were in danger of losing their ears and noses. At a banquet celebrating their release, Jonson reports, his 'old mother' produced a paper of poison which, if necessary, she had intended to administer to him to save him from this disgrace, and of which, she said, to show that she was 'no churl,' she would herself first have drunk.

Just before this incident, in 1603, Jonson had turned to tragedy and written 'Sejanus,' which marks the beginning of his most important decade. He followed up 'Sejanus' after several years with the less excellent 'Catiline,' but his most significant dramatic works, on the whole, are his four great satirical comedies. 'Volpone, or the Fox,' assails gross vice; 'Epicoene, the Silent Woman,' ridicules various sorts of absurd persons; 'The Alchemist' castigates quackery and its foolish encouragers; and 'Bartholomew Fair' is a coarse but overwhelming broadside at Puritan hypocrisy. Strange as it seems in the author of these masterpieces of frank realism, Jonson at the same time was showing himself the most gifted writer of the Court masks, which now, arrived at the last period of their evolution, were reaching the extreme of spectacular elaborateness.

Early in James' reign, therefore, Jonson was made Court Poet, and during the next thirty years he produced about forty masks, devoting to them much attention and care, and quarreling violently with Inigo Jones, the Court architect, who contrived the stage settings. During this period Jonson was under the patronage of various nobles, and he also reigned as dictator at the club of literary men which Sir Walter Raleigh had founded at the Mermaid Tavern (so called, like other inns, from its sign). A well-known poetical letter of the dramatist Francis Beaumont to Jonson celebrates the club meetings; and equally well known is a description given in the next generation from hearsay and inference by the antiquary Thomas Fuller: 'Many were the wit-combats betwixt Shakspere and Ben Jonson, which two I behold like a Spanish great galleon and an English man-of-war: Master Jonson, like the former, was built far higher in learning; solid, but slow in his performances; Shakespere, with the English man-of-war, lesser in bulk, but lighter in sailing, could turn with all tides, tack about and take advantage of all winds, by the quickness of his wit and invention.'

The last dozen years of Jonson's life were unhappy. Though he had a pension from the Court, he was sometimes in financial straits; and for a time he lost his position as Court Poet. He resumed the writing of regular plays, but his style no longer pleased the public; and he often suffered much from sickness. Nevertheless at the Devil Tavern he collected about him a circle of younger admirers, some of them among the oncoming poets, who were proud to be known as 'Sons of Ben,' and who largely accepted as authoritative his opinions on literary matters. Thus his life, which ended in 1637, did not altogether go out in gloom. On the plain stone which alone, for a long time, marked his grave in Westminster Abbey an unknown admirer inscribed the famous epitaph, 'O rare Ben Jonson.'

As a man Jonson, pugnacious, capricious, ill-mannered, sometimes surly, intemperate in drink and in other respects, is an object for only very qualified admiration; and as a writer he cannot properly be said to possess that indefinable thing, genius, which is essential to the truest greatness. But both as man and as writer he manifested great force; and in both drama and poetry he stands for several distinct literary principles and attainments highly important both in themselves and for their subsequent influence.

1. Most conspicuous in his dramas is his realism, often, as we have said, extremely coarse, and a direct reflection of his intellect, which was as strongly masculine as his body and altogether lacking, where the regular drama was concerned, in fineness of sentiment or poetic feeling. He early assumed an attitude of pronounced opposition to the Elizabethan romantic plays, which seemed to him not only lawless in artistic structure but unreal and trifling in atmosphere and substance. (That he was not, however, as has sometimes been said, personally hostile to Shakspere is clear, among other things, from his poetic tributes in the folio edition of Shakspere and from his direct statement elsewhere that he loved Shakspere almost to idolatry.) Jonson's purpose was to present life as he believed it to be; he was thoroughly acquainted with its worser side; and he refused to conceal anything that appeared to him significant. His plays, therefore, have very much that is flatly offensive to the taste which seeks in literature, prevailingly, for idealism and beauty; but they are, nevertheless, generally speaking, powerful portrayals of actual life.
2. Jonson's purpose, however, was never unworthy; rather, it was distinctly to uphold morality. His frankest plays, as we have indicated, are attacks on vice and folly, and sometimes, it is said, had important reformatory influence on contemporary manners. He held, indeed, that in the drama, even in comedy, the function of teaching was as important as that of giving pleasure. His attitude toward his audiences was that of a learned

schoolmaster, whose ideas they should accept with deferential respect; and when they did not approve his plays he was outspoken in indignant contempt.

3. Jonson's self-satisfaction and his critical sense of intellectual superiority to the generality of mankind produce also a marked and disagreeable lack of sympathy in his portrayal of both life and character. The world of his dramas is mostly made up of knaves, scoundrels, hypocrites, fools, and dupes; and it includes among its really important characters very few excellent men and not a single really good woman. Jonson viewed his fellow-men, in the mass, with complete scorn, which it was one of his moral and artistic principles not to disguise. His characteristic comedies all belong, further, to the particular type which he himself originated, namely, the 'Comedy of Humors.'

   Aiming in these plays to flail the follies of his time, he makes his chief characters, in spite of his realistic purpose, extreme and distorted 'humors,' each, in spite of individual traits, the embodiment of some one abstract vice--cowardice, sensualism, hypocrisy, or what not. Too often, also, the unreality is increased because Jonson takes the characters from the stock figures of Latin comedy rather than from genuine English life.

4. In opposition to the free Elizabethan romantic structure, Jonson stood for and deliberately intended to revive the classical style; though with characteristic good sense he declared that not all the classical practices were applicable to English plays. He generally observed unity not only of action but also of time (a single day) and place, sometimes with serious resultant loss of probability. In his tragedies, 'Sejanus' and 'Catiline,' he excluded comic material; for the most part he kept scenes of death and violence off the stage; and he very carefully and slowly constructed plays which have nothing, indeed, of the poetic greatness of Sophocles or Euripides (rather a Jonsonese broad solidity) but which move steadily to their climaxes and then on to the catastrophes in the compact classical manner. He carried his scholarship, however, to the point of pedantry, not

only in the illustrative extracts from Latin authors with which in the printed edition he filled the lower half of his pages, but in the plays themselves in the scrupulous exactitude of his rendering of the details of Roman life. The plays reconstruct the ancient world with much more minute accuracy than do Shakspere's; the student should consider for himself whether they succeed better in reproducing its human reality, making it a living part of the reader's mental and spiritual possessions.

5. Jonson's style in his plays, especially the blank verse of his tragedies, exhibits the same general characteristics. It is strong, compact, and sometimes powerful, but it entirely lacks imaginative poetic beauty--it is really only rhythmical prose, though sometimes suffused with passion.
6. The surprising skill which Jonson, author of such plays, showed in devising the court masks, daintily unsubstantial creations of moral allegory, classical myth, and Teutonic folklore, is rendered less surprising, perhaps, by the lack in the masks of any very great lyric quality. There is no lyric quality at all in the greater part of his non-dramatic verse, though there is an occasional delightful exception, as in the famous 'Drink to me only with thine eyes.' But of his non-dramatic verse we shall speak in the next chapter.
7. Last, and not least: Jonson's revolt from romanticism to classicism initiated, chiefly in non-dramatic verse, the movement for restraint and regularity, which, making slow headway during the next half century, was to issue in the triumphant pseudo-classicism of the generations of Dryden and Pope. Thus, notable in himself, he was significant also as one of the moving forces of a great literary revolution.

## THE OTHER DRAMATISTS

From the many other dramatists of this highly dramatic period, some of whom in their own day enjoyed a reputation fully equal to that of Shakspere and Jonson, we may merely select a few for brief mention. For not only does their light now pale hopelessly in the presence of Shakspere, but in many cases their violations of taste and moral restraint pass the limits of present-day tolerance. Most of them, like Shakspere, produced both comedies and tragedies, prevailingly romantic but with elements of realism; most of them wrote more often in collaboration than did Shakspere; they all shared the Elizabethan vigorously creative interest in life; but none of them attained either Shakspere's wisdom, his power, or his mastery of poetic beauty. One of the most learned of the group was George Chapman, whose verse has a Jonsonian solidity not unaccompanied with Jonsonian ponderousness.

He won fame also in non-dramatic poetry, especially by vigorous but rather clumsy verse translations of the 'Iliad' and 'Odyssey,' Another highly individual figure is that of Thomas Dekker, who seems to have been one of the completest embodiments of irrepressible Elizabethan cheerfulness, though this was joined in him with an irresponsibility which kept him commonly floundering in debt or confined in debtor's prison. His 'Shoemaker's Holiday' (1600), still occasionally chosen by amateur companies for reproduction, gives a rough-and-ready but (apart from its coarseness) charming romanticized picture of the life of London apprentices and whole-hearted citizens. Thomas Heywood, a sort of journalist before the days of newspapers, produced an enormous amount of work in various literary forms; in the drama he claimed to have had 'an entire hand, or at least a maine finger' in no less than two hundred and twenty plays. Inevitably, therefore, he is careless and slipshod, but some of his portrayals of sturdy English men and women and of romantic adventure (as in 'The Fair Maid of the West') are of refreshing naturalness and breeziness. Thomas Middleton, also a very prolific writer, often deals, like Jonson and Heywood, with sordid material. John Marston, as well, has too little delicacy or reserve; he also wrote catch-as-catch-can non-dramatic satires.

The sanity of Shakspere's plays, continuing and indeed increasing toward the end of his career, disguises for modern students the tendency to decline in the drama which set in at about the time of King James' accession. Not later than the end of the first decade of the century the dramatists as a class exhibit not only a decrease of originality in plot and characterization, but also a lowering of moral tone, which results largely from the closer identification of the drama with the Court party. There is a lack of seriousness of purpose, an increasing tendency to return, in more morbid spirit, to the sensationalism of the 1580's, and an anxious straining to attract and please the audiences by almost any means.

These tendencies appear in the plays of Francis Beaumont and John Fletcher, whose reputations are indissolubly linked together in one of the most famous literary partnerships of all time. Beaumont, however, was short-lived, and much the greater part of the fifty and more plays ultimately published under their joint names really belong to Fletcher alone or to Fletcher and other collaborators.

The scholarship of our day agrees with the opinion of their contemporaries in assigning to Beaumont the greater share of judgment and intellectual power and to Fletcher the greater share of spontaneity and fancy. Fletcher's style is very individual. It is peculiarly sweet; but its unmistakable mark is his constant tendency to break down the blank verse line by the use of extra syllables, both within the line and at the end. The lyrics which he scatters through his plays are beautifully smooth and musical.

The plays of Beaumont and Fletcher, as a group, are sentimentally romantic, often in an extravagant degree, though their charm often conceals the extravagance as well as the lack of true characterization. They are notable often for their portrayal of the loyal devotion of both men and women to king, lover, or friend. One of the best of them is 'Philaster, or Love Lies Bleeding,' while Fletcher's 'Faithful Shepherdess' is the most pleasing example in English of the artificial pastoral drama in the Italian and Spanish style.

The Elizabethan tendency to sensational horror finds its greatest artistic expression in two plays of John Webster, 'The White Devil, or Vittoria Corombona,' and 'The Duchess of Malfi.' Here the corrupt and brutal life of the Italian nobility of the Renaissance is presented with terrible frankness, but with an overwhelming sense for passion, tragedy, and pathos. The most moving pathos permeates some of the plays of John Ford (of the time of Charles I), for example, 'The Broken Heart'; but they are abnormal and unhealthy. Philip Massinger, a pupil and collaborator of Fletcher, was of thoughtful spirit, and apparently a sincere moralist at heart, in spite of much concession in his plays to the contrary demands of the time.

His famous comedy, 'A New Way to Pay Old Debts,' a satire on greed and cruelty, is one of the few plays of the period, aside from Shakspere's, which are still occasionally acted. The last dramatist of the whole great line was James Shirley, who survived the Commonwealth and the Restoration and died of exposure at the Fire of London in 1666. In his romantic comedies and comedies of manners Shirley vividly reflects the thoughtless life of the Court of Charles I and of the well-to-do contemporary London citizens and shows how surprisingly far that life had progressed toward the reckless frivolity and abandonment which after the interval of Puritan rule were to run riot in the Restoration period.

The great Elizabethan dramatic impulse had thus become deeply degenerate, and nothing could be more fitting than that it should be brought to a definite end. When the war broke out in 1642 one of the first acts of Parliament, now at last free to work its will on the enemies of Puritanism, was to decree that 'whereas public sports do not well agree with public calamities, nor public stage-plays with the seasons of humiliation,' all dramatic performances should cease. This law, fatal, of course, to the writing as well as the acting of plays, was enforced with only slightly relaxing rigor until very shortly before the Restoration of Charles II in 1660. Doubtless to the Puritans it seemed that their long fight against the theater had ended in permanent triumph; but this was only one of many respects in which the Puritans were to learn that human nature cannot be forced into permanent conformity with any rigidly over-severe standard, on however high ideals it may be based.

**SUMMARY**

The chief dramatists of the whole sixty years of the great period may be conveniently grouped as follows: I. Shakspere's early contemporaries, about 1580 to about 1593: Lyly, Peele, Greene, Kyd, Marlowe. II. Shakspere. III. Shakspere's later contemporaries, under Elizabeth and James I: Jonson, Chapman, Dekker, Heywood, Middleton, Marston, Beaumont and Fletcher, Webster. IV. The last group, under James I and Charles I, to 1642: Ford, Massinger, and Shirley.

# 8

# The Seventeenth Century, Prose and Poetry

The first half of the seventeenth century as a whole, compared with the Elizabethan age, was a period of relaxing vigor. The Renaissance enthusiasm had spent itself, and in place of the danger and glory which had long united the nation there followed increasing dissension in religion and politics and uncertainty as to the future of England and, indeed, as to the whole purpose of life. Through increased experience men were certainly wiser and more sophisticated than before, but they were also more self-conscious and sadder or more pensive. The output of literature did not diminish, but it spread itself over wider fields, in general fields of somewhat recondite scholarship rather than of creation. Nevertheless this period includes in prose one writer greater than any prose writer of the previous century, namely Francis Bacon, and, further, the book which unquestionably occupies the highest place in English literature, that is the King James version of the Bible; and in poetry it includes one of the very greatest figures, John Milton, together with a varied and highly interesting assemblage of lesser lyrists.

## FRANCIS BACON, VISCOUNT ST. ALBANS, 1561-1626

Francis Bacon, intellectually one of the most eminent Englishmen of all times, and chief formulator of the methods of modern science, was born in 1561 (three years before Shakspere), the son of Sir Nicholas Bacon, Lord Keeper of the Great Seal under Queen Elizabeth and one of her most trusted earlier advisers. The boy's precocity led the queen to call him her 'little Lord Keeper.' At the age of twelve he, like Wyatt, was sent to Cambridge, where his chief impression was of disgust at the unfruitful scholastic application of Aristotle's ideas, still supreme in spite of a century of Renaissance enlightenment.

A very much more satisfactory three years' residence in France in the household of the English ambassador was terminated in 1579 (the year of Spenser's 'Shepherd's Calendar') by the death of Sir Nicholas. Bacon was now ready to enter on the great career for which his talents fitted him, but his uncle by marriage, Lord Burghley, though all-powerful with the queen, systematically thwarted his progress, from jealous consciousness of his superiority to his own son. Bacon therefore studied law, and was soon chosen a member of Parliament, where he quickly became a leader. He continued, however, throughout his life to devote much of his time to study and scholarly scientific writing.

On the interpretation of Bacon's public actions depends the answer to the complex and much-debated question of his character. The most reasonable conclusions seem to be: that Bacon was sincerely devoted to the public good and in his earlier life was sometimes ready to risk his own interests in its behalf; that he had a perfectly clear theoretical insight into the principles of moral conduct; that he lacked the moral force of character to live on the level of his convictions, so that after the first, at least, his personal ambition was often stronger than his conscience; that he believed that public success could be gained only by conformity to the low standards of the age; that he fell into the fatal error of supposing that his own preeminent endowments and the services which they might enable him to render justified him in the use of unworthy means; that his sense of real as distinguished from apparent personal dignity was distressingly inadequate; and that, in general, like many men of great intellect, he was deficient in greatness of character, emotion, fine feeling, sympathy, and even in comprehension of the highest spiritual principles. He certainly shared to the full in the usual courtier's ambition for great place and wealth, and in the worldling's inclination to ostentatious display.

Having offended Queen Elizabeth by his boldness in successfully opposing an encroachment on the rights of the House of Commons, Bacon connected himself with the Earl of Essex and received from him many favors; but when Essex attempted a treasonable insurrection in 1601, Bacon, as one of the Queen's lawyers, displayed against him a subservient zeal which on theoretical grounds of patriotism might appear praiseworthy, but which in view of his personal obligations was grossly indecent. For the worldly prosperity which he sought, however, Bacon was obliged to wait until the accession of King James, after which his rise was rapid. The King appreciated his ability and often consulted him, and he frequently gave the wisest advice, whose acceptance might perhaps have averted the worst national disasters of the next fifty years.

The advice was above the courage of both the King and the age; but Bacon was advanced through various legal offices, until in 1613 he was made Attorney-General and in 1618 (two years after Shakspere's death) Lord High Chancellor of England, at the same time being raised to the peerage as Baron Verulam. During all this period, in spite of his better knowledge, he truckled with sorry servility to the King and his unworthy favorites and lent himself as an agent in their most arbitrary acts. Retribution overtook him in 1621, within a few days after his elevation to the dignity of Viscount St. Albans. The House of Commons, balked in an attack on the King and the Duke of Buckingham, suddenly turned on Bacon and impeached him for having received bribes in connection with his legal decisions as Lord Chancellor.

Bacon admitted the taking of presents (against which in one of his essays he had directly cautioned judges), and threw himself on the mercy of the House of Lords, with whom the sentence lay. He appears to have been sincere in protesting later that the presents had not influenced his decisions and that he was the justest judge whom England had had for fifty years; it seems that the giving of presents by the parties to a suit was a customary abuse. But he had technically laid himself open to the malice of his enemies and was condemned to very heavy penalties, of which two were enforced, namely, perpetual incapacitation from holding public office, and banishment from Court. Even after this he continued, with an astonishing lack of good taste, to live extravagantly and beyond his means (again in disregard of his own precepts), so that Prince Charles observed that he 'scorned to go out in a snuff.' He died in 1626 from a cold caught in the prosecution of his scientific researches, namely in an experiment on the power of snow to preserve meat.

Bacon's splendid mind and unique intellectual vision produced, perhaps inevitably, considering his public activity, only fragmentary concrete achievements. The only one of his books still commonly read is the series of 'Essays,' which consist of brief and comparatively informal jottings on various subjects. In their earliest form, in 1597, the essays were ten in number, but by additions from time to time they had increased at last in 1625 to fifty-eight. They deal with a great variety of topics, whatever Bacon happened to be interested in, from friendship to the arrangement of a house, and in their condensation they are more like bare synopses than complete discussions.

But their comprehensiveness of view, sureness of ideas and phrasing, suggestiveness, and apt illustrations reveal the pregnancy and practical force of Bacon's thought (though, on the other hand, he is not altogether free from the superstitions of his time and after the lapse of three hundred years sometimes seems commonplace). The whole general tone of the essays, also, shows the man, keen and worldly, not at all a poet or idealist. How to succeed and make the most of prosperity might be called the pervading theme of the essays, and subjects which in themselves suggest spiritual treatment are actually considered in accordance with a coldly intellectual calculation of worldly advantage.

The essays are scarcely less notable for style than for ideas. With characteristic intellectual independence Bacon strikes out for himself an extremely terse and clear manner of expression, doubtless influenced by such Latin authors as Tacitus, which stands in marked contrast to the formless diffuseness or artificial elaborateness of most Elizabethan and Jacobean prose. His unit of structure is always a short clause. The sentences are sometimes short, sometimes consist of a number of connected clauses; but they are always essentially loose rather than periodic; so that the thought is perfectly simple and its movement clear and systematic. The very numerous allusions to classical history and life are not the result of affectation, but merely indicate the natural furnishing of the mind of the educated Renaissance gentleman. The essays, it should be added, were evidently suggested and more or less influenced by those of the great French thinker, Montaigne, an earlier contemporary of Bacon. The hold of medieval scholarly tradition, it is further interesting to note, was still so strong that in order to insure their permanent preservation Bacon translated them into Latin--he took for granted that the English in which he first composed them and in which they will always be known was only a temporary vulgar tongue.

But Bacon's most important work, as we have already implied, was not in the field of pure literature but in the general advancement of knowledge, particularly knowledge of natural science; and of this great service we must speak briefly. His avowal to Burghley, made as early as 1592, is famous: 'I have taken all knowledge to be my province.' Briefly stated, his purposes, constituting an absorbing and noble ambition, were to survey all the learning of his time, in all lines of thought, natural science, morals, politics, and the rest, to overthrow the current method of a priori deduction, deduction resting, moreover, on very insufficient and long-antiquated bases of observation, and to substitute for it as the method of the future, unlimited fresh observation and experiment and inductive reasoning.

This enormous task was to be mapped out and its results summarized in a Latin work called 'Magna Instauratio Scientiarum' (The Great Renewal of Knowledge); but parts of this survey were necessarily to be left for posterity to formulate, and of the rest Bacon actually composed only a fraction. What may be called the first part appeared originally in English in 1605 and is known by the abbreviated title, "The Advancement of Learning'; the expanded Latin form has the title, 'De Augmentis Scientiarum.'

Its exhaustive enumeration of the branches of thought and knowledge, what has been accomplished in each and what may be hoped for it in the future, is thoroughly fascinating, though even here Bacon was not capable of passionate enthusiasm. However, the second part of the work, 'Novum Organum' (The New Method), written in Latin and published in 1620, is the most important. Most interesting here, perhaps, is the classification (contrasting with Plato's doctrine of divinely perfect controlling ideas) of the 'idols' (phantoms) which mislead the human mind. Of these Bacon finds four sorts: idols of the tribe, which are inherent in human nature; idols of the cave, the errors of the individual; idols of the market-place, due to mistaken reliance on words; and idols of the theater (that is, of the schools), resulting from false reasoning.

In the details of all his scholarly work Bacon's knowledge and point of view were inevitably imperfect. Even in natural science he was not altogether abreast of his time--he refused to accept Harvey's discovery of the manner of the circulation of the blood and the Copernican system of astronomy. Neither was he, as is sometimes supposed, the inventor of the inductive method of observation and reasoning, which in some degree is fundamental in all study. But he did, much more fully and clearly than any one before him, demonstrate the importance and possibilities of that method; modern experimental science and thought have proceeded directly in the path which he pointed out; and he is fully entitled to the great honor of being called their father, which certainly places him high among the great figures in the history of human thought.

## THE KING JAMES BIBLE, 1611

It was during the reign of James I that the long series of sixteenth century translations of the Bible reached its culmination in what we have already called the greatest of all English books (or rather, collections of books), the King James ('Authorized') version. In 1604 an ecclesiastical conference accepted a suggestion, approved by the king, that a new and more accurate rendering of the Bible should be made. The work was entrusted to a body of about fifty scholars, who divided themselves into six groups, among which the various books of the Bible were apportioned. The resulting translation, proceeding with the inevitable slowness, was completed in 1611, and then rather rapidly superseded all other English versions for both public and private use. This King James Bible is universally accepted as the chief masterpiece of English prose style.

The translators followed previous versions so far as possible, checking them by comparison with the original Hebrew and Greek, so that while attaining the greater correctness at which they aimed they preserved the accumulated stylistic excellences of three generations of their predecessors; and their language, properly varying according to the nature of the different books, possesses an imaginative grandeur and rhythm not unworthy--and no higher praise could be awarded--of the themes which it expresses.

The still more accurate scholarship of a later century demanded the Revised Version of 1881, but the superior literary quality of the King James version remains undisputed. Its style, by the nature of the case, was somewhat archaic from the outset, and of course has become much more so with the passage of time. This entails the practical disadvantage of making the Bible--events, characters, and ideas--seem less real and living; but on the other hand it helps inestimably to create the finer imaginative atmosphere which is so essential for the genuine religious spirit.

**MINOR PROSE WRITERS**

Among the prose authors of the period who hold an assured secondary position in the history of English literature three or four may be mentioned: Robert Burton, Oxford scholar, minister, and recluse, whose 'Anatomy of Melancholy' (1621), a vast and quaint compendium of information both scientific and literary, has largely influenced numerous later writers; Jeremy Taylor, royalist clergyman and bishop, one of the most eloquent and spiritual of English preachers, author of 'Holy Living' (1650) and 'Holy Dying' (1651); Izaak Walton, London tradesman and student, best known for his 'Compleat Angler' (1653), but author also of charming brief lives of Donne, George Herbert, and others of his contemporaries; and Sir Thomas Browne, a scholarly physician of Norwich, who elaborated a fastidiously poetic Latinized prose style for his pensively delightful 'Religio Medici' (A Physician's Religion--1643) and other works.

**LYRIC POETRY**

Apart from the drama and the King James Bible, the most enduring literary achievement of the period was in poetry. Milton--distinctly, after Shakspere, the greatest writer of the century--must receive separate consideration; the more purely lyric poets may be grouped together.

The absence of any sharp line of separation between the literature of the reign of Elizabeth and of those of James I and

Charles I is no less marked in the case of the lyric poetry than of the drama. Some of the poets whom we have already discussed in Chapter V continued writing until the second decade of the seventeenth century, or later, and some of those whom we shall here name had commenced their career well before 1600. Just as in the drama, therefore, something of the Elizabethan spirit remains in the lyric poetry; yet here also before many years there is a perceptible change; the Elizabethan spontaneous joyousness largely vanishes and is replaced by more self-conscious artistry or thought.

The Elizabethan note is perhaps most unmodified in certain anonymous songs and other poems of the early years of James I, such as the exquisite 'Weep you no more, sad fountains.' It is clear also in the charming songs of Thomas Campion, a physician who composed both words and music for several song-books, and in Michael Drayton, a voluminous poet and dramatist who is known to most readers only for his finely rugged patriotic ballad on the battle of Agincourt. Sir Henry Wotton, statesman and Provost (head) of Eton School, displays the Elizabethan idealism in 'The Character of a Happy Life' and in his stanzas in praise of Elizabeth, daughter of King James, wife of the ill-starred Elector-Palatine and King of Bohemia, and ancestress of the present English royal family.

The Elizabethan spirit is present but mingled with seventeenth century melancholy in the sonnets and other poems of the Scotch gentleman William Drummond of Hawthornden (the name of his estate near Edinburgh), who in quiet life-long retirement lamented the untimely death of the lady to whom he had been betrothed or meditated on heavenly things.

In Drummond appears the influence of Spenser, which was strong on many poets of the period, especially on some, like William Browne, who continued the pastoral form. Another of the main forces, in lyric poetry as in the drama, was the beginning of the revival of the classical spirit, and in lyric poetry also this was largely due to Ben Jonson.

As we have already said, the greater part of Jonson's non-dramatic poetry, like his dramas, expresses chiefly the downright strength of his mind and character. It is terse and unadorned, dealing often with commonplace things in the manner of the

Epistles and Satires of Horace, and it generally has more of the quality of intellectual prose than of real emotional poetry.

A very favorable representative of it is the admirable, eulogy on Shakspere included in the first folio edition of Shakspere's works. In a few instances, however, Jonson strikes the true lyric note delightfully. Every one knows and sings his two stanzas 'To Celia'--'Drink to me only with thine eyes,' which would still be famous without the exquisitely appropriate music that has come down to us from Jonson's own time, and which are no less beautiful because they consist largely of ideas culled from the Greek philosopher Theophrastus. In all his poems, however, Jonson aims consistently at the classical virtues of clearness, brevity, proportion, finish, and elimination of all excess.

These latter qualities appear also in the lyrics which abound in the plays of John Fletcher, and yet it cannot be said that Fletcher's sweet melody is more classical than Elizabethan. His other distinctive quality is the tone of somewhat artificial courtliness which was soon to mark the lyrics of the other poets of the Cavalier party. An avowed disciple of Jonson and his classicism and a greater poet than Fletcher is Robert Herrick, who, indeed, after Shakspere and Milton, is the finest lyric poet of these two centuries.

Herrick, the nephew of a wealthy goldsmith, seems, after a late graduation from Cambridge, to have spent some years about the Court and in the band of Jonson's 'sons.' Entering the Church when he was nearly forty, he received the small country parish of Dean Prior in the southwest (Devonshire), which he held for nearly twenty years, until 1647, when he was dispossessed by the victorious Puritans. After the Restoration he was reinstated, and he continued to hold the place until his death in old age in 1674. He published his poems (all lyrics) in 1648 in a collection which he called 'Hesperides and Noble Numbers.' The 'Hesperides' (named from the golden apples of the classical Garden of the Daughters of the Sun) are twelve hundred little secular pieces, the 'Noble Numbers' a much less extensive series of religious lyrics.

Both sorts are written in a great variety of stanza forms, all equally skilful and musical. Few of the poems extend beyond fifteen or twenty lines in length, and many are mere epigrams of four lines or even two. The chief secular subjects are: Herrick's devotion to various ladies, Julia, Anthea, Perilla, and sundry more, all presumably more or less imaginary; the joy and uncertainty of life; the charming beauty of Nature; country life, folk lore, and festivals; and similar light or familiar themes. Herrick's characteristic quality, so far as it can be described, is a blend of Elizabethan joyousness with classical perfection of finish. The finish, however, really the result of painstaking labor, such as Herrick had observed in his uncle's shop and as Jonson had enjoined, is perfectly unobtrusive; so apparently natural are the poems that they seem the irrepressible unmeditated outpourings of happy and idle moments.

In care-free lyric charm Herrick can certainly never be surpassed; he is certainly one of the most captivating of all the poets of the world. Some of the 'Noble Numbers' are almost as pleasing as the 'Hesperides,' but not because of real religious significance. For of anything that can be called spiritual religion Herrick was absolutely incapable; his nature was far too deficient in depth. He himself and his philosophy of life were purely Epicurean, Hedonistic, or pagan, in the sense in which we use those terms to-day. His forever controlling sentiment is that to which he gives perfect expression in his best-known song, 'Gather ye rosebuds,' namely the Horatian 'Carpe diem'--'Snatch all possible pleasure from the rapidly-fleeting hours and from this gloriously delightful world.' He is said to have performed his religious duties with regularity; though sometimes in an outburst of disgust at the stupidity of his rustic parishioners he would throw his sermon in their faces and rush out of the church. Put his religion is altogether conventional. He thanks God for material blessings, prays for their continuance, and as the conclusion of everything, in compensation for a formally orthodox life, or rather creed, expects when he dies to be admitted to Heaven. The simple naivete with which he expresses this skin-deep and primitive faith is, indeed, one of the chief sources of charm in the 'Noble Numbers.'

Herrick belongs in part to a group of poets who, being attached to the Court, and devoting some, at least, of their verses to conventional love-making, are called the Cavalier Poets. Among the others Thomas Carew follows the classical principles of Jonson in lyrics which are facile, smooth, and sometimes a little frigid. Sir John Suckling, a handsome and capricious representative of all the extravagances of the Court set, with whom he was enormously popular, tossed off with affected carelessness a mass of slovenly lyrics of which a few audaciously impudent ones are worthy to survive. From the equally chaotic product of Colonel Richard Lovelace stand out the two well-known bits of noble idealism, 'To Lucasta, Going to the Wars,' and 'To Althea, from Prison.' George Wither (1588-1667), a much older man than Suckling and Lovelace, may be mentioned with them as the writer in his youth of light-hearted love-poems. But in the Civil War he took the side of Parliament and under Cromwell he rose to the rank of major-general. In his later life he wrote a great quantity of Puritan religious verse, largely prosy in spite of his fluency.

The last important group among these lyrists is that of the more distinctly religious poets. The chief of these, George Herbert (1593-1633), the subject of one of the most delightful of the short biographies of Izaak Walton, belonged to a distinguished family of the Welsh Border, one branch of which held the earldom of Pembroke, so that the poet was related to the young noble who may have been Shakspere's patron. He was also younger brother of Lord Edward Herbert of Cherbury, an inveterate duellist and the father of English Deism. Destined by his mother to peaceful pursuits, he wavered from the outset between two forces, religious devotion and a passion for worldly comfort and distinction. For a long period the latter had the upper hand, and his life has been described by his best editor, Professor George Herbert Palmer, as twenty-seven years of vacillation and three of consecrated service. Appointed Public Orator, or showman, of his university, Cambridge, he spent some years in enjoying the somewhat trifling elegancies of life and in truckling to the great. Then, on the death of his patrons, he passed through a period of intense crisis from which he emerged wholly spiritualized.

The three remaining years of his life he spent in the little country parish of Bemerton, just outside of Salisbury, as a fervent High Church minister, or as he preferred to name himself, priest, in the strictest devotion to his professional duties and to the practices of an ascetic piety which to the usual

American mind must seem about equally admirable and conventional. His religious poems, published after his death in a volume called 'The Temple,' show mainly two things, first his intense and beautiful consecration to his personal God and Saviour, which, in its earnest sincerity, renders him distinctly the most representative poet of the Church of England, and second the influence of Donne, who was a close friend of his mother.

The titles of most of the poems, often consisting of a single word, are commonly fantastic and symbolical--for example, 'The Collar,' meaning the yoke of submission to God; and his use of conceits, though not so pervasive as with Donne, is equally contorted. To a present-day reader the apparent affectations may seem at first to throw doubt on Herbert's genuineness; but in reality he was aiming to dedicate to religious purposes what appeared to him the highest style of poetry. Without question he is, in a true if special sense, a really great poet.

The second of these religious poets, Richard Crashaw, whose life (1612-1649) was not quite so short as Herbert's, combined an ascetic devotion with a glowingly sensuous esthetic nature that seems rather Spanish than English. Born into an extreme Protestant family, but outraged by the wanton iconoclasm of the triumphant Puritans, and deprived by them of his fellowship, at Cambridge, he became a Catholic and died a canon in the church of the miracle-working Lady (Virgin Mary) of Loretto in Italy. His most characteristic poetry is marked by extravagant conceits and by ecstatic outbursts of emotion that have been called more ardent than anything else in English; though he sometimes writes also in a vein of calm and limpid beauty. He was a poetic disciple of Herbert, as he avowed by humbly entitling his volume 'Steps to the Temple.'

The life of Henry Vaughan (1621-1695) stands in contrast to those of Herbert and Crashaw both by its length and by its quietness. Vaughan himself emphasized his Welsh race by designating himself 'The Silurist' (native of South Wales). After an incomplete university course at Jesus College (the Welsh college), Oxford, and some apparently idle years in London among Jonson's disciples, perhaps also after serving the king in the war, he settled down in his native mountains to the self-denying life of a country physician. His important poems were mostly published at this time, in 1650 and 1655, in the collection which he named 'Silex Scintillans' (The Flaming Flint), a title explained by the frontispiece, which represents a flinty heart glowing under the lightning stroke of God's call. Vaughan's chief traits are a very fine and calm philosophic-religious spirit and a carefully observant love of external Nature, in which he sees mystic revelations of God. In both respects he is closely akin to the later and greater Wordsworth, and his 'Retreat' has the same theme as Wordsworth's famous 'Ode on Intimations of Immortality,' the idea namely that children have a greater spiritual sensitiveness than older persons, because they have come to earth directly from a former life in Heaven.

The contrast between the chief Anglican and Catholic religious poets of this period has been thus expressed by a discerning critic: 'Herrick's religious emotions are only as ripples on a shallow lake when compared to the crested waves of Crashaw, the storm-tides of Herbert, and the deep-sea stirrings of Vaughan.'

We may give a further word of mention to the voluminous Francis Quarles, who in his own day and long after enjoyed enormous popularity, especially among members of the Church of England and especially for his 'Emblems,' a book of a sort common in Europe for a century before his time, in which fantastic woodcuts, like Vaughan's 'Silex Scintillans,' were illustrated with short poems of religious emotion, chiefly dominated by fear. But Quarles survives only as an interesting curiosity.

Three other poets whose lives belong to the middle of the century may be said to complete this entire lyric group. Andrew Marvell, a very moderate Puritan, joined with Milton in his office of Latin Secretary under Cromwell, wrote much poetry of various sorts, some of it in the Elizabethan octosyllabic couplet. He voices a genuine love of Nature, like Wither often in the pastoral form; but his best-known poem is the 'Horatian Ode upon Cromwell's Return from Ireland,' containing the famous eulogy of King Charles' bearing at his execution.

Abraham Cowley, a youthful prodigy and always conspicuous for intellectual power, was secretary to Queen Henrietta Maria after her flight to France and later was a royalist spy in England. His most conspicuous poems are his so-called 'Pindaric Odes,' in which he supposed that he was imitating the structure of the Greek Pindar but really originated the pseudo-Pindaric Ode, a poem in irregular, non-correspondent stanzas. He is the last important representative of the 'Metaphysical' style. In his own day he was acclaimed as the greatest poet of all time, but as is usual in such cases his reputation very rapidly waned. Edmund Waller (1606-1687), a very wealthy gentleman in public life who played a flatly discreditable part in the Civil War, is most important for his share in shaping the riming pentameter couplet into the smooth pseudo-classical form rendered famous by Dryden and Pope; but his only notable single poems are two Cavalier love-lyrics in stanzas, 'On a Girdle' and 'Go, Lovely Rose.'

**JOHN MILTON, 1608-1674**

Conspicuous above all his contemporaries as the representative poet of Puritanism, and, by almost equally general consent, distinctly the greatest of English poets except Shakspere, stands John Milton. His life falls naturally into three periods: 1. Youth and preparation, 1608-1639, when he wrote his shorter poems. 2. Public life, 1639-1660, when he wrote, or at least published, in poetry, only a few sonnets. 3. Later years, 1660-1674, of outer defeat, but of chief poetic achievement, the period of 'Paradise Lost,' 'Paradise Regained,' and 'Samson Agonistes.'

Milton was born in London in December, 1608. His father was a prosperous scrivener, or lawyer of the humbler sort, and a Puritan, but broad-minded, and his children were brought up in the love of music, beauty, and learning. At the age of twelve the future poet was sent to St. Paul's School, and he tells us that from this time on his devotion to study seldom allowed him to leave his books earlier than midnight. At sixteen, in 1625, he entered Cambridge, where he remained during the seven years required for the M. A. degree, and where he was known as 'the lady of Christ's' [College], perhaps for his beauty, of which all his life he continued proud, perhaps for his moral scrupulousness. Milton was never, however, a conventional prig, and a quarrel with a self-important tutor led at one time to his informal suspension from the University. His nature, indeed, had many elements quite inconsistent with the usual vague popular conception of him. He was always not only inflexible in his devotion to principle, but--partly, no doubt, from consciousness of his intellectual superiority--haughty as well as reserved, self-confident, and little respectful of opinions and feelings that clashed with his own. Nevertheless in his youth he had plenty of animal spirits and always for his friends warm human sympathies.

To his college years belong two important poems. His Christmas hymn, the 'Ode on the Morning of Christ's Nativity,' shows the influence of his early poetical master, Spenser, and of contemporary pastoral poets, though it also contains some conceits--truly poetic conceits, however, not exercises in intellectual cleverness like many of those of Donne and his followers. With whatever qualifications, it is certainly one of the great English lyrics, and its union of Renaissance sensuousness with grandeur of conception and sureness of expression foretell clearly enough at twenty the poet of 'Paradise Lost.' The sonnet on his twenty-third birthday, further, is known to almost every reader of poetry as the best short expression in literature of the dedication of one's life and powers to God.

Milton had planned to enter the ministry, but the growing predominance of the High-Church party made this impossible for him, and on leaving the University in 1632 he retired to the country estate which his parents now occupied at Horton, twenty miles west of London. Here, for nearly six years, amid surroundings which nourished his poet's love for Nature, he devoted his time chiefly to further mastery of the whole range of approved literature, Greek, Latin, French, Italian, and English. His poems of these years also are few, but they too are of the very highest quality.

'L'Allegro' and 'Il Penseroso' are idealized visions, in the tripping Elizabethan octosyllabic couplet, of the pleasures of suburban life viewed in moods respectively of light-hearted happiness and of reflection. 'Comus,' the last of the Elizabethan and Jacobean masks, combines an exquisite poetic beauty and a real dramatic action more substantial than that of any other mask with a serious moral theme (the security of Virtue) in a fashion that renders it unique. 'Lycidas' is one of the supreme English elegies; though the grief which helps to create its power sprang more from the recent death of the poet's mother than from that of the nominal subject, his college acquaintance, Edward King, and though in the hands of a lesser artist the solemn denunciation of the false leaders of the English Church might not have been wrought into so fine a harmony with the pastoral form.

Milton's first period ends with an experience designed to complete his preparation for his career, a fifteen months' tour in France and Italy, where the highest literary circles received him cordially. From this trip he returned in 1639, sooner than he had planned, because, he said, the public troubles at home, foreshadowing the approaching war, seemed to him a call to service; though in fact some time intervened before his entrance on public life.

The twenty years which follow, the second period of Milton's career, developed and modified his nature and ideas in an unusual degree and fashion. Outwardly the occupations which they brought him appear chiefly as an unfortunate waste of his great poetic powers. The sixteen sonnets which belong here show how nobly this form could be adapted to the varied expression of the most serious thought, but otherwise Milton abandoned poetry, at least the publication of it, for prose, and for prose which was mostly ephemeral. Taking up his residence in London, for some time he carried on a small private school in his own house, where he much overworked his boys in the mistaken effort to raise their intellectual ambitions to the level of his own. Naturally unwilling to confine himself to a private sphere, he soon engaged in a prose controversy supporting the Puritan view against the Episcopal form of church government, that is against the office of bishops. There shortly followed the most regrettable incident in his whole career, which pathetically illustrates also the lack of a sense of humor which was perhaps his greatest defect.

At the age of thirty-four, and apparently at first sight, he suddenly married Mary Powell, the seventeen-year-old daughter of a royalist country gentleman with whom his family had long maintained some business and social relations. Evidently this daughter of the Cavaliers met a rude disillusionment in Milton's Puritan household and in his Old Testament theory of woman's inferiority and of a wife's duty of strict subjection to her husband;

a few weeks after the marriage she fled to her family and refused to return. Thereupon, with characteristic egoism, Milton put forth a series of pamphlets on divorce, arguing, contrary to English law, and with great scandal to the public, that mere incompatibility of temper was adequate ground for separation. He even proceeded so far as to make proposals of marriage to another woman.

But after two years and the ruin of the royalist cause his wife made unconditional submission, which Milton accepted, and he also received and supported her whole family in his house. Meanwhile his divorce pamphlets had led to the best of his prose writings. He had published the pamphlets without the license of Parliament, then required for all books, and a suit was begun against him. He replied with 'Areopagitica,' an, eloquent and noble argument against the licensing system and in favor of freedom of publication within the widest possible limits. (The name is an allusion to the condemnation of the works of Protagoras by the Athenian Areopagus.) In the stress of public affairs the attack on him was dropped, but the book remains, a deathless plea for individual liberty.

Now at last Milton was drawn into active public life. The execution of the King by the extreme Puritan minority excited an outburst of indignation not only in England but throughout Europe. Milton, rising to the occasion, defended the act in a pamphlet, thereby beginning a paper controversy, chiefly with the Dutch scholar Salmasius, which lasted for several years.

By 1652 it had resulted in the loss of Milton's eyesight, previously over-strained by his studies--a sacrifice in which he gloried but which lovers of poetry must always regret, especially since the controversy largely consisted, according to the custom of the time, in a disgusting exchange of personal scurrilities. Milton's championship of the existing government, however, together with his scholarship, had at once secured for him the position of Latin secretary, or conductor of the diplomatic correspondence of the State with foreign countries. He held this office, after the loss of his eyesight, with Marvell as a colleague, under both Parliament and Cromwell, but it is an error to suppose that he exerted any influence in the management of affairs or that he was on familiar terms with the Protector. At the Restoration he necessarily lost both the position and a considerable part of his property, and for a while he went into hiding; but through the efforts of Marvell and others he was finally included in the general amnesty.

In the remaining fourteen years which make the third period of his life Milton stands out for subsequent ages as a noble figure. His very obstinacy and egoism now enabled him, blind, comparatively poor, and the representative of a lost cause, to maintain his proud and patient dignity in the midst of the triumph of all that was most hateful to him, and, as he believed, to God. His isolation, indeed, was in many respects extreme, though now as always he found the few sympathetic friends on whom his nature was quite dependent. His religious beliefs had become what would at present be called Unitarian, and he did not associate with any of the existing denominations; in private theory he had even come to believe in polygamy.

At home he is said to have suffered from the coldness or more active antipathy of his three daughters, which is no great cause for wonder if we must credit the report that he compelled them to read aloud to him in foreign languages of which he had taught them the pronunciation but not the meaning. Their mother had died some years before, and he had soon lost the second wife who is the subject of one of his finest sonnets. In 1663, at the age of fifty-four, he was united in a third marriage to Elizabeth Minshull, a woman of twenty-four, who was to survive him for more than fifty years.

The important fact of this last period, however, is that Milton now had the leisure to write, or to complete, 'Paradise Lost.' For a quarter of a century he had avowedly cherished the ambition to produce 'such a work as the world would not willingly let die' and had had in mind, among others, the story of Man's Fall. Outlines for a treatment of it not in epic but in dramatic form are preserved in a list of a hundred possible subjects for a great work which he drew up as early as 1640, and during the Commonwealth period he seems not only to have been slowly maturing the plan but to have composed parts of the existing poem; nevertheless the actual work of composition belongs chiefly to the years following 1660. The story as told in Genesis had received much elaboration in Christian tradition from a very early period and Milton drew largely from this general tradition and no doubt to some extent from various previous treatments of the Bible narrative in several languages which he might naturally have read and kept in mind. But beyond the simple outline the poem, like every great work, is essentially the product of his own genius. He aimed, specifically, to produce a Christian epic which should rank with the great epics of antiquity and with those of the Italian Renaissance.

In this purpose he was entirely successful. As a whole, by the consent of all competent judges, 'Paradise Lost' is worthy of its theme, perhaps the greatest that the mind of man can conceive, namely 'to justify the ways of God.' Of course there are defects. The seventeenth century theology, like every successive theological, philosophical, and scientific system, has lost its hold on later generations, and it becomes dull indeed in the long expository passages of the poem. The attempt to express spiritual ideas through the medium of the secular epic, with its battles and councils and all the forms of physical life, is of course rationally paradoxical. It was early pointed out that in spite of himself Milton has in some sense made Satan the hero of the poem--a reader can scarcely fail to sympathize with the fallen archangel in his unconquerable Puritan-like resistance to the arbitrary decrees of Milton's despotic Deity. Further, Milton's personal, English, and Puritan prejudices sometimes intrude in various ways. But all these things are on the surface. In sustained imaginative grandeur of conception, expression, and imagery 'Paradise Lost' yields to no human work, and the majestic and varied movement of the blank verse, here first employed in a really great non-dramatic English poem, is as magnificent as anything else in literature.

It cannot be said that the later books always sustain the greatness of the first two; but the profusely scattered passages of sensuous description, at least, such as those of the Garden of Eden and of the beauty of Eve, are in their own way equally fine. Stately and more familiar passages alike show that however much his experience had done to harden Milton's Puritanism, his youthful Renaissance love of beauty for beauty's sake had lost none of its strength, though of course it could no longer be expressed with youthful lightness of fancy and melody. The poem is a magnificent example of classical art, in the best Greek spirit, united with glowing romantic feeling. Lastly, the value of Milton's scholarship should by no means be overlooked.

All his poetry, from the 'Nativity Ode' onward, is like a rich mosaic of gems borrowed from a great range of classical and modern authors, and in 'Paradise Lost' the allusions to literature and history give half of the romantic charm and very much of the dignity. The poem could have been written only by one who combined in a very high degree intellectual power, poetic feeling, religious idealism, profound scholarship and knowledge of literature, and also experienced knowledge of the actual world of men.

'Paradise Lost' was published in 1677. It was followed in 1671 by 'Paradise Regained,' only one-third as long and much less important; and by 'Samson Agonistes' (Samson in his Death Struggle). In the latter Milton puts the story of the fallen hero's last days into the majestic form of a Greek drama, imparting to it the passionate but lofty feeling evoked by the close similarity of Samson's situation to his own. This was his last work, and he died in 1674. Whatever his faults, the moral, intellectual and poetic greatness of his nature sets him apart as in a sense the grandest figure in English literature.

**JOHN BUNYAN**

Seventeenth century Puritanism was to find a supreme spokesman in prose fiction as well as in poetry; John Milton and John Bunyan, standing at widely different angles of experience, make one of the most interesting complementary pairs in all literature. By the mere chronology of his works, Bunyan belongs in our next period, but in his case mere chronology must be disregarded.

Bunyan was born in 1628 at the village of Elstow, just outside of Bedford, in central England. After very slight schooling and some practice at his father's trade of tinker, he was in 1644 drafted for two years and a half into garrison service in the Parliamentary army.

Released from this occupation, he married a poor but excellent wife and worked at his trade; but the important experiences of his life were the religious ones. Endowed by nature with great moral sensitiveness, he was nevertheless a person of violent impulses and had early fallen into profanity and laxity of conduct, which he later described with great exaggeration as a condition of abandoned wickedness.

But from childhood his abnormally active dramatic imagination had tormented him with dreams and fears of devils and hell-fire, and now he entered on a long and agonizing struggle between his religious instinct and his obstinate self-will. He has told the whole story in his spiritual autobiography, 'Grace Abounding to the Chief of Sinners,' which is one of the notable religious books of the world. A reader of it must be filled about equally with admiration for the force of will and perseverance that enabled Bunyan at last to win his battle, and pity for the fantastic morbidness that created out of next to nothing most of his well-nigh intolerable tortures.

One Sunday, for example, fresh from a sermon on Sabbath observance, he was engaged in a game of 'cat,' when he suddenly heard within himself the question, 'Wilt thou leave thy sins and go to heaven, or have thy sins and go to hell?' Stupefied, he looked up to the sky and seemed there to see the Lord Jesus gazing at him 'hotly displeased' and threatening punishment. Again, one of his favorite diversions was to watch bellmen ringing the chimes in the church steeples, and though his Puritan conscience insisted that the pleasure was 'vain,' still he would not forego it. Suddenly one day as he was indulging in it the thought occurred to him that God might cause one of the bells to fall and kill him, and he hastened to shield himself by standing under a beam. But, he reflected, the bell might easily rebound from the wall and strike him; so he shifted his position to the steeple-door. Then 'it came into his head, "How if the steeple itself should fall?"' and with that he fled alike from the controversy and the danger.

Relief came when at the age of twenty-four he joined a non-sectarian church in Bedford (his own point of view being Baptist). A man of so energetic spirit could not long remain inactive, and within two years he was preaching in the surrounding villages. A dispute with the Friends had already led to the beginning of his controversial writing when in 1660 the Restoration rendered preaching by persons outside the communion of the Church of England illegal, and he was arrested and imprisoned in Bedford jail. Consistently refusing to give the promise of submission and abstention from preaching which at any time would have secured his release, he continued in prison for twelve years, not suffering particular discomfort and working for the support of his family by fastening the ends onto shoestrings.

During this time he wrote and published several of the most important of his sixty books and pamphlets. At last, in 1672, the authorities abandoned the ineffective requirement of conformity, and he was released and became pastor of his church. Three years later he was again imprisoned for six months, and it was at that time that he composed the first part of 'The Pilgrim's Progress,' which was published in 1678. During the remaining ten years of his life his reputation and authority among the Dissenters almost equalled his earnest devotion and kindness, and won for him from his opponents the good-naturedly jocose title of 'the Baptist bishop.' He died in 1688.

Several of Bunyan's books are strong, but none of the others is to be named together with 'The Pilgrim's Progress.' This has been translated into nearly or quite a hundred languages and dialects--a record never approached by any other book of English authorship. The sources of its power are obvious. It is the intensely sincere presentation by a man of tremendous moral energy of what he believed to be the one subject of eternal and incalculable importance to every human being, the subject namely of personal salvation. Its language and style, further, are founded on the noble and simple model of the English Bible, which was almost the only book that Bunyan knew, and with which his whole being was saturated. His triumphant and loving joy in his religion enables him often to attain the poetic beauty and eloquence of his original; but both by instinct and of set purpose he rendered his own style even more simple and direct, partly by the use of homely vernacular expressions.

What he had said in 'Grace Abounding' is equally true here: 'I could have stepped into a style much higher... but I dare not. God did not play in convincing of me... wherefore I may not play in my relating of these experiences.' 'Pilgrim's Progress' is perfectly intelligible to any child, and further, it is highly dramatic and picturesque. It is, to be sure, an allegory, but one of those allegories which seem inherent in the human mind and hence more natural than the most direct narrative. For all men life is indeed a journey, and the Slough of Despond, Doubting Castle, Vanity Fair, and the Valley of Humiliation are places where in one sense or another every human soul has often struggled and suffered; so that every reader goes hand in hand with Christian and his friends, fears for them in their dangers and rejoices in their escapes.

The incidents, however, have all the further fascination of supernatural romance; and the union of this element with the homely sincerity of the style accounts for much of the peculiar quality of the book. Universal in its appeal, absolutely direct and vivid in manner--such a work might well become, as it speedily did, one of the most famous of world classics. It is interesting to learn, therefore, that Bunyan had expected its circulation to be confined to the common people; the early editions are as cheap as possible in paper, printing, and illustrations. Criticism, no doubt, easily discovers in 'Pilgrim's Progress' technical faults. The story often lacks the full development and balance of incidents and narration which a trained literary artist would have given it; the allegory is inconsistent in a hundred ways and places; the characters are only types; and Bunyan, always more preacher than artist, is distinctly unfair to the bad ones among them.

But these things are unimportant. Every allegory is inconsistent, and Bunyan repeatedly takes pains to emphasize that this is a dream; while the simplicity of character-treatment increases the directness of the main effect. When all is said, the book remains the greatest example in literature of what absolute earnestness may make possible for a plain and untrained man. Nothing, of course, can alter the fundamental distinctions. 'Paradise Lost' is certainly greater than 'Pilgrim's Progress,' because it is the work of a poet and a scholar as well as a religious enthusiast. But 'Pilgrim's Progress,' let it be said frankly, will always find a dozen readers where Milton has one by choice, and no man can afford to think otherwise than respectfully of achievements which speak powerfully and nobly to the underlying instincts and needs of all mankind.

The naturalness of the allegory, it may be added, renders the resemblance of 'Pilgrim's Progress' to many previous treatments of the same theme and to less closely parallel works like 'The Faerie Queene' probably accidental; in any significant sense Bunyan probably had no other source than the Bible and his own imagination.

# 9

# The Restoration

## GENERAL CONDITIONS AND CHARACTERISTICS

The repudiation of the Puritan rule by the English people and the Restoration of the Stuart kings in the person of Charles II, in 1660, mark one of the most decisive changes in English life and literature. The preceding half century had really been transitional, and during its course, as we have seen, the Elizabethan adventurous energy and half-naif greatness of spirit had more and more disappeared. With the coming of Charles II the various tendencies which had been replacing these forces seemed to crystallize into their almost complete opposites. This was true to a large extent throughout the country; but it was especially true of London and the Court party, to which literature of most sorts was now to be perhaps more nearly limited than ever before.

The revolt of the nation was directed partly against the irresponsible injustice of the Puritan military government but largely also against the excessive moral severity of the whole Puritan regime. Accordingly a large part of the nation, but particularly the Court, now plunged into an orgy of self-indulgence in which moral restraints almost ceased to be regarded. The new king and his nobles had not only been led by years of proscription and exile to hate on principle everything that bore the name of Puritan, but had spent their exile at the French Court, where utterly cynical and selfish pursuit of pleasure and licentiousness of conduct were merely masked by conventionally polished manners.

The upshot was that the quarter century of the renewed Stuart rule was in almost all respects the most disgraceful period of English history and life. In everything, so far as possible, the restored Cavaliers turned their backs on their immediate predecessors. The Puritans, in particular, had inherited the enthusiasm which had largely made the greatness of the Elizabethan period but had in great measure shifted it into the channel of their religion. Hence to the Restoration courtiers enthusiasm and outspoken emotion seemed marks of hypocrisy and barbarism. In opposition to such tendencies they aimed to realize the ideal of the man of the world, sophisticated, skeptical, subjecting everything to the scrutiny of the reason, and above all, well-bred. Well-bred, that is, according to the artificial social standards of a selfish aristocratic class; for the actual manners of the courtiers, as of such persons at all times, were in many respects disgustingly crude.

In religion most of them professed adherence to the English Church (some to the Catholic), but it was a conventional adherence to an institution of the State and a badge of party allegiance, not a matter of spiritual conviction or of any really deep feeling. The Puritans, since they refused to return to the English (Established) Church, now became known as Dissenters.

The men of the Restoration, then, deliberately repudiated some of the chief forces which seem to a romantic age to make life significant. As a natural corollary they concentrated their interest on the sphere of the practical and the actual. In science, particularly, they continued with marked success the work of Bacon and his followers. Very shortly after the Restoration the Royal Society was founded for the promotion of research and scientific knowledge, and it was during this period that Sir Isaac Newton (a man in every respect admirable) made his vastly important discoveries in physics, mathematics, and astronomy.

In literature, both prose and verse, the rationalistic and practical spirit showed itself in the enthroning above everything else of the principles of utility and common sense in substance and straightforward directness in style. The imaginative treatment of the spiritual life, as in 'Paradise Lost' or 'The Faerie Queene,' or the impassioned exaltation of imaginative beauty, as in much Elizabethan poetry, seemed to the typical men of the Restoration unsubstantial and meaningless, and they had no ambition to attempt flights in those realms. In anything beyond the tangible affairs of visible life, indeed, they had little real belief, and they preferred that literature should restrain itself within the safe limits of the known and the demonstrable.

Hence the characteristic Restoration verse is satire of a prosaic sort which scarcely belongs to poetry at all. More fortunate results of the prevailing spirit were the gradual abandonment of the conceits and irregularities of the 'metaphysical' poets, and, most important, the perfecting of the highly regular rimed pentameter couplet, the one great formal achievement of the time in verse. In prose style the same tendencies resulted in a distinct advance. Thitherto English prose had seldom attained to thorough conciseness and order; it had generally been more or less formless or involved in sentence structure or pretentious in general manner; but the Restoration writers substantially formed the more logical and clear-cut manner which, generally speaking, has prevailed ever since.

Quite consistent with this commonsense spirit, as the facts were then interpreted, was the allegiance which Restoration writers rendered to the literature of classical antiquity, an allegiance which has gained for this period and the following half-century, where the same attitude was still more strongly emphasized, the name 'pseudo-classical.' We have before noted that the enthusiasm for Greek and Latin literature which so largely underlay the Renaissance took in Ben Jonson and his followers, in part, the form of a careful imitation of the external technique of the classical writers. In France and Italy at the same time this tendency was still stronger and much more general.

The seventeenth century was the great period of French tragedy (Corneille and Racine), which attempted to base itself altogether on classical tragedy. Still more representative, however, were the numerous Italian and French critics, who elaborated a complex system of rules, among them, for tragedy, those of the 'three unities,' which they believed to dominate classic literature. Many of these rules were trivial and absurd, and the insistence of the critics upon them showed an unfortunate inability to grasp the real spirit of the classic, especially of Greek literature. In all this, English writers and critics of the Restoration period and the next half-century very commonly followed the French and Italians deferentially. Hence it is that the literature of the time is pseudo-classical (false classical) rather than true classical. But this reduction of art to strict order and decorum, it should be clear, was quite in accord with the whole spirit of the time.

One particular social institution of the period snould be mentioned for its connection with literature, namely the coffee houses, which, introduced about the middle of the century, soon became very popular and influential. They were, in our own idiom, cafes, where men met to sip coffee or chocolate and discuss current topics. Later, in the next century, they often developed into clubs.

**MINOR WRITERS**

The contempt which fell upon the Puritans as a deposed and unpopular party found stinging literary expression in one of the most famous of English satires, Samuel Butler's 'Hudibras.' Butler, a reserved and saturnine man, spent much of his uneventful life in the employ (sometimes as steward) of gentlemen and nobles, one of whom, a Puritan officer, Sir Samuel Luke, was to serve as the central lay-figure for his lampoon.

'Hudibras,' which appeared in three parts during a period of fifteen years, is written, like previous English satires, in rough-and-ready doggerel verse, in this case verse of octosyllabic couplets and in the form of a mock-epic. It ridicules the intolerance and sanctimonious hypocrisy of the Puritans as the Cavaliers insisted on seeing them in the person of the absurd Sir Hudibras and his squire Ralph (partly suggested by Cervantes' Don Quixote and Sancho).

These sorry figures are made to pass very unheroically through a series of burlesque adventures. The chief power of the production lies in its fire of witty epigrams, many of which have become familiar quotations, for example:

*He could distinguish, and divide, A hair 'twixt south and south-west side.*

*Compound for sins they are inclined to By damning those they have no mind to.*

Though the king and Court took unlimited delight in 'Hudibras' they displayed toward Butler their usual ingratitude and allowed him to pass his latter years in obscure poverty. Some of the other central characteristics of the age appear in a unique book, the voluminous 'Diary' which Samuel Pepys (pronounced Peps), a typical representative of the thrifty and unimaginative citizen class, kept in shorthand for ten years beginning in 1660. Pepys, who ultimately became Secretary to the Admiralty, and was a hard-working and very able naval official, was also astonishingly naif and vain. In his 'Diary' he records in the greatest detail, without the least reserve (and with no idea of publication) all his daily doings, public and private, and a large part of his thoughts.

The absurdities and weaknesses, together with the better traits, of a man spiritually shallow and yet very human are here revealed with a frankness unparalleled and almost incredible. Fascinating as a psychological study, the book also affords the fullest possible information about all the life of the period, especially the familiar life, not on dress-parade. In rather sharp contrast stands the 'Diary' of John Evelyn, which in much shorter space and virtually only in a series of glimpses covers seventy years of time. Evelyn was a real gentleman and scholar who occupied an honorable position in national life; his 'Diary,' also, furnishes a record, but a dignified record, of his public and private experience.

## THE RESTORATION DRAMA

The moral anarchy of the period is most strikingly exhibited in its drama, particularly in its comedy and 'comedy of manners.' These plays, dealing mostly with love-actions in the setting of the Court or of fashionable London life, and carrying still further the general spirit of those of Fletcher and Shirley a generation or two earlier, deliberately ridicule moral principles and institutions, especially marriage, and are always in one degree or another grossly indecent. Technically they are often clever; according to that definition of literature which includes a moral standard, they are not literature at all.

## JOHN DRYDEN, 1631-1700

No other English literary period is so thoroughly represented and summed up in the works of a single man as is the Restoration period in John Dryden, a writer in some respects akin to Ben Jonson, of prolific and vigorous talent without the crowning quality of genius.

Dryden, the son of a family of Northamptonshire country gentry, was born in 1631. From Westminster School and Cambridge he went, at about the age of twenty-six and possessed by inheritance of a minimum living income, to London, where he perhaps hoped to get political preferment through his relatives in the Puritan party. His serious entrance into literature was made comparatively late, in 1659, with a eulogizing poem on Cromwell on the occasion of the latter's death. When, the next year, Charles II was restored, Dryden shifted to the Royalist side and wrote some poems in honor of the king. Dryden's character should not be judged from this incident and similar ones in his later life too hastily nor without regard to the spirit of the times. Aside from the fact that Dryden had never professed, probably, to be a radical Puritan, he certainly was not, like Milton and Bunyan, a heroic person, nor endowed with deep and dynamic convictions; on the other hand, he was very far from being base or dishonorable--no one can read his works attentively without being impressed by their spirit of straightforward manliness.

Controlled, like his age, by cool common sense and practical judgment, he kept his mind constantly open to new impressions, and was more concerned to avoid the appearance of bigotry and unreason than to maintain that of consistency. In regard to politics and even religion he evidently shared the opinion, bred in many of his contemporaries by the wasteful strife of the previous generations, that beyond a few fundamental matters the good citizen should make no close scrutiny of details but rather render loyal support to the established institutions of the State, by which peace is preserved and anarchy restrained. Since the nation had recalled Charles II, overthrown Puritanism, and reestablished the Anglican Church, it probably appeared to Dryden an act of patriotism as well as of expediency to accept its decision.

Dryden's marriage with the daughter of an earl, two or three years after the Restoration, secured his social position, and for more than fifteen years thereafter his life was outwardly successful. He first turned to the drama. In spite of the prohibitory Puritan law (above, p. 150), a facile writer, Sir William Davenant, had begun, cautiously, a few years before the Restoration, to produce operas and other works of dramatic nature; and the returning Court had brought from Paris a passion for the stage, which therefore offered the best and indeed the only field for remunerative literary effort. Accordingly, although Dryden himself frankly admitted that his talents were not especially adapted to writing plays, he proceeded to do so energetically, and continued at it, with diminishing productivity, nearly down to the end of his life, thirty-five years later.

But his activity always found varied outlets. He secured a lucrative share in the profits of the King's Playhouse, one of the two theaters of the time which alone were allowed to present regular plays, and he held the mainly honorary positions of poet laureate and historiographer-royal. Later, like Chaucer, he was for a time collector of the customs of the port of London.

He was not much disturbed by 'The Rehearsal,' a burlesque play brought out by the Duke of Buckingham and other wits to ridicule current dramas and dramatists, in which he figured as chief butt under the name 'Bayes' (poet laureate); and he took more than full revenge ten years later when in 'Absalom and Achitophel' he drew the portrait of Buckingham as Zimri. But in 1680 an outrage of which he was the victim, a brutal and unprovoked beating inflicted by ruffians in the employ of the Earl of Rochester, seems to mark a permanent change for the worse in his fortunes, a change not indeed to disaster but to a permanent condition of doubtful prosperity.

The next year he became engaged in political controversy, which resulted in the production of his most famous work. Charles II was without a legitimate child, and the heir to the throne was his brother, the Duke of York, who a few years later actually became king as James II. But while Charles was outwardly, for political reasons, a member of the Church of England (at heart he was a Catholic), the Duke of York was a professed and devoted Catholic, and the powerful Whig party, strongly Protestant, was violently opposed to him. The monstrous fiction of a 'Popish Plot,' brought forward by Titus Oates, and the murderous frenzy which it produced, were demonstrations of the strength of the Protestant feeling, and the leader of the Whigs, the Earl of Shaftesbury, proposed that the Duke of York should be excluded by law from the succession to the throne in favor of the Duke of Monmouth, one of the king's illegitimate sons.

At last, in 1681, the nation became afraid of another civil war, and the king was enabled to have Shaftesbury arrested on the charge of treason. Hereupon Dryden, at the suggestion, it is said, of the king, and with the purpose of securing Shaftesbury's conviction, put forth the First Part of 'Absalom and Achitophel,' a masterly satire of Shaftesbury, Monmouth, and their associates in the allegorical disguise of the (somewhat altered) Biblical story of David and Absalom.

In 1685 Charles died and James succeeded him. At about the same time Dryden became a Catholic, a change which laid him open to the suspicion of truckling for royal favor, though in fact he had nothing to gain by it and its chief effect was to identify him with a highly unpopular minority. He had already, in 1682, written a didactic poem, 'Religio Laici' (A Layman's Religion), in which he set forth his reasons for adhering to the English Church. Now, in 1687, he published the much longer allegorical 'Hind and the Panther,' a defense of the Catholic Church and an attack on the English Church and the Dissenters.

The next year, King James was driven from the throne, his daughter Mary and her husband, William, Prince of Orange, succeeded him, and the supremacy of the Church of England was again assured. Dryden remained constant to Catholicism and his refusal to take the oath of allegiance to the new rulers cost him all his public offices and reduced him for the rest of his life to comparative poverty. He had the further mortification of seeing the very Shadwell whom he had so unsparingly ridiculed replace him as poet laureate.

These reverses, however, he met with his characteristic manly fortitude, and of his position as the acknowledged head of English letters he could not be deprived; his chair at 'Will's' coffee-house was the throne of an unquestioned monarch. His industry, also, stimulated by necessity, was unabated to the end. Among other work he continued, in accordance with the taste of the age, to make verse translations from the chief Latin poets, and in 1697 he brought out a version of all the poems of Vergil. He died in 1700, and his death may conveniently be taken, with substantial accuracy, as marking the end of the Restoration period.

Variety, fluency, and not ungraceful strength are perhaps the chief qualities of Dryden's work, displayed alike in his verse and in his prose. Since he was primarily a poet it is natural to speak first of his verse; and we must begin with a glance at the history of the rimed pentameter couplet, which he carried to the highest point of effectiveness thus far attained. This form had been introduced into English, probably from French, by Chaucer, who used it in many thousand lines of the 'Canterbury Tales.' It was employed to some extent by the Elizabethans, especially in scattered passages of their dramas, and in some poems of the early seventeenth century. Up to that time it generally had a free form, with frequent 'running-on' of the sense from one line to the next and marked irregularity of pauses. The process of developing it into the representative pseudo-classical measure of Dryden and Pope consisted in making the lines, or at least the couplets, generally end-stopt, and in securing a general regular movement, mainly by eliminating pronounced pauses within the line, except for the frequent organic cesura in the middle.

This process, like other pseudo-classical tendencies, was furthered by Ben Jonson, who used the couplet in more than half of his non-dramatic verse; but it was especially carried on by the wealthy politician and minor poet Edmund Waller (above, page 164), who for sixty years, from 1623 on, wrote most of his verse (no very great quantity) in the couplet. Dryden and all his contemporaries gave to Waller, rather too unreservedly, the credit of having first perfected the form, that is of first making it (to their taste) pleasingly smooth and regular. The great danger of the couplet thus treated is that of over-great conventionality, as was partly illustrated by Dryden's successor, Pope, who carried Waller's method to the farthest possible limit.

Dryden's vigorous instincts largely saved him from this fault; by skilful variations in accents and pauses and by terse forcefulness of expression he gave the couplet firmness as well as smoothness. He employed, also, two other more questionable means of variety, namely, the insertion (not original with him) of occasional Alexandrine lines and of frequent triplets, three lines instead of two riming together. A present-day reader may like the pentameter couplet or may find it frigid and tedious; at any rate Dryden employed it in the larger part of his verse and stamped it unmistakably with the strength of his strong personality.

In satiric and didactic verse Dryden is accepted as the chief English master, and here 'Absalom and Achitophel' is his greatest achievement. It is formally a narrative poem, but in fact almost nothing happens in it; it is really expository and descriptive--a very clever partisan analysis of a situation, enlivened by a series of the most skilful character sketches with very decided partisan coloring. The sketches, therefore, offer an interesting contrast with the sympathetic and humorous portraits of Chaucer's 'Prolog.' Among the secrets of Dryden's success in this particular field are his intellectual coolness, his vigorous masculine power of seizing on the salient points of character, and his command of terse, biting phraseology, set off by effective contrast.

Of Dryden's numerous comedies and 'tragi-comedies' (serious plays with a sub-action of comedy) it may be said summarily that some of them were among the best of their time but that they were as licentious as all the others. Dryden was also the chief author of another kind of play, peculiar to this period in England, namely the 'Heroic' (Epic) Play. The material and spirit of these works came largely from the enormously long contemporary French romances, which were widely read in England, and of which a prominent representative was 'The Great Cyrus' of Mlle. de Scudery, in ten volumes of a thousand pages or more apiece.

These romances, carrying further the tendency which appears in Sidney's 'Arcadia,' are among the most extravagant of all products of the romantic imagination--strange melanges of ancient history, medieval chivalry, pastoralism, seventeenth century artificial manners, and allegory of current events. The English 'heroic' plays, partly following along these lines, with influence also from Fletcher, lay their scenes in distant countries; their central interest is extravagant romantic love; the action is more that of epic adventure than of tragedy; and incidents, situations, characters, sentiments, and style, though not without power, are exaggerated or overstrained to an absurd degree. Breaking so violently through the commonplaceness and formality of the age, however, they offer eloquent testimony to the irrepressibility of the romantic instinct in human nature. Dryden's most representative play of this class is 'Almanzor and Almahide, or the Conquest of Granada,' in two long five-act parts.

We need do no more than mention two or three very bad adaptations of plays of Shakspere to the Restoration taste in which Dryden had a hand; but his most enduring dramatic work is his 'All for Love, or the World Well Lost,' where he treats without direct imitation, though in conscious rivalry, the story which Shakspere used in 'Antony and Cleopatra.' The two plays afford an excellent illustration of the contrast between the spirits of their periods. Dryden's undoubtedly has much force and real feeling; but he follows to a large extent the artificial rules of the pseudo-classical French tragedies and critics. He observes the 'three unities' with considerable closeness, and he complicates the love-action with new elements of Restoration jealousy and questions of formal honor. Altogether, the twentieth century reader finds in 'All for Love' a strong and skilful play, ranking, nevertheless, with its somewhat formal rhetoric and conventional atmosphere, far below Shakspere's less regular but magnificently emotional and imaginative masterpiece.

A word must be added about the form of Dryden's plays. In his comedies and in comic portions of the others he, like other English dramatists, uses prose, for its suggestion of every-day reality. In plays of serious tone he often turns to blank verse, and this is the meter of 'All for Love.' But early in his dramatic career he, almost contemporaneously with other dramatists, introduced the rimed couplet, especially in his heroic plays. The innovation was due in part to the influence of contemporary French tragedy, whose riming Alexandrine couplet is very similar in effect to the English couplet. About the suitability of the English couplet to the drama there has always been difference of critical opinion; but most English readers feel that it too greatly interrupts the flow of the speeches and is not capable of the dignity and power of blank verse. Dryden himself, at any rate, finally grew tired of it and returned to blank verse. Dryden's work in other forms of verse, also, is of high quality. In his dramas he inserted songs whose lyric sweetness is reminiscent of the similar songs of Fletcher. Early in his career he composed (in pentameter quatrains of alternate rime, like Gray's 'Elegy') 'Annus Mirabilis' (The Wonderful Year--namely 1666), a long and vigorous though far from faultless narrative of the war with the Dutch and of the Great Fire of London.

More important are the three odes in the 'irregular Pindaric' form introduced by Cowley. The first, that to Mrs. (i. e., Miss) Anne Killigrew, one of the Queen's maids of honor, is full, thanks to Cowley's example, of 'metaphysical' conceits and science. The two later ones, 'Alexander's Feast' and the 'Song for St. Cecilia's Day,' both written for a musical society's annual festival in honor of the patron saint of their art, are finely spirited and among the most striking, though not most delicate, examples of onomatopoeia in all poetry.

Dryden's prose, only less important than his verse, is mostly in the form of long critical essays, virtually the first in English, which are prefixed to many of his plays and poems. In them, following French example, he discusses fundamental questions of poetic art or of general esthetics. His opinions are judicious; independent, so far as the despotic authority of the French critics permitted, at least honest; and interesting. Mcst important, perhaps, is his attitude toward the French pseudo-classical formulas. He accepted French theory even in details which we now know to be absurd--agreed, for instance, that even Homer wrote to enforce an abstract moral (namely that discord destroys a state). In the field of his main interest, further, his reason was persuaded by the pseudo-classical arguments that English (Elizabethan) tragedy, with its violent contrasts and irregularity, was theoretically wrong. Nevertheless his greatness consists throughout partly in the common sense which he shares with the best English critics and thinkers of all periods; and as regards tragedy he concludes, in spite of rules and theory, that he 'loves Shakspere.'

In expression, still again, Dryden did perhaps more than any other man to form modern prose style, a style clear, straightforward, terse, forceful, easy and simple and yet dignified, fluent in vocabulary, varied, and of pleasing rhythm.

Dryden's general quality and a large part of his achievement are happily summarized in Lowell's epigram that he 'was the greatest poet who ever was or ever could be made wholly out of prose.' He can never again be a favorite with the general reading-public; but he will always remain one of the conspicuous figures in the history of English literature.

## THE OTHER DRAMATISTS

The other dramatists of the Restoration period may be dismissed with a few words. In tragedy the overdrawn but powerful plays of Thomas Otway, a man of short and pathetic life, and of Nathaniel Lee, are alone of any importance. In comedy, during the first part of the period, stand Sir George Etherege and William Wycherley. The latter's 'Country Wife' has been called the most heartless play ever written. To the next generation and the end of the period (or rather of the Restoration literature, which actually lasted somewhat beyond 1700), belong William Congreve, a master of sparkling wit, Sir John Vanbrugh, and George Farquhar.

So corrupt a form of writing as the Restoration comedy could not continue to flaunt itself indefinitely. The growing indignation was voiced from time to time in published protests, of which the last, in 1698, was the over-zealous but powerful 'Short View of the Immorality and Profaneness of the English Stage' by Jeremy Collier, which carried the more weight because the author was not a Puritan but a High-Church bishop and partisan of the Stuarts. Partly as a result of such attacks and partly by the natural course of events the pendulum, by the end of the period, was swinging back, and not long thereafter Restoration comedy died and the stage was left free for more decent, though, as it proved, not for greater, productions.

**10**

# Pseudo-classicism and the Beginnings of Modern Romanticism

## POLITICAL CONDITIONS

During the first part of the eighteenth century the direct connection between politics and literature was closer than at any previous period of English life; for the practical spirit of the previous generation continued to prevail, so that the chief writers were very ready to concern themselves with the affairs of State, and in the uncertain strife of parties ministers were glad to enlist their aid. On the death of King William in 1702, Anne, sister of his wife Queen Mary and daughter of James II, became Queen. Unlike King William she was a Tory and at first filled offices with members of that party. But the English campaigns under the Duke of Marlborough against Louis XIV were supported by the Whigs, who therefore gradually regained control, and in 1708 the Queen had to submit to a Whig ministry.

She succeeded in ousting them in 1710, and a Tory cabinet was formed by Henry Harley (afterwards Earl of Oxford) and Henry St. John (afterwards Viscount Bolingbroke). On the death of Anne in 1714 Bolingbroke, with other Tories, was intriguing for a second restoration of the Stuarts in the person of the son of James II (the 'Old Pretender'). But the nation decided for a Protestant German prince, a descendant of James I through his daughter Elizabeth, and this prince was crowned as George I--an event which brought England peace at the price of a century of rule by an unenlightened and sordid foreign dynasty. The Tories were violently turned out of office; Oxford was imprisoned, and Bolingbroke, having fled to the Pretender, was declared a traitor. Ten years later he was allowed to come back and attempted to oppose Robert Walpole, the Whig statesman who for twenty years governed England in the name of the first two Georges; but in the upshot Bolingbroke was again obliged to retire to France. How closely these events were connected with the fortunes of the foremost authors we shall see as we proceed.

## THE GENERAL SPIRIT OF THE PERIOD

The writers of the reigns of Anne and George I called their period the Augustan Age, because they flattered themselves that with them English life and literature had reached a culminating period of civilization and elegance corresponding to that which existed at Rome under the Emperor Augustus. They believed also that both in the art of living and in literature they had rediscovered and were practising the principles of the best periods of Greek and Roman life. In our own time this judgment appears equally arrogant and mistaken. In reality the men of the early eighteenth century, like those of the Restoration, largely misunderstood the qualities of the classical spirit, and thinking to reproduce them attained only a superficial, pseudo-classical, imitation. The main characteristics of the period and its literature continue, with some further development, those of the Restoration, and may be summarily indicated as follows:

1. Interest was largely centered in the practical well-being either of society as a whole or of one's own social class or set. The majority of writers, furthermore, belonged by birth or association to the upper social stratum and tended to overemphasize its artificial conventions, often looking with contempt on the other classes. To them conventional good breeding, fine manners, the pleasures of the leisure class, and the standards of 'The Town' (fashionable London society) were the only part of life much worth regarding.
2. The men of this age carried still further the distrust and dislike felt by the previous generation for emotion, enthusiasm, and strong individuality both in life and in literature, and exalted Reason and Regularity as their guiding stars. The terms 'decency' and 'neatness' were forever on their lips. They sought a conventional

uniformity in manners, speech, and indeed in nearly everything else, and were uneasy if they deviated far from the approved, respectable standards of the body of their fellows. Great poetic imagination, therefore, could scarcely exist among them, or indeed supreme greatness of any sort.

3. They had little appreciation for external Nature or for any beauty except that of formalized Art. A forest seemed to most of them merely wild and gloomy, and great mountains chiefly terrible, but they took delight in gardens of artificially trimmed trees and in regularly plotted and alternating beds of domestic flowers. The Elizabethans also, as we have seen, had had much more feeling for the terror than for the grandeur of the sublime in Nature, but the Elizabethans had had nothing of the elegant primness of the Augustans.
4. In speech and especially in literature, most of all in poetry, they were given to abstractness of thought and expression, intended to secure elegance, but often serving largely to substitute superficiality for definiteness and significant meaning. They abounded in personifications of abstract qualities and ideas ('Laughter, heavenly maid,' Honor, Glory, Sorrow, and so on, with prominent capital letters), a sort of a pseudo-classical substitute for emotion.
5. They were still more fully confirmed than the men of the Restoration in the conviction that the ancients had attained the highest possible perfection in literature, and some of them made absolute submission of judgment to the ancients, especially to the Latin poets and the Greek, Latin, and also the seventeenth century classicizing French critics. Some authors seemed timidly to desire to be under authority and to glory in surrendering their independence, individuality, and originality to foreign and long-established leaders and principles.
6. Under these circumstances the effort to attain the finished beauty of classical literature naturally resulted largely in a more or less shallow formal smoothness.

7. There was a strong tendency to moralizing, which also was not altogether free from conventionality and superficiality.

Although the 'Augustan Age' must be considered to end before the middle of the century, the same spirit continued dominant among many writers until near its close, so that almost the whole of the century may be called the period of pseudo-classicism.

**DANIEL DEFOE**

The two earliest notable writers of the period, however, though they display some of these characteristics, were men of strong individual traits which in any age would have directed them largely along paths of their own choosing. The first of them is Daniel Defoe, who belongs, furthermore, quite outside the main circle of high-bred and polished fashion.

Defoe was born in London about 1660, the son of James Foe, a butcher, to whose name the son arbitrarily and with characteristic eye to effect prefixed the 'De' in middle life. Educated for the Dissenting ministry, Defoe, a man of inexhaustible practical energy, engaged instead in several successive lines of business, and at the age of thirty-five, after various vicissitudes, was in prosperous circumstances. He now became a pamphleteer in support of King William and the Whigs. His first very significant work, a satire against the High-Church Tories entitled 'The Shortest Way with Dissenters,' belongs early in the reign of Queen Anne. Here, parodying extreme Tory bigotry, he argued, with apparent seriousness, that the Dissenters should all be hanged. The Tories were at first delighted, but when they discovered the hoax became correspondingly indignant and Defoe was set in the pillory, and (for a short time) imprisoned. In this confinement he began The Review, a newspaper which he continued for eleven years and whose department called 'The Scandal Club' suggested 'The Tatler' to Steele.

During many years following his release Defoe issued an enormous number of pamphlets and acted continuously as a secret agent and spy of the government. Though he was always at heart a thorough-going Dissenter and Whig, he served all the successive governments, Whig and Tory, alike; for his character and point of view were those of the 'practical' journalist and middle-class money-getter. This of course means that all his professed principles were superficial, or at least secondary, that he was destitute of real religious feeling and of the gentleman's sense of honor.

Defoe's influence in helping to shape modern journalism and modern every-day English style was large; but the achievement which has given him world-wide fame came late in life. In 1706 he had written a masterly short story, 'The Apparition of Mrs. Veal.' Its real purpose, characteristically enough, was the concealed one of promoting the sale of an unsuccessful religious book, but its literary importance lies first in the extraordinarily convincing mass of minute details which it casts about an incredible incident and second in the complete knowledge (sprung from Defoe's wide experience in journalism, politics, and business) which it displays of a certain range of middle-class characters and ideas.

It is these same elements, together with the vigorous presentation and emphasis of basal practical virtues, that distinguished 'Robinson Crusoe,' of which the First Part appeared in 1719, when Defoe was nearly or quite sixty years of age. The book, which must have been somewhat influenced by 'Pilgrim's Progress,' was more directly suggested by a passage in William Dampier's 'Voyage Round the World,' and also, as every one knows, by the experience of Alexander Selkirk, a sailor who, set ashore on the island of Juan Fernandez, off the coast of Chile, had lived there alone from 1709 to 1713. Selkirk's story had been briefly told in the year of his return in a newspaper of Steele, 'The Englishman'; it was later to inspire the most famous poem of William Cowper. 'Robinson Crusoe,' however, turned the material to account in a much larger, more clever, and more striking fashion.

Its success was immediate and enormous, both with the English middle class and with a wider circle of readers in the other European countries; it was followed by numerous imitations and it will doubtless always continue to be one of the best known of world classics. The precise elements of its power can be briefly indicated. As a story of unprecedented adventure in a distant and unknown region it speaks thrillingly to the universal human sense of romance. Yet it makes a still stronger appeal to the instinct for practical, every-day realism which is the controlling quality in the English dissenting middle class for whom Defoe was writing. Defoe has put himself with astonishingly complete dramatic sympathy into the place of his hero.

In spite of not a few errors and oversights (due to hasty composition) in the minor details of external fact, he has virtually lived Crusoe's life with him in imagination and he therefore makes the reader also pass with Crusoe through all his experiences, his fears, hopes and doubts. Here also, as we have implied, Defoe's vivid sense for external minutiae plays an important part. He tells precisely how many guns and cheeses and flasks of spirit Crusoe brought away from the wreck, how many days or weeks he spent in making his earthen vessels and his canoe--in a word, thoroughly actualizes the whole story. More than this, the book strikes home to the English middle class because it records how a plain Englishman completely mastered apparently insuperable obstacles through the plain virtues of courage, patience, perseverance, and mechanical ingenuity.

Further, it directly addresses the dissenting conscience in its emphasis on religion and morality. This is none the less true because the religion and morality are of the shallow sort characteristic of Defoe, a man who, like Crusoe, would have had no scruples about selling into slavery a dark-skinned boy who had helped him to escape from the same condition. Of any really delicate or poetic feeling, any appreciation for the finer things of life, the book has no suggestion. In style, like Defoe's other writings, it is straightforward and clear, though colloquially informal, with an entire absence of pretense or affectation. Structurally, it is a characteristic story of adventure--a series of loosely connected experiences not unified into an organic plot, and with no stress on character and little treatment of the really complex relations and struggles between opposing characters and groups of characters. Yet it certainly marks a step in the development of the modern novel, as will be indicated in the proper place.

Defoe's energy had not diminished with age and a hard life, and the success of 'Robinson Crusoe' led him to pour out a series of other works of romantic-realistic fiction. The second part of 'Robinson Crusoe' is no more satisfactory than any other similar continuation, and the third part, a collection of moralizings, is today entirely and properly forgotten. On the other hand, his usual method, the remarkable imaginative re-creation and vivifying of a host of minute details, makes of the fictitious 'Journal of the Plague Year' (1666) a piece of virtual history. Defoe's other later works are rather unworthy attempts to make profit out of his reputation and his full knowledge of the worst aspects of life; they are mostly very frank presentations of the careers of adventurers or criminals, real or fictitious. In this coarse realism they are picaresque, and in structure also they, like 'Robinson Crusoe,' are picaresque in being mere successions of adventures without artistic plot.

In Defoe's last years he suffered a great reverse of fortune, paying the full penalty for his opportunism and lack of ideals. His secret and unworthy long-standing connection with the Government was disclosed, so that his reputation was sadly blemished, and he seems to have gone into hiding, perhaps as the result of half-insane delusions. He died in 1731. His place in English literature is secure, though he owes it to the lucky accident of finding not quite too late special material exactly suited to his peculiar talent.

**JONATHAN SWIFT**

Jonathan Swift, another unique figure of very mixed traits, is like Defoe in that he connects the reign of William III with that of his successors and that, in accordance with the spirit of his age, he wrote for the most part not for literary but for practical purposes; in many other respects the two are widely different. Swift is one of the best representatives in English literature of sheer intellectual power, but his character, his aims, his environment, and the circumstances of his life denied to him also literary achievement of the greatest permanent significance. Swift, though of unmixed English descent, related to both Dryden and Robert Herrick, was born in Ireland, in 1667.

Brought up in poverty by his widowed mother, he spent the period between his fourteenth and twentieth years recklessly and without distinction at Trinity College, Dublin. From the outbreak attending the Revolution of 1688 he fled to England, where for the greater part of nine years he lived in the country as a sort of secretary to the retired statesman, Sir William Temple, who was his distant relative by marriage. Here he had plenty of time for reading, but the position of dependence and the consciousness that his great though still unformed powers of intellect and of action were rusting away in obscurity undoubtedly did much to increase the natural bitterness of his disposition. As the result of a quarrel he left Temple for a time and took holy orders, and on the death of Temple he returned to Ireland as chaplain to the English Lord Deputy.

He was eventually given several small livings and other church positions in and near Dublin, and at one of these, Laracor, he made his home for another nine years. During all this period and later the Miss Esther Johnson whom he has immortalized as 'Stella' holds a prominent place in his life. A girl of technically gentle birth, she also had been a member of Sir William Temple's household, was infatuated with Swift, and followed him to Ireland. About their intimacy there has always hung a mystery. It has been held that after many years they were secretly married, but this is probably a mistake; the essential fact seems to be that Swift, with characteristic selfishness, was willing to sacrifice any other possible prospects of 'Stella' to his own mere enjoyment of her society. It is certain, however, that he both highly esteemed her and reciprocated her affection so far as it was possible for him to love any woman.

In 1704 Swift published his first important works (written earlier, while he was living with Temple), which are among the masterpieces of his satirical genius. In 'The Battle of the Books' he supports Temple, who had taken the side of the Ancients in a hotly-debated and very futile quarrel then being carried on by French and English writers as to whether ancient or modern authors are the greater. 'The Tale of a Tub' is a keen, coarse, and violent satire on the actual irreligion of all Christian Churches. It takes the form of a burlesque history of three brothers, Peter (the Catholics, so called from St. Peter), Martin (the Lutherans and the Church of England, named from Martin Luther), and Jack (the Dissenters, who followed John Calvin); but a great part of the book is made up of irrelevant introductions and digressions in which Swift ridicules various absurdities, literary and otherwise, among them the very practice of digressions.

Swift's instinctive dominating impulse was personal ambition, and during this period he made long visits to London, attempting to push his fortunes with the Whig statesmen, who were then growing in power; attempting, that is, to secure a higher position in the Church; also, be it added, to get relief for the ill-treated English Church in Ireland. He made the friendship of Addison, who called him, perhaps rightly, 'the greatest genius of the age,' and of Steele, but he failed of his main purposes; and when in 1710 the Tories replaced the Whigs he accepted their solicitations and devoted his pen, already somewhat experienced in pamphleteering, to their service.

It should not be overlooked that up to this time, when he was already more than forty years of age, his life had been one of continual disappointment, so that he was already greatly soured. Now, in conducting a paper, 'The Examiner,' and in writing masterly political pamphlets, he found occupation for his tremendous energy and gave very vital help to the ministers. During the four years of their control of the government he remained in London on intimate terms with them, especially with Bolingbroke and Harley, exercising a very large advisory share in the bestowal of places of all sorts and in the general conduct of affairs. This was Swift's proper sphere; in the realization and exercise of power he took a fierce and deep delight.

His bearing at this time too largely reflected the less pleasant side of his nature, especially his pride and arrogance. Yet toward professed inferiors he could be kind; and real playfulness and tenderness, little evident in most of his other writings, distinguish his 'Journal to Stella,' which he wrote for her with affectionate regularity, generally every day, for nearly three years. The 'Journal' is interesting also for its record of the minor details of the life of Swift and of London in his day. His association, first and last, with literary men was unusually broad; when politics estranged him from Steele and Addison he drew close to Pope and other Tory writers in what they called the Scriblerus Club.

Despite his political success, Swift was still unable to secure the definite object of his ambition, a bishopric in England, since the levity with which he had treated holy things in 'A Tale of a Tub' had hopelessly prejudiced Queen Anne against him and the ministers could not act altogether in opposition to her wishes. In 1713 he received the unwelcome gift of the deanship of St. Patrick's Cathedral in Dublin, and the next year, when the Queen died and the Tory ministry fell, he withdrew to Dublin, as he himself bitterly said, 'to die like a poisoned rat in a hole.'

In Swift's personal life there were now events in which he again showed to very little advantage. In London he had become acquainted with a certain Hester Vanhomrigh, the 'Vanessa' of his longest poem, 'Cadenus and Vanessa' (in which 'Cadenus' is an anagram of 'Decanus,' Latin for 'Dean,' i. e., Swift). Miss Vanhomrigh, like 'Stella,' was infatuated with Swift, and like her followed him to Ireland, and for nine years, as has been said, he 'lived a double life' between the two. 'Vanessa' then died, probably of a broken heart, and 'Stella' a few years later. Over against this conduct, so far as it goes, may be set Swift's quixotic but extensive and constant personal benevolence and generosity to the poor.

In general, this last period of Swift's life amounted to thirty years of increasing bitterness. He devoted some of his very numerous pamphlets to defending the Irish, and especially the English who formed the governing class in Ireland, against oppression by England. Most important here were 'The Drapier's [i.e., Draper's, Cloth-Merchant's] Letters,' in which Swift aroused the country to successful resistance against a very unprincipled piece of political jobbery whereby a certain Englishman was to be allowed to issue a debased copper coinage at enormous profit to himself but to the certain disaster of Ireland.

'A Modest Proposal,' the proposal, namely, that the misery of the poor in Ireland should be alleviated by the raising of children for food, like pigs, is one of the most powerful, as well as one of the most horrible, satires which ever issued from any human imagination. In 1726 (seven years after 'Robinson Crusoe') appeared Swift's masterpiece, the only one of his works still widely known, namely, 'The Travels of Lemuel Gulliver.' The remarkable power of this unique work lies partly in its perfect combination of two apparently inconsistent things, first, a story of marvelous adventure which must always remain (in the first parts) one of the most popular of children's classics; and second, a bitter satire against mankind. The intensity of the satire increases as the work proceeds. In the first voyage, that to the Lilliputians, the tone is one mainly of humorous irony; but in such passages as the hideous description of the Struldbrugs in the third voyage the cynical contempt is unspeakably painful, and from the distorted libel on mankind in the Yahoos of the fourth voyage a reader recoils in indignant disgust.

During these years Swift corresponded with friends in England, among them Pope, whom he bitterly urged to 'lash the world for his sake,' and he once or twice visited England in the hope, even then, of securing a place in the Church on the English side of St. George's Channel. His last years were melancholy in the extreme. Long before, on noticing a dying tree, he had observed, with the pitiless incisiveness which would spare neither others nor himself: 'I am like that. I shall die first at the top.' His birthday he was accustomed to celebrate with lamentations. At length an obscure disease which had always afflicted him, fed in part, no doubt, by his fiery spirit and his fiery discontent, reached his brain.

After some years of increasing lethargy and imbecility, occasionally varied by fits of violent madness and terrible pain, he died in 1745, leaving all his money to found a hospital for the insane. His grave in St. Patrick's Cathedral bears this inscription of his own composing, the best possible epitome of his career: 'Ubi saeva indignatio cor ulterius lacerare nequit' (Where fierce indignation can no longer tear his heart).

The complexity of Swift's character and the great difference between the viewpoints of his age and of ours make it easy at the present time to judge him with too great harshness. Apart from his selfish egotism and his bitterness, his nature was genuinely loyal, kind and tender to friends and connections; and he hated injustice and the more flagrant kinds of hypocrisy with a sincere and irrepressible violence. Whimsicalness and a contemptuous sort of humor were as characteristic of him as biting sarcasm, and his conduct and writings often veered rapidly from the one to the other in a way puzzling to one who does not understand him. Nevertheless he was dominated by cold intellect and an instinct for the practical.

To show sentiment, except under cover, he regarded as a weakness, and it is said that when he was unable to control it he would retire from observation. He was ready to serve mankind to the utmost of his power when effort seemed to him of any avail, and at times he sacrificed even his ambition to his convictions; but he had decided that the mass of men were hopelessly foolish, corrupt, and inferior, personal sympathy with them was impossible to him, and his contempt often took the form of sardonic practical jokes, practised sometimes on a whole city. Says Sir Leslie Stephen in his life of Swift: 'His doctrine was that virtue is the one thing which deserves love and admiration, and yet that virtue in this hideous chaos of a world involves misery and decay.'

Of his extreme arrogance and brutality to those who offended him there are numerous anecdotes; not least in the case of women, whom he, like most men of his age, regarded as man's inferiors. He once drove a lady from her own parlor in tears by violent insistence that she should sing, against her will, and when he next met her, inquired, 'Pray, madam, are you as proud and ill-natured to-day as when I saw you last?' It seems, indeed, that throughout his life Swift's mind was positively abnormal, and this may help to excuse the repulsive elements in his writings. For metaphysics and abstract principles, it may be added, he had a bigoted antipathy. In religion he was a staunch and sincere High Churchman, but it was according to the formal fashion of many thinkers of his day; he looked on the Church not as a medium of spiritual life, of which he, like his generation, had little conception, but as one of the organized institutions of society, useful in maintaining decency and order.

Swift's 'poems' require only passing notice. In any strict sense they are not poems at all, since they are entirely bare of imagination, delicacy, and beauty. Instead they exhibit the typical pseudo-classical traits of matter-of-factness and clearness; also, as Swift's personal notes, cleverness, directness, trenchant intellectual power, irony, and entire ease, to which latter the prevailing octosyllabic couplet meter contributes. This is the meter of 'L'Allegro' and 'Il Penseroso,' and the contrast between these poems and Swift's is instructive.

Swift's prose style has substantially the same qualities. Writing generally as a man of affairs, for practical ends, he makes no attempt at elegance and is informal even to the appearance of looseness of expression. Of conscious refinements and also, in his stories, of technical artistic structural devices, he has no knowledge; he does not go out of the straight path in order to create suspense, he does not always explain difficulties of detail, and sometimes his narrative becomes crudely bare. He often displays the greatest imaginative power, but it is always a practical imagination; his similes, for example, are always from very matter-of-fact things. But more notable are his positive merits. He is always absolutely clear, direct, and intellectually forceful; in exposition and argument he is cumulatively irresistible; in description and narration realistically picturesque and fascinating; and he has the natural instinct for narration which gives vigorous movement and climax. Indignation and contempt often make his style burn with passion, and humor, fierce or bitterly mirthful, often enlivens it with startling flashes.

The great range of the satires which make the greater part of Swift's work is supported in part by variety of satiric method. Sometimes he pours out a savage direct attack. Sometimes, in a long ironical statement, he says exactly the opposite of what he really means to suggest. Sometimes he uses apparently logical reasoning where either, as in 'A Modest Proposal,' the proposition, or, as in the 'Argument Against Abolishing Christianity,' the arguments are absurd. He often shoots out incidental humorous or satirical shafts. But his most important and extended method is that of allegory.

The pigmy size of the Lilliputians symbolizes the littleness of mankind and their interests; the superior skill in rope-dancing which with them is the ground for political advancement, the political intrigues of real men; and the question whether eggs shall be broken on the big or the little end, which has embroiled Lilliput in a bloody war, both civil and foreign, the trivial causes of European conflicts. In Brobdingnag, on the other hand, the coarseness of mankind is exhibited by the magnifying process. Swift, like Defoe, generally increases the verisimilitude of his fictions and his ironies by careful accuracy in details, which is sometimes arithmetically genuine, sometimes only a hoax. In Lilliput all the dimensions are scientifically computed on a scale one-twelfth as large as that of man; in Brobdingnag, by an exact reversal, everything is twelve times greater than among men. But the long list of technical nautical terms which seem to make a spirited narrative at the beginning of the second of Gulliver's voyages is merely an incoherent hodge-podge.

Swift, then, is the greatest of English satirists and the only one who as a satirist claims large attention in a brief general survey of English literature. He is one of the most powerfully intellectual of all English writers, and the clear force of his work is admirable; but being first a man of affairs and only secondarily a man of letters, he stands only on the outskirts of real literature. In his character the elements were greatly mingled, and in our final judgment of him there must be combined something of disgust, something of admiration, and not a little of sympathy and pity.

### STEELE AND ADDISON AND 'THE TATLER' AND 'THE SPECTATOR'

The writings of Steele and Addison, of which the most important are their essays in 'The Tatler' and 'The Spectator,' contrast strongly with the work of Swift and are more broadly characteristic of the pseudo-classical period.

Richard Steele was born in Dublin in 1672 of an English father and an Irish mother. The Irish strain was conspicuous throughout his life in his warm-heartedness, impulsiveness and lack of self-control and practical judgment. Having lost his father early, he was sent to the Charterhouse School in London, where he made the acquaintance of Addison, and then to Oxford. He abandoned the university to enlist in the aristocratic regiment of Life Guards, and he remained in the army, apparently, for seven or eight years, though he seems not to have been in active service and became a recognized wit at the London coffee-houses.

Thackeray in 'Henry Esmond' gives interesting though freely imaginative pictures of him at this stage of his career and later. His reckless instincts and love of pleasure were rather strangely combined with a sincere theoretical devotion to religion, and his first noticeable work (1701), a little booklet called 'The

Christian Hero,' aimed, in opposition to fashionable license, to show that decency and goodness are requisites of a real gentleman. The resultant ridicule forced him into a duel (in which he seriously wounded his antagonist), and thenceforth in his writings duelling was a main object of his attacks.

During the next few years he turned with the same reforming zeal to comedy, where he attempted to exalt pure love and high ideals, though the standards of his age and class leave in his own plays much that to-day seems coarse. Otherwise his plays are by no means great; they initiated the weak 'Sentimental Comedy,' which largely dominated the English stage for the rest of the century. During this period Steele was married twice in rather rapid succession to wealthy ladies whose fortunes served only very temporarily to respite him from his chronic condition of debt and bailiff's duns.

Now succeeds the brief period of his main literary achievement. All his life a strong Whig, he was appointed in 1707 Gazetteer, or editor, of 'The London Gazette,' the official government newspaper. This led him in 1709 to start 'The Tatler.' English periodical literature, in forms which must be called the germs both of the modern newspaper and of the modern magazine, had begun in an uncertain fashion, of which the details are too complicated for record here, nearly a hundred years before, and had continued ever since with increasing vigor. The lapsing of the licensing laws in 1695 had given a special impetus.

Defoe's 'Review,' from 1704 to 1713, was devoted to many interests, including politics, the Church and commerce. Steele's 'Tatler' at first likewise dealt in each number with several subjects, such as foreign news, literary criticism, and morals, but his controlling instinct to inculcate virtue and good sense more and more asserted itself. The various departments were dated from the respective coffee-houses where those subjects were chiefly discussed, Poetry from 'Will's,' Foreign and Domestic News from 'St. James's,' and so on. The more didactic papers were ascribed to an imaginary Isaac Bickerstaff, a nom-de-plume which Steele borrowed from some of Swift's satires. Steele himself wrote two-thirds of all the papers, but before proceeding far he accepted Addison's offer of assistance and later he occasionally called in other contributors.

'The Tatler' appeared three times a week and ran for twenty-one months; it came to an end shortly after the return of the Tories to power had deprived Steele and Addison of some of their political offices. Its discontinuance may have been due to weariness on Steele's part or, since it was Whig in tone, to a desire to be done with partisan writing; at any rate, two months later, in March, 1711, of Marlborough's victory at Blenheim, secured the favor of the ministers of the day, and throughout almost all the rest of his life he held important political places, some even, thanks to Swift, during the period of Tory dominance. During his last ten years he was a member of Parliament; but though he was a delightful conversationalist in a small group of friends, he was unable to speak in public.

Addison's great fame as 'The Spectator' was increased when in 1713 he brought out the play 'Cato,' mostly written years before. This is a characteristic example of the pseudo-classical tragedies of which a few were produced during the first half of the eighteenth century. They are the stiffest and most lifeless of all forms of pseudo-classical literature; Addison, for his part, attempts not only to observe the three unities, but to follow many of the minor formal rules drawn up by the French critics, and his plot, characterization, and language are alike excessively pale and frigid. Paleness and frigidity, however, were taken for beauties at the time, and the moral idea of the play, the eulogy of Cato's devotion to liberty in his opposition to Caesar, was very much in accord with the prevailing taste, or at least the prevailing affected taste.

Both political parties loudly claimed the work as an expression of their principles, the Whigs discovering in Caesar an embodiment of arbitrary government like that of the Tories, the Tories declaring him a counterpart of Marlborough, a dangerous plotter, endeavoring to establish a military despotism. 'Cato,' further, was a main cause of a famous quarrel between Addison and Pope. Addison, now recognized as the literary dictator of the age, had greatly pleased Pope, then a young aspirant for fame, by praising his 'Essay on Criticism,' and Pope rendered considerable help in the final revision of 'Cato.' When John Dennis, a rather clumsy critic, attacked the play, Pope came to its defense with a reply written in a spirit of railing bitterness which sprang from injuries of his own. Addison, a real gentleman, disowned the defense, and this, with other slights suffered or imagined by Pope's jealous disposition, led to estrangement and soon to the composition of Pope's very clever and telling satire on Addison as 'Atticus,' which Pope did not publish, however, until he included it in his 'Epistle to Dr. Arbuthnot,' many years after Addison's death.

The few remaining years of Addison's life were rather unhappy. He married the widowed Countess of Warwick and attained a place in the Ministry as one of the Secretaries of State; but his marriage was perhaps incompatible and his quarrel with Steele was regrettable. He died in 1719 at the age of only forty-seven, perhaps the most generally respected and beloved man of his time. On his deathbed, with a somewhat self-conscious virtue characteristic both of himself and of the period, he called his stepson to come and 'see in what peace a Christian could die.'

'The Tatler' and the more important 'Spectator' accomplished two results of main importance: they developed the modern essay as a comprehensive and fluent discussion of topics of current interest; and they performed a very great service in elevating the tone of English thought and life. The later 'Tatlers' and all the 'Spectators' dealt, by diverse methods, with a great range of themes--amusements, religion, literature, art, dress, clubs, superstitions, and in general all the fashions and follies of the time. The writers, especially Addison, with his wide and mature scholarship, aimed to form public taste.

But the chief purpose of the papers, professedly, was 'to banish Vice and Ignorance' (though here also, especially in Steele's papers, the tone sometimes seems to twentieth-century readers far from unexceptionable). When the papers began to appear, in spite of some weakening of the Restoration spirit, the idea still dominated, or was allowed to appear dominant, that immorality and lawlessness were the proper marks of a gentleman. The influence of the papers is thus summarized by the poet Gray: 'It would have been a jest, some time since, for a man to have asserted that anything witty could be said in praise of a married state or that Devotion and Virtue were in any way necessary to the character of a fine gentleman.... Instead of complying with the false sentiments or vicious tastes of the age he [Steele] has boldly assured them that they were altogether in the wrong.... It is incredible to conceive the effect his writings have had upon the Town; how many thousand follies they have either quite banished or given a very great check to! how much countenance they have added to Virtue and Religion! how many people they have rendered happy by showing them it was their own faults if they were not so.'

An appeal was made, also, to women no less than to men. During the previous period woman, in fashionable circles, had been treated as an elegant toy, of whom nothing was expected but to be frivolously attractive. Addison and Steele held up to her the ideal of self-respecting intellectual development and of reasonable preparation for her own particular sphere.

The great effectiveness of 'The Spectator's' preaching was due largely to its tactfulness. The method was never violent denunciation, rather gentle admonition, suggestion by example or otherwise, and light or humorous raillery. Indeed, this almost uniform urbanity and good-nature makes the chief charm of the papers. Their success was largely furthered, also, by the audience provided in the coffee-houses, virtually eighteenth century middle-class clubs whose members and points of view they primarily addressed.

The external style has been from the first an object of unqualified and well-merited praise. Both the chief authors are direct, sincere, and lifelike, and the many short sentences which they mingle with the longer, balanced, ones give point and force. Steele is on the whole somewhat more colloquial and less finished, Addison more balanced and polished, though without artificial formality. Dr. Johnson's repeatedly quoted description of the style can scarcely be improved on--'familiar but not coarse, and elegant but not ostentatious.'

It still remains to speak of one particular achievement of 'The Spectator,' namely the development of the character-sketch, accomplished by means of the series of De Coverly papers, scattered at intervals among the others. This was important because it signified preparation for the modern novel with its attention to character as well as action. The character-sketch as a distinct form began with the Greek philosopher, Theophrastus, of the third century B. C., who struck off with great skill brief humorous pictures of typical figures--the Dissembler, the Flatterer, the Coward, and so on. This sort of writing, in one form or another, was popular in France and England in the seventeenth century. From it Steele, and following him Addison, really derived the idea for their portraits of Sir Roger, Will Honeycomb, Will Wimble, and the other members of the De Coverly group; but in each case they added individuality to the type traits. Students should consider how complete the resulting characterizations are, and in general just what additions and changes in all respects would be needed to transform the De Coverly papers into a novel of the nineteenth century type.

## ALEXANDER POPE, 1688-1744

The chief representative of pseudo-classicism in its most particular field, that of poetry, is Dryden's successor, Alexander Pope.

Pope was born in 1688 (just a hundred years before Byron), the son of a Catholic linen-merchant in London. Scarcely any other great writer has ever had to contend against such hard and cruel handicaps as he. He inherited a deformed and dwarfed body and an incurably sickly constitution, which carried with it abnormal sensitiveness of both nerves and mind. Though he never had really definite religious convictions of his own, he remained all his life formally loyal to his parents' faith, and under the laws of the time this closed to him all the usual careers of a gentleman.

But he was predestined by Nature to be a poet. Brought up chiefly at the country home near Windsor to which his father had retired, and left to himself for mental training, he never acquired any thoroughness of knowledge or power of systematic thought, but he read eagerly the poetry of many languages. He was one of the most precocious of the long list of precocious versifiers; his own words are: 'I lisped in numbers, for the numbers came.' The influences which would no doubt have determined his style in any case were early brought to a focus in the advice given him by an amateur poet and critic, William Walsh. Walsh declared that England had had great poets, 'but never one great poet that was correct' (that is of thoroughly regular style). Pope accepted this hint as his guiding principle and proceeded to seek correctness by giving still further polish to the pentameter couplet of Dryden.

At the age of twenty-one, when he was already on familiar terms with prominent literary men, he published some imitative pastorals, and two years later his 'Essay on Criticism.' This work is thoroughly representative both of Pope and of his period. In the first place the subject is properly one not for poetry but for expository prose. In the second place the substance is not original with Pope but is a restatement of the ideas of the Greek Aristotle, the Roman Horace, especially of the French critic Boileau, who was Pope's earlier contemporary, and of various other critical authorities, French and English.

But in terse and epigrammatic expression of fundamental or pseudo-classical principles of poetic composition and criticism the 'Essay' is amazingly brilliant, and it shows Pope already a consummate master of the couplet. The reputation which it brought him was very properly increased by the publication the next year of the admirable mock-epic 'The Rape of the Lock,' which Pope soon improved, against Addison's advice, by the delightful 'machinery' of the Rosicrucian sylphs. In its adaptation of means to ends and its attainment of its ends Lowell has boldly called this the most successful poem in English. Pope now formed his lifelong friendship with Swift (who was twice his age), with Bolingbroke, and other distinguished persons, and at twenty-five or twenty-six found himself acknowledged as the chief man of letters in England, with a wide European reputation.

For the next dozen years he occupied himself chiefly with the formidable task (suggested, no doubt, by Dryden's 'Virgil,' but expressive also of the age) of translating 'The Iliad' and 'The Odyssey.' 'The Iliad' he completed unaided, but then, tiring of the drudgery, he turned over half of 'The Odyssey' to two minor writers. So easy, however, was his style to catch that if the facts were not on record the work of his assistants would generally be indistinguishable from his own. From an absolute point of view many criticisms must be made of Pope's version. That he knew little Greek when he began the work and from first to last depended much on translations would in itself have made his rendering inaccurate.

Moreover, the noble but direct and simple spirit and language of Homer were as different as possible from the spirit and language of the London drawing-rooms for which Pope wrote; hence he not only expands, as every author of a verse-translation must do in filling out his lines, but inserts new ideas of his own and continually substitutes for Homer's expressions the periphrastic and, as he held, elegant ones of the pseudo-classic diction. The polished rimed couplet, also, pleasing as its precision and smoothness are for a while, becomes eventually monotonous to most readers of a romantic period. Equally serious is the inability which Pope shared with most of the men of his time to understand the culture of the still half-barbarous Homeric age.

He supposes (in his Preface) that it was by a deliberate literary artifice that Homer introduced the gods into his action, supposes, that is, that Homer no more believed in the Greek gods than did he, Pope, himself; and in general Pope largely obliterates the differences between the Homeric warrior-chief and the eighteenth century gentleman. The force of all this may be realized by comparing Pope's translation with the very sympathetic and skilful one made (in prose) in our own time by Messrs. Lang, Leaf, and Myers. A criticism of Pope's work which Pope never forgave but which is final in some aspects was made by the great Cambridge professor, Bentley: 'It's a pretty poem, Mr. Pope, but you must not call it Homer.' Yet after all, Pope merited much higher praise than this, and his work was really, a great achievement. It has been truly said that every age must have the great classics translated into its own dialect, and this work could scarcely have been better done for the early eighteenth century than it is done by Pope.

The publication of Pope's Homer marks an important stage in the development of authorship. Until the time of Dryden no writer had expected to earn his whole living by publishing works of real literature. The medieval minstrels and romancers of the higher class and the dramatists of the sixteenth and seventeenth centuries had indeed supported themselves largely or wholly by their works, but not by printing them. When, in Dryden's time, with the great enlargement of the reading public, conditions were about to change, the publisher took the upper hand; authors might sometimes receive gifts from the noblemen to whom they inscribed dedications, but for their main returns they must generally sell their works outright to the publisher and accept his price.

Pope's 'Iliad' and 'Odyssey' afforded the first notably successful instance of another method, that of publication by subscription--individual purchasers at a generous price being secured beforehand by solicitation and in acknowledgment having their names printed in a conspicuous list in the front of the book. From the two Homeric poems together, thanks to this device, Pope realized a profit of nearly L9000, and thus proved that an author might be independent of the publisher. On the success of 'The Iliad' alone Pope had retired to an estate at a London suburb, Twickenham (then pronounced 'Twitnam'), where he spent the remainder of his life. Here he laid out five acres with skill, though in the formal landscape-garden taste of his time. In particular, he excavated under the road a 'grotto,' which he adorned with mirrors and glittering stones and which was considered by his friends, or at least by himself, as a marvel of artistic beauty.

Only bare mention need here be made of Pope's edition of Shakspere, prepared with his usual hard work but with inadequate knowledge and appreciation, and published in 1725. His next production, 'The Dunciad,' can be understood only in the light of his personal character. Somewhat like Swift, Pope was loyal and kind to his friends and inoffensive to persons against whom he did not conceive a prejudice. He was an unusually faithful son, and, in a brutal age, a hater of physical brutality. But, as we have said, his infirmities and hardships had sadly warped his disposition and he himself spoke of 'that long disease, my life.' He was proud, vain, abnormally sensitive, suspicious, quick to imagine an injury, incredibly spiteful, implacable in resentment, apparently devoid of any sense of honesty--at his worst hateful and petty-minded beyond any other man in English literature. His trickiness was astonishing.

Dr. Johnson observes that he 'hardly drank tea without a stratagem,' and indeed he seems to have been almost constitutionally unable to do anything in an open and straightforward way. Wishing, for example, to publish his correspondence, he not only falsified it, but to preserve an appearance of modesty engaged in a remarkably complicated series of intrigues by which he trapped a publisher into apparently stealing a part of it--and then loudly protested at the theft and the publication. It is easy to understand, therefore, that Pope was readily drawn into quarrels and was not an agreeable antagonist. He had early taken a violent antipathy to the host of poor scribblers who are known by the name of the residence of most of them, Grub Street--an antipathy chiefly based, it would seem, on his contempt for their worldly and intellectual poverty. For some years he had been carrying on a pamphlet war against them, and now, it appears, he deliberately stirred them up to make new attacks upon him.

Determined, at any rate, to overwhelm all his enemies at once in a great satire, he bent all his energies, with the utmost seriousness, to writing 'The Dunciad' on the model of Dryden's 'Mac Flecknoe' and irresponsibly 'dealt damnation 'round the land.' Clever and powerful, the poem is still more disgusting--grossly obscene, pitifully rancorous against scores of insignificant creatures, and no less violent against some of the ablest men of the time, at whom Pope happened to have taken offense. Yet throughout the rest of his life Pope continued with keen delight to work the unsavory production over and to bring out new editions.

During his last fifteen years Pope's original work was done chiefly in two very closely related fields, first in a group of what he called 'Moral' essays, second in the imitation of a few of the Satires and Epistles of Horace, which Pope applied to circumstances of his own time. In the 'Moral' Essays he had intended to deal comprehensively with human nature and institutions, but such a systematic plan was beyond his powers. The longest of the essays which he accomplished, the 'Essay on Man,' aims, like 'Paradise Lost,' to 'vindicate the ways of God to man,' but as regards logic chiefly demonstrates the author's inability to reason. He derived the ideas, in fragmentary fashion, from Bolingbroke, who was an amateur Deist and optimist of the shallow eighteenth century type, and so far was Pope from understanding what he was doing that he was greatly disturbed when it was pointed out to him that the theology of the poem was Deistic rather than Christian. In this poem, as in all Pope's others of this period, the best things are the detached observations. Some of the other poems, especially the autobiographical 'Epistle to Dr. Arbuthnot,' are notable for their masterly and venomous satirical sketches of various contemporary characters.

Pope's physical disabilities brought him to premature old age, and he died in 1744. His declining years were saddened by the loss of friends, and he had never married, though his dependent and sensitive nature would have made marriage especially helpful to him. During the greater part of his life, however, he was faithfully watched over by a certain Martha Blount, whose kindness he repaid with only less selfishness than that which 'Stella' endured from Swift. Indeed, Pope's whole attitude toward woman, which appears clearly in his poetry, was largely that of the Restoration. Yet after all that must be said against Pope, it is only fair to conclude, as does his biographer, Sir Leslie Stephen: 'It was a gallant spirit which got so much work out of this crazy carcase, and kept it going, spite of all its feebleness, for fifty-six years.'

The question of Pope's rank among authors is of central importance for any theory of poetry. In his own age he was definitely regarded by his adherents as the greatest of all English poets of all time. As the pseudo-classic spirit yielded to the romantic this judgment was modified, until in the nineteenth century it was rather popular to deny that in any true sense Pope was a poet at all. Of course the truth lies somewhere between these extremes. Into the highest region of poetry, that of great emotion and imagination, Pope scarcely enters at all; he is not a poet in the same sense as Shakspere, Milton, Wordsworth, Shelley, or Browning; neither his age nor his own nature permitted it. In lyric, original narrative, and dramatic poetry he accomplished very little, though the success of his 'Elegy on an Unfortunate Lady' and 'Eloisa to Abelard' must be carefully weighed in this connection.

On the other hand, it may well be doubted if he can ever be excelled as a master in satire and kindred semi-prosaic forms. He is supreme in epigrams, the terse statement of pithy truths; his poems have furnished more brief familiar quotations to our language than those of any other writer except Shakspere. For this sort of effect his rimed couplet provided him an unrivalled instrument, and he especially developed its power in antithesis, very frequently balancing one line of the couplet, or one half of a line, against the other. He had received the couplet from Dryden, but he polished it to a greater finish, emphasizing, on the whole, its character as a single unit by making it more consistently end-stopped. By this means he gained in snap and point, though for purposes of continuous narrative or exposition he increased the monotony and somewhat decreased the strength.

Every reader must decide for himself how far the rimed couplet, in either Dryden's or Pope's use of it, is a proper medium for real poetry. But it is certain that within the limits which he laid down for himself, there never was a more finished artist than Pope. He chooses every word with the greatest care for its value as both sound and sense; his minor technique is well-night perfect, except sometimes in the matter of rimes; and in particular the variety which he secures, partly by skilful shifting of pauses and use of extra syllables, is remarkable; though it is a variety less forceful than Dryden's.

The judgments of certain prominent critics on the poetry of Pope and of his period may well be considered. Professor Lewis E. Gates has said: 'The special task of the pseudo-classical period was to order, to systematize, and to name; its favorite methods were, analysis and generalization. It asked for no new experience.

The abstract, the typical, the general--these were everywhere exalted at the expense of the image, the specific experience, the vital fact.' Lowell declares that it 'ignored the imagination altogether and sent Nature about her business as an impertinent baggage whose household loom competed unlawfully with the machine-made fabrics, so exquisitely uniform in pattern, of the royal manufactories.'

Still more hostile is Matthew Arnold: 'The difference between genuine poetry and the poetry of Dryden, Pope, and all their school, is briefly this: Their poetry is conceived and composed in their wits, genuine poetry is conceived and composed in the soul. The difference is immense.' Taine is contemptuous: 'Pope did not write because he thought, but thought in order to write. Inky paper, and the noise it makes in the world, was his idol.' Professor Henry A. Beers is more judicious: 'Pope did in some inadequate sense hold the mirror up to Nature.... It was a mirror in a drawing-room, but it gave back a faithful image of society, powdered and rouged, to be sure, and intent on trifles, yet still as human in its own way as the heroes of Homer in theirs, though not broadly human.'

It should be helpful also to indicate briefly some of the more specific mannerisms of pseudo-classical poetry, in addition to the general tendencies named above on page 190. Almost all of them, it will be observed, result from the habit of generalizing instead of searching for the pictorial and the particular.

There is a constant preference (to enlarge on what was briefly stated above) for abstract expressions instead of concrete ones, such expressions as 'immortal powers' or 'Heaven' for 'God.' These abstract expressions are especially noticeable in the descriptions of emotion, which the pseudo-classical writers often describe without really feeling it, in such colorless words as 'joys, 'delights,' and 'ecstasies,' and which they uniformly refer to the conventionalized 'heart, 'soul,' or 'bosom.' Likewise in the case of personal features, instead of picturing a face with blue eyes, rosy lips, and pretty color, these poets vaguely mention 'charms,' 'beauties,' 'glories,' 'enchantments,' and the like. These three lines from 'The Rape of the Lock' are thoroughly characteristic:

*The fair [the lady] each moment rises in her charms,*
*Repairs her smiles, awakens ev'ry grace, And calls forth all the, wonders of her face.*

The tendency reaches its extreme in the frequent use of abstract and often absurdly pretentious expressions in place of the ordinary ones which to these poets appeared too simple or vulgar. With them a field is generally a 'verdant mead'; a lock of hair becomes 'The long-contended honours of her head'; and a boot 'The shining leather that encased the limb.'

There is a constant use of generic or generalizing articles, pronouns, and adjectives, 'the,' 'a,' 'that,' 'every,' and 'each' as in some of the preceding and in the following examples: 'The wise man's passion and the vain man's boast.' 'Wind the shrill horn or spread the waving net.' 'To act a Lover's or a Roman's part.' 'That bleeding bosom.'

There is an excessive use of adjectives, often one to nearly every important noun, which creates monotony.

The vocabulary is largely conventionalized, with, certain favorite words usurping the place of a full and free variety, such words as 'conscious,' 'generous, 'soft,' and 'amorous.' The metaphors employed are largely conventionalized ones, like

'Now burns with glory, and then melts with love.' The poets imitate the Latin language to some extent; especially they often prefer long words of Latin origin to short Saxon ones, and Latin names to English--'Sol' for 'Sun, 'temple' for 'church,' 'Senate' for 'Parliament,' and so on.]

## SAMUEL JOHNSON, 1709-1784

To the informal position of dictator of English letters which had been held successively by Dryden, Addison, and Pope, succeeded in the third quarter of the eighteenth century a man very different from any of them, one of the most forcefully individual of all authors, Samuel Johnson. It was his fortune to uphold, largely by the strength of his personality, the pseudo-classical ideals which Dryden and Addison had helped to form and whose complete dominance had contributed to Pope's success, in the period when their authority was being undermined by the progress of the rising Romantic Movement.

Johnson was born in 1709, the son of a bookseller in Lichfield. He inherited a constitution of iron, great physical strength, and fearless self-assertiveness, but also hypochondria (persistent melancholy), uncouthness of body and movement, and scrofula, which disfigured his face and greatly injured his eyesight. In his early life as well as later, spasmodic fits of abnormal mental activity when he 'gorged' books, especially the classics, as he did food, alternated with other fits of indolence. The total result, however, was a very thorough knowledge of an extremely wide range of literature; when he entered Oxford in 1728 the Master of his college assured him that he was the best qualified applicant whom he had ever known. Johnson, on his side, was not nearly so well pleased with the University; he found the teachers incompetent, and his pride suffered intensely from his poverty, so that he remained at Oxford little more than a year.

The death of his father in 1731 plunged him into a distressingly painful struggle for existence which lasted for thirty years. After failing as a subordinate teacher in a boarding-school he became a hack-writer in Birmingham, where, at the age of twenty-five, he made a marriage with a widow, Mrs. Porter, an unattractive, rather absurd, but good-hearted woman of forty-six. He set up a school of his own, where he had only three pupils, and then in 1737 tramped with one of them, David

Garrick, later the famous actor, to London to try his fortune in another field.

When the two reached the city their combined funds amounted to sixpence. Sir Robert Walpole, ruling the country with unscrupulous absolutism, had now put an end to the employment of literary men in public life, and though Johnson's poem 'London,' a satire on the city written in imitation of the Roman poet Juvenal and published in 1738, attracted much attention, he could do no better for a time than to become one of that undistinguished herd of hand-to-mouth and nearly starving Grub Street writers whom Pope was so contemptuously abusing and who chiefly depended on the despotic patronage of magazine publishers. Living in a garret or even walking the streets at night for lack of a lodging, Johnson was sometimes unable to appear at a tavern because he had no respectable clothes.

It was ten years after the appearance of 'London' that he began to emerge, through the publication of his 'Vanity of Human Wishes,' a poem of the same kind as 'London' but more sincere and very powerful. A little later Garrick, who had risen very much more rapidly and was now manager of Drury Lane theater, gave him substantial help by producing his early play 'Irene,' a representative pseudo-classical tragedy of which it has been said that a person with a highly developed sense of duty may be able to read it through.

Meanwhile, by an arrangement with leading booksellers, Johnson had entered on the largest, and, as it proved, the decisive, work of his life, the preparation of his 'Dictionary of the English Language.' The earliest mentionable English dictionary had appeared as far back as 1604, 'containing 3000 hard words... gathered for the benefit and help of ladies, gentle women, or any other unskilful persons.'

Others had followed; but none of them was comprehensive or satisfactory. Johnson, planning a far more thorough work, contracted to do it for L1575--scanty pay for himself and his copyists, the more so that the task occupied more than twice as much time as he had expected, over seven years. The result, then, of very great labor, the 'Dictionary' appeared in 1755. It had distinct limitations.

The knowledge of Johnson's day was not adequate for tracing the history and etymology of words, and Johnson himself on being asked the reason for one of his numerous blunders could only reply, with his characteristic blunt frankness, 'sheer ignorance.' Moreover, he allowed his strong prejudices to intrude, even though he colored them with humor; for example in defining 'oats' as 'a grain which in England is generally given to horses, but in Scotland supports the people.' Jesting at himself he defined 'lexicographer' as 'a writer of dictionaries, a harmless drudge.' Nevertheless the work, though not creative literature, was a great and necessary one, and Johnson did it, on the whole, decidedly well. The 'Dictionary,' in successive enlargements, ultimately, though not until after Johnson's death, became the standard, and it gave him at once the definite headship of English literary life. Of course, it should be added, the English language has vastly expanded since his time, and Johnson's first edition contained only a tithe of the 400,000 words recorded in the latest edition of Webster (1910).

With the 'Dictionary' is connected one of the best-known incidents in English literary history. At the outset of the undertaking Johnson exerted himself to secure the patronage and financial aid of Lord Chesterfield, an elegant leader of fashion and of fashionable literature. At the time Chesterfield, not foreseeing the importance of the work, was coldly indifferent, but shortly before the Dictionary appeared, being better informed, he attempted to gain a share in the credit by commending it in a periodical. Johnson responded with a letter which is a perfect masterpiece of bitter but polished irony and which should be familiar to every student.

The hard labor of the 'Dictionary' had been the only remedy for Johnson's profound grief at the death of his wife, in 1752; and how intensively he could apply himself at need he showed again some years later when to pay his mother's funeral expenses he wrote in the evenings of a single week his 'Rasselas,' which in the guise of an Eastern tale is a series of philosophical discussions of life.

Great as were Johnson's labors during the eight years of preparation of the 'Dictionary' they made only a part of his activity. For about two years he earned a living income by carrying on the semi-weekly 'Rambler,' one of the numerous imitations of 'The Spectator.' He was not so well qualified as Addison or Steele for this work, but he repeated it some years later in 'The Idler.'

It was not until 1775 that Johnson received from Oxford the degree of LL.D. which gave him the title of 'Dr.,' now almost inseparable from his name; but his long battle with poverty had ended on the accession of George III in 1762, when the ministers, deciding to signalize the new reign by encouraging men of letters, granted Johnson a pension of L300 for life. In his Dictionary Johnson had contemptuously defined a pension thus: 'An allowance made to any one without an equivalent. In England, it is generally understood to mean pay given to a state hireling for treason to his country.'

This was embarrassing, but Johnson's friends rightly persuaded him to accept the pension, which he, at least, had certainly earned by services to society very far from treasonable. However, with the removal of financial pressure his natural indolence, increased by the strain of hardships and long-continued over-exertion, asserted itself in spite of his self-reproaches and frequent vows of amendment. Henceforth he wrote comparatively little but gave expression to his ideas in conversation, where his genius always showed most brilliantly. At the tavern meetings of 'The Club' (commonly referred to as 'The Literary Club'), of which Burke, Sir Joshua Reynolds, Goldsmith, Gibbon, and others, were members, he reigned unquestioned conversational monarch. Here or in other taverns with fewer friends he spent most of his nights, talking and drinking incredible quantities of tea, and going home in the small hours to lie abed until noon.

But occasionally even yet he aroused himself to effort. In 1765 appeared his long-promised edition of Shakspere. It displays in places much of the sound sense which is one of Johnson's most distinguishing merits, as in the terse exposure of the fallacies of the pseudo-classic theory of the three dramatic unities, and it made some interpretative contributions; but as a whole it was carelessly and slightly done. Johnson's last important production, his most important really literary work, was a series of 'Lives of the English Poets' from the middle of the seventeenth century, which he wrote for a publishers' collection of their works. The selection of poets was badly made by the publishers, so that many of the lives deal with very minor versifiers.

Further, Johnson's indolence and prejudices are here again evident; often when he did not know the facts he did not take the trouble to investigate; a thorough Tory himself he was often unfair to men of Whig principles; and for poetry of the delicately imaginative and romantic sort his rather painfully practical mind had little appreciation. Nevertheless he was in many respects well fitted for the work, and some of the lives, such as those of Dryden, Pope, Addison and Swift, men in whom he took a real interest, are of high merit.

Johnson's last years were rendered gloomy, partly by the loss of friends, partly by ill-health and a deepening of his lifelong tendency to morbid depression. He had an almost insane shrinking from death and with it a pathetic apprehension of future punishment. His melancholy was perhaps the greater because of the manly courage and contempt for sentimentality which prevented him from complaining or discussing his distresses. His religious faith, also, in spite of all intellectual doubts, was strong, and he died calmly, in 1784. He was buried in Westminster Abbey.

Johnson's picturesque surface oddities have received undue attention, thanks largely to his friend and biographer Boswell. Nearly every one knows, for example, that he superstitiously made a practice of entering doorways in a certain manner and would rather turn back and come in again than fail in the observance; that he was careless, even slovenly, in dress and person, and once remarked frankly that he had no passion for clean linen; that he ate voraciously, with a half-animal eagerness; that in the intervals of talking he 'would make odd sounds, a half whistle, or a clucking like a hen's, and when he ended an argument would blow out his breath like a whale.'

More important were his dogmatism of opinion, his intense prejudices, and the often seemingly brutal dictatorial violence with which he enforced them. Yet these things too were really on the surface. It is true that his nature was extremely conservative; that after a brief period of youthful free thinking he was fanatically loyal to the national Church and to the king (though theoretically he was a Jacobite, a supporter of the supplanted Stuarts as against the reigning House of Hanover);

and that in conversation he was likely to roar down or scowl down all innovators and their defenders or silence them with such observations as, 'Sir, I perceive you are a vile Whig.'

At worst it was not quite certain that he would not knock them down physically. Of women's preaching he curtly observed that it was like a dog walking on its hind legs: 'It is not done well, but you are surprised to find it done at all.' English insular narrowness certainly never had franker expression than in his exclamation: 'For anything I can see, all foreigners are fools.' For the American colonists who had presumed to rebel against their king his bitterness was sometimes almost frenzied; he characterized them as 'rascals, robbers and pirates.' His special antipathy to Scotland and its people led him to insult them repeatedly, though with some individual Scots he was on very friendly terms. Yet after all, many of these prejudices rested on important principles which were among the most solid foundations of Johnson's nature and largely explain his real greatness, namely on sound commonsense, moral and intellectual independence, and hatred of insincerity.

There was really something to be said for his refusal to listen to the Americans' demand for liberty while they themselves held slaves. Living in a period of change, Johnson perceived that in many cases innovations prove dangerous and that the progress of society largely depends on the continuance of the established institutions in which the wisdom of the past is summed up. Of course in specific instances, perhaps in the majority of them, Johnson was wrong; but that does not alter the fact that he thought of himself as standing, and really did stand, for order against a freedom which is always more or less in danger of leading to anarchy.

Johnson's personality, too, cannot be fairly judged by its more grotesque expression. Beneath the rough surface he was a man not only of very vigorous intellect and great learning, but of sincere piety, a very warm heart, unusual sympathy and kindness, and the most unselfish, though eccentric, generosity. Fine ladies were often fascinated by him, and he was no stranger to good society. On himself, during his later years, he spent only a third part of his pension, giving away the rest to a small army of beneficiaries. Some of these persons, through no claim on him but their need, he had rescued from abject distress and supported in his own house, where, so far from being grateful, they quarreled among themselves, complained of the dinner, or even brought their children to live with them.

Johnson himself was sometimes exasperated by their peevishness and even driven to take refuge from his own home in that of his wealthy friends the Thrales, where, indeed, he had a room of his own; but he never allowed any one else to criticize or speak harshly of them. In sum, no man was ever loved or respected more deeply, or with better reason, by those who really knew him, or more sincerely mourned when he died.

Johnson's importance as a conservative was greatest in his professional capacity of literary critic and bulwark of pseudo-classicism. In this case, except that a restraining influence is always salutary to hold a new movement from extremes, he was in opposition to the time-spirit; romanticism was destined to a complete triumph because it was the expression of vital forces which were necessary for the rejuvenation of literature. Yet it is true that romanticism carried with it much vague and insincere sentimentality, and it was partly against this that Johnson protested. Perhaps the twentieth-century mind is most dissatisfied with his lack of sympathy for the romantic return to an intimate appreciation of external Nature. Johnson was not blind to the charm of Nature and sometimes expresses it in his own writing; but for the most part his interest, like that of his pseudo-classical predecessors, was centered in the world of man. To him, as he flatly declared, Fleet Street, in the midst of the hurry of London life, was the most interesting place in the world.

In the substance of his work Johnson is most conspicuously, and of set purpose, a moralist. In all his writing, so far as the subject permitted, he aimed chiefly at the inculcation of virtue and the formation of character. His uncompromising resoluteness in this respect accounts for much of the dulness which it is useless to try to deny in his work. 'The Rambler' and 'The Idler' altogether lack Addison's lightness of touch and of humor; for Johnson, thoroughly Puritan at heart, and dealing generally with the issues of personal conduct and responsibility, can never greatly relax his seriousness, while Addison, a man of the world, is content if he can produce some effect on society as a whole.

Again, a present-day reader can only smile when he finds Johnson in his Preface to Shakspere blaming the great dramatist for omitting opportunities of instructing and delighting, as if the best moral teachers were always explicit. But Johnson's moral and religious earnestness is essentially admirable, the more so because his deliberate view of the world was thoroughly pessimistic. His own long and unhappy experience had convinced him that life is for the most part a painful tribulation, to be endured with as much patience and courage as possible, under the consciousness of the duty of doing our best where God has put us and in the hope (though with Johnson not a confident hope) that we shall find our reward in another world.

It has long been a popular tradition, based largely on a superficial page of Macaulay, that Johnson's style always represents the extreme of ponderous pedantry. As usual, the tradition must be largely discounted. It is evident that Johnson talked, on the whole, better than he wrote, that the present stimulus of other active minds aroused him to a complete exertion of his powers, but that in writing, his indolence often allowed him to compose half sleepily, at a low pressure. In some of his works, especially 'The Rambler,' where, it has been jocosely suggested, he was exercising the polysyllables that he wished to put into his 'Dictionary,' he does employ a stilted Latinized vocabulary and a stilted style, with too much use of abstract phrases for concrete ones, too many long sentences, much inverted order, and over-elaborate balance. His style is always in some respects monotonous, with little use, for instance, as critics have pointed out, of any form of sentence but the direct declarative, and with few really imaginative figures of speech. In much of his writing, on the other hand, the most conspicuous things are power and strong effective exposition. He often uses short sentences, whether or not in contrast to his long ones, with full consciousness of their value; when he will take the trouble, no one can express ideas with clearer and more forceful brevity; and in a very large part of his work his style carries the finely tonic qualities of his clear and vigorous mind.

## JAMES BOSWELL AND HIS 'LIFE OF JOHNSON'

It is an interesting paradox that while Johnson's reputation as the chief English man of letters of his age seems secure for all time, his works, for the most part, do not belong to the field of pure literature, and, further, have long ceased, almost altogether, to be read. His reputation is really due to the interest of his personality, and that is known chiefly by the most famous of all biographies, the life of him by James Boswell.

Boswell was a Scotch gentleman, born in 1740, the son of a judge who was also laird of the estate of Auchinleck in Ayrshire, near the English border. James Boswell studied law, but was never very serious in any regular activity. Early in life he became possessed by an extreme boyish-romantic admiration for Johnson's works and through them for their author, and at last in 1763 (only twenty years before Johnson's death) secured an introduction to him. Boswell took pains that acquaintance should soon ripen into intimacy, though it was not until nine years later that he could be much in Johnson's company.

Indeed it appears from Boswell's account that they were personally together, all told, only during a total of one hundred and eighty days at intermittent intervals, plus a hundred more continuously when in 1773 they went on a tour to the Hebrides. Boswell, however, made a point of recording in minute detail, sometimes on the spot, all of Johnson's significant conversation to which he listened, and of collecting with the greatest care his letters and all possible information about him. He is the founder and still the most thorough representative of the modern method of accurate biographical writing. After Johnson's death he continued his researches, refusing to be hurried or disturbed by several hasty lives of his subject brought out by other persons, with the result that when his work appeared in 1791 it at once assumed the position among biographies which it has ever since occupied. Boswell lived only four years longer, sinking more and more under the habit of drunkenness which had marred the greater part of his life.

Boswell's character, though absolutely different from Johnson's, was perhaps as unusual a mixture. He was shallow, extremely vain, often childishly foolish, and disagreeably jealous of Johnson's other friends. Only extreme lack of personal dignity can account for the servility of his attitude toward Johnson and his acceptance of the countless rebuffs from his idol some of which he himself records and which would have driven any other man away in indignation. None the less he was good-hearted, and the other members of Johnson's circle, though they were often vexed by him and admitted him to 'The Club' only under virtual compulsion by Johnson, seem on the whole, in the upshot, to have liked him. Certainly it is only by force of real genius of some sort, never by a mere lucky chance, that a man achieves the acknowledged masterpiece in any line of work.

Boswell's genius, one is tempted to say, consists partly of his absorption in the worship of his hero; more largely, no doubt, in his inexhaustible devotion and patience. If the bulk of his book becomes tiresome to some readers, it nevertheless gives a picture of unrivalled fulness and life-likeness. Boswell aimed to be absolutely complete and truthful. When the excellent Hannah More entreated him to touch lightly on the less agreeable traits of his subject he replied flatly that he would not cut off Johnson's claws, nor make a tiger a cat to please anybody. The only very important qualification to be made is that Boswell was not altogether capable of appreciating the deeper side of Johnson's nature. It scarcely needs to be added that Boswell is a real literary artist. He knows how to emphasize, to secure variety, to bring out dramatic contrasts, and also to heighten without essentially falsifying, as artists must, giving point and color to what otherwise would seem thin and pale.

## EDWARD GIBBON AND 'THE DECLINE AND FALL OF THE ROMAN EMPIRE'

The latter part of the eighteenth century produced not only the greatest of all biographies but also the history which can perhaps best claim the same rank, Edward Gibbon's 'Decline and Fall of the Roman Empire.' History of the modern sort, aiming at minute scientific accuracy through wide collection of materials and painstaking research, and at vivid reproduction of the life, situations and characters of the past, had scarcely existed anywhere, before Gibbon, since classical times. The medieval chroniclers were mostly mere annalists, brief mechanical recorders of external events, and the few more philosophic historians of the sixteenth and seventeenth centuries do not attain the first rank. The way was partly prepared for Gibbon by two Scottish historians, his early contemporaries, the philosopher David Hume and the clergyman William Robertson, but they have little of his scientific conscientiousness.

Gibbon, the son of a country gentleman in Surrey, was born in 1737. From Westminster School he passed at the age of fifteen to Oxford. Ill-health and the wretched state of instruction at the university made his residence there, according to his own exaggerated account, largely unprofitable, but he remained for little more than a year; for, continuing the reading of theological works, in which he had become interested as a child, he was converted to Catholicism, and was hurried by his father to the care of a Protestant pastor in Lausanne, Switzerland. The pastor reconverted him in a year, but both conversions were merely intellectual, since Gibbon was of all men the most incapable of spiritual emotion. Later in life he became a philosophic sceptic.

In Lausanne he fell in love with the girl who later actually married M. Necker, minister of finance under Louis XVI, and became the mother of the famous Mme. de Stael; but to Gibbon's father a foreign marriage was as impossible as a foreign religion, and the son, again, obediently yielded. He never again entertained the thought of marriage. In his five years of study at Lausanne he worked diligently and laid the broad foundation of the knowledge of Latin and Greek which was to be indispensable for his great work. His mature life, spent mostly on his ancestral estate in England and at a villa which he acquired in Lausanne, was as externally uneventful as that of most men of letters. He was for several years a captain in the English militia and later a member of Parliament and one of the Lords of Trade; all which positions were of course practically useful to him as a historian. He wrote a brief and interesting autobiography, which helps to reveal him as sincere and good-hearted, though cold and somewhat self-conceited, a rather formal man not of a large nature. He died in 1794.

The circumstances under which the idea of his history first entered his mind were highly dramatic, though his own account of the incident is brief and colorless. He was sitting at vespers on the Capitoline Hill in Rome, the center of ancient Roman greatness, and the barefooted Catholic friars were singing the service of the hour in the shabby church which has long since supplanted the Roman Capitol. Suddenly his mind was impressed with the vast significance of the transformation, thus suggested, of the ancient world into the modern one, a process which has rightly been called the greatest of all historical themes. He straightway resolved to become its historian, but it was not until five years later that he really began the work. Then three years of steady application produced his first volume, in 1773, and fourteen years more the remaining five.

The first source of the greatness of Gibbon's work is his conscientious industry and scholarship. With unwearied patience he made himself thoroughly familiar with the great mass of materials, consisting largely of histories and works of general literature in many languages, belonging to the fourteen hundred years with which he dealt. But he had also the constructive power which selects, arranges, and proportions, the faculty of clear and systematic exposition, and the interpretative historical vision which perceives and makes clear the broad tendencies in the apparent chaos of mere events. Much new information has necessarily been discovered since Gibbon wrote, but he laid his foundation so deep and broad that though his work may be supplemented it can probably never be superseded, and stands in the opinion of competent critics without an equal in the whole field of history except perhaps for that of the Greek Thucydides.

His one great deficiency is his lack of emotion. By intellectual processes he realizes and partly visualizes the past, with its dramatic scenes and moments, but he cannot throw himself into it (even if the material afforded by his authorities had permitted) with the passionate vivifying sympathy of later, romantic, historians. There are interest and power in his narratives of Julian's expedition into Assyria, of Zenobia's brilliant career, and of the capture of Constantinople by the Turks, but not the stirring power of Green or Froude or Macaulay. The most unfortunate result of this deficiency, however, is his lack of appreciation of the immense meaning of spiritual forces, most notoriously evident in the cold analysis, in his fifteenth chapter, of the reasons for the success of Christianity.

His style possesses much of the same virtues and limitations as his substance. He has left it on record that he composed each paragraph mentally as a whole before committing any part of it to paper, balancing and reshaping until it fully satisfied his sense of unity and rhythm. Something of formality and ponderousness quickly becomes evident in his style, together with a rather mannered use of potential instead of direct indicative verb forms; how his style compares with Johnson's and how far it should be called pseudo-classical, are interesting questions to consider. One appreciative description of it may be quoted: 'The language of Gibbon never flags; he walks forever as to the clash of arms, under an imperial banner; a military music animates his magnificent descriptions of battles, of sieges, of panoramic scenes of antique civilization.'

A longer eulogistic passage will sum up his achievement as a whole:

*'The historian of literature will scarcely reach the name of Edward Gibbon without emotion. It is not merely that with this name is associated one of the most splendid works which Europe produced in the eighteenth century, but that the character of the author, with all its limitations and even with all its faults, presents us with a typical specimen of the courage and singleheartedness of a great man of letters. Wholly devoted to scholarship without pedantry, and to his art without any of the petty vanity of the literary artist, the life of Gibbon was one long sacrifice to the purest literary enthusiasm.*

He lived to know, and to rebuild his knowledge in a shape as durable and as magnificent as a Greek temple. He was content for years and years to lie unseen, unheard of, while younger men rose past him into rapid reputation. No unworthy impatience to be famous, no sense of the uncertainty of life, no weariness or terror at the length or breadth of his self-imposed task, could induce him at any moment of weakness to give way to haste or discouragement in the persistent regular collection and digestion of his material or in the harmonious execution of every part of his design....

No man who honors the profession of letters, or regards with respect the higher and more enlightened forms of scholarship, will ever think without admiration of the noble genius of Gibbon.' It may be added that Gibbon is one of the conspicuous examples of a man whose success was made possible only by the possession and proper use of inherited wealth, with the leisure which it brings.

## EDMUND BURKE

The last great prose-writer of the eighteenth century, Edmund Burke, is also the greatest of English orators. Burke is the only writer primarily a statesman and orator who can be properly ranked among English authors of the first class. The reasons, operating in substantially the same way in all literature, are not hard to understand. The interests with which statesmen and orators deal are usually temporary; the spirit and style which give a spoken address the strongest appeal to an audience often have in them something of superficiality; and it is hard for the orator even to maintain his own mind on the higher level of rational thought and disinterested purpose. Occasionally, however, a man appears in public life who to the power of compelling speech and the personality on which it is based adds intellect, a philosophic temperament, and the real literary, poetic, quality. Such men were Demosthenes, Cicero, Webster, and at times Lincoln, and beside them in England stands Burke. It is certainly an interesting coincidence that the chief English representatives of four outlying regions of literature should have been closely contemporaneous--Johnson the moralist and hack writer, Boswell the biographer, Gibbon the historian, and Burke the orator.

Burke was born in Dublin in 1729 of mixed English and Irish parentage. Both strains contributed very important elements to his nature. As English we recognize his indomitable perseverance, practical good sense, and devotion to established principles; as largely Irish his spontaneous enthusiasm, ardent emotion, and disinterested idealism. Always brilliant, in his earlier years he was also desultory and somewhat lawless. From Trinity College in Dublin he crossed over to London and studied law, which he soon abandoned. In 1756 he began his career as an author with 'A Vindication of Natural Society,' a skilful satire on the philosophic writings which Bolingbroke (the friend of Swift and Pope) had put forth after his political fall and which, while nominally expressing the deistic principles of natural religion, were virtually antagonistic to all religious faith.

Burke's 'Philosophical Inquiry into the Origin of our Ideas on the Sublime and Beautiful,' published the same year, and next in time after Dryden among important English treatises on esthetics, has lost all authority with the coming of the modern science of psychology, but it is at least sincere and interesting. Burke now formed his connection with Johnson and his circle. An unsatisfactory period as secretary to an official in Ireland proved prolog to the gift of a seat in Parliament from a Whig lord, and thus at the age of thirty-six Burke at last entered on the public life which was his proper sphere of action. Throughout his life, however, he continued to be involved in large debts and financial difficulties, the pressure of which on a less buoyant spirit would have been a very serious handicap.

As a politician and statesman Burke is one of the finest figures in English history. He was always a devoted Whig, because he believed that the party system was the only available basis for representative government; but he believed also, and truly, that the Whig party, controlled though it was by a limited and largely selfish oligarchy of wealthy nobles, was the only effective existing instrument of political and social righteousness. To this cause of public righteousness, especially to the championing of freedom, Burke's whole career was dedicated; he showed himself altogether possessed by the passion for truth and justice. Yet equally conspicuous was his insistence on respect for the practicable. Freedom and justice, he always declared, agreeing thus far with Johnson, must be secured not by hasty violence but under the forms of law, government, and religion which represent the best wisdom of past generations.

Of any proposal he always asked not only whether it embodied abstract principles of right but whether it was workable and expedient in the existing circumstances and among actual men. No phrase could better describe Burke's spirit and activity than that which Matthew Arnold coined of him--'the generous application of ideas to life.' It was England's special misfortune that, lagging far behind him in both vision and sympathy, she did not allow him to save her from the greatest disaster of her history. Himself she repaid with the usual reformer's reward.

Though he soon made himself 'the brains of the Whig party,' which at times nothing but his energy and ability held together, and though in consequence he was retained in Parliament virtually to the end of his life, he was never appointed to any office except that of Paymaster of the Forces, which he accepted after he had himself had the annual salary reduced from L25,000 to L4,000, and which he held for only a year.

During all the early part of his public career Burke steadily fought against the attempts of the King and his Tory clique to entrench themselves within the citadel of irresponsible government. At one time also he largely devoted his efforts to a partly successful attack on the wastefulness and corruption of the government; and his generous effort to secure just treatment of Ireland and the Catholics was pushed so far as to result in the loss of his seat as member of Parliament from Bristol. But the permanent interest of his thirty years of political life consists chiefly in his share in the three great questions, roughly successive in time, of what may be called England's foreign policy, namely the treatment of the English colonies in America, the treatment of the native population of the English empire in India, and the attitude of England toward the French Revolution.

In dealing with the first two of these questions Burke spoke with noble ardor for liberty and the rights of man, which he felt the English government to be disregarding. Equally notable with his zeal for justice, however, was his intellectual mastery of the facts. Before he attempted to discuss either subject he had devoted to it many years of the most painstaking study--in the case of India no less than fourteen years; and his speeches, long and highly complicated, were filled with minute details and exact statistics, which his magnificent memory enabled him to deliver without notes.

His most important discussions of American affairs are the 'Speech on American Taxation' (1774), the 'Speech on Conciliation with America' (1775), both delivered in Parliament while the controversy was bitter but before war had actually broken out, and 'A Letter to the Sheriffs of Bristol' (1777). Burke's plea was that although England had a theoretical constitutional right to tax the colonies it was impracticable to do so against their will, that the attempt was therefore useless and must lead to disaster, that measures of conciliation instead of force should be employed, and that the attempt to override the liberties of Englishmen in America, those liberties on which the greatness of England was founded, would establish a dangerous precedent for a similar course of action in the mother country itself. In the fulfilment of his prophecies which followed the rejection of his argument Burke was too good a patriot to take satisfaction.

In his efforts in behalf of India Burke again met with apparent defeat, but in this case he virtually secured the results at which he had aimed. During the seventeenth century the English East India Company, originally organized for trade, had acquired possessions in India, which, in the middle of the eighteenth century and later, the genius of Clive and Warren Hastings had increased and consolidated into a great empire. The work which these men had done was rough work and it could not be accomplished by scrupulous methods; under their rule, as before, there had been much irregularity and corruption, and part of the native population had suffered much injustice and misery.

Burke and other men saw the corruption and misery without realizing the excuses for it and on the return of Hastings to England in 1786 they secured his impeachment. For nine years Burke, Sheridan, and Fox conducted the prosecution, vying with one another in brilliant speeches, and Burke especially distinguished himself by the warmth of sympathetic imagination with which he impressed on his audiences the situation and sufferings of a far-distant and alien race. The House of Lords ultimately acquitted Hastings, but at the bar of public opinion Burke had brought about the condemnation and reform, for which the time was now ripe, of the system which Hastings had represented.

While the trial of Hastings was still in progress all Europe was shaken by the outbreak of the French Revolution, which for the remainder of his life became the main and perturbing subject of Burke's attention. Here, with an apparent change of attitude, for reasons which we will soon consider, Burke ranged himself on the conservative side, and here at last he altogether carried the judgment of England with him. One of the three or four greatest movements in modern history, the French Revolution exercised a profound influence on English thought and literature, and we must devote a few words to its causes and progress.

During the two centuries while England had been steadily winning her way to constitutional government, France had past more and more completely under the control of a cynically tyrannical despotism and a cynically corrupt and cruel feudal aristocracy.

For a generation, radical French philosophers had been opposing to the actual misery of the peasants the ideal of the natural right of all men to life, liberty, and the pursuit of happiness, and at last in 1789 the people, headed by the lawyers and thinkers of the middle class, arose in furious determination, swept away their oppressors, and after three years established a republic. The outbreak of the Revolution was hailed by English liberals with enthusiasm as the commencement of an era of social justice; but as it grew in violence and at length declared itself the enemy of all monarchy and of religion, their attitude changed; and in 1793 the execution of the French king and queen and the atrocities of the Reign of Terror united all but the radicals in support of the war against France in which England joined with the other European countries. During the twenty years of struggle that followed the portentous figure of Napoleon soon appeared, though only as Burke was dying, and to oppose and finally to suppress him became the duty of all Englishmen, a duty not only to their country but to humanity.

At the outbreak of the Revolution Burke was already sixty, and the inevitable tendency of his mind was away from the enthusiastic liberalism which had so strongly moved him in behalf of the Americans and the Hindoos. At the very outset he viewed the Revolution with distrust, and this distrust soon changed to the most violent opposition. Of actual conditions in France he had no adequate understanding. He failed to realize that the French people were asserting their most elementary rights against an oppression a hundred times more intolerable than anything that the Americans had suffered; his imagination had long before been dazzled during a brief stay in Paris by the external glitter of the French Court; his own chivalrous sympathy was stirred by the sufferings of the queen; and most of all he saw in the Revolution the overthrow of what he held to be the only safe foundations of society--established government, law, social distinctions, and religion--by the untried abstract theories which he had always held in abhorrence.

Moreover, the activity of the English supporters of the French revolutionists seriously threatened an outbreak of anarchy in England also. Burke, therefore, very soon began to oppose the whole movement with all his might. His 'Reflections on the Revolution in France,' published in 1790, though very one-sided, is a most powerful model of reasoned denunciation and brilliant eloquence; it had a wide influence and restored Burke to harmony with the great majority of his countrymen. His remaining years, however, were increasingly gloomy. His attitude caused a hopeless break with the liberal Whigs, including Fox; he gave up his seat in Parliament to his only son, whose death soon followed to prostrate him; and the successes of the French plunged him into feverish anxiety. After again pouring out a flood of passionate eloquence in four letters entitled 'Thoughts on the Prospect of a Regicide Peace' (with France) he died in 1797.

We have already indicated many of the sources of Burke's power as a speaker and writer, but others remain to be mentioned. Not least important are his faculties of logical arrangement and lucid statement. He was the first Englishman to exemplify with supreme skill all the technical devices of exposition and argument--a very careful ordering of ideas according to a plan made clear, but not too conspicuous, to the hearer or reader; the use of summaries, topic sentences, connectives; and all the others. In style he had made himself an instinctive master of rhythmical balance, with something, as contrasted with nineteenth century writing, of eighteenth century formality.

Yet he is much more varied, flexible, and fluent than Johnson or Gibbon, with much greater variety of sentence forms and with far more color, figurativeness and picturesqueness of phrase. In his most eloquent and sympathetic passages he is a thorough poet, splendidly imaginative and dramatic. J. R. Greene in his 'History of England' has well spoken of 'the characteristics of his oratory--its passionate ardor, its poetic fancy, its amazing prodigality of resources; the dazzling succession in which irony, pathos, invective, tenderness, the most brilliant word pictures, the coolest argument, followed each other.' Fundamental, lastly, in Burke's power, is his philosophic insight, his faculty of correlating facts and penetrating below this surface, of viewing events in the light of their abstract principles, their causes and their inevitable results. In spite of all this, in the majority of cases Burke was not a successful speaker. The overwhelming logic and feeling of his speech 'On the Nabob of Arcot's Debts' produced so little effect at its delivery that the ministers against whom it was directed did not even think necessary to answer it. One of Burke's contemporaries has recorded that he left the Parliament house (crawling under the benches to avoid Burke's notice) in order to escape hearing one of his speeches which when it was published he read with the most intense interest. In the latter part of his life Burke was even called 'the dinner-bell of the House' because his rising to speak was a signal for a general exodus of the other members. The reasons for this seeming paradox are apparently to be sought in something deeper than the mere prejudice of Burke's opponents. He was prolix, but, chiefly, he was undignified in appearance and manner and lacked a good delivery. It was only when the sympathy or interest of his hearers enabled them to forget these things that they were swept away by the force of his reason or the contagion of his wit or his emotion. On such occasions, as in his first speech in the impeachment of Hastings, he was irresistible.

From what has now been said it must be evident that while Burke's temperament and mind were truly classical in some of their qualities, as in his devotion to order and established institutions, and in the clearness of his thought and style, and while in both spirit and style he manifests a regard for decorum and formality which connects him with the pseudo-classicists, nevertheless he shared to at least as great a degree in those qualities of emotion and enthusiasm which the pseudo-classic writers generally lacked and which were to distinguish the romantic writers of the nineteenth century. How the romantic movement had begun, long before Burke came to maturity, and how it had made its way even in the midst of the pseudo-classical period, we may now consider.

## THE ROMANTIC MOVEMENT

The reaction which was bound to accompany the triumph of Pseudo-classicism, as a reassertion of those instincts in human nature which Pseudo-classicism disregarded, took the form of a distinct Romantic Revival. Beginning just about as Pope's reputation was reaching its climax, and gathering momentum throughout the greater part of the eighteenth century, this movement eventually gained a predominance as complete as that which Pseudo-classicism had enjoyed, and became the chief force, not only in England but in all Western Europe, in the literature of the whole nineteenth century. The impulse was not confined to literature, but permeated all the life of the time.

In the sphere of religion, especially, the second decade of the eighteenth century saw the awakening of the English church from lethargy by the great revival of John and Charles Wesley, whence, quite contrary to their original intention, sprang the Methodist denomination. In political life the French Revolution was a result of the same set of influences. Romanticism showed itself partly in the supremacy of the Sentimental Comedy and in the great share taken by Sentimentalism in the development of the novel, of both of which we shall speak hereafter; but its fullest and most steadily progressive manifestation was in non-dramatic poetry. Its main traits as they appear in the eighteenth century are as clearly marked as the contrasting ones of Pseudo-classicism, and we can enumerate them distinctly, though it must of course be understood that they appear in different authors in very different degrees and combinations.

1. There is, among the Romanticists, a general breaking away not only from the definite pseudo-classical principles, but from the whole idea of submission to fixed authority. Instead there is a spirit of independence and revolt, an insistence on the value of originality and the right of the individual to express himself in his own fashion.
2. There is a strong reassertion of the value of emotion, imagination, and enthusiasm. This naturally involves some reaction against the pseudo-classic, and also the true classic, regard for finished form.
3. There is a renewal of genuine appreciation and love for external Nature, not least for her large and great aspects, such as mountains and the sea. The contrast between the pseudo-classical and the romantic attitude in this respect is clearly illustrated, as has often been pointed out, by the difference between the impressions recorded by Addison and by the poet Gray in the presence of the

Alps. Addison, discussing what he saw in Switzerland, gives most of his attention to the people and politics. One journey he describes as 'very troublesome,' adding: 'You can't imagine how I am pleased with the sight of a plain.' In the mountains he is conscious chiefly of difficulty and danger, and the nearest approach to admiration which he indicates is 'an agreeable kind of horror.' Gray, on the other hand, speaks of the Grande Chartreuse as 'one of the most solemn, the most romantic, and the most astonishing scenes.... I do not remember to have gone ten paces without an exclamation that there was no restraining. Not a precipice, not a torrent, nor a cliff, but is pregnant with religion and poetry.'

4. The same passionate appreciation extends with the Romanticists to all full and rich beauty and everything grand and heroic.
5. This is naturally connected also with a love for the remote, the strange, and the unusual, for mystery, the supernatural, and everything that creates wonder. Especially, there is a great revival of interest in the Middle Ages, whose life seemed to the men of the eighteenth century, and indeed to a large extent really was, picturesque and by comparison varied and adventurous. In the eighteenth century this particular revival was called 'Gothic,' a name which the Pseudo-classicists, using it as a synonym for 'barbarous,' had applied to the Middle Ages and all their works, on the mistaken supposition that all the barbarians who overthrew the Roman Empire and founded the medieval states were Goths.
6. In contrast to the pseudo-classical preference for abstractions, there is, among the Romanticists, a devotion to concrete things, the details of Nature and of life. In expression, of course, this brings about a return to specific words and phraseology, in the desire to picture objects clearly and fully.
7. There is an increasing democratic feeling, a breaking away from the interest in artificial social life and a conviction that every human being is worthy of respect. Hence sprang the sentiment of universal brotherhood

and the interest in universal freedom, which finally extended even to the negroes and resulted in the abolition of slavery.

But from the beginning there was a reawakening of interest in the life of the common people--an impulse which is not inconsistent with the love of the remote and unusual, but rather means the discovery of a neglected world of novelty at the very door of the educated and literary classes. 8. There is a strong tendency to melancholy, which is often carried to the point of morbidness and often expresses itself in meditation and moralizing on the tragedies of life and the mystery of death. This inclination is common enough in many romantic-spirited persons of all times, and it is always a symptom of immaturity or lack of perfect balance. Among the earlier eighteenth century Romanticists there was a very nourishing crop of doleful verse, since known from the place where most of it was located, as the 'Graveyard poetry.'

Even Gray's 'Elegy in a Country Churchyard' is only the finest representative of this form, just as Shakspere's 'Hamlet' is the culmination of the crude Elizabethan tragedy of blood. So far as the mere tendency to moralize is concerned, the eighteenth century Romanticists continue with scarcely any perceptible change the practice of the Pseudo-classicists. 9. In poetic form, though the Romanticists did not completely abandon the pentameter couplet for a hundred years, they did energetically renounce any exclusive allegiance to it and returned to many other meters. Milton was one of their chief masters, and his example led to the revival of blank verse and of the octo-syllabic couplet. There was considerable use also of the Spenserian stanza, and development of a great variety of lyric stanza forms, though not in the prodigal profusion of the Elizabethan and Jacobean period.

## JAMES THOMSON

The first author in whom the new impulse found really definite expression was the Scotsman James Thomson. At the age of twenty-five, Thomson, like many of his countrymen during his century and the previous one, came fortune-hunting to London, and the next year, 1726, while Pope was issuing his translation of 'The Odyssey,' he published a blank-verse poem of several hundred lines on 'Winter.' Its genuine though imperfect appreciation and description of Nature as she appears on the broad sweeps of the Scottish moors, combined with its novelty, gave it great success, and Thomson went on to write also of Summer, Spring and Autumn, publishing the whole work as 'The Seasons' in 1730.

He was rewarded by the gift of sinecure offices from the government and did some further writing, including, probably, the patriotic lyric, 'Rule, Britannia,' and also pseudo-classical tragedies; but his only other poem of much importance is 'The Castle of Indolence' (a subject appropriate to his own good-natured, easy-going disposition), which appeared just before his death, in 1748. In it he employs Spenser's stanza, with real skill, but in a half-jesting fashion which the later eighteenth-century Romanticists also seem to have thought necessary when they adopted it, apparently as a sort of apology for reviving so old-fashioned a form.

'The Seasons' was received with enthusiasm not only in England but in France and Germany, and it gave an impulse for the writing of descriptive poetry which lasted for a generation; but Thomson's romantic achievement, though important, is tentative and incomplete, like that of all beginners. He described Nature from full and sympathetic first-hand observation, but there is still a certain stiffness about his manner, very different from the intimate and confident familiarity and power of spiritual interpretation which characterizes the great poets of three generations later.

Indeed, the attempt to write several thousand lines of pure descriptive poetry was in itself ill-judged, since as the German critic Lessing later pointed out, poetry is the natural medium not for description but for narration; and Thomson himself virtually admitted this in part by resorting to long dedications and narrative episodes to fill out his scheme. Further, romantic as he was in spirit, he was not able to free himself from the pseudo-classical mannerisms; every page of his poem abounds with the old lifeless phraseology--'the finny tribes' for 'the fishes,' 'the vapoury whiteness' for 'the snow' or 'the hard-won treasures of the year' for 'the crops.' His blank verse, too, is comparatively clumsy--padded with unnecessary words and the lines largely end-stopped.

## WILLIAM COLLINS

There is marked progress in romantic feeling and power of expression as we pass from Thomson to his disciple, the frail lyric poet, William Collins. Collins born at Chichester, was an undergraduate at Oxford when he published 'Persian Eclogues' in rimed couplets to which the warm feeling and free metrical treatment give much of romantic effect. In London three years later (1746) Collins put forth his significant work in a little volume of 'Odes.' Discouraged by lack of appreciation, always abnormally high-strung and neurasthenic, he gradually lapsed into insanity, and died at the age of thirty-seven. Collins' poems show most of the romantic traits and their impetuous emotion often expresses itself in the form of the false Pindaric ode which Cowley had introduced.

His 'Ode on the Popular Superstitions of the Highlands,' further, was one of the earliest pieces of modern literature to return for inspiration to the store of medieval supernaturalism, in this case to Celtic supernaturalism. But Collins has also an exquisiteness of feeling which makes others of his pieces perfect examples of the true classical style. The two poems in 'Horatian' ode forms, that is in regular short stanzas, the 'Ode Written in the Year 1746' and the 'Ode to Evening' (unrimed), are particularly fine. With all this, Collins too was not able to escape altogether from pseudo-classicism. His subjects are often abstract--'The Passions,' 'Liberty,' and the like; his characters, too, in almost all his poems, are merely the old abstract personifications, Fear, Fancy, Spring, and many others; and his phraseology is often largely in the pseudo-classical fashion. His work illustrates, therefore, in an interesting way the conflict of poetic forces in his time and the influence of environment on a poet's mind. The true classic instinct and the romanticism are both his own; the pseudo-classicism belongs to the period.

## THOMAS GRAY

Precisely the same conflict of impulses appears in the lyrics of a greater though still minor poet of the same generation, a man of perhaps still more delicate sensibilities than Collins, namely Thomas Gray. Gray, the only survivor of many sons of a widow who provided for him by keeping a millinery shop, was born in 1716. At Eton he became intimate with Horace Walpole, the son of the Prime Minister, who was destined to become an amateur leader in the Romantic Movement, and after some years at Cambridge the two traveled together on the Continent. Lacking the money for the large expenditure required in the study of law, Gray took up his residence in the college buildings at Cambridge, where he lived as a recluse, much annoyed by the noisy undergraduates.

During his last three years he held the appointment and salary of professor of modern history, but his timidity prevented him from delivering any lectures. He died in 1771. He was primarily a scholar and perhaps the most learned man of his time. He was familiar with the literature and history not only of the ancient world but of all the important modern nations of western Europe, with philosophy, the sciences of painting, architecture, botany, zoology, gardening, entomology (he had a large collection of insects), and even heraldry. He was himself an excellent musician. Indeed almost the only subject of contemporary knowledge in which he was not proficient was mathematics, for which he had an aversion, and which prevented him from taking a college degree.

The bulk of Gray's poetry is very small, no larger, in fact, than that of Collins. Matthew Arnold argued in a famous essay that his productivity was checked by the uncongenial pseudo-classic spirit of the age, which, says Arnold, was like a chill north wind benumbing his inspiration, so that 'he never spoke out.' The main reason, however, is really to be found in Gray's own over-painstaking and diffident disposition. In him, as in Hamlet, anxious and scrupulous striving for perfection went far to paralyze the power of creation; he was unwilling to write except at his best, or to publish until he had subjected his work to repeated revisions, which sometimes, as in the case of his 'Elegy Written in a Country Churchyard,' extended over many years.

He is the extreme type of the academic poet. His work shows, however, considerable variety, including real appreciation for Nature, as in the 'Ode on the Spring,' delightful quiet humor, as in the 'Ode on a Favorite Cat,' rather conventional moralizing, as in the 'Ode on a Distant Prospect of Eton College,' magnificent expression of the fundamental human emotions, as in the 'Elegy,' and warlike vigor in the

'Norse Ode' translated from the 'Poetic Edda' in his later years. In the latter he manifests his interest in Scandinavian antiquity, which had then become a minor object of romantic enthusiasm. The student should consider for himself the mingling of the true classic, pseudo-classic, and romantic elements in the poems, not least in the 'Elegy,' and the precise sources of their appeal and power. In form most of them are regular 'Horatian' odes, but 'The Bard' and 'The Progress of Poesy' are the best English examples of the genuine Pindaric ode.

## OLIVER GOLDSMITH

Next in order among the romantic poets after Gray, and more thoroughly romantic than Gray, was Oliver Goldsmith, though, with characteristic lack of the power of self-criticism, he supposed himself to be a loyal follower of Johnson and therefore a member of the opposite camp. Goldsmith, as every one knows, is one of the most attractive and lovable figures in English literature. Like Burke, of mixed English and Irish ancestry, the son of a poor country curate of the English Church in Ireland, he was born in 1728. Awkward, sensitive, and tender-hearted, he suffered greatly in childhood from the unkindness of his fellows. As a poor student at the University of Dublin he was not more happy, and his lack of application delayed the gaining of his degree until two years after the regular time.

The same Celtic desultoriness characterized all the rest of his life, though it could not thwart his genius. Rejected as a candidate for the ministry, he devoted three years to the nominal study of medicine at the Universities of Edinburgh and Leyden (in Holland). Next he spent a year on a tramping trip through Europe, making his way by playing the flute and begging. Then, gravitating naturally to London, he earned his living by working successively for a druggist, for the novelist-printer Samuel Richardson, as a teacher in a boys' school, and as a hack writer. At last at the age of thirty-two he achieved success with a series of periodical essays later entitled 'The Citizen of the World,' in which he criticized European politics and society with skill and insight.

Bishop Percy now introduced him to Johnson, who from this time watched over him and saved him from the worst results of his irresponsibility. He was one of the original members of 'The Club.' In 1764 occurred the well-known and characteristic incident of the sale of 'The Vicar of Wakefield.' Arrested for debt at his landlady's instance, Goldsmith sent for Johnson and showed him the manuscript of the book. Johnson took it to a publisher, and though without much expectation of success asked and received L60 for it. It was published two years later. Meanwhile in 1764 appeared Goldsmith's descriptive poem, 'The Traveler,' based on his own experiences in Europe. Six years later it was followed by 'The Deserted Village,' which was received with the great enthusiasm that it merited.

Such high achievement in two of the main divisions of literature was in itself remarkable, especially as Goldsmith was obliged to the end of his life to spend much of his time in hack writing, but in the later years of his short life he turned also with almost as good results to the drama (comedy). We must stop here for the few words of general summary which are all that the eighteenth century drama need receive in a brief survey like the present one. During the first half of the century, as we have seen, an occasional pseudo-classical tragedy was written, none of them of any greater excellence than Addison's 'Cato' and Johnson's 'Irene'.

The second quarter of the century was largely given over to farces and burlesques, which absorbed the early literary activity of the novelist Henry Fielding, until their attacks on Walpole's government led to a severe licensing act, which suppressed them. But the most distinctive and predominant forms of the middle and latter half of the century were, first, the Sentimental Comedy, whose origin may be roughly assigned to Steele, and, second, the domestic melodrama, which grew out of it. In the Sentimental Comedy the elements of mirth and romance which are the legitimate bases of comedy were largely subordinated to exaggerated pathos, and in the domestic melodrama the experiences of insignificant persons of the middle class were presented for sympathetic consideration in the same falsetto fashion.

Both forms (indeed, they were one in spirit) were extreme products of the romantic return to sentiment and democratic feeling. Both were enormously popular and, crossing the Channel, like Thomson's poetic innovation, exerted a great influence on the drama of France and Germany (especially in the work of Lessing), and in general on the German Romantic Movement. Goldsmith was inferior to no one in genuine sentiment, but he was disgusted at the sentimental excesses of these plays.

His 'Good Natured Man,' written with the express purpose of opposing them, and brought out in 1768, was reasonably successful, and in 1771 his far superior 'She Stoops to Conquer' virtually put an end to Sentimental Comedy. This is one of the very few English comedies of a former generation which are still occasionally revived on the stage to-day. Goldsmith's comedies, we may add here for completeness, were shortly followed by the more brilliant ones of another Irish-Englishman, Richard Brinsley Sheridan, who displayed Congreve's wit without his cynicism. These were 'The Rivals,' produced in 1775, when Sheridan was only twenty-four, and 'The School for Scandal,' 1777. Sheridan, a reckless man of fashion, continued most of his life to be owner of Drury Lane Theater, but he soon abandoned playwriting to become one of the leaders of the Whig party. With Burke and Fox, as we have seen, he conducted the impeachment of Hastings.

'She Stoops to Conquer' was Goldsmith's last triumph. A few months later, in 1774, he died at the age of only forty-five, half submerged, as usual, in foolish debts, but passionately mourned not only by his acquaintances in the literary and social worlds, but by a great army of the poor and needy to whom he had been a benefactor. In the face of this testimony to his human worth his childish vanities and other weaknesses may well be pardoned. All Goldsmith's literary work is characterized by one main quality, a charming atmosphere of optimistic happiness which is the expression of the best side of his own nature. The scene of all his most important productions, very appropriately, is the country--the idealized English country.

Very much, to be sure, in all his works has to be conceded to the spirit of romance. Both in 'The Vicar of Wakefield' and in 'She Stoops to Conquer' characterization is mostly conventional, and events are very arbitrarily manipulated for the sake of the effects in rather free-and-easy disregard of all principles of motivation. But the kindly knowledge of the main forces in human nature, the unfailing sympathy, and the irrepressible conviction that happiness depends in the last analysis on the individual will and character make Goldsmith's writings, especially 'The Vicar,' delightful and refreshing.

All in all, however, 'The Deserted Village' is his masterpiece, with its romantic regret, verging on tragedy but softened away from it, and its charming type characterizations, as incisive as those of Chaucer and Dryden, but without any of Dryden's biting satire. In the choice of the rimed couplet for 'The Traveler' and 'The Deserted Village' the influence of pseudo-classicism and of Johnson appears; but Goldsmith's treatment of the form, with his variety in pauses and his simple but fervid eloquence, make it a very different thing from the rimed couplet of either Johnson or Pope. 'The Deserted Village,' it should be added, is not a description of any actual village, but a generalized picture of existing conditions. Men of wealth in England and Ireland were enlarging their sheep pastures and their hunting grounds by buying up land and removing villages, and Goldsmith, like Sir Thomas More, two hundred years earlier, and likewise patriots of all times, deeply regretted the tendency.

## PERCY, MACPHERSON, AND CHATTERTON

The appearance of Thomson's 'Winter' in 1726 is commonly taken as conveniently marking the beginning of the Romantic Movement. Another of its conspicuous dates is 1765, the year of the publication of the 'Reliques [pronounced Relics] of Ancient English Poetry' of the enthusiastic antiquarian Thomas (later Bishop) Percy. Percy drew from many sources, of which the most important was a manuscript volume, in which an anonymous seventeenth century collector had copied a large number of old poems and which Percy rescued just in the nick of time, as the maids in the house of one of his friends were beginning to use it as kindling for the fires.

His own book consisted of something less than two hundred very miscellaneous poems, ranging in date from the fourteenth century to his own day. Its real importance, however, lies in the fact that it contained a number of the old popular ballads. Neither Percy himself nor any one else in his time understood the real nature of these ballads and their essential difference from other poetry, and Percy sometimes tampered with the text and even filled out gaps with stanzas of his own, whose sentimental style is ludicrously inconsistent with the primitive vigor of the originals. But his book, which attained great popularity, marks the beginning of the special study of the ballads and played an important part in the revival of interest in medieval life.

Still greater interest was aroused at the time by the Ossianic poems of James Macpherson. From 1760 to 1763 Macpherson, then a young Highland Scots schoolmaster, published in rapid succession certain fragments of Gaelic verse and certain more extended works in poetical English prose which, he asserted, were part of the originals, discovered by himself, and translations, of the poems of the legendary Scottish bard Ossian, of the third Christian century. These productions won him substantial material rewards in the shape of high political offices throughout the rest of his long life. About the genuineness of the compositions, however, a violent controversy at once arose, and Dr. Johnson was one of the skeptics who vigorously denounced Macpherson as a shameless impostor.

The general conviction of scholars of the present day is that while Macpherson may have found some fragments of very ancient Gaelic verse in circulation among the Highlanders, he fabricated most of what he published. These works, however, 'Fingal' and the rest, certainly contributed to the Romantic Movement; and they are not only unique productions, but, in small quantities, still interesting. They can best be described as reflections of the misty scenes of Macpherson's native Highlands--vague impressionistic glimpses, succeeding one another in purposeless repetition, of bands of marching warriors whose weapons intermittently flash and clang through the fog, and of heroic women, white-armed and with flowing hair, exhorting the heroes to the combat or lamenting their fall.

A very minor figure, but one of the most pathetic in the history of English literature, is that of Thomas Chatterton. While he was a boy in Bristol, Chatterton's imagination was possessed by the medieval buildings of the city, and when some old documents fell into his hands he formed the idea of composing similar works in both verse and prose and passing them off as medieval productions which he had discovered. To his imaginary author he gave the name of Thomas Rowley. Entirely successful in deceiving his fellow-townsmen, and filled with a great ambition, Chatterton went to London, where, failing to secure patronage, he committed suicide as the only resource against the begging to which his proud spirit could not submit.

This was in 1770, and he was still only eighteen years old. Chatterton's work must be viewed under several aspects. His imitation of the medieval language was necessarily very imperfect and could mislead no one to-day; from this point of view the poems have no permanent significance. The moral side of his action need not be seriously weighed, as Chatterton never reached the age of responsibility and if he had lived would soon have passed from forgery to genuine work. That he might have achieved much is suggested by the evidences of real genius in his boyish output, which probably justify Wordsworth's description, of him as 'the marvelous boy.' That he would have become one of the great English poets, however, is much more open to question.

**WILLIAM COWPER**

Equally pathetic is the figure of William Cowper (pronounced either Cowper or Cooper), whose much longer life (1731-1800) and far larger literary production give him a more important actual place than can be claimed for Chatterton, though his natural ability was far less and his significance to-day is chiefly historical. Cowper's career, also, was largely frustrated by the same physical weaknesses which had ruined Collins, present in the later poet in still more distressing degree. Cowper is clearly a transition poet, sharing largely, in a very mild fashion, in some of the main romantic impulses, but largely pseudo-classical in his manner of thought and expression.

His life may be briefly summarized. Morbid timidity and equally morbid religious introspection, aggravated by disappointments in love, prevented him as a young man from accepting a very comfortable clerkship in the House of Lords and drove him into intermittent insanity, which closed more darkly about him in his later years. He lived the greater part of his mature life in the household of a Mrs. Unwin, a widow for whom he had a deep affection and whom only his mental affliction prevented him from marrying. A long residence in the wretched village of Olney, where he forced himself to cooperate in all phases of religious work with the village clergyman, the stern enthusiast John Newton, produced their joint collection of 'Olney Hymns,' many of which deservedly remain among the most popular in our church song-books; but it inevitably increased Cowper's disorder. After this he resigned himself to a perfectly simple life, occupied with the writing of poetry, the care of pets, gardening, and carpentry.

The bulk of his work consists of long moralizing poems, prosy, prolix, often trivial, and to-day largely unreadable. Same of them are in the rimed couplet and others in blank verse. His blank-verse translation of Homer, published in 1791, is more notable, and 'Alexander Selkirk' and the humorous doggerel 'John Gilpin' are famous; but his most significant poems are a few lyrics and descriptive pieces in which he speaks out his deepest feelings with the utmost pathetic or tragic power. In the expression of different moods of almost intolerable sadness 'On the Receipt of My Mother's Picture' and 'To Mary' (Mrs. Unwin) can scarcely be surpassed, and 'The Castaway' is final as the restrained utterance of morbid religious despair. Even in his long poems, in his minutely loving treatment of Nature he is the most direct precursor of Wordsworth, and he is one of the earliest outspoken opponents of slavery and cruelty to animals. How unsuited in all respects his delicate and sensitive nature was to the harsh experiences of actual life is suggested by Mrs. Browning with vehement sympathy in her poem, 'Cowper's Grave.'

## WILLIAM BLAKE

Still another utterly unworldly and frankly abnormal poet, though of a still different temperament, was William Blake (1757-1827), who in many respects is one of the most extreme of all romanticists. Blake, the son of a London retail shopkeeper, received scarcely any book education, but at fourteen he was apprenticed to an engraver, who stimulated his imagination by setting him to work at making drawings in Westminster Abbey and other old churches. His training was completed by study at the Royal Academy of Arts, and for the rest of his life he supported himself, in poverty, with the aid of a devoted wife, by keeping a print-and-engraving shop. Among his own engravings the best known is the famous picture of Chaucer's Canterbury Pilgrims, which is not altogether free from the weird strangeness that distinguished most of his work in all lines. For in spite of his commonplace exterior life Blake was a thorough mystic to whom the angels and spirits that he beheld in trances were at least as real as the material world. When his younger brother died he declared that he saw the released soul mount through the ceiling, clapping its hands in joy.

The bulk of his writing consists of a series of 'prophetic books' in verse and prose, works, in part, of genius, but of unbalanced genius, and virtually unintelligible. His lyric poems, some of them composed when he was no more than thirteen years old, are unlike anything else anywhere, and some of them are of the highest quality. Their controlling trait is childlikeness; for Blake remained all his life one of those children of whom is the Kingdom of Heaven. One of their commonest notes is that of childlike delight in the mysterious joy and beauty of the world, a delight sometimes touched, it is true, as in 'The Tiger,' with a maturer consciousness of the wonderful and terrible power behind all the beauty.

Blake has intense indignation also for all cruelty and everything which he takes for cruelty, including the shutting up of children in school away from the happy life of out-of-doors. These are the chief sentiments of 'Songs of Innocence.' In 'Songs of Experience' the shadow of relentless fact falls somewhat more perceptibly across the page, though the prevailing ideas are the same. Blake's significant product is very small, but it deserves much greater reputation than it has actually attained. One characteristic external fact should be added. Since Blake's poverty rendered him unable to pay for having his books printed, he himself performed the enormous labor of engraving them, page by page, often with an ornamental margin about the text.

### ROBERT BURNS

Blake, deeply romantic as he is by nature, virtually stands by himself, apart from any movement or group, and the same is equally true of the somewhat earlier lyrist in whom eighteenth century poetry culminates, namely Robert Burns. Burns, the oldest of the seven children of two sturdy Scotch peasants of the best type, was born in 1759 in Ayrshire, just beyond the northwest border of England. In spite of extreme poverty, the father joined with some of his neighbors in securing the services of a teacher for their children, and the household possessed a few good books, including Shakspere and Pope, whose influence on the future poet was great. But the lot of the family was unusually hard.

The father's health failed early and from childhood the boys were obliged to do men's work in the field. Robert later declared, probably with some bitter exaggeration, that his life had combined 'the cheerless gloom of a hermit with the unceasing moil of a galley slave.' His genius, however, like his exuberant spirit, could not be crushed out.

His mother had familiarized him from the beginning with the songs and ballads of which the country was full, and though he is said at first to have had so little ear for music that he could scarcely distinguish one tune from another, he soon began to compose songs (words) of his own as he followed the plough. In the greatness of his later success his debt to the current body of song and music should not be overlooked. He is only the last of a long succession of rural Scottish song-writers; he composed his own songs to accompany popular airs; and many of them are directly based on fragments of earlier songs. None the less his work rises immeasurably above all that had gone before it.

The story of Burns' mature life is the pathetic one of a very vigorous nature in which genius, essential manliness, and good impulses struggled against and were finally overcome by violent passions, aggravated by the bitterness of poverty and repeated disappointments. His first effort, at eighteen, to better his condition, by the study of surveying at a neighboring town, resulted chiefly in throwing him into contact with bad companions; a venture in the business of flax-dressing ended in disaster; and the same ill-fortune attended the several successive attempts which he made at general farming.

He became unfortunately embroiled also with the Church, which (the Presbyterian denomination) exercised a very strict control in Scotland. Compelled to do public penance for some of his offenses his keen wit could not fail to be struck by the inconsistency between the rigid doctrines and the lives of some of the men who were proceeding against him; and he commemorated the feud in his series of overwhelming but painfully flippant satires.

His brief period of dazzling public success dawned suddenly out of the darkest moment of his fortunes. At the age of twenty-seven, abandoning the hope which he had already begun to cherish of becoming the national poet of Scotland, he had determined in despair to emigrate to Jamaica to become an overseer on a plantation. (That this chief poet of democracy, the author of 'A Man's a Man for a' That,' could have planned to become a slave-driver suggests how closely the most genuine human sympathies are limited by habit and circumstances.) To secure the money for his voyage Burns had published his poems in a little volume.

This won instantaneous and universal popularity, and Burns, turning back at the last moment, responded to the suggestion of some of the great people of Edinburgh that he should come to that city and see what could be done for him. At first the experiment seemed fortunate, for the natural good breeding with which this untrained countryman bore himself for a winter as the petted lion of the society of fashion and learning (the University) was remarkable. None the less the situation was unnatural and necessarily temporary, and unluckily Burns formed associations also with such boon companions of the lower sort as had hitherto been his undoing.

After a year Edinburgh dropped him, thus supplying substantial fuel for his ingrained poor man's jealousy and rancor at the privileged classes. Too near his goal to resume the idea of emigrating, he returned to his native moors, rented another farm, and married Jean Armour, one of the several heroines of his love-poems. The only material outcome of his period of public favor was an appointment as internal revenue collector, an unpopular and uncongenial office which he accepted with reluctance and exercised with leniency. It required him to occupy much of his time in riding about the country, and contributed to his final failure as a farmer. After the latter event he removed to the neighboring market-town of Dumfries, where he again renewed his companionship with unworthy associates. At last prospects for promotion in the revenue service began to open to him, but it was too late; his naturally robust constitution had given way to over-work and dissipation, and he died in 1796 at the age of thirty-seven. Burns' place among poets is perfectly clear. It is chiefly that of a song-writer, perhaps the greatest songwriter of the world.

At work in the fields or in his garret or kitchen after the long day's work was done, he composed songs because he could not help it, because his emotion was irresistibly stirred by the beauty and life of the birds and flowers, the snatch of a melody which kept running through his mind, or the memory of the girl with whom he had last talked. And his feelings expressed themselves with spontaneous simplicity, genuineness, and ease. He is a thoroughly romantic poet, though wholly by the grace of nature, not at all from any conscious intention--he wrote as the inspiration moved him, not in accordance with any theory of art.

The range of his subjects and emotions is nearly or quite complete--love; comradeship; married affection, as in 'John Anderson, My Jo'; reflective sentiment; feeling for nature; sympathy with animals; vigorous patriotism, as in 'Scots Wha Hae' (and Burns did much to revive the feeling of Scots for Scotland); deep tragedy and pathos; instinctive happiness; delightful humor; and the others.

It should be clearly recognized, however, that this achievement, supreme as it is in its own way, does not suffice to place Burns among the greatest poets. The brief lyrical outbreaks of the song-writer are no more to be compared with the sustained creative power and knowledge of life and character which make the great dramatist or narrative poet than the bird's song is to be compared with an opera of Wagner.

But such comparisons need not be pressed; and the song of bird or poet appeals instantly to every normal hearer, while the drama or narrative poem requires at least some special accessories and training. Burns' significant production, also, is not altogether limited to songs. 'The Cotter's Saturday Night' (in Spenser's stanza) is one of the perfect descriptive poems of lyrical sentiment; and some of Burns' meditative poems and poetical epistles to acquaintances are delightful in a free-and-easy fashion. The exuberant power in the religious satires and the narrative 'Tam o' Shanter' is undeniable, but they belong to a lower order of work.

Many of Burns' poems are in the Lowland Scots dialect; a few are wholly in ordinary English; and some combine the two idioms. It is an interesting question whether Burns wins distinctly greater success in one than in the other. In spite of his prevailing literary honesty, it may be observed, his English shows some slight traces of the effort to imitate Pope and the feeling that the pseudo-classical style with its elegance was really the highest--a feeling which renders some of his letters painfully affected.

## THE NOVEL

We have traced the literary production of the eighteenth century in many different forms, but it still remains to speak of one of the most important, the novel, which in the modern meaning of the word had its origin not long before 1750. Springing at that time into apparently sudden popularity, it replaced the drama as the predominant form of literature and has continued such ever since. The reasons are not hard to discover. The drama is naturally the most popular literary form in periods like the Elizabethan when the ability (or inclination) to read is not general, when men are dominated by the zest for action, and when cities have become sufficiently large to keep the theaters well filled.

It is also the natural form in such a period as that of the Restoration, when literary life centers about a frivolous upper class who demand an easy and social form of entertainment. But the condition is very different when, as in the eighteenth and still more in the nineteenth century, the habit of reading, and some recognition of its educating influence, had spread throughout almost all classes and throughout the country, creating a public far too large, too scattered, and too varied to gain access to the London and provincial theaters or to find all their needs supplied by a somewhat artificial literary form. The novel, on the other hand, gives a much fuller portrayal of life than does the drama, and allows the much more detailed analysis of characters and situations which the modern mind has come more and more to demand.

The novel, which for our present purpose must be taken to include the romance, is, of course, only a particular and highly developed kind of long story, one of the latest members of the family of fiction, or the larger family of narrative, in prose and verse. The medieval romances, for example, included most of the elements of the novel, even, sometimes, psychological analysis; but the romances usually lacked the unity, the complex and careful structure, the thorough portrayal of character, and the serious attention to the real problems of life which in a general way distinguish the modern novel. Much the same is true of the Elizabethan 'novels,' which, besides, were generally short as well as of small intellectual and ethical caliber.

During the Restoration period and a little later there began to appear several kinds of works which perhaps looked more definitely toward the later novel. Bunyan's religious allegories may likely enough have had a real influence on it, and there were a few English tales and romances of chivalry (above, pages 184-5), and a few more realistic pieces of fiction. The habit of journal writing and the letters about London life sent by some persons in the city to their friends in the country should also be mentioned. The De Coverly papers in 'The Spectator' approach distinctly toward the novel. They give real presentation of both characters and setting (social life) and lack only connected treatment of the story (of Sir Roger). Defoe's fictions, picaresque tales of adventure, come still closer, but lack the deeper artistic and moral purpose and treatment suggested a moment ago. The case is not very different with Swift's 'Gulliver's Travels,' which, besides, is primarily a satire. Substantially, therefore, all the materials were now ready, awaiting only the fortunate hand which should arrange and shape them into a real novel. This proved to be the hand of a rather unlikely person, the outwardly commonplace printer, Samuel Richardson.

## SAMUEL RICHARDSON

It is difficult, because of the sentimental nature of the period and the man, to tell the story of Richardson's career without an appearance of farcical burlesque. Born in 1689, in Derbyshire, he early gave proof of his special endowments by delighting his childish companions with stories, and, a little later, by becoming the composer of the love letters of various young women. His command of language and an insistent tendency to moralize seemed to mark him out for the ministry, but his father was unable to pay for the necessary education and apprenticed him to a London printer. Possessed of great fidelity and all the quieter virtues, he rose steadily and became in time the prosperous head of his own printing house, a model citizen, and the father of a large family of children. Before he reached middle life he was a valetudinarian. His household gradually became a constant visiting place for a number of young ladies toward whom he adopted a fatherly attitude and who without knowing it were helping him to prepare for his artistic success.

When he was not quite fifty his great reputation among his acquaintances as a letter-writer led some publishers to invite him to prepare a series of 'Familiar [that is, Friendly] Letters' as models for inexperienced young people. Complying, Richardson discovered the possibilities of the letter form as a means of telling stories, and hence proceeded to write his first novel, 'Pamela, [Footnote: He wrongly placed the accent on the first syllable.] or Virtue Rewarded,' which was published in 1740. It attained enormous success, which he followed up by writing his masterpiece, 'Clarissa Harlowe' (1747-8), and then 'The History of Sir Charles Grandison' (1753). He spent his latter years, as has been aptly said, in a sort of perpetual tea-party, surrounded by bevies of admiring ladies, and largely occupied with a vast feminine correspondence, chiefly concerning his novels. He died of apoplexy in 1761.

At this distance of time it is easy to summarize the main traits of Richardson's novels.

1. He gave form to the modern novel by shaping it according to a definite plot with carefully selected incidents which all contributed directly to the outcome. In this respect his practice was decidedly stricter than that of most of his English successors down to the present time. Indeed, he avowedly constructed his novels on the plan of dramas, while later novelists, in the desire to present a broader picture of life, have generally allowed themselves greater range of scenes and a larger number of characters. In the instinct for suspense, also, no one has surpassed Richardson; his stories are intense, not to say sensational, and once launched upon them we follow with the keenest interest to the outcome.

2. Nevertheless, he is always prolix. That the novels as published varied in length from four to eight volumes is not really significant, since these were the very small volumes which (as a source of extra profit) were to be the regular form for novels until after the time of Scott. Even 'Clarissa,' the longest, is not longer than some novels of our own day. Yet they do much exceed the average in length and would undoubtedly gain by condensation. Richardson, it may be added, produced each of them in the space of a few months, writing, evidently, with the utmost fluency, and with little need for revision.
3. Most permanently important, perhaps, of all Richardson's contributions, was his creation of complex characters, such as had thitherto appeared not in English novels but only in the drama. In characterization Richardson's great strength lay with his women--he knew the feminine mind and spirit through and through. His first heroine, Pamela, is a plebeian serving-maid, and his second, Clarissa, a fine-spirited young lady of the wealthy class, but both are perfectly and completely true and living, throughout all their terribly complex and trying experiences. Men, on the other hand, those beyond his own particular circle, Richardson understood only from the outside. Annoyed by criticisms to this effect, he attempted in the hero of his last book to present a true gentleman, but the result is only a mechanical ideal figure of perfection whose wooden joints creak painfully as he moves slowly about under the heavy load of his sternly self-conscious goodness and dignity.
4. Richardson's success in his own time was perhaps chiefly due to his striking with exaggerated emphasis the note of tender sentiment to which the spirit of his generation was so over-ready to respond. The substance of his books consists chiefly of the sufferings of his heroines under ingeniously harrowing persecution at the hands of remorseless scoundrels. Pamela, with her serving-maid's practical efficiency, proves able to take care of herself, but the story of the high-bred and noble-minded

Clarissa is, with all possible deductions, one of the most deeply-moving tragedies ever committed to paper. The effect in Richardson's own time may easily be imagined; but it is also a matter of record that his novels were commonly read aloud in the family circle (a thing which some of their incidents would render impossible at the present day) and that sometimes when the emotional strain became too great the various listeners would retire to their own rooms to cry out their grief. Richardson appealed directly, then, to the prevailing taste of his generation, and no one did more than he to confirm its hold on the next generation, not only in England, but also in France and Germany.

5. We have not yet mentioned what according to Richardson's own reiterated statement was his main purpose in writing, namely, the conveying of moral and religious instruction. He is extremely anxious to demonstrate to his readers that goodness pays and that wickedness does not, generally even in this world (though in 'Clarissa' his artistic sense refuses to be turned aside from the inevitable tragic outcome). The spiritual vulgarity of the doctrine, so far as material things are concerned, is clearly illustrated in the mechanically virtuous Pamela, who, even in the midst of the most outrageous besetments of Squire B----, is hoping with all her soul for the triumph which is actually destined for her, of becoming his wife and so rising high above her original humble station. Moreover, Richardson often goes far and tritely out of his way in his preaching. At their worst, however, his sentimentality and moralizing were preferable to the coarseness which disgraced the works of some of his immediate successors.

6. Lastly must be mentioned the form of his novels. They all consist of series of letters, which constitute the correspondence between some of the principal characters, the great majority being written in each case by the heroine. This method of telling a story requires special concessions from the reader; but even more than the other first-personal method, exemplified in 'Robinson Crusoe,' it has the great advantage of giving the most

> intimate possible revelation of the imaginary writer's mind and situation. Richardson handles it with very great skill, though in his anxiety that his chief characters may not be misunderstood he occasionally commits the artistic blunder of inserting footnotes to explain their real motives.

Richardson, then, must on the whole be called the first of the great English novelists--a striking case of a man in whom one special endowment proved much weightier than a large number of absurdities and littlenesses.

## HENRY FIELDING

Sharply opposed to Richardson stands his later contemporary and rival, Henry Fielding. Fielding was born of an aristocratic family in Somersetshire in 1707. At Eton School and the University of Leyden (in Holland) he won distinction, but at the age of twenty he found himself, a vigorous young man with instincts for fine society, stranded in London without any tangible means of support. He turned to the drama and during the next dozen years produced many careless and ephemeral farces, burlesques, and light plays, which, however, were not without value as preparation for his novels. Meanwhile he had other activities--spent the money which his wife brought him at marriage in an extravagant experiment as gentleman-farmer; studied law and was admitted to the bar; and conducted various literary periodicals.

His attacks on the government in his plays helped to produce the severe licensing act which put an end to his dramatic work and that of many other light playwrights. When Richardson's 'Pamela' appeared Fielding was disgusted with what seemed to him its hypocritical silliness, and in vigorous artistic indignation he proceeded to write 'The History of Joseph Andrews,' representing Joseph as the brother of Pamela and as a serving-man, honest, like her, in difficult circumstances. Beginning in a spirit of sheer burlesque, Fielding soon became interested in his characters, and in the actual result produced a rough but masterful picture of contemporary life. The coarse Parson Trulliber and the admirable Parson Adams are among the famous characters of fiction. But even in the later part of the book Fielding did not altogether abandon his ridicule of

Richardson. He introduced among the characters the 'Squire B----' of 'Pamela,' only filling out the blank by calling him 'Squire Booby,' and taking pains to make him correspondingly ridiculous.

Fielding now began to pay the penalty for his youthful dissipations in failing health, but he continued to write with great expenditure of time and energy. 'The History of Jonathan Wild the Great,' a notorious ruffian whose life Defoe also had narrated, aims to show that great military conquerors are only bandits and cutthroats really no more praiseworthy than the humbler individuals who are hanged without ceremony. Fielding's masterpiece, 'The History of Tom Jones,' followed hard after Richardson's 'Clarissa,' in 1749. His last novel, 'Amelia,' is a half autobiographic account of his own follies. His second marriage, to his first wife's maid, was intended, as he frankly said, to provide a nurse for himself and a mother for his children, but his later years were largely occupied with heroic work as a police justice in Westminster, where, at the sacrifice of what health remained to him, he rooted out a specially dangerous band of robbers. Sailing for recuperation, but too late, to Lisbon, he died there at the age of forty-seven, in 1754.

The chief characteristics of Fielding's nature and novels, mostly directly opposite or complementary to those of Richardson, are these:

1. He is a broad realist, giving to his romantic actions a very prominent background of actual contemporary life. The portrayal is very illuminating; we learn from Fielding a great deal, almost everything, one is inclined to say, about conditions in both country and city in his time--about the state of travel, country inns, city jails, and many other things; but with his vigorous masculine nature he makes abundant use of the coarser facts of life and character which a finer art avoids. However, he is extremely human and sympathetic; in view of their large and generous naturalness the defects of his character and works are at least pardonable.
2. His structure is that of the rambling picaresque story of adventure, not lacking, in his case, in definite progress toward a clearly-designed end, but admitting many

digressions and many really irrelevant elements. The number of his characters, especially in 'Tom Jones,' is enormous. Indeed, the usual conception of a novel in his day, as the word 'History,' which was generally included in the title, indicates, was that of the complete story of the life of the hero or heroine, at least up to the time of marriage. It is virtually the old idea of the chronicle-history play. Fielding himself repeatedly speaks of his masterpiece as an 'epic.'

3. His point of view is primarily humorous. He avowedly imitates the manner of Cervantes in 'Don Quixote' and repeatedly insists that he is writing a mock-epic. His very genuine and clear-sighted indignation at social abuses expresses itself through his omnipresent irony and satire, and however serious the situations he almost always keeps the ridiculous side in sight. He offends some modern readers by refusing to take his art in any aspect over-seriously; especially, he constantly asserts and exercises his 'right' to break off his story and chat quizzically about questions of art or conduct in a whole chapter at a time.
4. His knowledge of character, that of a generous-hearted man of the world, is sound but not subtile, and is deeper in the case of men than of women, especially in the case of men who resemble himself. Tom Jones is virtually Henry Fielding in his youth and is thoroughly lifelike, but Squire Allworthy, intended as an example of benevolent perfection, is no less of a pale abstraction than Sir Charles Grandison. The women, cleverly as their typical feminine traits are brought out, are really viewed only from without.

## THE OTHER SENTIMENTALISTS AND REALISTS

Richardson and Fielding set in motion two currents, of sentimentalism and realism, respectively, which flowed vigorously in the novel during the next generation, and indeed (since they are of the essence of life), have continued, with various modifications, down to our own time. Of the succeeding realists the most important is Tobias Smollett, a Scottish ex-physician of violent and brutal nature, who began to produce his picaresque stories of adventure during the lifetime of Fielding. He made ferociously unqualified attacks on the statesmen of his day, and in spite of much power, the coarseness of his works renders them now almost unreadable.

But he performed one definite service; in 'Roderick Random,' drawing on his early experiences as a ship's surgeon, he inaugurated the out-and-out sea story, that is the story which takes place not, like 'Robinson Crusoe,' in small part, but mainly, on board ship. Prominent, on the other hand, among the sentimentalists is Laurence Sterne, who, inappropriately enough, was a clergyman, the author of 'Tristram Shandy.' This book is quite unlike anything else ever written.

Sterne published it in nine successive volumes during almost as many years, and he made a point of almost complete formlessness and every sort of whimsicality. The hero is not born until the third volume, the story mostly relates to other people and things, pages are left blank to be filled out by the reader--no grotesque device or sudden trick can be too fantastic for Sterne.

But he has the gift of delicate pathos and humor, and certain episodes in the book are justly famous, such as the one where Uncle Toby carefully puts a fly out of the window, refusing to 'hurt a hair of its head,' on the ground that 'the world surely is wide enough to hold both thee and me.' The best of all the sentimental stories is Goldsmith's 'Vicar of Wakefield' (1766), of which we have already spoken. With its kindly humor, its single-hearted wholesomeness, and its delightful figure of Dr. Primrose it remains, in spite of its artlessness, one of the permanent landmarks of English fiction.

## HISTORICAL AND 'GOTHIC' ROMANCES

Stories which purported to reproduce the life of the Past were not unknown in England in the seventeenth century, but the real beginning of the historical novel and romance belongs to the later part of the eighteenth century. The extravagance of romantic writers at that time, further, created a sort of subspecies called in its day and since the 'Gothic' romance. These 'Gothic' stories are nominally located in the Middle Ages, but their main object is not to give an accurate picture of medieval life, but to arouse terror in the reader, by means of a fantastic apparatus of gloomy castles, somber villains, distressed and sentimental heroines, and supernatural mystery.

The form was inaugurated by Horace Walpole, the son of the former Prime Minister, who built near Twickenham (Pope's home) a pseudo-medieval house which he named Strawberry Hill, where he posed as a center of the medieval revival. Walpole's 'Castle of 'Otranto,' published in 1764, is an utterly absurd little story, but its novelty at the time, and the author's prestige, gave it a great vogue.

The really best 'Gothic' romances are the long ones written by Mrs. Ann Radcliffe in the last decade of the century, of which 'The Mysteries of Udolpho,' in particular, was popular for two generations. Mrs. Radcliffe's books overflow with sentimentality, but display real power, especially in imaginative description. Of the more truly historical romances the best were the 'Thaddeus of Warsaw' and 'Scottish Chiefs' of Miss Jane Porter, which appeared in the first decade of the nineteenth century.

None of all these historical and 'Gothic' romances attains the rank of great or permanent literature, but they were historically important, largely because they prepared the way for the novels of Walter Scott, which would hardly have come into being without them, and which show clear signs of the influence of even their most exaggerated features.

## NOVELS OF PURPOSE

Still another sort of novel was that which began to be written in the latter part of the century with the object of exposing some particular abuse in society. The first representatives of the class aimed, imitating the French sentimentalist Rousseau, to improve education, and in accordance with the sentimental Revolutionary misconception which held that all sin and sorrow result from the corruptions of civilization, often held up the primitive savage as a model of all the kindly virtues.

The most important of the novels of purpose, however, were more thorough-going attacks on society composed by radical revolutionists, and the least forgotten is the 'Caleb Williams' of William Godwin (1794), which is intended to demonstrate that class-distinctions result in hopeless moral confusion and disaster.

## MISS BURNEY AND THE FEMININE NOVEL OF MANNERS

The most permanent results of the latter part of the century in fiction were attained by three women who introduced and successively continued the novel which depicts, from the woman's point of view, with delicate satire, and at first in the hope of accomplishing some reform, or at least of showing the beauty of virtue and morality, the contemporary manners of well-to-do 'society.' The first of these authoresses was Miss Frances Burney, who later became Madame D'Arblay, but is generally referred to familiarly as Fanny Burney.

The unassuming daughter of a talented and much-esteemed musician, acquainted in her own home with many persons of distinction, such as Garrick and Sir Joshua Reynolds, and given from girlhood to the private writing of stories and of a since famous Diary, Miss Burney composed her 'Evelina' in leisure intervals during a number of years, and published it when she was twenty-five, in 1778. It recounts, in the Richardsonian letter form, the experiences of a country girl of good breeding and ideally fine character who is introduced into the life of London high society, is incidentally brought into contact with disagreeable people of various types, and soon achieves a great triumph by being acknowledged as the daughter of a repentant and wealthy man of fashion and by marrying an impossibly perfect young gentleman, also of great wealth.

Structure and substance in 'Evelina' are alike somewhat amateurish in comparison with the novels of the next century; but it does manifest, together with some lack of knowledge of the real world, genuine understanding of the core, at least, of many sorts of character; it presents artificial society life with a light and pleasing touch; and it brought into the novel a welcome atmosphere of womanly purity and delicacy. 'Evelina' was received with great applause and Miss Burney wrote other books, but they are without importance. Her success won her the friendship of Dr. Johnson and the position of one of the Queen's waiting women, a sort of gilded slavery which she endured for five years. She was married in middle-age to a French emigrant officer, Monsieur D'Arblay, and lived in France and England until the age of nearly ninety, latterly an inactive but much respected figure among the writers of a younger generation.

## MISS EDGEWORTH

Much more voluminous and varied was the work of Miss Burney's successor, Maria Edgeworth, who devoted a great part of her long life (1767-1849) to active benevolence and to attendance on her father, an eccentric and pedantic English gentleman who lived mostly on his estate in Ireland and who exercised the privilege of revising or otherwise meddling with most of her books. In the majority of her works Miss Edgeworth followed Miss Burney, writing of the experiences of young ladies in fashionable London life.

In these novels her purpose was more obviously moral than Miss Burney's--she aimed to make clear the folly of frivolity and dissipation; and she also wrote moral tales for children which though they now seem old-fashioned were long and widely popular. Since she had a first-hand knowledge of both Ireland and England, she laid the scenes of some of her books partly in both countries, thereby creating what was later called 'the international novel.' Her most distinctive achievement, however, was the introduction of the real Irishman (as distinct from the humorous caricature) into fiction. Scott testified that it was her example that suggested to him the similar portrayal of Scottish character and life.

## JANE AUSTEN

Much the greatest of this trio of authoresses is the last, Jane Austen, who perhaps belongs as much to the nineteenth century as the eighteenth. The daughter of a clergyman, she past an absolutely uneventful life of forty-two years (1775-1817) in various villages and towns in Southern England. She had finished her masterpiece, 'Pride and Prejudice,' at the age of twenty-two, but was unable for more than a dozen years to find a publisher for this and her other earlier works. When at last they were brought out she resumed her writing, but the total number of her novels is only six.

Her field, also, is more limited than that of any other great English novelist; for she deliberately restricted herself, with excellent judgment, to portraying what she knew at first-hand, namely the life of the well-to-do classes of her own 'provincial' region. Moreover, her theme is always love; desirable marriage for themselves or their children seems to be the single object of almost all her characters; and she always conducts her heroine successfully to this goal. Her artistic achievement, like herself, is so well-bred and unobtrusive that a hasty reader may easily fail to appreciate it. Her understanding of character is almost perfect, her sense for structure and dramatic scenes (quiet ones) equally good, and her quiet and delightful humor and irony all-pervasive.

Scott, with customary generosity, praised her 'power of rendering ordinary things and characters interesting from the truth of her portrayal,' in favorable contrast with his own facility in 'the Big Bow-Wow strain.' Nevertheless the assertion of some present-day critics that she is the greatest of all English authoresses is certainly extravagant. Her novels, though masterly in their own field and style, do not have the fulness of description or the elaboration of action which add beauty and power to most later ones, and her lack of a sense for the greater issues of life denies her legitimate comparison with such a writer as George Eliot.

## SUMMARY

The variety of the literary influences in eighteenth century England was so great that the century can scarcely be called a literary unit; yet as a whole it contrasts clearly enough both with that which goes before and with that which follows. Certainly its total contribution to English literature was great and varied.

# 11

# The Romantic Triumph

## THE GREAT WRITERS OF 1798-1830

As we look back to-day over the literature of the last three quarters of the eighteenth century, here just surveyed, the progress of the Romantic Movement seems the most conspicuous general fact which it presents. But at the, death of Cowper in 1800 the movement still remained tentative and incomplete, and it was to arrive at full maturity only in the work of the great writers of the following quarter century, who were to create the finest body of literature which England had produced since the Elizabethan period. All the greatest of these writers were poets, wholly or in part, and they fall roughly into two groups: first, William Wordsworth, Samuel Taylor Coleridge, Robert Southey, and Walter Scott; and second, about twenty years younger, Lord Byron, Percy Bysshe Shelley, and John Keats.

This period of Romantic Triumph, or of the lives of its authors, coincides in time, and not by mere accident, with the period of the success of the French Revolution, the prolonged struggle of England and all Europe against Napoleon (above, page 233), and the subsequent years when in Continental Europe despotic government reasserted itself and sternly suppressed liberal hopes and uprisings, while in England liberalism and democracy steadily and doggedly gathered force until by the Reform Bill of 1832 political power was largely transferred from the former small governing oligarchy to the middle class.

How all these events influenced literature we shall see as we proceed. The beginning of the Romantic triumph is found, by general consent, in the publication in 1798 of the little volume of 'Lyrical Ballads' which contained the first significant poetry of Wordsworth and Coleridge.

Even during this its greatest period, however, Romanticism had for a time a hard battle to fight, and a chief literary fact of the period was the founding and continued success of the first two important English literary and political quarterlies, 'The Edinburgh Review' and 'The Quarterly Review,' which in general stood in literature for the conservative eighteenth century tradition and violently attacked all, or almost all, the Romantic poets.

These quarterlies are sufficiently important to receive a few words in passing. In the later eighteenth century there had been some periodicals devoted to literary criticism, but they were mere unauthoritative booksellers' organs, and it was left for the new reviews to inaugurate literary journalism of the modern serious type.

'The Edinburgh Review,' suggested and first conducted, in 1802, by the witty clergyman and reformer Sydney Smith, passed at once to the hands of Francis (later Lord) Jeffrey, a Scots lawyer who continued to edit it for nearly thirty years. Its politics were strongly liberal, and to oppose it the Tory 'Quarterly Review' was founded in 1808, under the editorship of the satirist William Gifford and with the cooperation of Sir Walter Scott, who withdrew for the purpose from his connection with the 'Edinburgh.' These reviews were followed by other high-class periodicals, such as 'Blackwood's Magazine,' and most of the group have maintained their importance to the present day.

## SAMUEL TAYLOR COLERIDGE

The poets Wordsworth and Coleridge are of special interest not only from the primary fact that they are among the greatest of English authors, but also secondarily because in spite of their close personal association each expresses one of the two main contrasting or complementary tendencies in the Romantic movement; Coleridge the delight in wonder and mystery, which he has the power to express with marvelous poetic suggestiveness, and Wordsworth, in an extreme degree, the belief in the simple and quiet forces, both of human life and of Nature.

To Coleridge, who was slightly the younger of the two, attaches the further pathetic interest of high genius largely thwarted by circumstances and weakness of will. Born in Devonshire in 1772, the youngest of the many children of a self-made clergyman and schoolmaster, he was a precocious and abnormal child, then as always a fantastic dreamer, despised by other boys and unable to mingle with them. After the death of his father he was sent to Christ's Hospital, the 'Blue-Coat' charity school in London, where he spent nine lonely years in the manner briefly described in an essay of Charles Lamb, where Coleridge appears under a thin disguise. The very strict discipline was no doubt of much value in giving firmness and definite direction to his irregular nature, and the range of his studies, both in literature and in other fields, was very wide.

Through the aid of scholarships and of contributions from his brothers he entered Cambridge in 1791, just after Wordsworth had left the University; but here his most striking exploit was a brief escapade of running away and enlisting in a cavalry troop. Meeting Southey, then a student at Oxford, he drew him into a plan for a 'Pantisocracy' (a society where all should be equal), a community of twelve young couples to be founded in some 'delightful part of the new back settlements' of America on the principles of communistic cooperation in all lines, broad mental culture, and complete freedom of opinion. Naturally, this plan never past beyond the dream stage.

Coleridge left the University in 1794 without a degree, tormented by a disappointment in love. He had already begun to publish poetry and newspaper prose, and he now attempted lecturing. He and Southey married two sisters, whom Byron in a later attack on Southey somewhat inaccurately described as 'milliners of Bath'; and Coleridge settled near Bristol. After characteristically varied and unsuccessful efforts at conducting a periodical, newspaper writing, and preaching as a Unitarian (a creed which was then considered by most Englishmen disreputable and which Coleridge later abandoned), he moved with his wife in 1797 to Nether Stowey in Somersetshire.

Expressly in order to be near him, Wordsworth and his sister Dorothy soon leased the neighboring manor-house of Alfoxden, and there followed the memorable year of intellectual and emotional stimulus when Coleridge's genius suddenly expanded into short-lived but wonderful activity and he wrote most of his few great poems, 'The Ancient Mariner,' 'Kubla Khan,' and the First Part of 'Christabel.' 'The Ancient Mariner' was planned by Coleridge and Wordsworth on one of their frequent rambles, and was to have been written in collaboration; but as it proceeded, Wordsworth found his manner so different from that of Coleridge that he withdrew altogether from the undertaking. The final result of the incident, however, was the publication in 1798 of 'Lyrical Ballads,' which included of Coleridge's work only this one poem, but of Wordsworth's several of his most characteristic ones.

Coleridge afterwards explained that the plan of the volume contemplated two complementary sorts of poems. He was to present supernatural or romantic characters, yet investing them with human interest and semblance of truth; while Wordsworth was to add the charm of novelty to everyday things and to suggest their kinship to the supernatural, arousing readers from their accustomed blindness to the loveliness and wonders of the world around us. No better description could be given of the poetic spirit and the whole poetic work of the two men. Like some other epoch-marking books, 'Lyrical Ballads' attracted little attention. Shortly after its publication Coleridge and the Wordsworths sailed for Germany, where for the greater part of a year Coleridge worked hard, if irregularly, at the language, literature, and philosophy.

The remaining thirty-five years of his life are a record of ambitious projects and fitful efforts, for the most part turned by ill-health and lack of steady purpose into melancholy failure, but with a few fragmentary results standing out brilliantly. At times Coleridge did newspaper work, at which he might have succeeded; in 1800, in a burst of energy, he translated Schiller's tragedy 'Wallenstein' into English blank verse, a translation which in the opinion of most critics surpasses the original; and down to 1802, and occasionally later, he wrote a few more poems of a high order. For a few years from 1800 on he lived at Greta Hall in the village of Keswick (pronounced Kesick), in the northern end of the Lake Region (Westmoreland), fifteen miles from Wordsworth; but his marriage was incompatible (with the fault on his side), and he finally left his wife and children, who were thenceforward supported largely by Southey, his successor at Greta Hall. Coleridge himself was maintained chiefly by the generosity of friends; later, in part, by public pensions.

It was apparently about 1800, to alleviate mental distress and great physical suffering from neuralgia, that he began the excessive use of opium (laudanum) which for many years had a large share in paralyzing his will. For a year, in 1804-5, he displayed decided diplomatic talent as secretary to the Governor of Malta. At several different times, also, he gave courses, of lectures on Shakspere and Milton; as a speaker he was always eloquent; and the fragmentary notes of the lectures which have been preserved rank very high in Shaksperean criticism.

His main interest, however, was now in philosophy; perhaps no Englishman has ever had a more profoundly philosophical mind; and through scattered writings and through his stimulating though prolix talks to friends and disciples he performed a very great service to English thought by introducing the viewpoint and ideas of the German transcendentalists, such as Kant, Schelling, and Fichte. During his last eighteen years he lived mostly in sad acceptance of defeat, though still much honored, in the house of a London physician. He died in 1834.

As a poet Coleridge's first great distinction is that which we have already pointed out, namely that he gives wonderfully subtile and appealing expression to the Romantic sense for the strange and the supernatural, and indeed for all that the word 'Romance' connotes at the present day. He accomplishes this result partly through his power of suggesting the real unity of the inner and outer worlds, partly through his skill, resting in a large degree on vivid impressionistic description, in making strange scenes appear actual, in securing from the reader what he himself called 'that willing suspension of disbelief which constitutes poetic faith.' Almost every one has felt the weird charm of 'The Ancient Mariner,' where all the unearthly story centers about a moral and religious idea, and where we are dazzled by a constant succession of such pictures as these:

*And ice, mast-high, came floating by,*

*As green as emerald.*

*We were the first that ever burst Into that silent sea.*

*The western wave was all aflame:*
*The day was well nigh done:*
*Almost upon the western wave*
*Rested the broad, bright sun;*
*When that strange shape drove suddenly*
*Betwixt us and the sun.*

'Christabel' achieves what Coleridge himself described as the very difficult task of creating witchery by daylight; and 'Kubla Khan,' worthy, though a brief fragment, to rank with these two, is a marvelous glimpse of fairyland.

In the second place, Coleridge is one of the greatest English masters of exquisite verbal melody, with its tributary devices of alliteration and haunting onomatopoeia. In this respect especially his influence on subsequent English poetry has been incalculable. The details of his method students should observe for themselves in their study of the poems, but one particular matter should be mentioned. In 'Christabel' and to a somewhat less degree in 'The Ancient Mariner' Coleridge departed as far as possible from eighteenth century tradition by greatly varying the number of syllables in the lines, while keeping a regular number of stresses. Though this practice, as we have seen, was customary in Old English poetry and in the popular ballads, it was supposed by Coleridge and his contemporaries to be a new discovery, and it proved highly suggestive to other romantic poets. From hearing 'Christabel' read (from manuscript) Scott caught the idea for the free-and-easy meter of his poetical romances.

With a better body and will Coleridge might have been one of the supreme English poets; as it is, he has left a small number of very great poems and has proved one of the most powerful influences on later English poetry.

## WILLIAM WORDSWORTH, 1770-1850

William Wordsworth [Footnote: The first syllable is pronounced like the common noun 'words'] was born in 1770 in Cumberland, in the 'Lake Region,' which, with its bold and varied mountains as well as its group of charming lakes, is the most picturesque part of England proper. He had the benefit of all the available formal education, partly at home, partly at a 'grammar' school a few miles away, but his genius was formed chiefly by the influence of Nature, and, in a qualified degree, by that of the simple peasant people of the region. Already as a boy, though normal and active, he began to be sensitive to the Divine Power in Nature which in his mature years he was to express with deeper sympathy than any poet before him.

Early left an orphan, at seventeen he was sent by his uncles to Cambridge University. Here also the things which most appealed to him were rather the new revelations of men and life than the formal studies, and indeed the torpid instruction of the time offered little to any thoughtful student. On leaving Cambridge he was uncertain as to his life-work. He said that he did not feel himself 'good enough' for the Church, he was not drawn toward law, and though he fancied that he had capacity for a military career, he felt that 'if he were ordered to the West Indies his talents would not save him from the yellow fever.' At first, therefore, he spent nearly a year in London in apparent idleness, an intensely interested though detached spectator of the city life, but more especially absorbed in his mystical consciousness of its underlying current of spiritual being.

After this he crossed to France to learn the language. The Revolution was then (1792) in its early stages, and in his 'Prelude' Wordsworth has left the finest existing statement of the exultant anticipations of a new world of social justice which the movement aroused in himself and other young English liberals. When the Revolution past into the period of violent bloodshed he determined, with more enthusiasm than judgment, to put himself forward as a leader of the moderate Girondins. From the wholesale slaughter of this party a few months later he was saved through the stopping of his allowance by his more cautious uncles, which compelled him, after a year's absence, to return to England.

For several years longer Wordsworth lived uncertainly. When, soon after his return, England, in horror at the execution of the French king, joined the coalition of European powers against France, Wordsworth experienced a great shock--the first, he tells us, that his moral nature had ever suffered--at seeing his own country arrayed with corrupt despotisms against what seemed to him the cause of humanity. The complete degeneration of the Revolution into anarchy and tyranny further served to plunge him into a chaos of moral bewilderment, from which he was gradually rescued partly by renewed communion with Nature and partly by the influence of his sister Dorothy, a woman of the most sensitive nature but of strong character and admirable good sense.

From this time for the rest of her life she continued to live with him, and by her unstinted and unselfish devotion contributed very largely to his poetic success. He had now begun to write poetry (though thus far rather stiffly and in the rimed couplet), and the receipt of a small legacy from a friend enabled him to devote his life to the art. Six or seven years later his resources were several times multiplied by an honorable act of the new Lord Lonsdale, who voluntarily repaid a sum of money owed by his predecessor to Wordsworth's father.

In 1795 Wordsworth and his sister moved from the Lake Region to Dorsetshire, at the other end of England, likewise a country of great natural beauty. Two years later came their change (of a few miles) to Alfoxden, the association with Coleridge, and 'Lyrical Ballads,' containing nineteen of Wordsworth's poems (above, page 267). After their winter in Germany the Wordsworths settled permanently in their native Lake Region, at first in 'Dove Cottage,' in the village of Grasmere.

This simple little stone house, buried, like all the others in the Lake Region, in brilliant flowers, and opening from its second story onto the hillside garden where Wordsworth composed much of his greatest poetry, is now the annual center of pilgrimage for thousands of visitors, one of the chief literary shrines of England and the world. Here Wordsworth lived frugally for several years; then after intermediate changes he took up his final residence in a larger house, Rydal Mount, a few miles away. In 1802 he married Mary Hutchinson, who had been one of his childish schoolmates, a woman of a spirit as fine as that of his sister, whom she now joined without a thought of jealousy in a life of self-effacing devotion to the poet.

Wordsworth's poetic inspiration, less fickle than that of Coleridge, continued with little abatement for a dozen years; but about 1815, as he himself states in his fine but pathetic poem 'Composed upon an Evening of Extraordinary Splendour,' it for the most part abandoned him. He continued, however, to produce a great deal of verse, most of which his admirers would much prefer to have had unwritten. The plain Anglo-Saxon yeoman strain which was really the basis of his nature now asserted itself in the growing conservatism of ideas which marked the last forty years of his life. His early love of simplicity hardened into a rigid opposition not only to the materialistic modern industrial system but to all change--the Reform Bill, the reform of education, and in general all progressive political and social movements. It was on this abandonment of his early liberal principles that Browning based his spirited lyric 'The Lost Leader.'

During the first half or more of his mature life, until long after he had ceased to be a significant creative force, Wordsworth's poetry, for reasons which will shortly appear, had been met chiefly with ridicule or indifference, and he had been obliged to wait in patience while the slighter work first of Scott and then of Byron took the public by storm. Little by little, however, he came to his own, and by about 1830 he enjoyed with discerning readers that enthusiastic appreciation of which he is certain for all the future. The crowning mark of recognition came in 1843 when on the death of his friend Southey he was made Poet Laureate. The honor, however, had been so long delayed that it was largely barren. Ten years earlier his life had been darkened by the mental decay of his sister and the death of Coleridge; and other personal sorrows now came upon him. He died in 1850 at the age of eighty.

Wordsworth, as we have said, is the chief representative of some (especially one) of the most important principles in the Romantic Movement; but he is far more than a member of any movement; through his supreme poetic expression of some of the greatest spiritual ideals he belongs among the five or six greatest English poets. First, he is the profoundest interpreter of Nature in all poetry. His feeling for Nature has two aspects. He is keenly sensitive, and in a more delicately discriminating way than any of his predecessors, to all the external beauty and glory of Nature, especially inanimate Nature--of mountains, woods and fields, streams and flowers, in all their infinitely varied aspects. A wonderfully joyous and intimate sympathy with them is one of his controlling impulses.

But his feeling goes beyond the mere physical and emotional delight of Chaucer and the Elizabethans; for him Nature is a direct manifestation of the Divine Power, which seems to him to be everywhere immanent in her; and communion with her, the communion into which he enters as he walks and meditates among the mountains and moors, is to him communion with God. He is literally in earnest even in his repeated assertion that from observation of Nature man may learn (doubtless by the proper attuning of his spirit) more of moral truth than from all the books and sages. To Wordsworth Nature is man's one great and sufficient teacher.

It is for this reason that, unlike such poets as Keats and Tennyson, he so often views Nature in the large, giving us broad landscapes and sublime aspects. Of this mystical semi-pantheistic Nature-religion his 'Lines composed above Tintern Abbey' are the noblest expression in literature. All this explains why Wordsworth considered his function as a poet a sacred thing and how his intensely moral temperament found complete satisfaction in his art.

It explains also, in part, the limitation of his poetic genius. Nature indeed did not continue to be to him, as he himself says that it was in his boyhood, absolutely 'all in all'; but he always remained largely absorbed in the contemplation and interpretation of it and never manifested, except in a few comparatively short and exceptional poems, real narrative or dramatic power (in works dealing with human characters or human life).

In the second place, Wordsworth is the most consistent of all the great English poets of democracy, though here as elsewhere his interest is mainly not in the external but in the spiritual aspect of things. From his insistence that the meaning of the world for man lies not in the external events but in the development of character results his central doctrine of the simple life. Real character, he holds, the chief proper object of man's effort, is formed by quietly living, as did he and the dalesmen around him, in contact with Nature and communion with God rather than by participation in the feverish and sensational struggles of the great world. Simple country people, therefore, are nearer to the ideal than are most persons who fill a larger place in the activities of the world.

This doctrine expresses itself in a striking though one-sided fashion in his famous theory of poetry--its proper subjects, characters, and diction. He stated his theory definitely and at length in a preface to the second edition of 'Lyrical Ballads,' published in 1800, a discussion which includes incidentally some of the finest general critical interpretation ever made of the nature and meaning of poetry. Wordsworth declared: 1. Since the purpose of poetry is to present the essential emotions of men, persons in humble and rustic life are generally the fittest subjects for treatment in it, because their natures and manners are simple and more genuine than those of other men, and are kept so by constant contact with the beauty and serenity of Nature. 2. Not only should artificial poetic diction (like that of the eighteenth century) be rejected, but the language of poetry should be a selection from that of ordinary people in real life, only purified of its vulgarities and heightened so as to appeal to the imagination. (In this last modification lies the justification of rime.) There neither is nor can be any essential difference between the language of prose and that of poetry.

This theory, founded on Wordsworth's disgust at eighteenth century poetic artificiality, contains a very important but greatly exaggerated element of truth. That the experiences of simple and common people, including children, may adequately illustrate the main spiritual aspects of life Wordsworth unquestionably demonstrated in such poems as 'The Reverie of Poor Susan,' 'Lucy Gray,' and 'Michael.' But to restrict poetry largely to such characters and subjects would be to eliminate not only most of the external interest of life, which certainly is often necessary in giving legitimate body to the spiritual meanings, but also a great range of significant experiences which by the nature of things can never come to lowly and simple persons.

That the characters of simple country people are on the average inevitably finer and more genuine than those of others is a romantic theory rather than a fact, as Wordsworth would have discovered if his meditative nature had, allowed him to get into really direct and personal contact with the peasants about him. As to the proper language of poetry, no one to-day (thanks partly to Wordsworth) defends artificiality, but most of Wordsworth's own best work, as well as that of all other poets, proves clearly that there is an essential difference between the language of prose and that of poetry, that much of the meaning of poetry results from the use of unusual, suggestive, words and picturesque expressions, which create the essential poetic atmosphere and stir the imagination in ways distinctly different from those of prose. Wordsworth's obstinate adherence to his theory in its full extent, indeed, produced such trivial and absurd results as 'Goody Blake and Harry Gill,' 'The Idiot Boy,' and 'Peter Bell,' and great masses of hopeless prosiness in his long blank-verse narratives.

This obstinacy and these poems are only the most conspicuous result of Wordsworth's chief temperamental defect, which was an almost total lack of the sense of humor. Regarding himself as the prophet of a supremely important new gospel, he never admitted the possibility of error in his own point of view and was never able to stand aside from his poetry and criticise it dispassionately. This somewhat irritating egotism, however, was perhaps a necessary element in his success; without it he might not have been able to live serenely through the years of misunderstanding and ridicule which would have silenced or embittered a more diffident spirit.

The variety of Wordsworth's poetry deserves special mention; in addition to his short lyric and narrative poems of Nature and the spiritual life several kinds stand out distinctly. A very few poems, the noble 'Ode to Duty,' 'Laodamia,' and 'Dion,' are classical in inspiration and show the finely severe repression and finish of classic style. Among his many hundreds of sonnets is a very notable group inspired by the struggle of England against Napoleon. Wordsworth was the first English poet after Milton who used the sonnet powerfully and he proves himself a worthy successor of Milton. The great bulk of his work, finally, is made up of his long poems in blank-verse. 'The Prelude,' written during the years 1799-1805, though not published until after his death, is the record of the development of his poet's mind, not an outwardly stirring poem, but a unique and invaluable piece of spiritual autobiography. Wordsworth intended to make this only an introduction to another work of enormous length which was to have presented his views of Man, Nature, and Society. Of this plan he completed two detached parts, namely the fragmentary 'Recluse' and 'The

Excursion,' which latter contains some fine passages, but for the most part is uninspired.

Wordsworth, more than any other great English poet, is a poet for mature and thoughtful appreciation; except for a very small part of his work many readers must gradually acquire the taste for him. But of his position among the half dozen English poets who have made the largest contribution to thought and life there can be no question; so that some acquaintance with him is a necessary part of any real education.

## ROBERT SOUTHEY

Robert Southey (1774-1843), a voluminous writer of verse and prose who from his friendship with Wordsworth and Coleridge has been associated with them as third in what has been inaptly called 'The Lake School' of poets, was thought in his own day to be their equal; but time has relegated him to comparative obscurity. An insatiate reader and admirable man, he wrote partly from irrepressible instinct and partly to support his own family and at times, as we have seen, that of Coleridge. An ardent liberal in youth, he, more quickly than Wordsworth, lapsed into conservatism, whence resulted his appointment as Poet Laureate in 1813 and the unremitting hostility of Lord Byron. His rather fantastic epics, composed with great facility and much real spirit, are almost forgotten; he is remembered chiefly by three or four short poems--'The Battle of Blenheim,' 'My days among the dead are past,' 'The Old Man's Comforts' (You are old, Father William,' wittily parodied by 'Lewis Carroll' in 'Alice in Wonderland')--and by his excellent short prose 'Life of Nelson.'

## WALTER SCOTT

In the eighteenth century Scotland had contributed Thomson and Burns to the Romantic movement; now, early in the nineteenth, she supplied a writer of unexcelled and marvelous creative energy, who confirmed the triumph of the movement with work of the first importance in both verse and prose, namely Walter Scott. Scott, further, is personally one of the most delightful figures in English literature, and he is probably the most famous of all the Scotsmen who have ever lived. He was descended from an ancient Border fighting clan, some of whose pillaging heroes he was to celebrate in his poetry, but he himself was born, in 1771, in Edinburgh, the son of an attorney of a privileged, though not the highest, class. In spite of some serious sicknesses, one of which left him permanently lame, he was always a very active boy, more distinguished at school for play and fighting than for devotion to study. But his unconscious training for literature began very early; in his childhood his love of poetry was stimulated by his mother, and he always spent much time in roaming about the country and picking up old ballads and traditional lore. Loyalty to his father led him to devote six years of hard work to the uncongenial study of the law, and at twenty he was admitted to the Edinburgh bar as an advocate. Though his geniality and high-spirited brilliancy made him a social favorite he never secured much professional practice; but after a few years he was appointed permanent Sheriff of Selkirk, a county a little to the south of Edinburgh, near the English Border. Later, in 1806, he was also made one of the Principal Clerks of Session, a subordinate but responsible office with a handsome salary which entailed steady attendance and work at the metropolitan law court in Edinburgh during half of each year.

His instinct for literary production was first stimulated by the German Romantic poets. In 1796 he translated Burger's fiery and melodramatic ballad 'Lenore,' and a little later wrote some vigorous though hasty ballads of his own. In 1802-1803 he published 'Minstrelsy of the Scottish Border,' a collection of Scottish ballads and songs, which he carefully annotated. He went on in 1805, when he was thirty-four, to his first original verse-romance, 'The Lay of the Last Minstrel.' Carelessly constructed and written, this poem was nevertheless the most spirited reproduction of the life of feudal chivalry which the Romantic Movement had yet brought forth, and its popularity was immediate and enormous.

Always writing with the greatest facility, though in brief hours snatched from his other occupations, Scott followed up 'The Lay' during the next ten years with the much superior 'Marmion,' 'The Lady of the Lake,' and other verse-romances, most of which greatly increased both his reputation and his income. In 1813 he declined the offer of the Poet Laureateship, then considered a position of no great dignity for a successful man, but secured the appointment of Southey, who was his friend. In 1811 he moved from the comparatively modest country house which he had been occupying to the estate of Abbotsford, where he proceeded to fulfill his ambition of building a great mansion and making himself a sort of feudal chieftain. To this project he devoted for years a large part of the previously unprecedented profits from his writings.

For a dozen years before, it should be added, his inexhaustible energy had found further occupation in connection with a troop of horse which he had helped to organize on the threat of a French invasion and of which he acted as quartermaster, training in barracks, and at times drilling for hours before breakfast.

The amount and variety of his literary work was much greater than is understood by most of his admirers today. He contributed largely, in succession, to the 'Edinburgh' and 'Quarterly' reviews, and having become a secret partner in the printing firm of the Ballantyne brothers, two of his school friends, exerted himself not only in the affairs of the company but in vast editorial labors of his own, which included among other things voluminously annotated editions of Dryden and Swift. His productivity is the more astonishing because after his removal to Abbotsford he gave a great part of his time not only to his family but also to the entertainment of the throngs of visitors who pressed upon him in almost continuous crowds. The explanation is to be found partly in his phenomenally vigorous constitution, which enabled him to live and work with little sleep; though in the end he paid heavily for this indiscretion.

The circumstances which led him to turn from poetry to prose fiction are well known. His poetical vein was really exhausted when in 1812 and 1813 Byron's 'Childe Harold' and flashy Eastern tales captured the public fancy. Just about as Scott was goodnaturedly confessing to himself that it was useless to dispute Byron's supremacy he accidentally came across the first chapters of 'Waverley,' which he had written some years before and had thrown aside in unwillingness to risk his fame by a venture in a new field. Taking it up with renewed interest, in the evenings of three weeks he wrote the remaining two-thirds of it; and he published it with an ultimate success even greater than that of his poetry.

For a long time, however, Scott did not acknowledge the authorship of 'Waverley' and the novels which followed it (which, however, was obvious to every one), chiefly because he feared that the writing of prose fiction would seem undignified in a Clerk of Session. The rapidity of the appearance of his novels testified to the almost unlimited accumulation of traditions and incidents with which his astonishing memory was stored; in seventeen years he published nearly thirty 'Waverley' novels, equipping most of them, besides, with long fictitious introductions, which the present-day reader almost universally skips. The profits of Scott's works, long amounting apparently to from ten to twenty thousand pounds a year, were beyond the wildest dream of any previous author, and even exceeded those of most popular authors of the twentieth century, though partly because the works were published in unreasonably expensive form, each novel in several volumes. Still more gratifying were the great personal popularity which Scott attained and his recognition as the most eminent of living Scotsmen, of which a symbol was his elevation to a baronetcy in 1820.

But the brightness of all this glory was to be pathetically dimmed. In 1825 a general financial panic, revealing the laxity of Scott's business partners, caused his firm to fail with liabilities of nearly a hundred and twenty thousand pounds. Always magnanimous and the soul of honor, Scott refused to take advantage of the bankruptcy laws, himself assumed the burden of the entire debt, and set himself the stupendous task of paying it with his pen. Amid increasing personal sorrows he labored on for six years and so nearly attained his object that the debt was actually extinguished some years after his death. But in the effort he completed the exhaustion of his long-overtaxed strength, and, a trip to Italy proving unavailing, returned to Abbotsford, and died, a few weeks after Goethe, in 1832.

As a man Scott was first of all a true and thorough gentleman, manly, open hearted, friendly and lovable in the highest degree. Truthfulness and courage were to him the essential virtues, and his religious faith was deep though simple and unobtrusive. Like other forceful men, he understood his own capacity, but his modesty was extreme; he always insisted with all sincerity that the ability to compose fiction was not for a moment to be compared with the ability to act effectively in practical activities; and he was really displeased at the suggestion that he belonged among the greatest men of the age.

In spite of his Romantic tendencies and his absolute simplicity of character, he clung strongly to the conservatism of the feudal aristocracy with which he had labored so hard to connect himself; he was vigorously hostile to the democratic spirit, and, in his later years, to the Reform Bill; and he felt and expressed almost childish delight in the friendship of the contemptible George IV, because George IV was his king. The conservatism was closely connected, in fact, with his Romantic interest in the past, and in politics it took the form, theoretically, of Jacobitism, loyalty to the worthless Stuart race whose memory his novels have done so much to keep alive. All these traits are made abundantly clear in the extended life of Scott written by his son-in-law, J. G. Lockhart, which is one of the two or three greatest English biographies.

Scott's long poems, the best of them, are the chief examples in English of dashing verse romances of adventure and love. They are hastily done, as we have said, and there is no attempt at subtilty of characterization or at any moral or philosophical meaning; nevertheless the reader's interest in the vigorous and picturesque action is maintained throughout at the highest pitch. Furthermore, they contain much finely sympathetic description of Scottish scenery, impressionistic, but poured out with enthusiasm. Scott's numerous lyrics are similarly stirring or moving expressions of the primal emotions, and some of them are charmingly musical.

The qualities of the novels, which represent the culmination of Romantic historical fiction, are much the same. Through his bold and active historical imagination Scott vivifies the past magnificently; without doubt, the great majority of English readers know English history chiefly through his works. His dramatic power, also, at its best, is superb; in his great scenes and crises he is masterly as narrator and describer. In the presentation of the characters there is often much of the same superficiality as in the poems, but there is much also of the highest skill.

The novels may be roughly divided into three classes: first those, like 'Ivanhoe,' whose scene is laid in the twelfth or thirteenth century; second those, like 'Kenilworth,' which are located in the fifteenth or sixteenth; and third, those belonging to England and Scotland of the seventeenth and eighteenth. In the earlier ones sheer romance predominates and the hero and heroine are likely to be more or less conventional paragons, respectively, of courage and tender charm; but in the later ones Scott largely portrays the life and people which he himself knew; and he knew them through and through. His Scottish characters in particular, often especially the secondary ones, are delightfully realistic portraits of a great variety of types. Mary Queen of Scots in 'The Abbot' and Caleb Balderstone in 'The Bride of Lammermoor' are equally convincing in their essential but very personal humanity. Descriptions of scenery are correspondingly fuller in the novels than in the poems and are equally useful for atmosphere and background.

In minor matters, in the novels also, there is much carelessness. The style, more formal than that of the present day, is prevailingly wordy and not infrequently slipshod, though its vitality is a much more noticeable characteristic. The structure of the stories is far from compact. Scott generally began without any idea how he was to continue or end and sent off each day's instalment of his manuscript in the first draft as soon as it was written; hence the action often wanders, or even, from the structural point of view, drags. But interest seldom greatly slackens until the end, which, it must be further confessed, is often suddenly brought about in a very inartistic fashion. It is of less consequence that in the details of fact Scott often commits errors, not only, like all historical novelists, deliberately manipulating the order and details of the actual events to suit his purposes, but also making frequent sheer mistakes. In 'Ivanhoe,' for example, the picture of life in the twelfth century is altogether incorrect and misleading. In all these matters scores of more self-conscious later writers are superior to Scott, but mere correctness counts for far less than genius.

When all is said, Scott remains the greatest historical novelist, and one of the greatest creative forces, in world literature.

## THE LAST GROUP OF ROMANTIC POETS

Coleridge, Wordsworth, Southey, and Scott had mostly ceased to produce poetry by 1815. The group of younger men, the last out-and-out Romanticists, who succeeded them, writing chiefly from about 1810 to 1825, in some respects contrast strongly with them. Byron and Shelley were far more radically revolutionary; and Keats, in his poetry, was devoted wholly to the pursuit and worship of beauty with no concern either for a moral philosophy of life or for vigorous external adventure. It is a striking fact also that these later men were all very short-lived; they died at ages ranging only from twenty-six to thirty-six.

Lord Byron, 1788-1824. Byron (George Gordon Byron) expresses mainly the spirit of individual revolt, revolt against all existing institutions and standards. This was largely a matter of his own personal temperament, but the influence of the time also had a share in it, the time when the apparent failure of the French Revolution had thrown the pronounced liberals back upon their own resources in bitter dissatisfaction with the existing state of society. Byron was born in 1788. His father, the violent and worthless descendant of a line of violent and worthless nobles, was just then using up the money which the poet's mother had brought him, and soon abandoned her.

She in turn was wildly passionate and uncontrolled, and in bringing up her son indulged alternately in fits of genuine tenderness and capricious outbursts of mad rage and unkindness. Byron suffered also from another serious handicap; he was born with deformed feet, so that throughout life he walked clumsily--a galling irritation to his sensitive pride. In childhood his poetic instincts were stimulated by summers spent among the scenery of his mother's native Scottish Highlands. At the age of ten, on the death of his great-uncle, he succeeded to the peerage as Lord Byron, but for many years he continued to be heavily in debt, partly because of lavish extravagance, which was one expression of his inherited reckless wilfulness. Throughout his life he was obliged to make the most heroic efforts to keep in check another inherited tendency, to corpulence; he generally restricted his diet almost entirely to such meager fare as potatoes and soda-water, though he often broke out also into periods of unlimited self-indulgence.

From Harrow School he passed to Trinity College, Cambridge, where Macaulay and Tennyson were to be among his successors. Aspiring to be an athlete, he made himself respected as a fighter, despite his deformity, by his strength of arm, and he was always a powerful swimmer. Deliberately aiming also at the reputation of a debauchee, he lived wildly, though now as later probably not altogether so wickedly as he represented. After three years of irregular attendance at the University his rank secured him the degree of M. A., in 1808. He had already begun to publish verse, and when 'The Edinburgh Review' ridiculed his very juvenile 'Hours of Idleness' he added an attack on Jeffrey to a slashing criticism of contemporary poets which he had already written in rimed couplets (he always professed the highest admiration for Pope's poetry), and published the piece as 'English Bards and Scotch Reviewers.'

He was now settled at his inherited estate of Newstead Abbey (one of the religious foundations given to members of the nobility by Henry VIII when he confiscated them from the Church), and had made his appearance in his hereditary place in the House of Lords; but following his instinct for excitement and for doing the expensively conspicuous thing he next spent two years on a European tour, through Spain, Greece, and Turkey. In Greece he traveled, as was necessary, with a large native guard, and he allowed reports to become current that he passed through a succession of romantic and reckless adventures. The first literary result of his journey was the publication in 1812 of the first two cantos of 'Childe Harold's Pilgrimage.'

This began as the record of the wanderings of Childe Harold, a dissipated young noble who was clearly intended to represent the author himself; but Byron soon dropped this figure as a useless impediment in the series of descriptions of Spain and Greece of which the first two cantos consist. He soon abandoned also the attempt to secure an archaic effect by the occasional use of Spenserian words, but he wrote throughout in Spenser's stanza, which he used with much power. The public received the poem with the greatest enthusiasm; Byron summed up the case in his well-known comment: 'I awoke one morning and found myself famous.' In fact, 'Childe Harold' is the best of all

Byron's works, though the third and fourth cantos, published some years later, and dealing with Belgium, the battle of Waterloo, and central Europe, are superior to the first two.

Its excellence consists chiefly in the fact that while it is primarily a descriptive poem, its pictures, dramatically and finely vivid in themselves, are permeated with intense emotion and often serve only as introductions to passionate rhapsodies, so that the effect is largely lyrical.

Though Byron always remained awkward in company he now became the idol of the world of fashion. He followed up his first literary success by publishing during the next four years his brief and vigorous metrical romances, most of them Eastern in setting, 'The Giaour' (pronounced by Byron 'Jower'), 'The Bride of Abydos,' 'The Corsair,' 'Lara,' 'The Siege of Corinth,' and 'Parisina.' These were composed not only with remarkable facility but in the utmost haste, sometimes a whole poem in only a few days and sometimes in odds and ends of time snatched from social diversions. The results are only too clearly apparent; the meter is often slovenly, the narrative structure highly defective, and the characterization superficial or flatly inconsistent.

In other respects the poems are thoroughly characteristic of their author. In each of them stands out one dominating figure, the hero, a desperate and terrible adventurer, characterized by Byron himself as possessing 'one virtue and a thousand crimes,' merciless and vindictive to his enemies, tremblingly obeyed by his followers, manifesting human tenderness only toward his mistress (a delicate romantic creature to whom he is utterly devoted in the approved romantic-sentimental fashion), and above all inscrutably enveloped in a cloud of pretentious romantic melancholy and mystery. Like Childe Harold, this impossible and grandiose figure of many incarnations was well understood by every one to be meant for a picture of Byron himself, who thus posed for and received in full measure the horrified admiration of the public. But in spite of all this melodramatic clap-trap the romances, like 'Childe Harold,' are filled with the tremendous Byronic passion, which, as in 'Childe Harold,' lends great power alike to their narrative and their description.

Byron now made a strangely ill-judged marriage with a Miss Milbanke, a woman of the fashionable world but of strict and perhaps even prudish moral principles. After a year she left him, and 'society,' with characteristic inconsistency, turned on him in a frenzy of superficial indignation. He shortly (1816) fled from England, never to return, both his colossal vanity and his truer sensitive self stung by the injustice to fury against the hypocrisy and conventionalities of English life, which, in fact, he had always despised. He spent the following seven years as a wanderer over Italy and central Europe. He often lived scandalously; sometimes he was with the far more fine-spirited Shelley; and he sometimes furnished money to the Italians who were conducting the agitation against their tyrannical foreign governments.

All the while he was producing a great quantity of poetry. In his half dozen or more poetic dramas he entered a new field. In the most important of them, 'Manfred,' a treatment of the theme which Marlowe and Goethe had used in 'Faust,' his real power is largely thwarted by the customary Byronic mystery and swagger. 'Cain' and 'Heaven and Earth,' though wretchedly written, have also a vaguely vast imaginative impressiveness. Their defiant handling of Old Testament material and therefore of Christian theology was shocking to most respectable Englishmen and led Southey to characterize Byron as the founder of the 'Satanic School' of English poetry. More significant is the longest and chief of his satires, 'Don Juan,' on which he wrote intermittently for years as the mood took him. It is ostensibly the narrative of the adventures of a young Spaniard, but as a story it rambles on formlessly without approaching an end, and its real purpose is to serve as an utterly cynical indictment of mankind, the institutions of society, and accepted moral principles. Byron often points the cynicism by lapsing into brilliant doggerel, but his double nature appears in the occasional intermingling of tender and beautiful passages.

Byron's fiery spirit was rapidly burning itself out. In his uncontrolled zest for new sensations he finally tired of poetry, and in 1823 he accepted the invitation of the European committee in charge to become a leader of the Greek revolt against Turkish oppression. He sailed to the Greek camp at the malarial town of Missolonghi, where he showed qualities of leadership but died of fever after a few months, in 1824, before he had time to accomplish anything.

It is hard to form a consistent judgment of so inconsistent a being as Byron. At the core of his nature there was certainly much genuine goodness--generosity, sympathy, and true feeling. However much we may discount his sacrifice of his life in the cause of a foreign people, his love of political freedom and his hatred of tyranny were thoroughly and passionately sincere, as is repeatedly evident in such poems as the sonnet on 'Chillon,' 'The Prisoner of Chillon,' and the 'Ode on Venice.' On the other hand his violent contempt for social and religious hypocrisy had as much of personal bitterness as of disinterested principle; and his persistent quest of notoriety, the absence of moderation in his attacks on religious and moral standards, his lack of self-control, and his indulgence in all the vices of the worser part of the titled and wealthy class require no comment. Whatever allowances charity may demand on the score of tainted heredity, his character was far too violent and too shallow to approach to greatness.

As a poet he continues to occupy a conspicuous place (especially in the judgment of non-English-speaking nations) through the power of his volcanic emotion. It was this quality of emotion, perhaps the first essential in poetry, which enrolled among his admirers a clear spirit in most respects the antithesis of his own, that of Matthew Arnold. In 'Memorial Verses' Arnold says of him:

*He taught us little, but our soul*
*Had felt him like the thunder's roll.*
*With shivering heart the strife we saw*
*Of passion with eternal law.*

His poetry has also an elemental sweep and grandeur. The majesty of Nature, especially of the mountains and the ocean, stirs him to feeling which often results in superb stanzas, like the well-known ones at the end of 'Childe Harold' beginning 'Roll on, thou deep and dark blue Ocean, roll'! Too often, however, Byron's passion and facility of expression issue in bombast and crude rhetoric. Moreover, his poetry is for the most part lacking in delicacy and fine shading; scarcely a score of his lyrics are of the highest order. He gives us often the blaring music of a military band or the loud, swelling volume of an organ, but very seldom the softer tones of a violin or symphony.

To his creative genius and power the variety as well as the amount of his poetry offers forceful testimony.

In moods of moral and literary severity, to summarize, a critic can scarcely refrain from dismissing Byron with impatient contempt; nevertheless his genius and his in part splendid achievement are substantial facts. He stands as the extreme but significant exponent of violent Romantic individualism in a period when Romantic aspiration was largely disappointed and disillusioned, but was indignantly gathering its strength for new efforts.

## PERCY BYSSHE SHELLEY, 1792-1832

Shelley resembles Byron in his thorough-going revolt against society, but he is totally unlike Byron in several important respects. His first impulse was an unselfish love for his fellow-men, with an aggressive eagerness for martyrdom in their behalf; his nature was unusually, even abnormally, fine and sensitive; and his poetic quality was a delicate and ethereal lyricism unsurpassed in the literature of the world. In both his life and his poetry his visionary reforming zeal and his superb lyric instinct are inextricably intertwined.

Shelley, born in 1792, belonged to a family of Sussex country gentry; a baronetcy bestowed on his grandfather during the poet's youth passed from his father after his own death to his descendants. Matthew Arnold has remarked that while most of the members of any aristocracy are naturally conservative, confirmed advocates of the system under which they enjoy great privileges, any one of them who happens to be endowed with radical ideas is likely to carry these to an extreme. In Shelley's case this general tendency was strengthened by reaction against the benighted Toryism of his father and by most of the experiences of his life from the very outset. At Eton his hatred of tyranny was fiercely aroused by the fagging system and the other brutalities of an English school; he broke into open revolt and became known as 'mad Shelley,' and his schoolfellows delighted in driving him into paroxysms of rage.

Already at Eton he read and accepted the doctrines of the French pre-Revolutionary philosophers and their English interpreter William Godwin. He came to believe not only that human nature is essentially good, but that if left to itself it can be implicitly trusted; that sin and misery are merely the results of the injustice springing from the institutions of society, chief of which are organized government, formal religion, law, and formal marriage; and that the one essential thing is to bring about a condition where these institutions can be abolished and where all men may be allowed to follow their own inclinations.

The great advance which has been made since Shelley's time in the knowledge of history and the social sciences throws a pitiless light on the absurdity of this theory, showing that social institutions, terribly imperfect as they are, are by no means chiefly bad but rather represent the slow gains of thousands of years of painful progress; none the less the theory was bound to appeal irresistibly to such an impulsive and inexperienced idealism as that of Shelley.

It was really, of course, not so much against social institutions themselves that Shelley revolted as against their abuses, which were still more flagrantly apparent in his time than in ours. When he repudiated Christianity and declared himself an atheist, what he actually had in mind was the perverted parody of religion mainly offered by the Church of his time; and, as some one has observed, when he pronounced for love without marriage it was because of the tragedies that he had seen in marriages without love. Much must be ascribed also to his sheer radicalism--the instinct to fly violently against whatever was conventionally accepted and violently to flaunt his adherence to whatever was banned.

In 1810 Shelley entered Oxford, especially exasperated by parental interference with his first boyish love, and already the author of some crude prose-romances and poetry. In the university he devoted his time chiefly to investigating subjects not included or permitted in the curriculum, especially chemistry; and after a few months, having written a pamphlet on 'The Necessity of Atheism' and sent it with conscientious zeal to the heads of the colleges, he was expelled. Still a few months later, being then nineteen years old, he allowed himself to be led, admittedly only through pity, into a marriage with a certain Harriet Westbrook, a frivolous and commonplace schoolgirl of sixteen.

For the remaining ten years of his short life he, like Byron, was a wanderer, sometimes in straits for money, though always supported, after some time generously enough, by his father. At first he tried the career of a professional agitator; going to Ireland he attempted to arouse the people against English tyranny by such devices as scattering copies of addresses from his window in Dublin or launching them in bottles in the Bristol Channel; but he was soon obliged to flee the country.

It is hard, of course, to take such conduct seriously; yet in the midst of much that was wild, his pamphlets contained also much of solid wisdom, no small part of which has since been enacted into law.

Unselfish as he was in the abstract, Shelley's enthusiast's egotism and the unrestraint of his emotions rendered him fitful, capricious, unable to appreciate any point of view but his own, and therefore when irritated or excited capable of downright cruelty in concrete cases. The most painful illustration is afforded by his treatment of his first wife. Three years after his marriage he informed her that he considered the connection at an end and abandoned her to what proved a few years of a wretched existence. Shelley himself formed a union with Mary Wollstonecraft Godwin, the daughter of his revolutionary teacher.

Her sympathetic though extravagant admiration for his genius, now beginning to express itself in really great poetry, was of the highest value to him, the more so that from this time on he was viewed by most respectabie Englishman with the same abhorrence which they felt for Byron. In 1818 the Shelleys also abandoned England (permanently, as it proved) for Italy, where they moved from place to place, living sometimes, as we have said, with Byron, for whose genius, in spite of its coarseness, Shelley had a warm admiration.

Shelley's death came when he was only thirty, in 1822, by a sudden accident--he was drowned by the upsetting of his sailboat in the Gulf of Spezia, between Genoa and Pisa. His body, cast on the shore, was burned in the presence of Byron and another radical, Leigh Hunt, and the ashes were buried in the Protestant cemetery just outside the wall of Rome, where Keats had been interred only a year earlier.

Some of Shelley's shorter poems are purely poetic expressions of poetic emotion, but by far the greater part are documents (generally beautiful also as poetry) in his attack on existing customs and cruelties. Matthew Arnold, paraphrasing Joubert's description of Plato, has characterized him as 'a beautiful and ineffectual angel, beating in the void his luminous wings in vain.' This is largely true, but it overlooks the sound general basis and the definite actual results which belong to his work, as to that of every great idealist.

On the artistic side the most conspicuous thing in his poetry is the ecstatic aspiration for Beauty and the magnificent embodiment of it. Shelley is the poetic disciple, but a thoroughly original disciple, of Coleridge. His esthetic passion is partly sensuous, and he often abandons himself to it with romantic unrestraint. His 'lyrical cry,' of which Matthew Arnold has spoken, is the demand, which will not be denied, for beauty that will satisfy his whole being. Sensations, indeed, he must always have, agreeable ones if possible, or in default of them, painful ones; this explains his occasional touches of repulsive morbidness. But the repulsive strain is exceptional. No other poetry is crowded in the same way as his with pictures glorious and delicate in form, light, and color, or is more musically palpitating with the delight which they create.

To Shelley as a follower of Plato, however, the beauty of the senses is only a manifestation of ideal Beauty, the spiritual force which appears in other forms as Intellect and Love; and Intellect and Love as well are equal objects of his unbounded devotion. Hence his sensuousness is touched with a real spiritual quality. In his poetic emotion, as in his social ambitions, Shelley is constantly yearning for the unattainable. One of our best critics has observed: 'He never shows his full power in dealing separately with intellectual or moral or physical beauty. His appropriate sphere is swift sensibility, the intersecting line between the sensuous and the intellectual or moral. Mere sensation is too literal for him, mere feeling too blind and dumb, mere thought too cold.... Wordsworth is always exulting in the fulness of Nature, Shelley is always chasing its falling stars.'

The contrast, here hinted at, between Shelley's view of Nature and that of Wordsworth, is extreme and entirely characteristic; the same is true, also, when we compare Shelley and Byron. Shelley's excitable sensuousness produces in him in the presence of Nature a very different attitude from that of Wordsworth's philosophic Christian-mysticism. For the sensuousness of Shelley gets the upper hand of his somewhat shadowy Platonism, and he creates out of Nature mainly an ethereal world of delicate and rapidly shifting sights and sounds and sensations. And while he is not unresponsive to the majestic greatness of Nature in her vast forms and vistas, he is never impelled, like Byron, to claim with them the kinship of a haughty elemental spirit.

A rather long passage of appreciative criticism is sufficiently suggestive for quotation:

"From the world of [Shelley's] imagination the shapes of the old world had disappeared, and their place was taken by a stream of radiant vapors, incessantly forming, shifting, and dissolving in the 'clear golden dawn,' and hymning with the voices of seraphs, to the music of the stars and the 'singing rain,' the sublime ridiculous theories of Godwin. In his heart were emotions that responded to the vision--an aspiration or ecstasy, a dejection or despair, like those of spirits rapt into Paradise or mourning over its ruin. And he wrote not like Shakspere or Pope, for Londoners sitting in a theatre or a coffee-house, intelligence's vivid enough but definitely embodied in a definite society, able to fly, but also able to sit; he wrote, or rather he sang, to his own soul, to other spirit-sparks of the fire of Liberty scattered over the dark earth, to spirits in the air, to the boundless spirit of Nature or Freedom or Love, his one place of rest and the one source of his vision, ecstasy, and sorrow.

He sang to this, and he sang of it, and of the emotions it inspired, and of its world-wide contest with such shapes of darkness as Faith and Custom. And he made immortal music; now in melodies as exquisite and varied as the songs of Schubert, and now in symphonies where the crudest of Philosophies of History melted into golden harmony. For although there was something always working in Shelley's mind and issuing in those radiant vapors, he was far deeper and truer than his philosophic creed; its expression and even its development were constantly checked or distorted by the hard and narrow framework of his creed. And it was one which in effect condemned nine-tenths of the human nature that has formed the material of the world's great poems."

The finest of Shelley's poems, are his lyrics. 'The Skylark' and 'The Cloud' are among the most dazzling and unique of all outbursts of poetic genius. Of the 'Ode to the West Wind,' a succession of surging emotions and visions of beauty swept, as if by the wind itself, through the vast spaces of the world, Swinburne exclaims: 'It is beyond and outside and above all criticism, all praise, and all thanksgiving.' The 'Lines Written among the Euganean Hills,' 'The Indian Serenade,' 'The Sensitive Plant' (a brief narrative), and not a few others are also of the highest quality. In 'Adonais,' an elegy on Keats and an invective against the reviewer whose brutal criticism, as Shelley wrongly supposed, had helped to kill him, splendid poetic power, at least, must be admitted. Much less satisfactory but still fascinating are the longer poems, narrative or philosophical, such as the early 'Alastor,' a vague allegory of a poet's quest for the beautiful through a gorgeous and incoherent succession of romantic wildernesses; the 'Hymn to Intellectual Beauty'; 'Julian and Maddalo,' in which Shelley and Byron (Maddalo) are portrayed; and 'Epipsychidion,' an ecstatic poem on the love which is spiritual sympathy. Shelley's satires may be disregarded.

To the dramatic form belong his two most important long poems. 'Prometheus Unbound' partly follows AEschylus in treating the torture of the Titan who is the champion or personification of Mankind, by Zeus, whom Shelley makes the incarnation of tyranny and on whose overthrow the Golden Age of Shelleyan anarchy succeeds. The poem is a lyrical drama, more on the Greek than on the English model. There is almost no action, and the significance lies first in the lyrical beauty of the profuse choruses and second in the complete embodiment of Shelley's passionate hatred of tyranny. 'The Cenci' is more dramatic in form, though the excess of speech over action makes of it also only a 'literary drama.'

The story, taken from family history of the Italian Renaissance, is one of the most horrible imaginable, but the play is one of the most powerful produced in English since the Elizabethan period. That the quality of Shelley's genius is unique is obvious on the slightest acquaintance with him, and it is equally certain that in spite of his premature death and all his limitations he occupies an assured place among the very great poets. On the other hand, the vagueness of his imagination and expression has recently provoked severe criticism. It has even been declared that the same mind cannot honestly enjoy both the carefully wrought classical beauty of Milton's 'Lycidas' and Shelley's mistily shimmering 'Adonais.' The question goes deep and should receive careful consideration.

## JOHN KEATS, 1795-1821

No less individual and unique than the poetry of Byron and Shelley is that of the third member of this group, John Keats, who is, in a wholesome way, the most conspicuous great representative in English poetry since Chaucer of the spirit of 'Art for Art's sake.' Keats was born in London in 1795, the first son of a livery-stable keeper. Romantic emotion and passionateness were among his chief traits from the start; but he was equally distinguished by a generous spirit, physical vigor (though he was very short in build), and courage. His younger brothers he loved intensely and fought fiercely. At boarding-school, however, he turned from headstrong play to enthusiastic reading of Spenser and other great English and Latin poets and of dictionaries of Greek and Roman mythology and life. An orphan at fourteen, the mismanagement of his guardians kept him always in financial difficulties, and he was taken from school and apprenticed to a suburban surgeon. After five years of study and hospital practice the call of poetry proved too strong, and he abandoned his profession to revel in Spenser, Shakspere, and the Italian epic authors. He now became an enthusiastic disciple of the literary and political radical, Leigh Hunt, in whose home at Hampstead he spent much time. Hunt was a great poetic stimulus to Keats, but he is largely responsible for the flippant jauntiness and formlessness of Keats' earlier poetry, and the connection brought on Keats from the outset the relentless hostility of the literacy critics, who had dubbed Hunt and his friends 'The Cockney [i.e., Vulgar] School of Poetry.'

Keats' first little volume of verse, published in 1817, when he was twenty-one,-contained some delightful poems and clearly displayed most of his chief tendencies. It was followed the next year by his longest poem, 'Endymion,' where he uses, one of the vaguely beautiful Greek myths as the basis for the expression of his own delight in the glory of the world and of youthful sensations.

As a narrative the poem is wandering, almost chaotic; that it is immature Keats himself frankly admitted in his preface; but in luxuriant loveliness of sensuous imagination it is unsurpassed. Its theme, and indeed the theme of all Keats' poetry, may be said to be found in its famous first line--'A thing of beauty is a joy forever.' The remaining three years of Keats' life were mostly tragic. 'Endymion' and its author were brutally attacked in 'The Quarterly Review' and 'Blackwood's Magazine.' The sickness and death, from consumption, of one of Keats' dearly-loved brothers was followed by his infatuation with a certain Fanny Brawne, a commonplace girl seven years younger than himself.

This infatuation thenceforth divided his life with poetry and helped to create in him a restless impatience that led him, among other things, to an unhappy effort to force his genius, in the hope of gain, into the very unsuitable channel of play-writing. But restlessness did not weaken his genuine and maturing poetic power; his third and last volume, published in 1820, and including 'The Eve of St. Agnes,' 'Isabella,' 'Lamia,' the fragmentary 'Hyperion,' and his half dozen great odes, probably contains more poetry of the highest order than any other book of original verse, of so small a size, ever sent from the press. By this time, however, Keats himself was stricken with consumption, and in the effort to save his life a warmer climate was the last resource.

Lack of sympathy with Shelley and his poetry led him to reject Shelley's generous offer of entertainment at Pisa, and he sailed with his devoted friend the painter Joseph Severn to southern Italy. A few months later, in 1821, he died at Rome, at the age of twenty-five. His tombstone, in a neglected corner of the Protestant cemetery just outside the city wall, bears among other words those which in bitterness of spirit he himself had dictated: 'Here lies one whose name was writ in water.' But, in fact, not only had he created more great poetry than was ever achieved by any other man at so early an age, but probably no other influence was to prove so great as his on the poets of the next generation.

The most important qualities of his poetry stand out clearly:

1. He is, as we have implied, the great apostle of full though not unhealthy enjoyment of external Beauty, the beauty of the senses. He once said: 'I feel sure I should write, from the mere yearning and tenderness I have for the beautiful, even if my night's labors should be burnt every morning and no eye ever rest upon them.' His use of beauty in his poetry is marked at first by passionate Romantic abandonment and always by lavish Romantic richness. This passion was partly stimulated in him by other poets, largely by the Italians, and especially by Spenser, from one of whose minor poems Keats chose the motto for his first volume: 'What more felicity can fall to creature than to enjoy delight with liberty?' Shelley's enthusiasm for Beauty, as we have seen, is somewhat similar to that of Keats.

   But for both Spenser and Shelley, in different fashions, external Beauty is only the outer garment of the Platonic spiritual Beauty, while to Keats in his poetry it is, in appearance at least, almost everything. He once exclaimed, even, 'Oh for a life of sensations rather than of thoughts!' Notable in his poetry is the absence of any moral purpose and of any interest in present-day life and character, particularly the absence of the democratic feeling which had figured so largely in most of his Romantic predecessors. These facts must not be over-emphasized, however. His famous final phrasing of the great poetic idea--'Beauty is truth, truth beauty'--itself shows consciousness of realities below the surface, and the inference which is sometimes hastily drawn that he was personally a fiberless dreamer is as far as possible from the truth.

   In fact he was always vigorous and normal, as well as sensitive; he was always devoted to outdoor life; and his very attractive letters, from which his nature can best be judged, are not only overflowing with unpretentious and cordial human feeling but testify that he was not really unaware of specific social and moral issues. Indeed, occasional passages in his poems indicate that he intended to deal with these issues in other poems when he should feel his powers adequately matured. Whether, had he lived, he would have proved capable of handling them significantly is one of the questions which must be left to conjecture, like the other question whether his power of style would have further developed.

Almost all of Keats' poems are exquisite and luxuriant in their embodiment of sensuous beauty, but 'The Eve of St. Agnes,' in Spenser's richly lingering stanza, must be especially mentioned.

2. Keats is one of the supreme masters of poetic expression, expression the most beautiful, apt, vivid, condensed, and imaginatively suggestive. His poems are noble storehouses of such lines as these:

*The music, yearning like a God in pain.*

*Into her dream he melted, as the rose*

*Blendeth its odour with the violet.*

*magic casements, opening on the foam*

*Of perilous seas, in faery lands forlorn.*

It is primarily in this respect that he has been the teacher of later poets.

3. Keats never attained dramatic or narrative power or skill in the presentation of individual character. In place of these elements he has the lyric gift of rendering moods. Aside from ecstatic delight, these are mostly moods of pensiveness, languor, or romantic sadness, like the one so magically suggested in the 'Ode to a Nightingale,' of Ruth standing lonely and 'in tears amid the alien corn.'

4. Conspicuous in Keats is his spiritual kinship with the ancient Greeks. He assimilated with eager delight all the riches of the Greek imagination, even though he never learned the language and was dependent on the dull mediums of dictionaries and translations. It is not only that his recognition of the permanently significant and beautiful embodiment of the central facts of life in the Greek stories led him to select some of them as the

> subjects for several of his most important poems; but his whole feeling, notably his feeling for Nature, seems almost precisely that of the Greeks, especially, perhaps, of the earlier generations among whom their mythology took shape. To him also Nature appears alive with divinities. Walking through the woods he almost expects to catch glimpses of hamadryads peering from their trees, nymphs rising from the fountains, and startled fauns with shaggy skins and cloven feet scurrying away among the bushes.

In his later poetry, also, the deeper force of the Greek spirit led him from his early Romantic formlessness to the achievement of the most exquisite classical perfection of form and finish. His Romantic glow and emotion never fade or cool, but such poems as the Odes to the Nightingale and to a Grecian Urn, and the fragment of 'Hyperion,' are absolutely flawless and satisfying in structure and expression.

## SUMMARY

One of the best comments on the poets whom we have just been considering is a single sentence of Lowell: 'Three men, almost contemporaneous with each other, Wordsworth, Keats, and Byron, were the great means of bringing back English poetry from the sandy deserts of rhetoric and recovering for her her triple inheritance of simplicity, sensuousness, and passion.' But justice must be done also to the 'Renaissance of Wonder' in Coleridge, the ideal aspiration of Shelley, and the healthy stirring of the elementary instincts by Scott.

## LESSER WRITERS

Throughout our discussion of the nineteenth century it will be more than ever necessary to pass by with little or no mention various authors who are almost of the first rank. To our present period belong: Thomas Campbell (1777-1844), author of 'Ye Mariners of England,' 'Hohenlinden,' and other spirited battle lyrics; Thomas Moore (1779-1852), a facile but over-sentimental Irishman, author of 'Irish Melodies,' 'Lalla Rookh,' and a famous life of Byron; Charles. Lamb (1775-1834), the delightfully whimsical essayist and lover of Shakspere; William Hazlitt (1778-1830), a romantically dogmatic but sympathetically appreciative critic; Thomas de Quincey (1785-1859), a capricious and voluminous author, master of a poetic prose style, best known for his 'Confessions of an English Opium-Eater'; Walter Savage Landor (1775-1864), the best nineteenth century English representative, both in prose and in lyric verse, of the pure classical spirit, though his own temperament was violently romantic; Thomas Love Peacock (1785-1866), author of some delightful satirical and humorous novels, of which 'Maid Marian' anticipated 'Ivanhoe'; and Miss Mary Russell Mitford (1787-1855), among whose charming prose sketches of country life 'Our Village' is best and best-known.

# 12

# The Victorian Period

## GENERAL CONDITIONS

The last completed period of English literature, almost coincident in extent with the reign of the queen whose name it bears (Victoria, queen 1837-1901), stands nearly beside The Elizabethan period in the significance and interest of its work. The Elizabethan literature to be sure, in its imaginative and spiritual enthusiasm, is the expression of a period more profoundly great than the Victorian; but the Victorian literature speaks for an age which witnessed incomparably greater changes than any that had gone before in all the conditions of life--material comforts, scientific knowledge, and, absolutely speaking, in intellectual and spiritual enlightenment. Moreover, to twentieth century students the Victorian literature makes a specially strong appeal because it is in part the literature of our own time and its ideas and point of view are in large measure ours. We must begin by glancing briefly at some of the general determining changes and conditions to which reference has just been made, and we may naturally begin with the merely material ones.

Before the accession of Queen Victoria the 'industrial revolution,' the vast development of manufacturing made possible in the latter part of the eighteenth century by the introduction of coal and the steam engine, had rendered England the richest nation in the world, and the movement continued with steadily accelerating momentum throughout the period. Hand in hand with it went the increase of population from less than thirteen millions in England in 1825 to nearly three times as many at the end of the period. The introduction of the steam railway and the steamship, at the beginning of the period, in place of the lumbering stagecoach and the sailing vessel, broke up the old stagnant and stationary habits of life and increased the amount of travel at least a thousand times.

The discovery of the electric telegraph in 1844 brought almost every important part of Europe, and eventually of the world, nearer to every town dweller than the nearest county had been in the eighteenth century; and the development of the modern newspaper out of the few feeble sheets of 1825 (dailies and weeklies in London, only weeklies elsewhere), carried full accounts of the doings of the whole world, in place of long-delayed fragmentary rumors, to every door within a few hours. No less striking was the progress in public health and the increase in human happiness due to the enormous advance in the sciences of medicine, surgery, and hygiene. Indeed these sciences in their modern form virtually began with the discovery of the facts of bacteriology about 1860, and the use of antiseptics fifteen years later, and not much earlier began the effective opposition to the frightful epidemics which had formerly been supposed to be dependent only on the will of Providence.

Political and social progress, though less astonishing, was substantial. In 1830 England, nominally a monarchy, was in reality a plutocracy of about a hundred thousand men--landed nobles, gentry, and wealthy merchants--whose privileges dated back to fifteenth century conditions. The first Reform Bill, of 1832, forced on Parliament by popular pressure, extended the right of voting to men of the 'middle class,' and the subsequent bills of 1867 and 1885 made it universal for men. Meanwhile the House of Commons slowly asserted itself against the hereditary House of Lords, and thus England became perhaps the most truly democratic of the great nations of the world. At the beginning of the period the social condition of the great body of the population was extremely bad. Laborers in factories and mines and on farms were largely in a state of virtual though not nominal slavery, living, many of them, in unspeakable moral and physical conditions.

Little by little improvement came, partly by the passage of laws, partly by the growth of trades-unions. The substitution in the middle of the century of free-trade for protection through the passage of the 'Corn-Laws' afforded much relief by lowering the price of food. Socialism, taking shape as a definite movement in the middle of the century, became one to be reckoned with before its close, though the majority of the more well-to-do classes failed to understand even then the growing necessity for far-reaching economic and social changes. Humanitarian consciousness, however, gained greatly during the period. The middle and upper classes awoke to some extent to their duty to the poor, and sympathetic benevolent effort, both organized and informal, increased very largely in amount and intelligence. Popular education, too, which in 1830 had no connection with the State and was in every respect very incomplete, was developed and finally made compulsory as regards the rudiments.

Still more permanently significant, perhaps, was the transformation of the former conceptions of the nature and meaning of the world and life, through the discoveries of science. Geology and astronomy now gradually compelled all thinking people to realize the unthinkable duration of the cosmic processes and the comparative littleness of our earth in the vast extent of the universe. Absolutely revolutionary for almost all lines if thought was the gradual adoption by almost all thinkers of the theory of Evolution, which, partly formulated by Lamarck early in the century, received definite statement in 1859 in Charles Darwin's 'Origin of Species.' The great modification in the externals of religious belief thus brought about was confirmed also by the growth of the science of historical criticism.

This movement of religious change was met in its early stages by the very interesting reactionary 'Oxford' or 'Tractarian' Movement, which asserted the supreme authority of the Church and its traditional doctrines. The most important figure in this movement, who connects it definitely with literature, was John Henry Newman (1801-90), author of the hymn 'Lead, Kindly Light,' a man of winning personality and great literary skill. For fifteen years, as vicar of the Oxford University Church, Newman was a great spiritual force in the English communion, but the series of 'Tracts for the Times' to which he largely contributed, ending in 1841 in the famous Tract 90, tell the story of his gradual progress toward Rome.

Thereafter as an avowed Roman Catholic and head of a monastic establishment Newman showed himself a formidable controversialist, especially in a literary encounter with the clergyman-novelist Charles Kingsley which led to Newman's famous 'Apologia pro Vita Sua' (Apology for My Life), one of the secondary literary masterpieces of the century.

His services to the Catholic Church were recognized in 1879 by his appointment as a Cardinal. More than one of the influences thus hastily surveyed combine in creating the moral, social, and intellectual strenuousness which is one of the main marks of the literature of the period. More conspicuously than ever before the majority of the great writers, not least the poets and novelists, were impelled not merely by the emotional or dramatic creative impulse but by the sense of a message for their age which should broaden the vision and elevate the ideals of the masses of their fellows. The literature of the period, therefore, lacks the disinterested and joyous spontaneity of, for example, the Elizabethan period, and its mood is far more complex than that of the partly socially-minded pseudo-classicists.

While all the new influences were manifesting themselves in Victorian literature they did not, of course, supersede the great general inherited tendencies. This literature is in the main romantic. On the social side this should be evident; the Victorian social humanitarianism is merely the developed form of the eighteenth century romantic democratic impulse. On the esthetic side the romantic traits are also present, though not so aggressively as in the previous period; with romantic vigor the Victorian literature often combines exquisite classical finish; indeed, it is so eclectic and composite that all the definite older terms take on new and less sharply contrasting meanings when applied to it.

So long a period naturally falls into sub-divisions; during its middle part in particular, progress and triumphant romanticism, not yet largely attacked by scientific scepticism, had created a prevailing atmosphere of somewhat passive sentiment and optimism both in society and in literature which has given to the adjective 'mid-Victorian' a very definite denotation. The adjective and its period are commonly spoken of with contempt in our own day by those persons who pride themselves on their complete sophistication and superiority to all intellectual and emotional weakness. But during the 'mid-Victorian' years, there was also a comparative healthiness in the lives of the well-to-do classes and in literature which had never before been equalled and which may finally prove no less praiseworthy than the rather self-conscious freedom and unrestraint of the early twentieth century.

The most important literature of the whole period falls under the three heads of essays, poetry, and prose fiction, which we may best consider in that order.

**LORD MACAULAY**

The first great figure, chronologically, in the period, and one of the most clearly-defined and striking personalities in English literature, is Thomas Babington Macaulay, [Footnote: The details of Macaulay's life are known from the; famous biography of him by his nephew, Sir George Trevelyan.] who represents in the fullest degree the Victorian vigor and delight in material progress, but is quite untouched by the Victorian spiritual striving. The descendant of Scottish ministers and English Quakers, Macaulay was born in 1800. His father was a tireless and devoted member of the group of London anti-slavery workers (Claphamites), and was Secretary of the company which conducted Sierra Leone (the African state for enfranchised negroes); he had also made a private fortune in African trade.

From his very babyhood the son displayed almost incredible intellectual precocity and power of memory. His voracious reading began at the age of three, when he 'for the most part lay on the rug before the fire, with his book on the floor, and a piece of bread-and-butter in his hand.' Once, in his fifth year, when a servant had spilled an urn of hot coffee over his legs, he replied to the distressed inquiries of the lady of the house, 'Thank you, madam, the agony is abated.' From the first it seems to have been almost impossible for him to forget anything which had ever found lodgment in, or even passed through, his mind. His childish production of both verse and prose was immense. These qualities and accomplishments, however, did not make him a prig. Both as child and as man, though he was aggressive and showed the prejudices of his class, he was essentially natural and unaffected; and as man he was one of the most cordial and affectionate of companions, lavish of his time with his friends, and one of the most interesting of conversationalists. As he grew toward maturity he proved unique in his manner, as well as in his power, of reading. It is said that he read books faster than other people skimmed them, and skimmed them as fast as any one else could turn the leaves, this, however, without superficiality. One of the habits of his middle life was to walk through London, even the most crowded parts, 'as fast as other people walked, and reading a book a great deal faster than anybody else could read.' His remarkable endowments, however, were largely counterbalanced by his deficiency in the spiritual sense. This appears most seriously in his writings, but it shows itself also in his personal tastes.

For Nature he cared little; like Dr. Johnson he 'found London the place for him.' One occasion when he remarked on the playing of 'God save the Queen' is said to have been the only one when he ever appeared to distinguish one tune from another. Even on the material side of life he had limitations very unusual in an English gentleman. Except for walking, which might almost be called a main occupation with him, he neither practised nor cared for any form of athletic exercise, 'could neither swim nor row nor drive nor skate nor shoot,' nor scarcely ride.

From private schools Macaulay proceeded to Trinity College, Cambridge, where he remained through the seven years required for the Master's degree. In spite of his aversion for mathematics, he finally won a 'lay' fellowship, which did not involve residence at the University nor any other obligation, but which almost sufficed for his support during the seven years of its duration. At this time his father failed in his business, and during several years Macaulay was largely occupied with the heavy task of reestablishing it and paying the creditors. In college he had begun to write in prose and verse for the public literary magazines, and in 1825 appeared his essay on Milton, the first of the nearly forty literary, historical, and biographical essays which during the next thirty years or more he contributed to 'The Edinburgh Review.'

He also nominally studied law, and was admitted to the bar in 1826, but he took no interest in the profession. In 1828 he was made a Commissioner of Bankruptcy and in 1830 he attained the immediate object of his ambition by receiving from a nobleman who controlled it a seat in Parliament. Here he at once distinguished himself as orator and worker. Heart and soul a Liberal, he took a prominent part in the passage of the first Reform Bill, of 1832, living at the same time a busy social life in titled society.

The Ministry rewarded his services with a position on the Board of Control, which represented the government in its relations with the East India Company, and in 1834, in order to earn the fortune which seemed to him essential to his continuance in the unremunerative career of public life, he accepted the position of legal adviser to the Supreme Council of India, which carried with it a seat in that Council and a salary of L10,000 a year. During the three months voyage to India he 'devoured' and in many cases copiously annotated a vast number of books in 'Greek, Latin, Spanish, Italian, French, and English; folios, quartos, octavos, and duodecimos.' Under the pressure of actual necessity he now mastered the law, and the most important parts of the astonishing mass of work that he performed during his three and a half years in India consisted in redrafting the penal code and in helping to organize education.

Soon after his return to England he was elected to Parliament as member for Edinburgh, and for two years he was in the Cabinet. Somewhat later the publication of his 'Lays of Ancient Rome' and of his collected essays brought him immense fame as a writer, and in 1847 his defeat at Edinburgh for reelection to Parliament gave him time for concentrated labor on the 'History of England' which he had already begun as his crowning work. To it he thenceforth devoted most of his energies, reading and sifting the whole mass of available source-material and visiting the scenes of the chief historical events.

The popular success of the five volumes which he succeeded in preparing and published at intervals was enormous. In 1852 he was reelected to Parliament at Edinburgh, but ill-health resulting from his long-continued excessive expenditure of energy warned him that he had not long to live. He was made a baron in 1857 and died in 1859, deeply mourned both because of his manly character and because with him perished mostly unrecorded a knowledge of the facts of English history more minute, probably, than that of any one else who has ever lived.

Macaulay never married, but, warm-hearted as he was, always lived largely in his affection for his sisters and for the children of one of them, Lady Trevelyan. In his public life he displayed as an individual a fearless and admirable devotion to principle, modified somewhat by the practical politician's devotion to party. From every point of view, his character was remarkable, though bounded by his very definite limitations.

Least noteworthy among Macaulay's works are his poems, of which the 'Lays of Ancient Rome' are chief. Here his purpose is to embody his conception of the heroic historical ballads which must have been current among the early Romans as among the medieval English--to recreate these ballads for modern readers.

For this sort of verse Macaulay's temperament was precisely adapted, and the 'Lays' present the simple characters, scenes, and ideals of the early Roman republican period with a sympathetic vividness and in stirring rhythms which give them an unlimited appeal to boys. None the less the 'Lays' really make nothing else so clear as that in the true sense of the word Macaulay was not at all a poet. They show absolutely nothing of the finer feeling which adds so much, for example, to the descriptions in Scott's somewhat similar romances, and they are separated by all the breadth of the world from the realm of delicate sensation and imagination to which Spenser and Keats and all the genuine poets are native-born.

The power of Macaulay's prose works, as no critic has failed to note, rests on his genius as an orator. For oratory he was rarely endowed. The composition of a speech was for him a matter of a few hours; with almost preternatural mental activity he organized and sifted the material, commonly as he paced up and down his garden or his room; then, the whole ready, nearly verbatim, in his mind, he would pass to the House of Commons to hold his colleagues spell-bound during several hours of fervid eloquence. Gladstone testified that the announcement of Macaulay's intention to speak was 'like a trumpet call to fill the benches.' The great qualities, then, of his essays and his 'History' are those which give success to the best sort of popular oratory--dramatic vividness and clearness, positiveness, and vigorous, movement and interest. He realizes characters and situations, on the external side, completely, and conveys his impression to his readers with scarcely any diminution of force.

Of expository structure he is almost as great a master as Burke, though in his essays and 'History' the more concrete nature of his material makes him prevailingly a narrator. He sees and presents his subjects as wholes, enlivening them with realistic details and pictures, but keeping the subordinate parts subordinate and disposing of the less important events in rapid summaries. Of clear and trenchant, though metallic, narrative and expository style he is a master. His sentences, whether long or short, are always lucid; he knows the full value of a short sentence suddenly snapped out after a prolonged period; and no other writer has ever made such' frequent and striking (though somewhat monotonous) use of deliberate oratorical balance of clauses and strong antithesis, or more illuminating use of vivid resumes. The best of his essays, like those on the Earl of Chatham and on the two men who won India for England, Clive and Warren Hastings, are models of the comparatively brief comprehensive dissertation of the form employed by Johnson in his 'Lives of the Poets.'

Macaulay, however, manifests the, defects even of his virtues. His positiveness, fascinating and effective as it is for an uncritical reader, carries with it extreme self-confidence and dogmatism, which render him violently intolerant of any interpretations of characters and events except those that he has formed, and formed sometimes hastily and with prejudice. The very clearness and brilliancy of his style are often obtained at the expense of real truth; for the force of his sweeping statements and his balanced antitheses often requires much heightening or even distortion of the facts; in making each event and each character stand out in the plainest outline he has often stripped it of its background of qualifying circumstances. These specific limitations, it will be evident, are outgrowths of his great underlying deficiency--the deficiency in spiritual feeling and insight.

Macaulay is a masterly limner of the external side of life, but he is scarcely conscious of the interior world in which the finer spirits live and work out their destinies. Carlyle's description of his appearance is significant: 'I noticed the homely Norse features that you find everywhere in the Western Isles, and I thought to myself, "Well, any one can see that you are an honest, good sort of fellow, made out of oatmeal." Macaulay's eminently clear, rapid, and practical mind comprehended fully and respected whatever could be seen and understood by the intellect; things of more subtle nature he generally disbelieved in or dismissed with contempt. In dealing with complex or subtle characters he cannot reveal the deeper spiritual motives from which their action sprang; and in his view of history he does not include the underlying and controlling spiritual forces.

Macaulay was the most brilliant of those whom the Germans have named Philistines, the people for whom life consists of material things; specifically he was the representative of the great body of middle-class early-Victorian liberals, enthusiastically convinced that in the triumphs of the Liberal party, of democracy, and of mechanical invention, the millennium was being rapidly realized. Macaulay wrote a fatal indictment of himself when in praising Bacon as the father of modern science he depreciated Plato, the idealist. Plato's philosophy, said Macaulay, 'began in words and ended in words,' and he added that 'an acre in Middlesex is better than a peerage in Utopia.' In his literary and personal essays, therefore, such as the famous ones on Milton and Bacon, which belong early in his career, all his immense reading did not suffice to produce sympathetic and sensitive judgments; there is often more pretentiousness of style than significance of interpretation. In later life he himself frankly expressed regret that he had ever written these essays.

Macaulay's 'History of England' shows to some degree the same faults as the essays, but here they are largely corrected by the enormous labor which he devoted to the work. His avowed purpose was to combine with scientific accuracy the vivid picturesqueness of fiction, and to 'supersede the last fashionable novel on the tables of young ladies.' His method was that of an unprecedented fulness of details which produces a crowded pageant of events and characters extremely minute but marvelously lifelike. After three introductory chapters which sketch the history of England down to the death of Charles II, more than four large volumes are occupied with the following seventeen years; and yet Macaulay had intended to continue to the death of George IV, nearly a hundred and thirty years later. For absolute truthfulness of detail the 'History' cannot always be depended on, but to the general reader its great literary merits are likely to seem full compensation for its inaccuracies.

**THOMAS CARLYLE**

The intense spiritual striving which was so foreign to Macaulay's practical nature first appears among the Victorians in the Scotsman Thomas Carlyle, a social and religious prophet, lay-preacher, and prose-poet, one of the most eccentric but one of the most stimulating of all English writers. The descendant of a warlike Scottish Border clan and the son of a stone-mason who is described as 'an awful fighter,' Carlyle was born in 1795 in the village of Ecclefechan, just across the line from England, and not far from Burns' county of Ayr. His fierce, intolerant, melancholy, and inwardly sensitive spirit, together with his poverty, rendered him miserable throughout his school days, though he secured, through his father's sympathy, a sound elementary education. He tramped on foot the ninety miles from Ecclefechan to Edinburgh University, and remained there for four years; but among the subjects of study he cared only for mathematics, and he left at the age of seventeen without receiving a degree.

From this time for many years his life was a painful struggle, a struggle to earn his living, to make a place in the world, and to find himself in the midst of his spiritual doubts and the physical distress caused by lifelong dyspepsia and insomnia. For some years and in various places he taught school and received private pupils, for very meager wages, latterly in Edinburgh, where he also did literary hack-work. He had planned at first to be a minister, but the unorthodoxy of his opinions rendered this impossible; and he also studied law only to abandon it. One of the most important forces in this period of his slow preparation was his study of German and his absorption of the idealistic philosophy of Kant, Schelling, and Fichte, of the broad philosophic influence of Goethe, and the subtile influence of Richter. A direct result was his later very fruitful continuation of Coleridge's work in turning the attention of Englishmen to German thought and literature. In 1821 he passed through a sudden spiritual crisis, when as he was traversing Leith Walk in Edinburgh his then despairing view of the Universe as a soulless but hostile mechanism all at once gave way to a mood of courageous self-assertion. He afterward looked on this experience as a spiritual new birth, and describes it under assumed names at the end of the great chapter in 'Sartor Resartus' on 'The Everlasting No.'

In 1825 his first important work, a 'Life of Schiller,' was published, and in 1826 he was married to Miss Jane Welsh. She was a brilliant but quiet woman, of social station higher than his; for some years he had been acting as counselor in her reading and intellectual development. No marriage in English Literature has been more discussed, a result, primarily, of the publication by Carlyle's friend and literary executor, the historian J. A. Froude, of Carlyle's autobiographical Reminiscences and Letters. After Mrs. Carlyle's death Carlyle blamed himself bitterly for inconsiderateness toward her, and it is certain that his erratic and irritable temper, partly exasperated by long disappointment and by constant physical misery, that his peasant-bred lack of delicacy, and his absorption in his work, made a perpetual and vexatious strain on Mrs. Carlyle's forbearance throughout the forty years of their life together. The evidence, however, does not show that the marriage was on the whole really unfortunate or indeed that it was not mainly a happy one.

For six years beginning in 1828 the Carlyles lived on (though they did not themselves carry on) the lonely farm of Craigenputtock, the property of Mrs. Carlyle. This was for both of them a period of external hardship, and they were chiefly dependent on the scanty income from Carlyle's laborious work on periodical essays (among which was the fine-spirited one on Burns). Here Carlyle also wrote the first of his chief works, 'Sartor Resartus,' for which, in 1833-4, he finally secured publication, in 'Fraser's Magazine,' to the astonishment and indignation of most of the readers. The title means 'The Tailor Retailored,' and the book purports to be an account of the life of a certain mysterious German, Professor Teufelsdrockh (pronounced Toyfelsdreck) and of a book of his on The Philosophy of Clothes. Of course this is allegorical, and Teufelsdrockh is really Carlyle, who, sheltering himself under the disguise, and accepting only editorial responsibility, is enabled to narrate his own spiritual struggles and to enunciate his deepest convictions, sometimes, when they are likely to offend his readers, with a pretense of disapproval.

The Clothes metaphor (borrowed from Swift) sets forth the central mystical or spiritual principle toward which German philosophy had helped Carlyle, the idea, namely, that all material things, including all the customs and forms of society, such as government and formalized religion, are merely the comparatively insignificant garments of the spiritual reality and the spiritual life on which men should center their attention. Even Time and Space and the whole material world are only the shadows of the true Reality, the spiritual Being that cannot perish.

Carlyle has learned to repudiate, and he would have others repudiate, 'The Everlasting No,' the materialistic attitude of unfaith in God and the spiritual world, and he proclaims 'The Everlasting Yea,' wherein are affirmed, the significance of life as a means of developing character and the necessity of accepting life and its requirements with manly self-reliance and moral energy. 'Seek not Happiness,' Carlyle cries, 'but Blessedness. Love not pleasure; love God.'

This is the central purport of the book. In the second place and as a natural corollary Carlyle vigorously denounces, throughout, all shams and hypocrisies, the results of inert or dishonest adherence to outgrown ideas or customs. He attacks, for instance, all empty ostentation; war, as both foolish and wicked; and the existing condition of society with its terrible contrast between the rich and the poor.

Again, he urges still a third of the doctrines which were to prove most characteristic of him, that Gospel of Work which had been proclaimed so forcibly, from different premises, five hundred years before by those other uncompromising Puritans, the authors of 'Piers Plowman.' In courageous work, Carlyle declares, work whether physical or mental, lies the way of salvation not only for pampered idlers but for sincere souls who are perplexed and wearied with over-much meditation on the mysteries of the universe, 'Be no, longer a Chaos,' he urges, 'but a World, or even Worldkin. Produce! Produce! Were it but the pitifullest infinitesimal, fraction of a Product, produce it, in God's name! 'Tis the utmost thou hast in thee: out with it, then. Up, up! Whatsoever thy hand findeth to do, do it with thy whole might. Work while it is called Today; for the Night cometh, wherein no man can work.'

It will probably now be evident that the mainspring of the undeniable and volcanic power of 'Sartor Resartus' (and the same is true of Carlyle's other chief works) is a tremendous moral conviction and fervor. Carlyle is eccentric and perverse--more so in 'Sartor Resartus' than elsewhere--but he is on fire with his message and he is as confident as any Hebrew prophet that it is the message most necessary for his generation. One may like him or be repelled by him, but a careful reader cannot remain unmoved by his personality and his ideas.

One of his most striking eccentricities is the remarkable style which he deliberately invented for 'Sartor Resartus' and used thenceforth in all his writings (though not always in so extreme a form). Some of the specific peculiarities of this style are taken over, with exaggeration, from German usage; some are Biblical or other archaisms; others spring mainly from Carlyle's own amazing mind. His purpose in employing, in the denunciation of shams and insincerities, a form itself so far removed from directness and simplicity was in part, evidently, to shock people into attention; but after all, the style expresses appropriately his genuine sense of the incoherence and irony of life, his belief that truth can be attained only by agonizing effort, and his contempt for intellectual and spiritual commonplaceness.

In 1834 Carlyle moved to London, to a house in Cheyne (pronounced Cheeny) Row, Chelsea, where he lived for his remaining nearly fifty years. Though he continued henceforth in large part to reiterate the ideas of 'Sartor Resartus,' he now turned from biography, essays, and literary criticism to history, and first published 'The French Revolution.' He had almost decided in despair to abandon literature, and had staked his fortune on this work; but when the first volume was accidentally destroyed in manuscript he proceeded with fine courage to rewrite it, and he published the whole book in 1837. It brought him the recognition which he sought. Like 'Sartor Resartus' it has much subjective coloring, which here results in exaggeration of characters and situations, and much fantasy and grotesqueness of expression; but as a dramatic and pictorial vilification of a great historic movement it was and remains unique, and on the whole no history is more brilliantly enlightening and profoundly instructive. Here, as in most of his later works, Carlyle throws the emphasis on the power of great personalities.

During the next years he took advantage of his success by giving courses of lectures on literature and history, though he disliked the task and felt himself unqualified as a speaker. Of these courses the most important was that on 'Heroes and Hero-Worship,' in which he clearly stated the doctrine on which thereafter he laid increasing stress, that the strength of humanity is in its strong men, the natural leaders, equipped to rule by power of intellect, of spirit, and of executive force. Control by them is government by the fit, whereas modern democracy is government by the unfit. Carlyle called democracy 'mobocracy' and considered it a mere bad piece of social and political machinery, or, in his own phrase, a mere 'Morrison's pill,' foolishly expected to cure all evils at one gulp. Later on Carlyle came to express this view, like all his others, with much violence, but it is worthy of serious consideration, not least in twentieth century America.

Of Carlyle's numerous later works the most important are 'Past and Present,' in which he contrasts the efficiency of certain strong men of medieval Europe with the restlessness and uncertainty of contemporary democracy and humanitarianism and attacks modern political economy; 'Oliver Cromwell's Letters and Speeches,' which revolutionized the general opinion of Cromwell, revealing him as a true hero or strong man instead of a hypocritical fanatic; and 'The History of Frederick the Great,' an enormous work which occupied Carlyle for fourteen years and involved thorough personal examination of the scenes of Frederick's life and battles. During his last fifteen years Carlyle wrote little of importance, and the violence of his denunciation of modern life grew shrill and hysterical.

That society was sadly wrong he was convinced, but he propounded no definite plan for its regeneration. He had become, however, a much venerated as well as a picturesque figure; and he exerted a powerful and constructive influence, not only directly, but indirectly through the preaching of his doctrines, in the main or in part, by the younger essayists and the chief Victorian poets and novelists, and in America by Emerson, with whom he maintained an almost lifelong friendship and correspondence. Carlyle died in 1881.

Carlyle was a strange combination of greatness and narrowness. Like Macaulay, he was exasperatingly blind and bigoted in regard to the things in which he had no personal interest, though the spheres of their respective enthusiasms and antipathies were altogether different. Carlyle viewed pleasure and merely esthetic art with the contempt of the Scottish Covenanting fanatics, refusing even to read poetry like that of Keats; and his insistence on moral meanings led him to equal intolerance of such story-tellers as Scott. In his hostility to the materialistic tendencies so often deduced from modern science he dismissed Darwin's 'Origin of Species' with the exclamation that it showed up the capricious stupidity of mankind and that he never could read a page of it or would waste the least thought upon it. He mocked at the anti-slavery movement in both America and the English possessions, holding that the negroes were an inferior race probably better off while producing something under white masters than if left free in their own ignorance and sloth. Though his obstinacy was a part of his national temperament, and his physical and mental irritability in part a result of his ill-health, any candid estimate of his life cannot altogether overlook them. On the whole, however, there is no greater ethical, moral, and spiritual force in English Literature than Carlyle, and so much of his thought has passed into the common possession of all thinking persons to-day that we are all often his debtors when we are least conscious of it.

## JOHN RUSKIN

Among the other great Victorian writers the most obvious disciple of Carlyle in his opposition to the materialism of modern life is John Ruskin. But Ruskin is much more than any man's disciple; and he also contrasts strongly with Carlyle, first because a large part of his life was devoted to the study of Art--he is the single great art-critic in English Literature--and also because he is one of the great preachers of that nineteenth century humanitarianism at which Carlyle was wont to sneer.

Ruskin's parents were Scotch, but his father, a man of artistic tastes, was established as a wine-merchant in London and had amassed a fortune before the boy's birth in 1819. The atmosphere of the household was sternly Puritan, and Ruskin was brought up under rigid discipline, especially by his mother, who gave him most of his early education. He read, wrote, and drew precociously; his knowledge of the Bible, in which his mother's training was relentlessly thorough, of Scott, Pope, and Homer, dates from his fifth or sixth year. For many years during his boyhood he accompanied his parents on long annual driving trips through Great Britain and parts of Europe, especially the Alps. By these experiences his inborn passion for the beautiful and the grand in Nature and Art was early developed. During seven years he was at Oxford, where his mother lived with him and watched over him; until her death in his fifty-second year she always continued to treat him like a child, an attitude to which, habit and affection led him to submit with a matter-of-course docility that his usual wilfulness and his later fame render at first sight astonishing. At Oxford, as throughout his life, he showed himself brilliant but not a close or careful student, and he was at that time theologically too rigid a Puritan to be interested in the Oxford Movement, then in its most intense stage.

His career as a writer began immediately after he left the University. It falls naturally into two parts, the first of about twenty years, when he was concerned almost altogether with Art, chiefly Painting and Architecture; and the second somewhat longer, when he was intensely absorbed in the problems of society and strenuously working as a social reformer. From the outset, however, he was actuated by an ardent didactic purpose; he wrote of Art in order to awake men's spiritual natures to a joyful delight in the Beautiful and thus to lead, them to God, its Author.

The particular external direction of Ruskin's work in Art was given, as usual, more or less by accident. His own practice in water-color drawing led him as a mere youth to a devoted admiration for the landscape paintings of the contemporary artist J.M.W. Turner. Turner, a romantic revolutionist against the eighteenth century theory of the grand style, was then little appreciated; and when Ruskin left the University he began, with characteristic enthusiasm, an article on 'Modern Painters,' designed to demonstrate Turner's superiority to all possible rivals. Even the first part of this work expanded itself into a volume, published in 1843, when Ruskin was only twenty-four;

and at intervals during the next seventeen years he issued four additional volumes, the result of prolonged study both of Nature and of almost all the great paintings in Europe.

The completed book is a discursive treatise, the various volumes necessarily written from more or less different view-points, on many of the main aspects, general and technical, of all art, literary as well as pictorial. For Ruskin held, and brilliantly demonstrated, that the underlying principles of all the Fine Arts are identical, and 'Modern Painters' contains some of the most famous and suggestive passages of general literary criticism ever written, for example those on The Pathetic Fallacy and The Grand Style. Still further, to Ruskin morality and religion are inseparable from Art, so that he deals searchingly, if incidentally, with those subjects as well. Among his fundamental principles are the ideas that a beneficent God has created the world and its beauty directly for man's use and pleasure; that all true art and all true life are service of God and should be filled with a spirit of reverence; that art should reveal truth; and that really great and good art can spring only from noble natures and a sound national life.

The style of the book is as notable as the substance. It is eloquent with Ruskin's enthusiastic admiration for Beauty and with his magnificent romantic rhetoric (largely the result, according to his own testimony, of his mother's exacting drill in the Bible), which here and elsewhere make him one of the greatest of all masters of gorgeous description and of fervid exhortation. The book displays fully, too, another of his chief traits, an intolerant dogmatism, violently contemptuous of any judgments but his own. On the religious side, especially, Ruskin's Protestantism is narrow, and even bigoted, but it softens as the book proceeds (and decidedly more in his later years). With all its faults, 'Modern Painters' is probably the greatest book ever written on Art and is an immense storehouse, of noble material, and suggestion.

In the intervals of this work Ruskin published others less comprehensive, two of which are of the first importance. 'The Seven Lamps of Architecture' argues that great art, as the supreme expression of life, is the result of seven moral and religious principles, Sacrifice, Truth, Power, and the like. 'The Stones of Venice' is an, impassioned exposition of the beauty of Venetian Gothic architecture, and here as always Ruskin expresses his vehement preference for the Gothic art of the Middle Ages as contrasted with the less original and as it seems to him less sincere style of the Renaissance.

The publication of the last volume of 'Modern Painters' in 1860 roughly marks the end of Ruskin's first period. Several influences had by this time begun to sadden him. More than ten years before, with his usual filial meekness, he had obeyed his parents in marrying a lady who proved uncongenial and who after a few years was divorced from him. Meanwhile acquaintance with Carlyle had combined with experience to convince him of the comparative ineffectualness of mere art-criticism as a social and religious force. He had come to feel with increasing indignation that the modern industrial system, the materialistic political economy founded on it, and the whole modern organization of society reduce the mass of men to a state of intellectual, social, and religious squalor and blindness, and that while they continue in this condition it is of little use to talk to them about Beauty.

He believed that some of the first steps in the necessary redemptive process must be the education of the poor and a return to what he conceived (certainly with much exaggeration) to have been the conditions of medieval labor, when each craftsman was not a mere machine but an intelligent and original artistic creator; but the underlying essential was to free industry from the spirit of selfish money-getting and permeate it with Christian sympathy and respect for man as man. The ugliness of modern life in its wretched city tenements and its hideous factories Ruskin would have utterly destroyed, substituting such a beautiful background (attractive homes and surroundings) as would help to develop spiritual beauty. With his customary vigor Ruskin proceeded henceforth to devote himself to the enunciation, and so far as possible the realization of these beliefs, first by delivering lectures and writing books.

He was met, like all reformers, with a storm of protest, but most of his ideas gradually became the accepted principles of social theory. Among his works dealing with these subjects may be named 'Unto This Last,' 'Munera Pulveris' (The Rewards of the Dust--an attack on materialistic political economy), and 'Fors Clavigera' (Fortune the Key-Bearer), the latter a series of letters to workingmen extending over many years. To 1865 belongs his most widely-read book, 'Sesame and Lilies,' three lectures on the spiritual meaning of great literature in contrast to materialism, the glory of womanhood, and the mysterious significance of life.

From the death of his mother in 1871 Ruskin began to devote his large inherited fortune to 'St. George's Guild,' a series of industrial and social experiments in which with lavish generosity he attempted to put his theories into practical operation. All these experiments, as regards direct results, ended in failure, though their general influence was great. Among other movements now everywhere taken for granted 'social settlements' are a result of his efforts.

All this activity had not caused Ruskin altogether to abandon the teaching of art to the members of the more well-to-do classes, and beginning in 1870 he held for three or four triennial terms the newly-established professorship of Art at Oxford and gave to it much hard labor. But this interest was now clearly secondary in his mind.

Ruskin's temper was always romantically high-strung, excitable, and irritable. His intense moral fervor, his multifarious activities, and his disappointments were also constant strains on his nervous force. In 1872, further, he was rejected in marriage by a young girl for whom he had formed a deep attachment and who on her death-bed, three years later, refused, with strange cruelty, to see him. In 1878 his health temporarily failed, and a few years later he retired to the home, 'Brantwood,' at Coniston in the Lake Region, which he had bought on the death of his mother. Here his mind gradually gave way, but intermittently, so that he was still able to compose 'Praterita' (The Past), a delightful autobiography. He died in 1900.

Ruskin, like Carlyle, was a strange compound of genius, nobility, and unreasonableness, but as time goes on his dogmatism and violence may well be more and more forgotten, while his idealism, his penetrating interpretation of art and life, his fruitful work for a more tolerable social order, and his magnificent mastery of style and description assure him a permanent place in the history of English literature and of civilization.

**MATTHEW ARNOLD**

Contemporary with Carlyle and Ruskin and fully worthy to rank with them stands still a third great preacher of social and spiritual regeneration, Matthew Arnold, whose personality and message, however, were very different from theirs and who was also one of the chief Victorian poets. Arnold was born in 1822, the son--and this is decidedly significant--of the Dr. Thomas Arnold who later became the famous headmaster of Rugby School and did more than any other man of the century to elevate the tone of English school life. Matthew Arnold proceeded from Rugby to Oxford (Balliol College), where he took the prize for original poetry and distinguished himself as a student. This was the period of the Oxford Movement, and Arnold was much impressed by Newman's fervor and charm, but was already too rationalistic in thought to sympathize with his views.

After graduation Arnold taught Greek for a short time at Rugby and then became private secretary to Lord Lansdoune, who was minister of public instruction. Four years later, in 1851, Arnold was appointed an inspector of schools, a position which he held almost to the end of his life and in which he labored very hard and faithfully, partly at the expense of his creative work. His life was marked by few striking outward events. His marriage and home were happy. Up to 1867 his literary production consisted chiefly of poetry, very carefully composed and very limited in amount, and for two five-year terms, from 1857 to 1867, he held the Professorship of Poetry at Oxford.

At the expiration of his second term he did not seek for reappointment, because he did not care to arouse the opposition of Gladstone--then a power in public affairs--and stir up religious controversy. His retirement from this position virtually marks the very distinct change from the first to the second main period of his career. For with deliberate self-sacrifice he now turned from poetry to prose essays, because he felt that through the latter medium he could render what seemed to him a more necessary public service. With characteristic self-confidence, and obeying his inherited tendency to didacticism, he appointed himself, in effect, a critic of English national life, beliefs, and taste, and set out to instruct the public in matters of literature, social relations, politics and religion. In many essays, published separately or in periodicals, he persevered in this task until his death in 1888.

As a poet Arnold is generally admitted to rank among the Victorians next after Tennyson and Browning. The criticism, partly true, that he was not designed by Nature to be a poet but made himself one by hard work rests on his intensely, and at the outset coldly, intellectual and moral temperament. He himself, in modified Puritan spirit, defined poetry as a criticism of life; his mind was philosophic; and in his own verse, inspired by Greek poetry, by Goethe and Wordsworth, he realized his definition. In his work, therefore, delicate melody and sensuous beauty were at first much less conspicuous than a high moral sense, though after the first the elements of external beauty greatly developed, often to the finest effect.

In form and spirit his poetry is one of the very best later reflections of that of Greece, dominated by thought, dignified, and polished with the utmost care. 'Sohrab and Rustum,' his most ambitious and greatest single poem, is a very close and admirable imitation of 'The Iliad.' Yet, as the almost intolerable pathos of 'Sohrab and Rustum' witnesses, Arnold is not by any means deficient, any more than the Greek poets were, in emotion. He affords, in fact, a striking example of classical form and spirit united with the deep, self-conscious, meditative feeling of modern Romanticism.

In substance Arnold's poetry is the expression of his long and tragic spiritual struggle. To him religion, understood as a reverent devotion to Divine things, was the most important element in life, and his love of pure truth was absolute; but he held that modern knowledge had entirely disproved the whole dogmatic and doctrinal scheme of historic Christianity and that a new spiritual revelation was necessary. To his Romantic nature, however, mere knowledge and mere modern science, which their followers were so confidently exalting, appeared by no means adequate to the purpose; rather they seemed to him largely futile, because they did not stimulate the emotions and so minister to the spiritual life.

Further, the restless stirrings of his age, beginning to arouse itself from the social lethargy of centuries, appeared to him pitifully unintelligent and devoid of results. He found all modern life, as he says in 'The Scholar-Gypsy,' a 'strange disease,' in which men hurry wildly about in a mad activity which they mistake for achievement. In Romantic melancholy he looked wistfully back by contrast to periods when 'life was fresh and young' and could express itself vigorously and with no torturing introspection. The exaggerated pessimism in this part of his outcry is explained by his own statement, that he lived in a transition time, when the old faith was (as he held) dead, and the new one (partly realized in our own generation) as yet 'powerless to be born.'

Arnold's poetry, therefore, is to be viewed as largely the expression, monotonous but often poignantly beautiful, of a temporary mood of questioning protest. But if his conclusion is not positive, it is at least not weakly despairing. Each man, he insists, should diligently preserve and guard in intellectual and moral integrity the fortress of his own soul, into which, when necessary, he can retire in serene and stoical resignation, determined to endure and to 'see life steadily and see it whole.' Unless the man himself proves traitor, the littlenesses of life are powerless to conquer him. In fact, the invincible courage of the thoroughly disciplined spirit in the midst of doubt and external discouragement has never been, more nobly expressed than by Arnold in such poems as 'Palladium' and (from a different point of view) 'The Last Word.'

There is a striking contrast (largely expressing an actual change of spirit and point of view) between the manner of Arnold's poetry and that of his prose. In the latter he entirely abandons the querulous note and assumes instead a tone of easy assurance, jaunty and delightfully satirical. Increasing maturity had taught him that merely to sit regarding the past was useless and that he himself had a definite doctrine, worthy of being preached with all aggressiveness.

We have already said that his essays fall into four classes, literary, social, religious, and political, though they cannot always be sharply distinguished. As a literary critic he is uneven, and, as elsewhere, sometimes superficial, but his fine appreciation and generally clear vision make him refreshingly stimulating. His point of view is unusually broad, his chief general purpose being to free English taste from its insularity, to give it sympathetic acquaintance with the peculiar excellences of other literatures. Some of his essays, like those on 'The Function of Criticism at the Present Time,' 'Wordsworth,' and 'Byron,' are among the best in English, while his 'Essays on Translating Homer' present the most famous existing interpretation of the spirit and style of the great Greek epics.

In his social essays, of which the most important form the volume entitled 'Culture and Anarchy,' he continues in his own way the attacks of Carlyle and Ruskin. Contemporary English life seems to him a moral chaos of physical misery and of the selfish, unenlightened, violent expression of untrained wills. He too looks with pitying contempt on the material achievements of science and the Liberal party as being mere 'machinery,' means to an end, which men mistakenly worship as though it possessed a real value in itself. He divides English society into three classes:

1. The Aristocracy, whom he nick-names 'The Barbarians,' because, like the Germanic tribes who overthrew the Roman Empire, they vigorously assert their own privileges and live in the external life rather than in the life of the spirit.
2. The Middle Class, which includes the bulk of the nation. For them he borrows from German criticism the name 'Philistines,' enemies of the chosen people, and he finds their prevailing traits to be intellectual and spiritual narrowness and a fatal and superficial satisfaction with mere activity and material prosperity.
3. 'The Populace,' the 'vast raw and half-developed residuum.' For them Arnold had sincere theoretical sympathy (though his temperament made it impossible for him to enter into the same sort of personal sympathy with them as did Ruskin); but their whole environment and conception of life seemed to him hideous. With his usual uncomplimentary frankness Arnold summarily described the three groups as 'a materialized upper class, a vulgarized middle class, and a brutalized lower class.'

For the cure of these evils Arnold's proposed remedy was Culture, which he defined as a knowledge of the best that has been thought and done in the world and a desire to make the best ideas prevail. Evidently this Culture is not a mere knowledge of books, unrelated to the rest of life. It has indeed for its basis a very wide range of knowledge, acquired by intellectual processes, but this knowledge alone Arnold readily admitted to be 'machinery.'

The real purpose and main part of Culture is the training, broadening, and refining of the whole spirit, including the emotions as well as the intellect, into sympathy with all the highest ideals, and therefore into inward peace and satisfaction. Thus Culture is not indolently selfish, but is forever exerting itself to 'make the best ideas'--which Arnold also defined as 'reason and the will, of God'--'prevail.'

Arnold felt strongly that a main obstacle to Culture was religious narrowness. He held that the English people had been too much occupied with the 'Hebraic' ideal of the Old Testament, the interest in morality or right conduct, and though he agreed that this properly makes three quarters of life, he insisted that it should be joined with the Hellenic (Greek) ideal of a perfectly rounded nature. He found the essence of Hellenism expressed in a phrase which he took from Swift, 'Sweetness and Light,' interpreting Sweetness to mean the love of Beauty, material and spiritual, and Light, unbiased intelligence; and he urged that these forces be allowed to have the freest play.

He vigorously attacked the Dissenting denominations, because he believed them to be a conspicuous embodiment of Philistine lack of Sweetness and Light, with an unlovely insistence on unimportant external details and a fatal blindness to the meaning of real beauty and real spirituality. Though he himself was without a theological creed, he was, and held that every Englishman should be, a devoted adherent of the English Church, as a beautiful, dignified, and national expression of essential religion, and therefore a very important influence for Culture.

Toward democracy Arnold took, not Carlyle's attitude of definite opposition, but one of questioning scrutiny. He found that one actual tendency of modern democracy was to 'let people do as they liked,' which, given the crude violence of the Populace, naturally resulted in lawlessness and therefore threatened anarchy. Culture, on the other hand, includes the strict discipline of the will and the sacrifice of one's own impulses for the good of all, which means respect for Law and devotion to the State. Existing democracy, therefore, he attacked with unsparing irony, but he did not condemn its principle. One critic has said that 'his ideal of a State can best be described as an Educated Democracy, working by Collectivism in Government, Religion and Social Order.' But in his own writings he scarcely gives expression to so definite a conception.

Arnold's doctrine, of course, was not perfectly comprehensive nor free from prejudices; but none could be essentially more useful for his generation or ours. We may readily grant that it is, in one sense or another, a doctrine for chosen spirits, but if history makes anything clear it is that chosen spirits are the necessary instruments of all progress and therefore the chief hope of society.

The differences between Arnold's teaching and that of his two great contemporaries are probably now clear. All three are occupied with the pressing necessity of regenerating society. Carlyle would accomplish this end by means of great individual characters inspired by confidence in the spiritual life and dominating their times by moral strength; Ruskin would accomplish it by humanizing social conditions and spiritualizing and refining all men's natures through devotion to the principles of moral Right and esthetic Beauty; Arnold would leaven the crude mass of society, so far as possible, by permeating it with all the myriad influences of spiritual, moral, and esthetic culture. All three, of course, like every enlightened reformer, are aiming at ideal conditions which can be actually realized only in the distant future.

Arnold's style is one of the most charming features of his work. Clear, direct, and elegant, it reflects most attractively his own high breeding; but it is also eminently forceful, and marked by very skilful emphasis and reiteration. One of his favorite devices is a pretense of great humility, which is only a shelter from which he shoots forth incessant and pitiless volleys of ironical raillery, light and innocent in appearance, but irresistible in aim and penetrating power. He has none of the gorgeousness of Ruskin or the titanic strength of Carlyle, but he can be finely eloquent, and he is certainly one of the masters of polished effectiveness.

## ALFRED TENNYSON

In poetry, apart from the drama, the Victorian period is the greatest in English literature. Its most representative, though not its greatest, poet is Alfred Tennyson. Tennyson, the fourth of a large family of children, was born in Somersby, Lincolnshire, in 1809. That year, as it happened, is distinguished by the birth of a large number of eminent men, among them Gladstone, Darwin, and Lincoln. Tennyson's father was a clergyman, holding his appointments from a member of the landed gentry; his mother was peculiarly gentle and benevolent. From childhood the poet, though physically strong, was moody and given to solitary dreaming; from early childhood also he composed poetry, and when he was seventeen he and one of his elder brothers brought out a volume of verse, immature, but of distinct poetic feeling and promise.

The next year they entered Trinity College, Cambridge, where Tennyson, too reserved for public prominence, nevertheless developed greatly through association with a gifted group of students. Called home by the fatal illness of his father shortly before his four year's were completed, he decided, as Milton had done, and as Browning was even then doing, to devote himself to his art; but, like Milton, he equipped himself, now and throughout his life, by hard and systematic study of many of the chief branches of knowledge, including the sciences. His next twenty years were filled with difficulty and sorrow.

Two volumes of poems which he published in 1830 and 1832 were greeted by the critics with their usual harshness, which deeply wounded his sensitive spirit and checked his further publication for ten years; though the second of these volumes contains some pieces which, in their later, revised, form, are among his chief lyric triumphs. In 1833 his warm friend Arthur Hallam, a young man of extraordinary promise, who was engaged, moreover, to one of Tennyson's sisters, died suddenly without warning. Tennyson's grief, at first overwhelming, was long a main factor in his life and during many years found slow artistic expression in 'In Memoriam' and other poems. A few years later came another deep sorrow. Tennyson formed an engagement of marriage with Miss Emily Sellwood, but his lack of worldly prospects led her relatives to cancel it.

Tennyson now spent much of his time in London, on terms of friendship with many literary men, including Carlyle, who almost made an exception in his favor from his general fanatical contempt for poetry. In 1842 Tennyson published two volumes of poems, including the earlier ones revised; he here won an undoubted popular success and was accepted by the best judges as the chief living productive English poet. Disaster followed in the shape of an unfortunate financial venture which for a time reduced his family to serious straits and drove him with shattered nerves to a sanitarium. Soon, however, he received from the government as a recognition of his poetic achievement a permanent annual pension of two hundred pounds, and in 1847 he published the strange but delightful 'Princess.' The year 1850 marked the decisive turning point of his career. He was enabled to renew his engagement and be married; the publication of 'In Memoriam' established him permanently in a position of such popularity as few living poets have ever enjoyed; and on the death of Wordsworth he was appointed Poet Laureate.

The prosperity of the remaining half of his life was a full recompense for his earlier struggles, though it is marked by few notable external events. Always a lover of the sea, he soon took up his residence in the Isle of Wight. His production of poetry was steady, and its variety great. The largest of all his single achievements was the famous series of 'Idylls of the King,' which formed a part of his occupation for many years. In much of his later work there is a marked change from his earlier elaborate decorativeness to a style of vigorous strength. At the age of sixty-five, fearful that he had not yet done enough to insure his fame, he gave a remarkable demonstration of poetic vitality by striking out into the to him new field of poetic drama.

His important works here are the three tragedies in which he aimed to complete the series of Shakspere's chronicle-history plays; but he lacked the power of dramatic action, and the result is rather three fine poems than successful plays. In 1883, after having twice refused a baronetcy, he, to the regret of his more democratic friends, accepted a peerage (barony). Tennyson disliked external show, but he was always intensely loyal to the institutions of England, he felt that literature was being honored in his person, and he was willing to secure a position of honor for his son, who had long rendered him devoted service.

He died quietly in 1892, at the age of eighty-three, and was buried in Westminster Abbey beside Browning, who had found a resting-place there three years earlier. His personal character, despite some youthful morbidness, was unusually delightful, marked by courage, honesty, sympathy, and straightforward manliness. He had a fine voice and took undisguised pleasure in reading his poems aloud. The chief traits of his poetry in form and substance may be suggested in a brief summary.

1. Most characteristic, perhaps, is his exquisite artistry (in which he learned much from Keats). His appreciation for sensuous beauty, especially color, is acute; his command of poetic phraseology is unsurpassed; he suggests shades of, feeling and elusive aspiration with, marvelously subtile power; his descriptions are magnificently beautiful, often with much detail; and his melody is often the perfection of sweetness. Add the truth and tenderness of his emotion, and it results that he is one of the finest and most moving of lyric poets. Nor is all this beauty vague and unsubstantial. Not only was he the most careful of English poets, revising his works with almost unprecedented pains, but his scientific habit of mind insists on the greatest accuracy; in his allusions to Nature he often introduces scientific facts in a way thitherto unparalleled, and sometimes even only doubtfully poetic.

   The influence of the classic literatures on his style and expression was great; no poet combines more harmoniously classic perfection and romantic feeling.
2. The variety of his poetic forms is probably greater than that of any other English poet. In summary catalogue may be named: lyrics, both delicate and stirring; ballads; romantic dreams and fancies; descriptive poems; sentimental reveries, and idyls; long narratives, in which he displays perfect narrative skill; delightfully realistic character-sketches, some of them in dialect; dramas; and meditative poems, long and short, on religious, ethical, and social questions. In almost all these forms he has produced numerous masterpieces.

3. His chief deficiency is in the dramatic quality. No one can present more finely than he moods (often carefully set in a harmoniously appropriate background of external nature) or characters in stationary position; and there is splendid spirit in his narrative passages of vigorous action. Nevertheless his genius and the atmosphere of his poems are generally dreamy, romantic, and aloof from actual life. A brilliant critic has caustically observed that he 'withdraws from the turmoil of the real universe into the fortress of his own mind, and beats the enemy in toy battles with toy soldiers.' He never succeeded in presenting to the satisfaction of most good critics a vigorous man in vigorous action.
4. The ideas of his poetry are noble and on the whole clear. He was an independent thinker, though not an innovator, a conservative liberal, and was so widely popular because he expressed in frank but reverent fashion the moderately advanced convictions of his time. His social ideals, in which he is intensely interested, are those of Victorian humanitarianism. He hopes ardently for a steady amelioration of the condition of the masses, proceeding toward a time when all men shall have real opportunity for full development; and freedom is one of his chief watchwords. But with typical English conservatism he believes that progress must be gradual, and that it should be controlled by order, loyalty, and reverence. Like a true Englishman, also, he is sure that the institutions of England are the best in the world, so that he is a strong supporter of the monarchy and the hereditary aristocracy. In religion, his inherited belief, rooted in his deepest fibers, early found itself confronted by the discoveries of modern science, which at first seemed to him to proclaim that the universe is much what it seemed to the young Carlyle, a remorseless monster, 'red in tooth and claw,' scarcely thinkable as the work of a Christian God who cares for man.

Tennyson was too sincere to evade the issue, and after years of inner struggle he arrived at a positive faith in the central principles of Christianity, broadly interpreted, though it was avowedly a faith based on instinct and emotional need rather than on unassailable reasoning. His somewhat timid disposition, moreover, never allowed him to enunciate his conclusions with anything like the buoyant aggressiveness of his contemporary, Robert Browning. How greatly science had influenced his point of view appears in the conception which is central in his later poetry, namely that the forces of the universe are governed by unchanging Law, through which God works. The best final expression of his spirit is the lyric 'Crossing the Bar,' which every one knows and which at his own request is printed last in all editions of his works.

## ELIZABETH BARRETT BROWNING AND ROBERT BROWNING

Robert Browning, Tennyson's chief poetic contemporary, stands in striking artistic contrast to Tennyson--a contrast which perhaps serves to enhance the reputation of both. Browning's life, if not his poetry, must naturally be considered in connection with that of Elizabeth Barrett Browning, with whom he was united in what appears the most ideal marriage of two important writers in the history of literature.

Elizabeth Barrett, the daughter of a country gentleman of Herefordshire (the region of the Malvern Hills and of 'Piers Plowman'), was born in 1806. She was naturally both healthy and intellectually precocious; the writing of verse and outdoor life divided all her early life, and at seventeen she published, a volume of immature poems. At fifteen, however, her health was impaired by an accident which happened as she was saddling her pony, and at thirty, after a removal of the family to London, it completely failed. From that time on for ten years she was an invalid, confined often to her bed and generally to her chamber, sometimes apparently at the point of death. Nevertheless she kept on with persistent courage and energy at her study and writing. The appearance of her poems in two volumes in 1844 gave her a place among the chief living poets and led to her acquaintance with Browning.

Browning was born in a London suburb in 1812 (the same year with Dickens), of very mixed ancestry, which may partly explain the very diverse traits in his nature and poetry. His father, a man of artistic and cultured tastes, held a subordinate though honorable position in the Bank of England. The son inherited a strong instinct for all the fine arts, and though he composed verses before he could write, seemed for years more likely to become a musician than a poet. His formal schooling was irregular, but he early began to acquire from his father's large and strangely-assorted library the vast fund of information which astonishes the reader of his poetry, and he too lived a healthy out-of-door life.

His parents being Dissenters, the universities were not open to him, and when he was seventeen his father somewhat reluctantly consented to his own unhesitating choice of poetry as a profession. For seventeen years more he continued in his father's home, living a normal life among his friends, writing continuously, and gradually acquiring a reputation among some good critics, but making very little impression on the public. Some of his best short poems date from these years, such as 'My Last Duchess' and 'The Bishop Orders His Tomb'; but his chief effort went into a series of seven or eight poetic dramas, of which 'Pippa Passes' is best known and least dramatic. They are noble poetry, but display in marked degree the psychological subtilety which in part of his poetry demands unusually close attention from the reader.

In one of the pieces in her volumes of 1844 Elizabeth Barrett mentioned Browning, among other poets, with generous praise. This led to a correspondence between the two, and soon to a courtship, in which Browning's earnestness finally overcame Miss Barrett's scrupulous hesitation to lay upon him (as she felt) the burden of her invalidism. Indeed her invalidism at last helped to turn the scales in Browning's favor, for the physicians had declared that Miss Barrett's life depended on removal to a warmer climate, but to this her father, a well-intentioned but strangely selfish man, absolutely refused to consent. The record of the courtship is given in Mrs. Browning's 'Sonnets from the Portuguese' (a whimsical title, suggested by Mrs.

Browning's childhood nickname, 'The Little Portuguese'), which is one of the finest of English sonnet-sequences. The marriage, necessarily clandestine, took place in 1846; Mrs. Browning's father thenceforth treated her as one dead, but the removal from her morbid surroundings largely restored her health for the remaining fifteen years of her life. During these fifteen years the two poets resided chiefly in various cities of

Italy, with a nominal home in Florence, and Mrs. Browning had an inherited income which sufficed for their support until their poetry became profitable. Their chief works during this period were Mrs. Browning's 'Aurora Leigh' (1856), a long 'poetic novel' in blank verse dealing with the relative claims of Art and Social Service and with woman's place in the world; and Browning's most important single publication, his two volumes of 'Men and Women' (1855), containing fifty poems, many of them among his very best.

Mrs. Browning was passionately interested in the Italian struggle for independence against Austrian tyranny, and her sudden death in 1861 seems to have been hastened by that of the Italian statesman Cavour. Browning, at first inconsolable, soon returned with his son to London, where he again made his home, for the rest of his life. Henceforth he published much poetry, for the most part long pieces of subtile psychological and spiritual analysis. In 1868-9 he brought out his characteristic masterpiece, 'The Ring and the Book,' a huge psychological epic, which proved the tardy turning point in his reputation. People might not understand the poem, but they could not disregard it, the author became famous, almost popular, and a Browning cult arose, marked by the spread of Browning societies in both England and America. Browning enjoyed his success for twenty years and died quietly in 1889 at the home of his son in Venice.

Browning earnestly reciprocated his wife's loyal devotion and seemed really to believe, as he often insisted, that her poetry was of a higher order than his own. Her achievement, indeed, was generally overestimated, in her own day and later, but it is now recognized that she is scarcely a really great artist. Her intense emotion, her fine Christian idealism, and her very wide reading give her real power; her womanly tenderness is admirable; and the breadth of her interests and sometimes the clearness of her judgment are notable; but her secluded life of ill-health rendered her often sentimental, high-strung, and even hysterical.

She has in her the impulses and material of great poetry, but circumstances and her temperament combined to deny her the patient self-discipline necessary for the best results. She writes vehemently to assert the often-neglected rights of women and children or to denounce negro slavery and all oppression; and sometimes, as when in 'The Cry of the Children' she revealed the hideousness of child-labor in the factories, she is genuine and irresistible; but more frequently she produces highly romantic or mystical imaginary narrations (often in medieval settings). She not seldom mistakes enthusiasm or indignation for artistic inspiration, and she is repeatedly and inexcusably careless in meter and rime. Perhaps her most satisfactory poems, aside from those above mentioned, are 'The Vision of Poets' and 'The Rime of the Duchess May.'

In considering the poetry of Robert Browning the inevitable first general point is the nearly complete contrast with Tennyson. For the melody and exquisite beauty of phrase and description which make so large a part of Tennyson's charm, Browning cares very little; his chief merits as an artist lie mostly where Tennyson is least strong; and he is a much more independent and original thinker than Tennyson. This will become more evident in a survey of his main characteristics.

1. Browning is the most thoroughly vigorous and dramatic of all great poets who employ other forms than the actual drama. Of his hundreds of poems the great majority set before the reader a glimpse of actual life and human personalities--an action, a situation, characters, or a character--in the clearest and most vivid possible way. Sometimes the poem is a ringing narration of a fine exploit, like 'How They Brought the Good News'; sometimes it is quieter and more reflective. Whatever the style, however, in the great majority of cases Browning employs the form which without having actually invented it he developed into an instrument of thitherto unsuspected power, namely the dramatic monolog in which a character discusses his situation or life or some central part or incident, of it, under circumstances which reveal with wonderful completeness its significance and his own essential character. To portray and interpret life in this way, to give his readers a sudden vivid understanding of its main forces and conditions in representative moments, may be called the first obvious purpose, or perhaps rather instinct, of Browning and his poetry. The dramatic economy of

downright careless in such details as sentence
But the difficulty arising from these various ecce
occurs chiefly in his longer poems, and ofter
mainly as a mental stimulus. Equally striking, pe
is his frequent grotesqueness in choice of subjec
in treatment, which seems to result chiefly from
wish to portray the world as it actually is, keeping
close touch with genuine everyday reality; partly al
from his instinct to break away from placid and fiberles
conventionality.

4. Browning is decidedly one of those who hold the poet to be a teacher, and much, indeed most, of his poetry is occupied rather directly with the questions of religion and the deeper meanings of life. Taken all together, that is, his poetry constitutes a very extended statement of his philosophy of life. The foundation of his whole theory is a confident and aggressive optimism. He believes, partly on the basis of intellectual reasoning, but mainly on what seems to him the convincing testimony of instinct, that the universe is controlled by a loving God, who has made life primarily a thing of happiness for man. Man should accept life with gratitude and enjoy to the full all its possibilities. Evil exists only to demonstrate the value of Good and to develop character, which can be produced only by hard and sincere struggle. Unlike Tennyson, therefore, Browning has full confidence in present reality--he believes that life on earth is predominantly good.

Nevertheless earthly life is evidently incomplete in itself, and the central law of existence is Progress, which gives assurance of a future life where man may develop the spiritual nature which on earth seems to have its beginning and distinguishes man from the brutes. This future life, however, is probably not one but many, a long succession of lives, the earlier ones not so very different, perhaps, from the present one on earth; and even the worst souls, commencing the next life, perhaps, as a result of their failure here, at a spiritual stage lower than the present one, must ultimately pass through all stages of the spiritual process, and come to stand with all the others near the perfection of God himself. This whole theory, which, because later thought has largely adopted it from Browning, seems much less original to-day than when he first propounded it, is stated and reiterated in his poems with a dynamic idealizing power which, whether or not one assents to it in details, renders it magnificently stimulating. It is rather fully expressed as a whole, in two of Browning's best known and finest poems, 'Rabbi ben Ezra,' and 'Abt Vogler.' Some critics, it should be added, however, feel that Browning is too often and too insistently a teacher in his poetry and that his art would have gained if he had introduced his philosophy much more incidentally.

5. In his social theory Browning differs not only from Tennyson but from the prevailing thought of his age, differs in that his emphasis is individualistic. Like all the other Victorians he dwells on the importance of individual devotion to the service of others, but he believes that the chief results of such effort must be in the development of the individual's character, not greatly in the actual betterment of the world. The world, indeed, as it appears to him, is a place of probation and we cannot expect ever to make it over very radically; the important thing is that the individual soul shall use it to help him on his 'lone way' to heaven. Browning, accordingly, takes almost no interest in the specific social and political questions of his day, a fact which certainly will not operate against the permanence of his fame. More detrimental, no doubt, aside from the actual faults which we have mentioned, will be his rather extravagant Romanticism--the vehemence of his passion and his insistence on the supreme value of emotion. With these characteristics classically minded critics have always been highly impatient, and they will no doubt prevent him from ultimately taking a place beside Shakspere and the serene Milton; but they will not seriously interfere, we may be certain, with his recognition as one of the very great English poets.

## ROSSETTI AND THE PRE-RAPHAELITE MOVEMENT

Many of the secondary Victorian poets must here be passed by, but several of them are too important to be dismissed without at least brief notice. The middle of the century is marked by a new Romantic impulse, the Pre-Raphaelite Movement, which begins with Dante Gabriel Rossetti. Rossetti was born in London in 1828. His father was an Italian, a liberal refugee from the outrageous government of Naples, and his mother was also half Italian. The household, though poor, was a center for other Italian exiles, but this early and tempestuous political atmosphere created in the poet, by reaction, a lifelong aversion for politics. His desultory education was mostly in the lines of painting and the Italian and English poets. His own practice in poetry began as early as is usual with poets, and before he was nineteen, by a special inspiration, he wrote his best and most famous poem, 'The Blessed Damosel.' In the school of the Royal Academy of Painting, in 1848, he met William Holman Hunt and John E. Millais, and the three formed the Pre-Raphaelite Brotherhood, in which Rossetti, whose disposition throughout his life was extremely self-assertive, or even domineering, took the lead.

The purpose of the Brotherhood was to restore to painting and literature the qualities which the three enthusiasts found in the fifteenth century Italian painters, those who just preceded Raphael. Rossetti and his friends did not decry the noble idealism of Raphael himself, but they felt that in trying to follow his grand style the art of their own time had become too abstract and conventional. They wished to renew emphasis on serious emotion, imagination, individuality, and fidelity to truth; and in doing so they gave special attention to elaboration of details in a fashion distinctly reminiscent of medievalism. Their work had much, also, of medieval mysticism and symbolism. Besides painting pictures they published a very short-lived periodical, 'The Germ,' containing both literary material and drawings. Ruskin, now arriving at fame and influence, wrote vigorously in their favor, and though the Brotherhood did not last long as an organization, it has exerted a great influence on subsequent painting.

Rossetti's impulses were generous, but his habits were eccentric and selfish, and his life unfortunate. His engagement with Miss Eleanor Siddal, a milliner's apprentice (whose face appears in many of his pictures), was prolonged by his lack of means for nine years; further, he was an agnostic, while she held a simple religious faith, and she was carrying on a losing struggle with tuberculosis. Sixteen months after their marriage she died, and on a morbid impulse of remorse for inconsiderateness in his treatment of her Rossetti buried his poems, still unpublished, in her coffin. After some years, however, he was persuaded to disinter and publish them. Meanwhile he had formed friendships with the slightly younger artists William Morris and Edward Burne-Jones, and they established a company for the manufacture of furniture and other articles, to be made beautiful as well as useful, and thus to aid in spreading the esthetic sense among the English people.

After some years Rossetti and Burne-Jones withdrew from the enterprise, leaving it to Morris. Rossetti continued all his life to produce both poetry and paintings. His pictures are among the best and most gorgeous products of recent romantic art--'Dante's Dream,' 'Beata Beatrix,' 'The Blessed Damosel,' and many others. During his later years he earned a large income, and he lived in a large house in Cheyne Row, Chelsea (near Carlyle), where for a while, as long as his irregular habits permitted, the novelist George Meredith and the poet Swinburne were also inmates. He gradually grew more morbid, and became a rather pitiful victim of insomnia, the drug chloral, and spiritualistic delusions about his wife. He died in 1882.

Rossetti's poetry is absolutely unlike that of any other English poet, and the difference is clearly due in large part to his Italian race and his painter's instinct. He has, in the didactic sense, absolutely no religious, moral, or social interests; he is an artist almost purely for art's sake, writing to give beautiful embodiment to moods, experiences, and striking moments. If it is true of Tennyson, however, that he stands aloof from actual life, this is far truer of Rossetti. His world is a vague and languid region of enchantment, full of whispering winds, indistinct forms of personified abstractions, and the murmur of hidden streams; its landscape sometimes bright, sometimes shadowy, but always delicate, exquisitely arranged for luxurious decorative effect. In his ballad-romances, to be sure, such as, 'The King's Tragedy,' there is much dramatic vigor; yet there is still more of medieval weirdness. Rossetti, like Dante, has much of spiritual mysticism, and his interest centers in the inner rather than the outer life; but his method, that of a painter and a southern Italian, is always highly sensuous. His melody is superb and depends partly on a highly Latinized vocabulary, archaic pronunciations, and a delicate genius in sound-modulation, the effect being heightened also by frequent alliteration and masterly use of refrains. 'Sister Helen,' obviously influenced by the popular ballad 'Edward, Edward,' derives much of its tremendous tragic power from the refrain, and in the use of this device is perhaps the most effective poem in the world. Rossetti is especially facile also with the sonnet. His sonnet sequence, 'The House of Life,' one of the most notable in English, exalts earthly Love as the central force in the world and in rather fragmentary fashion traces the tragic influence of Change in both life and love.

## WILLIAM MORRIS

William Morris, a man of remarkable versatility and tremendous energy, which expressed themselves in poetry and many other ways, was the son of a prosperous banker, and was born in London in 1834. At Oxford in 1853-55 he became interested in medieval life and art, was stimulated by the poetry of Mrs. Browning and Tennyson, became a friend of Burne-Jones, wrote verse and prose, and was a member of a group called 'The Brotherhood,' while a little later published for a year a monthly magazine not unlike 'The Germ.' He apprenticed himself to an architect, but at the same time also practised several decorative arts, such as woodcarving, illuminating manuscripts, and designing furniture, stained glass and embroidery.

Together with Burne-Jones, moreover, he became an enthusiastic pupil of Rossetti in painting. His first volume of verse, 'The Defence of Guinevere and Other Poems,' put forth in 1858, shows the influence of Rossetti and Pre-Raphaelitism, but it mainly gives vivid presentation to the spirit of fourteenth-century French chivalry. In 1861 came the foundation of the decorative-art firm of Morris and Co., which after some years grew into a large business, continued to be Morris' main occupation to the end of his life, and has exercised a great influence, both in England and elsewhere, on the beautifying of the surroundings of domestic life.

Meanwhile Morris had turned to the writing of long narrative poems, which he composed with remarkable fluency. The most important is the series of versions of Greek and Norse myths and legends which appeared in 1868-70 as 'The Earthly Paradise.' Shortly after this he became especially interested in Icelandic literature and published versions of some of its stories; notably one of the Siegfried tale, 'Sigurd the Volsung.' In the decade from 1880 to 1890 he devoted most of his energy to work for the Socialist party, of which he became a leader. His ideals were largely identical with those of Ruskin; in particular he wished to restore (or create) in the lives of workingmen conditions which should make of each of them an independent artist. The practical result of his experience was bitter disappointment, he was deposed from his leadership, finally abandoned the party, and returned to art and literature. He now published a succession of prose romances largely inspired by the Icelandic sagas and composed in a strange half-archaic style. He also established the 'Kelmscott Press,' which he made famous for its production of elaborate artistic editions of great books. He died in 1896.

Morris' shorter poems are strikingly dramatic and picturesque, and his longer narrations are remarkably facile and often highly pleasing. His facility, however, is his undoing. He sometimes wrote as much as eight hundred lines in a day, and he once declared: 'If a chap can't compose an epic poem while he's weaving tapestry, he had better shut up; he'll never do any good at all.' In reading his work one always feels that there is the material of greatness, but perhaps nothing that he wrote is strictly great. His prose will certainly prove less permanent than his verse.

## SWINBURNE

A younger disciple of the Pre-Raphaelite Movement but also a strongly original artist was Algernon Charles Swinburne. Born in 1837 into a wealthy family, the son of an admiral, he devoted himself throughout his life wholly to poetry, and his career was almost altogether devoid of external incident. After passing through Eton and Oxford he began as author at twenty-three by publishing two plays imitative of Shakspere. Five years later he put forth 'Atalanta in Calydon,' a tragedy not only drawn from Greek heroic legend, but composed in the ancient Greek manner, with long dialogs and choruses. These two volumes express the two intensely vigorous forces which were strangely combined in his nature; for while no man has ever been a more violent romanticist than Swinburne, yet, as one critic has said, 'All the romantic riot in his blood clamored for Greek severity and Greek restraint.'

During the next fifteen years he was partly occupied with a huge poetic trilogy in blank verse on Mary Queen of Scots, and from time to time he wrote other dramas and much prose criticism, the latter largely in praise of the Elizabethan dramatists and always wildly extravagant in tone. He produced also some long narrative poems, of which the chief is 'Tristram of Lyonesse.' His chief importance, however, is as a lyric poet, and his lyric production was large. His earlier poems in this category are for the most part highly objectionable in substance or sentiment, but he gradually worked into a better vein. He was a friend of George Meredith, Burne-Jones, Morris, Rossetti (to whom he loyally devoted himself for years), and the painter Whistler. He died in 1909.

Swinburne carried his radicalism into all lines. Though an ardently patriotic Englishman, he was an extreme republican; and many of his poems are dedicated to the cause of Italian independence or to liberty in general. The significance of his thought, however, is less than that of any other English poet who can in any sense be called great; his poetry is notable chiefly for its artistry, especially for its magnificent melody. Indeed, it has been cleverly said that he offers us an elaborate service of gold and silver, but with little on it except salt and pepper. In his case, however, the mere external beauty and power often seem their own complete and satisfying justification. His command of different meters is marvelous; he uses twice as many as Browning, who is perhaps second to him in this respect, and his most characteristic ones are those of gloriously rapid anapestic lines with complicated rime-schemes.

Others of his distinctive traits are lavish alliteration, rich sensuousness, grandiose vagueness of thought and expression, a great sweep of imagination, and a corresponding love of vastness and desolation. He makes much decorative use of Biblical imagery and of vague abstract personifications--in general creates an atmosphere similar to that of Rossetti. Somewhat as in the case of Morris, his fluency is almost fatal--he sometimes pours out his melodious but vague emotion in forgetfulness of all proportion and restraint. From the intellectual and spiritual point of view he is nearly negligible, but as a musician in words he has no superior, not even Shelley.

## OTHER VICTORIA POETS

Among the other Victorian poets, three, at least, must be mentioned. Arthur Hugh Clough (1819-1861), tutor at Oxford and later examiner in the government education office, expresses the spiritual doubt and struggle of the period in noble poems similar to those of Matthew Arnold, whose fine elegy 'Thyrsis' commemorates him. Edward Fitzgerald (1809-1883), Irish by birth, an eccentric though kind-hearted recluse, and a friend of Tennyson, is known solely for his masterly paraphrase (1859) of some of the Quatrains of the skeptical eleventh-century Persian astronomer-poet Omar Khayyam. The similarity of temper between the medieval oriental scholar and the questioning phase of the Victorian period is striking (though the spirit of Fitzgerald's verse is no doubt as much his own as Omar's), and no poetry is more poignantly beautiful than the best of this.

Christina Rossetti (1830-94), the sister of Dante Gabriel Rossetti, lived in London with her mother in the greatest seclusion, occupied with an ascetic devotion to the English Church, with her poetry, and with the composition, secondarily, of prose articles and short stories. Her poetry is limited almost entirely to the lyrical expression of her spiritual experiences, much of it is explicitly religious, and all of it is religious in feeling. It is tinged with the Pre-Raphaelite mystic medievalism; and a quiet and most affecting sadness is its dominant trait; but the power and beauty of a certain small part of it perhaps entitle her to be called the chief of English poetesses.

## THE EARLIER SECONDARY NOVELISTS

To Scott's position of unquestioned supremacy among romancers and novelists Charles Dickens succeeded almost immediately on Scott's death, but certain secondary early

Victorian novelists may be considered before him. In the lives of two of these, Bulwer-Lytton and Benjamin Disraeli, there are interesting parallels. Both were prominent in politics, both began writing as young men before the commencement of the Victorian period, and both ended their literary work only fifty years later. Edward Bulwer, later created Sir Edward Bulwer-Lytton, and finally raised to the peerage as Lord Lytton (1803-1873), was almost incredibly fluent and versatile. Much of his life a member of Parliament and for a while of the government, he was a vigorous pamphleteer. His sixty or more really literary works are of great variety; perhaps the best known of them are his second novel, the trifling 'Pelham' (1828), which inaugurated a class of so-called 'dandy' novels, giving sympathetic presentation to the more frivolous social life of the 'upper' class, and the historical romances 'The Last Days of Pompeii' (1834) and 'Harold' (1843). In spite of his real ability, Bulwer was a poser and sentimentalist, characteristics for which he was vigorously ridiculed by Thackeray.

Benjamin Disraeli, later Earl of Beaconsfield (1804-1881), a much less prolific writer, was by birth a Jew. His immature earliest novel, 'Vivian Grey' (1826), deals, somewhat more sensibly, with the same social class as Bulwer's 'Pelham.' In his novels of this period, as in his dress and manner, he deliberately attitudinized, a fact which in part reflected a certain shallowness of character, in part was a device to attract attention for the sake of his political ambition. After winning his way into Parliament he wrote in 1844-7 three political novels,' Coningsby,' 'Sybil,' and 'Tancred,' which set forth his Tory creed of opposition to the dominance of middle-class Liberalism. For twenty-five years after this he was absorbed in the leadership of his party, and he at last became Prime Minister. In later life he so far returned to literature as to write two additional novels.

Vastly different was the life and work of Charlotte Bronte (1816-1855). Miss Bronte, a product and embodiment of the strictest religious sense of duty, somewhat tempered by the liberalizing tendency of the time, was the daughter of the rector of a small and bleak Yorkshire village, Haworth, where she was brought up in poverty. The two of her sisters who reached maturity, Emily and Anne, both still more short-lived than she, also wrote novels, and Emily produced some lyrics which strikingly express the stern, defiant will that characterized all the children of the family. Their lives were pitifully bare, hard, and morbid, scarcely varied or enlivened except by a year which Charlotte and Emily spent when Charlotte was twenty-six in a private school in Brussels, followed on Charlotte's part by a return to the same school for a year as teacher. In 1847 Charlotte's novel 'Jane Eyre' (pronounced like the word 'air') won a great success. Her three later novels are less significant. In 1854 she was married to one of her father's curates, a Mr. Nicholls, a sincere but narrow-minded man. She was happy in the marriage, but died within a few months, worn out by the unremitting physical and moral strain of forty years.

The significance of 'Jane Eyre' can be suggested by calling it the last striking expression of extravagant Romanticism, partly Byronic, but grafted on the stern Bronte moral sense. One of its two main theses is the assertion of the supreme authority of religious duty, but it vehemently insists also on the right of the individual conscience to judge of duty for itself, in spite of conventional opinion, and, difficult as this may be to understand to-day, it was denounced at the time as irreligious. The Romanticism appears further in the volcanic but sometimes melodramatic power of the love story, where the heroine is a somewhat idealized double of the authoress and where the imperfect portrayal of the hero reflects the limitations of Miss Bronte's own experience.

Miss Bronte is the subject of one of the most delightfully sympathetic of all biographies, written by Mrs. Elizabeth Cleghorn Gaskell. Mrs. Gaskell was authoress also of many stories, long and short, of which the best known is 'Cranford' (1853), a charming portrayal of the quaint life of a secluded village.

## CHARLES DICKENS

The most popular of all English novelists, Charles Dickens, was born in 1812, the son of an unpractical and improvident government navy clerk whom, with questionable taste, he later caricatured in 'David Copperfield' as Mr. Micawber. The future novelist's schooling was slight and irregular, but as a boy he read much fiction, especially seventeenth and eighteenth century authors, whose influence is apparent in the picaresque lack of structure of his own works. From childhood also he showed the passion for the drama and the theater which resulted from the excitably dramatic quality of his own temperament and which always continued to be the second moving force of his life. When he was ten years old his father was imprisoned for debt (like Micawber, in the Marshalsea prison), and he was put to work in the cellar of a London shoe-blacking factory.

On his proud and sensitive disposition this humiliation, though it lasted only a few months, inflicted a wound which never thoroughly healed; years after he was famous he would cross the street to avoid the smell from an altogether different blacking factory, with its reminder 'of what he once was.' To this experience, also, may evidently be traced no small part of the intense sympathy with the oppressed poor, especially with helpless children, which is so prominent in his novels. Obliged from the age of fifteen to earn his own living, for the most part, he was for a while a clerk in a London lawyer's office, where he observed all sorts and conditions of people with characteristic keenness. Still more valuable was his five or six years' experience in the very congenial and very active work of a newspaper reporter, where his special department was political affairs. This led up naturally to his permanent work. The successful series of lively 'Sketches by Boz' dealing with people and scenes about London was preliminary to 'The Pickwick Papers,' which made the author famous at the age of twenty-four.

During the remaining thirty-three years of his life Dickens produced novels at the rate of rather more than one in two years. He composed slowly and carefully but did not revise greatly, and generally published by monthly installments in periodicals which, latterly, he himself established and edited. Next after 'The Pickwick Papers' came 'Oliver Twist,' and 'David Copperfield' ten years later. Of the others, 'Martin Chuzzlewit,' 'Dombey and Son,' 'Bleak House,' and 'A Tale of Two Cities,' are among the best. For some years Dickens also published an annual Christmas story, of which the first two, 'A Christmas Carol' and 'The Chimes,' rank highest.

His exuberant physical energy gave to his life more external variety than is common with authors. At the age of thirty he made a visit to the United States and travelled as far as to the then extreme western town of St. Louis, everywhere received and entertained with the most extravagant enthusiasm. Even before his return to England, however, he excited a reaction, by his abundantly justified but untactful condemnation of American piracy of English books; and this reaction was confirmed by his subsequent caricature of American life in 'American Notes' and 'Martin Chuzzlewit.' For a number of years during the middle part of his career Dickens devoted a vast amount of energy to managing and taking the chief part in a company of amateur actors, who performed at times in various cities. Later on he substituted for this several prolonged series of semi-dramatic public readings from his works, an effort which drew heavily on his vitality and shortened his life, but which intoxicated him with its enormous success. One of these series was delivered in America, where, of course, the former ill-feeling had long before worn away.

Dickens lived during the greater part of his life in London, but in his later years near Rochester, at Gadshill, the scene of Falstaff's exploit. He made long sojourns also on the Continent. Much social and outdoor life was necessary to him; he had a theory that he ought to spend as much time out of doors as in the house. He married early and had a large family of children, but pathetically enough for one whose emotions centered so largely about the home, his own marriage was not well-judged; and after more than twenty years he and his wife (the Dora Spenlow of 'David Copperfield') separated, though with mutual respect. He died in 1870 and was buried in Westminster Abbey in the rather ostentatiously unpretentious way which, with his deep-seated dislike for aristocratic conventions, he had carefully prescribed in his will.

Dickens' popularity, in his own day and since, is due chiefly: (1) to his intense human sympathy; (2) to his unsurpassed emotional and dramatic power; and (3) to his aggressive humanitarian zeal for the reform of all evils and abuses, whether they weigh upon the oppressed classes or upon helpless individuals. Himself sprung from the lower middle class, and thoroughly acquainted with the life of the poor and apparently of sufferers in all ranks, he is one of the most moving spokesmen whom they have ever had. The pathos and tragedy of their experiences--aged and honest toilers subjected to pitiless task-masters or to the yoke of social injustice; lonely women uncomplainingly sacrificing their lives for unworthy men; sad-faced children, the victims of circumstances, of cold-blooded parents, or of the worst criminals--these things play a large part in almost all of Dickens' books. In almost all, moreover, there is present, more or less in the foreground, a definite humanitarian aim, an attack on some time-consecrated evil--the poor-house system, the cruelties practised in private schools, or the miscarriage of justice in the Court of Chancery. In dramatic vividness his great scenes are masterly, for example the storm in 'David Copperfield,' the pursuit and discovery of Lady Dedlock in 'Bleak House,' and the interview between Mrs. Dombey and James Carker in 'Dombey and Son.'

Dickens' magnificent emotional power is not balanced, however, by a corresponding intellectual quality; in his work, as in his temperament and bearing, emotion is always in danger of running to excess. One of his great elements of strength is his sense of humor, which has created an almost unlimited number of delightful scenes and characters; but it very generally becomes riotous and so ends in sheer farce and caricature, as the names of many of the characters suggest at the outset. Indeed Dickens has been rightly designated a grotesque novelist--the greatest of all grotesque novelists. Similarly his pathos is often exaggerated until it passes into mawkish sentimentality, so that his humbly-bred heroines, for example, are made to act and talk with all the poise and certainty which can really spring only from wide experience and broad education. Dickens' zeal for reform, also, sometimes outruns his judgment or knowledge and leads him to assault evils that had actually been abolished long before he wrote.

No other English author has approached Dickens in the number of characters whom he has created; his twenty novels present literally thousands of persons, almost all thoroughly human, except for the limitations that we have already noted. Their range is of course very great, though it never extends successfully into the 'upper' social classes. For Dickens was violently prejudiced against the nobility and against all persons of high social standing, and when he attempted to introduce them created only pitifully wooden automatons. For the actual English gentleman we must pass by his Sir Leicester Dedlocks and his Mr. Veneerings to novelists of a very different viewpoint, such as Thackeray and Meredith. Dickens' inexhaustible fertility in characters and scenes is a main cause of the rather extravagant lack of unity which is another conspicuous feature of his books. He usually made a good preliminary general plan and proceeded on the whole with firm movement and strong suspense. But he always introduces many characters and sub-actions not necessary to the main story, and develops them quite beyond their real artistic importance. Not without influence here was the necessity of filling a specified number of serial instalments, each of a definite number of pages, and each requiring a striking situation at the end. Moreover, Dickens often follows the eighteenth-century picaresque habit of tracing the histories of his heroes from birth to marriage. In most respects, however, Dickens' art improved as he proceeded. The love element, it should be noted, as what we have already said implies, plays a smaller part than usual among the various aspects of life which his books present.

Not least striking among Dickens' traits is his power of description. His observation is very quick and keen, though not fine; his sense for the characteristic features, whether of scenes in Nature or of human personality and appearance, is unerring; and he has never had a superior in picturing and conveying the atmosphere both of interiors and of all kinds of scenes of human life. London, where most of his novels are wholly or chiefly located, has in him its chief and most comprehensive portrayer.

Worthy of special praise, lastly, is the moral soundness of all Dickens' work, praise which is not seriously affected by present-day sneers at his 'middle-class' and 'mid-Victorian' point of view. Dickens' books, however, like his character, are destitute of the deeper spiritual quality, of poetic and philosophic idealism. His stories are all admirable demonstrations of the power and beauty of the nobler practical virtues, of kindness, courage, humility, and all the other forms of unselfishness; but for the underlying mysteries of life and the higher meanings of art his positive and self-formed mind had very little feeling. From first to last he speaks authentically for the common heart of humanity, but he is not one of the rarer spirits, like Spenser or George Eliot or Meredith, who transport us into the realm of the less tangible realities. All his limitations, indeed, have become more conspicuous as time has passed; and critical judgment has already definitely excluded him from the select ranks of the truly greatest authors.

## WILLIAM M. THACKERAY

Dickens' chief rival for fame during his later lifetime and afterward was Thackeray, who presents a strong contrast with him, both as man and as writer.

Thackeray, the son of an East India Company official, was born at Calcutta in 1811. His father died while he was a child and he was taken to England for his education; he was a student in the Charterhouse School and then for a year at Cambridge. Next, on the Continent, he studied drawing, and though his unmethodical and somewhat idle habits prevented him from ever really mastering the technique of the art, his real knack for it enabled him later on to illustrate his own books in a semi-grotesque but effective fashion. Desultory study of the law was interrupted when he came of age by the inheritance of a comfortable fortune, which he managed to lose within a year or two by gambling, speculations, and an unsuccessful effort at carrying on a newspaper. Real application to newspaper and magazine writing secured him after four years a place on 'Eraser's Magazine,' and he was married. Not long after, his wife became insane, but his warm affection for his daughters gave him throughout his life genuine domestic happiness.

For ten years Thackeray's production was mainly in the line of satirical humorous and picaresque fiction, none of it of the first rank. During this period he chiefly attacked current vices, snobbishness, and sentimentality, which latter quality, Thackeray's special aversion, he found rampant in contemporary life and literature, including the novels of Dickens. The appearance of his masterpiece, 'Vanity Fair' (the allegorical title taken from a famous incident in 'Pilgrim's Progress'), in 'Fraser's Magazine' in 1847-8 (the year before Dickens' 'David Copperfield') brought him sudden fame and made him a social lion. Within the next ten years he produced his other important novels, of which the best are 'Pendennis,' 'Henry Esmond,' and 'The Newcomes,' and also his charming essays (first delivered as lectures) on the eighteenth century in England, namely

spirit and even its literary style with an approach to perfection that has never been rivaled. On other grounds as well the book ranks almost if not quite beside 'Vanity Pair.' Henry Esmond himself is Thackeray's most thoroughly wise and good character, and Beatrix is as real and complex a woman as even Becky Sharp.

## GEORGE ELIOT

The perspective of time has made it clear that among the Victorian novelists, as among the poets, three definitely surpass the others. With Dickens and Thackeray is to be ranked only 'George Eliot' (Mary Anne Evans).

George Eliot was born in 1819 in the central county of Warwick from which Shakspere had sprung two centuries and a half before. Her father, a manager of estates for various members of the landed gentry, was to a large extent the original both of her Adam Bede and of Caleb Garth in 'Middlemarch,' while her own childish life is partly reproduced in the experiences of Maggie in "The Mill on the Floss.' Endowed with one of the strongest minds that any woman has ever possessed, from her very infancy she studied and read widely. Her nature, however, was not one-sided; all her life she was passionately fond of music; and from the death of her mother in her eighteenth year she demonstrated her practical capacity in the management of her father's household.

Circumstances. combined with her unusual ability to make her entire life one of too high pressure, and her first struggle was religious. She was brought up a Methodist, and during her girlhood was fervently evangelical, in the manner of Dinah Morris in 'Adam Bede'; but moving to Coventry she fell under the influence of some rationalistic acquaintances who led her to adopt the scientific Positivism of the French philosopher Comte. Her first literary work, growing out of the same interest, was the formidable one of translating the 'Life of Jesus' of the German professor Strauss. Some years of conscientious nursing of her father, terminated by his death, were followed by one in Geneva, nominally a year of vacation, but she spent it largely in the study of experimental physics. On her return to England she became a contributor and soon assistant editor of the liberal periodical 'The Westminster Review.'

This connection was most important in its personal results; it brought her into contact with a versatile man of letters, George Henry Lewes, and in 1854 they were united as man and wife. Mr. Lewes had been unhappily married years before to a woman who was still alive, and English law did not permit the divorce which he would have secured in America. Consequently the new union was not a legal marriage, and English public opinion was severe in its condemnation. In the actual result the sympathetic companionship of Mr. Lewes was of the greatest value to George Eliot and brought her much happiness; yet she evidently felt keenly the equivocal social position, and it was probably in large part the cause of the increasing sadness of her later years.

She was already thirty-six when in 1856 she entered on creative authorship with the three 'Scenes from Clerical Life.' The pseudonym which she adopted for these and her later stories originated in no more substantial reason than her fondness for 'Eliot' and the fact that Mr. Lewes' first name was 'George.' 'Adam Bede' in 1859 completely established her reputation, and her six or seven other books followed as rapidly as increasingly laborious workmanship permitted. 'Romola.' in 1863, a powerful but perhaps over-substantial historical novel, was the outcome partly of residence in Florence. Not content with prose, she attempted poetry also, but she altogether lacked the poet's delicacy of both imagination and expression. The death of Mr. Lewes in 1878 was a severe blow to her, since she was always greatly dependent on personal sympathy; and after a year and a half, to the surprise of every one, she married Mr. John W. Cross, a banker much younger than herself. But her own death followed within a few months in 1880.

George Eliot's literary work combines in an interesting way the same distinct and even strangely contrasting elements as her life, and in her writings their relative proportions alter rather markedly during the course of her career. One of the most attractive qualities, especially in her earlier books, is her warm and unaffected human sympathy, which is temperamental, but greatly enlarged by her own early experience. The aspiration, pathos and tragedy of life, especially among the lower and middle classes in the country and the small towns, can scarcely be interpreted with more feeling, tenderness, or power than in her pages. But her sympathy does not blind her to the world of comedy; figures like Mrs. Poyser in 'Adam Bede' are delightful. Even from the beginning, however, the really controlling forces in George Eliot's work were intellectual and moral.

She started out with the determination to render the facts of life with minute and conscientious accuracy, an accuracy more complete than that of Mrs. Gaskell, who was in large degree her model; and as a result her books, from the beginning, are masterpieces of the best sort of realism. The characters, life, and backgrounds of many of them are taken from her own Warwickshire acquaintances and country, and for the others she made the most painstaking study. More fundamental than her sympathy, indeed, perhaps even from the outset, is her instinct for scientific analysis. Like a biologist or a botanist, and with much more deliberate effort than most of her fellow-craftsmen, she traces and scrutinizes all the acts and motives of her characters until she reaches and reveals their absolute inmost truth.

This objective scientific method has a tendency to become sternly judicial, and in extreme cases she even seems to be using her weak or imperfect characters as deterrent examples. Inevitably, with her disposition, the scientific tendency grew upon her. Beginning with 'Middlemarch' (1872), which is perhaps her masterpiece, it seems to some critics decidedly too preponderant, giving to her novels too much the atmosphere of psychological text-books; and along with it goes much introduction of the actual facts of nineteenth century science. Her really primary instinct, however, is the moral one. The supremacy of moral law may fairly be called the general theme of all her works; to demonstrating it her scientific method is really in the main auxiliary; and in spite of her accuracy it makes of her more an idealist than a realist. With unswerving logic she traces the sequence of act and consequence, showing how apparently trifling words and deeds reveal the springs of character and how careless choices and seemingly insignificant self-indulgences may altogether determine the issues of life. The couplet from Aeschylus which she prefixed to one of the chapters of 'Felix Holt' might stand at the outset of all her work:

*'Tis law as steadfast as the throne of Zeus-- Our days are heritors of days gone by.*

Her conviction, or at least her purpose, is optimistic, to show that by honest effort the sincere and high-minded man or woman may win happiness in the face of all difficulties and disappointments; but her own actual judgment of life was somber, not altogether different from that which Carlyle repudiated in 'The Everlasting Yea'; so that the final effect of her books, though stimulating, is subdued rather than cheerful.

In technique her very hard work generally assured mastery. Her novels are firmly knit and well-proportioned, and have the inevitable movement of life itself; while her great scenes equal those of Thackeray in dramatic power and, at their best, in reserve and suggestiveness. Perhaps her chief technical faults are tendencies to prolixity and too much expository analysis of characters and motives.

## SECONDARY MIDDLE AND LATER VICTORIAN NOVELISTS

Several of the other novelists of the mid-century and later produced work which in a period of less prolific and less highly developed art would have secured them high distinction. Charles Kingsley (1819-1875) spent most of his life, by his own self-renouncing choice, as curate and rector of the little Hampshire parish of Eversley, though for some years he also held the professorship of history at Cambridge. An aggressive Protestant, he drifted in his later years into the controversy with Cardinal Newman which opened the way for Newman's 'Apologia.' From the outset, Kingsley was an enthusiastic worker with F. D. Maurice in the Christian Socialist movement which aimed at the betterment of the conditions of life among the working classes.

'Alton Locke' and 'Yeast,' published in 1849, were powerful but reasonable and very influential expressions of his convictions--fervid arguments in the form of fiction against existing social injustices. His most famous books are 'Hypatia' (1853), a novel dealing with the Church in its conflict with Greek philosophy in fifth-century Alexandria, and 'Westward Ho!' (1855) which presents with sympathetic largeness of manner the adventurous side of Elizabethan life. His brief 'Andromeda' is one of the best English poems in the classical dactylic hexameter.

Charles Reade (1814-1884), a man of dramatic disposition somewhat similar to that of Dickens (though Reade had a University education and was admitted to the bar), divided his interest and fiery energies between the drama and the novel. But while his plays were of such doubtful quality that he generally had to pay for having them acted, his novels were often strong and successful. Personally he was fervently evangelical, and like Dickens he was often inspired to write by indignation at social wrongs.

His 'Hard Cash' (1863), which attacks private insane asylums, is powerful; but his most important work is 'The Cloister and the Hearth' (1861), one of the most informing and vivid of all historical novels, with the father of Erasmus for its hero. No novelist can, be more thrilling and picturesque than Reade, but he lacks restraint and is often highly sensational and melodramatic.

Altogether different is the method of Anthony Trollope (1815-1882) in his fifty novels. Trollope, long a traveling employe in the post-office service, was a man of very assertive and somewhat commonplace nature.

Partly a disciple of Thackeray, he went beyond Thackeray's example in the refusal to take his art altogether seriously as an art; rather, he treated it as a form of business, sneering at the idea of special inspiration, and holding himself rigidly to a mechanical schedule of composition--a definite and unvarying number of pages in a specified number of hours on each of his working days. The result is not so disastrous as might have been expected; his novels have no small degree of truth and interest.

The most notable are the half dozen which deal with ecclesiastical life in his imaginary county of Barsetshire, beginning with 'The Warden' and 'Barchester Towers.' His 'Autobiography' furnishes in some of its chapters one of the noteworthy existing discussions of the writer's art by a member of the profession.

Richard Blackmore (1825-1900), first a lawyer, later manager of a market-garden, was the author of numerous novels, but will be remembered only for 'Lorna Doone' (1869), a charming reproduction of Devonshire country life assigned to the romantic setting of the time of James II. Its simple-minded and gigantic hero John Ridd is certainly one of the permanent figures of English fiction.

Joseph H. Shorthouse (1834-1903), a Birmingham chemical manufacturer, but a man of very fine nature, is likewise to be mentioned for a single book, 'John Inglesant' (1881). Located in the middle of the seventeenth century, when the strife of religious and political parties afforded material especially available for the author's purpose, this is a spiritual romance, a High Churchman's assertion of the supremacy of the inner over the outer life. From this point of view it is one of the most significant of English novels, and though much of it is philosophical and though it is not free from technical faults, parts of it attain the extreme limit of absorbing narrative interest.

Walter Pater (1839-1894), an Oxford Fellow, also represents distinctly the spirit of unworldliness, which in his case led to a personal aloofness from active life. He was the master of a delicately-finished, somewhat over-fastidious, style, which he employed in essays on the Renaissance and other historical and artistic topics and in a spiritual romance, 'Marius the Epicurean' (1885). No less noteworthy than 'John Inglesant,' and better constructed, this latter is placed in the reign of the Roman Emperor Marcus Aurelius, but its atmosphere is only in part historically authentic.

## GEORGE MEREDITH (1828-1910)

Except for a lack of the elements which make for popularity, George Meredith would hold an unquestioned place in the highest rank of novelists. In time he is partly contemporary with George Eliot, as he began to publish a little earlier than she. But he long outlived her and continued to write to the end of his life; and his recognition was long delayed; so that he may properly be placed in the group of later Victorian novelists. His long life was devoid of external incident; he was long a newspaper writer and afterward literary reader for a publishing house; he spent his later years quietly in Surrey, enjoying the friendship of Swinburne and other men of letters.

Among novelists he occupies something the same place which Browning, a person of very different temperament and ideas, holds among poets. He writes only for intelligent and thoughtful people and aims to interpret the deeper things of life and character, not disregarding dramatic external incident, but using it as only one of the means to his main purpose. His style is brilliant, epigrammatic, and subtile; and he prefers to imply many things rather than to state them directly. All this makes large, perhaps sometimes too large, demands on the reader's attention, but there is, of course, corresponding stimulation. Meredith's general attitude toward life is the fine one of serene philosophic confidence, the attitude in general of men like Shakspere and Goethe.

He despises sentimentality, admires chiefly the qualities of quiet strength and good breeding which are exemplified among the best members of the English aristocracy; and in all his interpretation is very largely influenced by modern science. His virile courage and optimism are as pronounced as those of Browning; he wrote a noteworthy 'Essay on Comedy' and oftentimes insists on emphasizing the comic rather than the tragic aspect of things, though he can also be powerful in tragedy; and his enthusiasms for the beauty of the world and for the romance of youthful love are delightful. He may perhaps best be approached through 'Evan Harrington' (1861) and 'The Ordeal of Richard Feverel' (1859). 'The Egoist' (1879) and 'Diana of the Crossways' (1885) are among his other strongest books. In his earlier years he wrote a considerable body of verse, which shows much the same qualities as his prose. Some of it is rugged in form, but other parts magnificently dramatic, and some few poems, like the unique and superb 'Love in the Valley,' charmingly beautiful.

### THOMAS HARDY

In Thomas Hardy (born 1840) the pessimistic interpretation of modern science is expressed frankly and fully, with much the same pitiless consistency that distinguishes contemporary European writers such as Zola. Mr. Hardy early turned to literature from architecture and he has lived a secluded life in southern England, the ancient Wessex, which he makes the scene of all his novels. His knowledge of life is sure and his technique in all respects masterly. He has preferred to deal chiefly with persons in the middle and poorer classes of society because, like Wordsworth, though with very different emphasis, he feels that in their experiences the real facts of life stand out most truly. His deliberate theory is a sheer fatalism--that human character and action are the inevitable result of laws of heredity and environment over which man has no control. 'The Return of the Native' (1878) and 'Far from the Madding Crowd' (1874) are among his best novels, though the sensational frankness of 'Tess of the D'Urbervilles' (1891) has given it greater reputation.

**STEVENSON**

Robert Louis Stevenson (1850-1894), the first of the rather prominent group of recent Scotch writers of fiction, is as different as possible from Hardy. Destined for the career of civil engineer and lighthouse builder in which his father and grandfather were distinguished, he proved unfitted for it by lack both of inclination and of health, and the profession of law for which he later prepared himself was no more congenial.

From boyhood he, like Scott, studied human nature with keen delight in rambles about the country, and unlike Scott he was incessantly practising writing merely for the perfection of his style.

As an author he won his place rather slowly; and his whole mature life was a wonderfully courageous and persistent struggle against the sickness which generally prevented him from working more than two or three hours a day and often kept him for months in bed unable even to speak.

A trip to California in an emigrant train in 1879-1880 brought him to death's door but accomplished its purpose, his marriage to an American lady, Mrs. Osbourne, whom he had previously met in artist circles in France. He first secured a popular success with the boys' pirate story, 'Treasure Island,' in 1882.

'A Child's Garden of Verses' (1885) was at once accepted as one of the most irresistibly sympathetic of children's classics; and 'The Strange Case of Dr. Jekyll and Mr. Hyde' (1886), a unique and astonishingly powerful moral lesson in the form of a thrilling little romance which strangely anticipates the later discoveries of psychology, made in its different way a still stronger impression.

Stevenson produced, considering his disabilities, a remarkably large amount of work--essays, short stories, and romances--but the only others of his books which need here be mentioned are the four romances of Scotch life in the eighteenth century which belong to his later years; of these 'The Master of Ballantrae' and the fragmentary 'Weir of Hermiston' are the best. His letters, also, which, like his widely-circulated prayers, reveal his charming and heroic personality, are among the most interesting in the history of English Literature.

His bodily weakness, especially tuberculosis, which had kept him wandering from one resort to another, at last drove him altogether from Europe to the South Seas.

He finally settled in Samoa, where for the last half dozen years of his life he was busy not only with clearing his land, building his house, and writing, but with energetic efforts to serve the natives, then involved in broils among themselves and with England, Germany, and the United States. His death came suddenly when he was only forty-four years old, and the Samoans, who ardently appreciated what he had done for them, buried him high up on a mountain overlooking both his home and the sea.

Stevenson, in the midst of an age perhaps too intensely occupied with the deeper questions, stood for a return to the mere spirit of romance, and for occasional reading he furnishes delightful recreation. In the last analysis, however, his general lack of serious significance condemns him at most to a secondary position. At his best his narrative technique (as in 'The Master of Ballantrae') is perfect; his portrayal of men (he almost never attempted women) is equally certain; his style has no superior in English; and his delicate sensibility and keenness of observation render him a master of description.

But in his attitude toward life he never reached full maturity (perhaps because of the supreme effort of will necessary for the maintenance of his cheerfulness); not only did he retain to the end a boyish zest for mere adventure, but it is sometimes adventure of a melodramatic and unnecessarily disagreeable kind, and in his novels and short stories he offers virtually no interpretation of the world. No recent English prose writer has exercised a wider influence than he, but none is likely to suffer as time goes on a greater diminution of reputation.

## RUDYARD KIPLING

The name which naturally closes the list of Victorian writers is that of Rudyard Kipling, though he belongs, perhaps, as much to the twentieth century as to the one preceding. The son of a professor of architecture and sculpture in the University of Bombay, India, he was born in that city in 1865. Educated in England in the United Services College (for officers in the army and navy), he returned at the age of seventeen to India, where he first did strenuous editorial work on newspapers in Lahore, in the extreme northwestern part of the country.

He secured his intimate knowledge of the English army by living, through the permission of the commanding general, with the army on the frontiers. His instinct for story-telling in verse and prose had showed itself from his boyhood, but his first significant appearance in print was in 1886, with a volume of poems later included among the 'Departmental Ditties.' 'Plain Tales from the Hills' in prose, and other works, followed in rapid succession and won him enthusiastic recognition. In 1890 he removed to the United States, where he married and remained for seven years. Since then he has lived in England, with an interval in South Africa. He wrote prolifically during the '90's; since then both the amount of his production and its quality have fallen off.

Kipling is the representative of the vigorous life of action as led by manly and efficient men, and of the spirit of English imperialism. His poem "The White Man's Burden" sums up his imperialism--the creed that it is the duty of the higher races to civilize the lower ones with a strong hand; and he never doubts that the greater part of this obligation rests at present upon England--a theory, certainly, to which history lends much support. Kipling is endowed with the keenest power of observation, with the most genuine and most democratic human sympathies, and with splendid dramatic force.

Consequently he has made a unique contribution to literature in his portrayals, in both prose and verse, of the

English common soldier and of English army life on the frontiers of the Empire. On the other hand his verse is generally altogether devoid of the finer qualities of poetry. 'Danny Deever,' 'Pharaoh and the Sergeant,' 'Fuzzy Wuzzy,' 'The Ballad of East and West,' 'The Last Chantey,' 'Mulholland's Contract,' and many others, are splendidly stirring, but their colloquialism and general realism put them on a very different level from the work of the great masters who express the deeper truths in forms of permanent beauty.

At times, however, Kipling too gives voice to religious feelings, of a simple sort, in an impressive fashion, as in 'McAndrews' Hymn,' 'The Recessional,' and 'When earth's last picture is painted.' His sweeping rhythms and his grandiose forms of expression, suggestive of the vast spaces of ocean and plain and of inter-stellar space with which he delights to deal, have been very widely copied by minor verse-writers.

His very vivid and active imagination enables him not only to humanize animal life with remarkable success, as in the prose 'Jungle-Books,' but to range finely in the realms of the mysterious, as in the short stories 'They' and 'The Brushwood Boy.' Of short-stories he is the most powerful recent writer, as witness 'The Man Who Would Be King,' 'The Man Who Was,' 'Without Benefit of Clergy,' and 'Wee Willie Winkie'; though with all the frankness of modern realism he sometimes leads us into scenes of extreme physical horror. With longer stories he is generally less successful; 'Kim,' however, has much power.

## THE HISTORIANS

The present book, as a brief sketch of English Literature rather strictly defined, has necessarily disregarded the scientists, economists, and philosophers whose writings did much to mold the course of thought during the Victorian period. Among the numerous prominent historians, however, two must be mentioned for the brilliant literary quality of their work.

James Anthony Froude (1818-1894) was a disciple of Carlyle, from whom he took the idea of making history center around its great men and of giving to it the vivid effectiveness of the drama. With Froude too this results in exaggeration, and further he is sadly inaccurate, but his books are splendidly fascinating. His great 'History of England from the Fall of Wolsey to the

Armada' is his longest work; his 'Sketch' of Julius Casar is certainly one of the most interesting books of biography and history ever written. John Richard Green (1837-1883), who was a devoted clergyman before he became a historian, struggled all his life against the ill-health which finally cut short his career.

His 'History of the English People' is an admirable representative of the modern historical spirit, which treats general social conditions as more important than mere external events; but as a narrative it vies in interest with the very different one of Macaulay. Very honorable mention should be made also of W. E. H. Lecky, who belongs to the conscientiously scientific historical school. His 'History of Rationalism in Europe,' for example, is a very fine monument of the most thorough research and most effective statement; but to a mature mind its interest is equally conspicuous.

## THE TWENTIETH CENTURY

Beginning as early as the latter part of the eighteenth century literary production, thanks largely to the tremendous increase of education and of newspapers and magazines, has steadily grown, until now it has reached be wildering volume and complexity, in which the old principles are partly merged together and the new tendencies, for contemporary observers, at least, scarcely stand out with decisive distinctness.

Most significant to-day, perhaps, are the spirit of independence, now carried in some respects beyond the farthest previous Romantic limits, and the realistic impulse, in which the former impulses of democracy and humanitarianism play a large part.

Facts not to be disregarded are the steady advance of the short story, beginning early in the Victorian period or before, to a position of almost chief prominence with the novel; and the rise of American literature to a position approaching equality with that of England. Of single authors none have yet certainly achieved places of the first rank, but two or three may be named.

Mr. William De Morgan, by profession a manufacturer of artistic pottery, has astonished the world by beginning to publish at the age of sixty-five a series of novels which show no small amount of Thackeray's power combined with too large a share of Thackeray's diffuseness. Mr. Alfred Noyes (born 1880) is a refreshingly true lyric poet and balladist, and Mr. John Masefield has daringly enlarged the field of poetry by frank but very sincere treatment of extremely realistic subjects. But none of these authors can yet be termed great. About the future it is useless to prophesy, but the horrible war of 1914 is certain to exert for many years a controlling influence on the thought and literature of both England and the whole world, an influence which, it may be hoped, will ultimately prove stimulating and renovating.

Whatever may be true of the future, the record of the past is complete. No intelligent person can give even hasty study to the fourteen existing centuries of English Literature without being deeply impressed by its range and power, or without coming to realize that it stands conspicuous as one of the noblest and fullest achievements of the human race.

# Bibliography


Abercrombie, D.: *Elements of General Ponetics*, Edinburgh, Edinburgh University Press, 1967.

Ailsby, Christopher: *Roll of Infamy*, Osceola, MBI, 1997.

Allen, Ernst: *The English Novel: a Short Critical History*, London: Phoenix House, 1954.

Amitav Ghosh's: *The Shadow Lines: Critical Essays*, New Delhi, Atlantic, 2002.

Arthur Miller: *As a Critic of Drama*, New Delhi, Anmol, 2004.

Authors, Texts, Issues: *Essays on Indian Literature*, Delhi, Pencraft International, 2003.

Ayoni and Other Stories: *A Collection of Telugu Short Stories*, New Delhi, Stree Katha, 2001.

Ball, M. J. : *Phonetics: The Science of Speech*, London, Arnold, 1999.

Bennett, J. A. W.: *Middle English Literature*, Oxford, Clarendon Press, 1986.

Bentley, Eades: *The Jacobean and Caroline Stage*, Oxford, Clarendon Press, 1941.

Beyond Borders: *An Anthology of SAARC Poetry*, Noida, Rainbow, 2002.

Bhattacharyya, Nath: *Indian Religious Historiography*, New Delhi, Munshiram Manoharlal Publishers, 1996.

Brown, G.: *Listening to Spoken English*, Harlow, Longman, 1990.

Brown, J. M.: *Ireland in Fiction; a Guide to Irish Novels, Tales, Romances, and Folk-lore*, London: Maunsel, 1919.

Bush, Douglas: *English Literature in the Earlier Seventeenth Century, 1600-1660*, Oxford, Clarendon Press, 1962.

Cahalan, M.: *The Irish Novel: a Critical History*, Boston, Twayne Publishers, 1988.

Caidin, Martin: *The Tigers are Burning*, NY, Hawthorn Books, 1974.

Cavanagh, John: *British Theatre: a Bibliography, 1901 to 1985*, Hampshire, Motley, 1989.

Chambers, Kerchever: *English Literature at the Close of the Middle Ages*, New York: Oxford University Press, 1947.

Classe, A.: *The Rhythm of English Prose*, Oxford, Blackwell, 1939.

Couper-Kuhlen, E.: *An Introduction to English Prosody*, London, Edward Arnold, 1986.

Courthope, John: *A History of English Poetry*, London, MacMillan and Co., 1903.

Crystal, D.: *Prosodic Systems and Intonation in English*, Cambridge, Cambridge University Press, 1969.

Davis, Brian L. : *Uniforms and Insignia of the Luftwaffe*, London, Arms and Armor, 1999.

Davis, Gwenn: *Drama by Women to 1900: a Bibliography of American and British Writers*, London, Mansell, 1992.

Derek, Albert: *Old English and Middle English Poetry*, London, Routledge & K. Paul, 1977.

Dobree, Bonamy: *English Literature in the Early Eighteenth Century, 1700-1740*, Oxford, Clarendon Press, 1959.

Edmund Spenser: *A Critical Study*, New Delhi, Anmol Pub., 2005.

Edmund, Kerchever: *English Literature at the Close of the Middle Ages*, New York: Oxford University Press, 1947.

Ferrence, G.: *Deadly Fashion: the Rise and Fall of Cigarette Smoking in North America*, New York, Garland, 1989.

Francis, Russell: *The Scottish Novel: from Smollett to Spark*, Cambridge, Harvard University Press, 1978.

Gerald, Eades: *The Jacobean and Caroline Stage*, Oxford, Clarendon Press, 1941.

Halliday, M. A. K.: *Intonation and Grammar in British English*, The Hague, Mouton, 1967.

Harivansh R.B.: *In the Afternoon of Time: An Autobiography*, New Delhi, Penguin, 2001.

Hart, Russell: *The Scottish Novel: from Smollett to Spark*, Cambridge, Harvard University Press, 1978.

Hogan, Robert Goode: *The Modern Irish Drama: a Documentary History*, NJ: Humanities Press, 1975.

Jack, Ian Robert James: *English Literature, 1815-1832,* Oxford, Clarendon Press, 1963.

James Baldwin: *Protest and Beyond: A Study of Afro-American Fiction*, New Delhi, Rajat Pub., 2005.

James, Ernest: *Principles of Textual Criticism*, San Marino, Huntington Library, 1972.

James, Runcieman: *English Literature of the Late Seventeenth Century*, New York, Oxford University Press, 1969.

Jhumpa Lahiri: *The Master Storyteller: A Critical Response to Interpreter of Maladies*, New Delhi, KPH, 2002.

John Milton: *A Critical Study*, New Delhi, Anmol, 2005.

Knowles, G.: *Patterns of Spoken English: An Introduction to English Phonetics*, London, Longman, 1987.

Laver, J.: *Principles of Phonetics*, Cambridge, Cambridge University Press, 1994.

Logan, P.: *The Later Jacobean and Caroline Dramatists*, Lincoln, University of Nebraska Press, 1978.

Matricardi, Paolo: *Complete Book of World War II Combat Aircraft*, NY, Military Press, 1988

Naipaul, V.S. : *A House for Mr. Biswas: With an Introduction by Ian Buruma*, New Delhi, Penguin, 1992.

Nath, Narendra: *Indian Religious Historiography*, New Delhi, Munshiram Manoharlal Publishers, 1996.

Neil Bissoondath: *Indo-Caribbean-Canadian Diaspora*, New Delhi, Rawat, 2005.

Nicoll, Allardyce: *A History of English Drama, 1660-1900*, Cambridge, University Press, 1952-65.

Perkins, David: *A History of Modern Poetry*, Cambridge, Belknap Press of Harvard University Press, 1976.

Philip Roth: *A Novelist in Crisis*, New Delhi, Classical Publishing, 2001.

Pierre, Turner: *Uniforms and Insignia of the Luftwaffe*, London, Arms and Armor, 1999.

Rahilly, J.: *Phonetics: The Science of Speech*, London, Arnold, 1999.

Raja Rao: *The Fictionist*, Delhi, B.R. Publishing, 2003.

Robert, Lewis: *The Black Corps*, Madison, University of Wisconsin Press, 1983.

Rogers, H.: *The Sounds of Language: An Introduction to Phonetics*, Harlow, Longman, 2000.

Royle, Trevor: *The Macmillan Companion to Scottish Literature*, London, MacMillan Reference Books, 1983.

Salzman, Paul: *English Prose Fiction, 1558-1700: a Critical History*, Oxford, Clarendon Press, 1985.

Seidlhofer, B.: *Pronunciation, Oxford*, Oxford University Press, 1994.

Stevenson, Lionel: *Victorian Fiction: a Guide to Research*, Cambridge, Harvard University Press, 1966.

Sutherland, John: *The Stanford Companion to Victorian Fiction*, Stanford, Stanford University Press, 1989.

Terence, P.: *The Later Jacobean and Caroline Dramatists*, Lincoln, University of Nebraska Press, 1978.

Underhill, A.: *Sound Foundations*, London, Heineman, 1994.

Vann, J. Don: *Victorian Novels in Serial*, New York, Modern Language Association of America, 1985.

Vikram Seth: *Multiple Locations, Multiple Affiliation*, New Delhi, Rawat, 2001.

Walter, Ernest: *Tradition and Dream : the English and American Novel from the Twenties to Our Time*, London: Hogarth Press, 1986.

Wearing, J. P.: *The London Stage, 1890-1899: a Calendar of Plays and Players*, NJ, Scarecrow Press, 1976.

Wickham, Glynne William Gladstone: *Early English Stages, 1300 to 1660*, London, Routledge and Paul; 1959.

William Blake: *A Critical Study*, New Delhi, Anmol, 2005.

William, John: *A History of English Poetry*, London, MacMillan and Co., 1903.

Yeats, W.B. : *Poetry and Plays*, New Delhi, Atlantic, 2002.

# Index

## J



## K



## L



## M